# THE
# EXPANDING ROLES
## OF
# CHINESE AMERICANS
## IN
# U.S.-CHINA RELATIONS

# THE
# EXPANDING ROLES
## OF
# CHINESE AMERICANS
## IN
# U.S.-CHINA RELATIONS

Transnational
Networks and Trans-Pacific
Interactions

Peter H. Koehn
and Xiao-huang Yin
editors

AN EAST GATE BOOK

*M.E. Sharpe*
Armonk, New York
London, England

An East Gate Book

**Library of Congress Cataloging-in-Publication Data**

The expanding roles of Chinese Americans in U.S.–China relations : transnational
networks and trans-Pacific interactions / edited by Peter H. Koehn and Xiao-huang Yin.
    p. cm.
    "An east gate book"
    Includes bibliographical references and index.
    ISBN 0-7656-0949-5 (cloth: alk. paper); ISBN 0-7656-0950-9 (pbk.: alk. paper)
    1. Chinese Americans. 2. United States—Relations—China. 3. China—Relations—United
States. I. Koehn, Peter H. II. Yin, Xiao-huang.

E184.C5 E9 2002
305.895'1073—dc21                                        2001057688

Printed in the United States of America

The paper used in this publication meets the minimum requirements of
American National Standard for Information Sciences
Permanence of Paper for Printed Library Materials,
ANSI Z 39.48-1984.

| BM (c) | 10 | 9 | 8 | 7 | 6 | 5 | 4 | 3 | 2 | 1 |
| BM (p) | 10 | 9 | 8 | 7 | 6 | 5 | 4 | 3 | 2 | 1 |

# Contents

# List of Tables and Figure

**Tables**

**Figure**

# Explanation of Chinese Materials

A few mechanical details about Chinese materials in this volume merit explanation. For readers' convenience and to save space, in most cases we have cited the English translation of a Chinese title only after providing its romanization in the first citation. In addition, to maintain consistency, we have spelled Chinese names according to the Chinese custom, which places one's surname before the given name. Also, Chinese characters are romanized based on the *pinyin* system with the following exceptions: the names and titles that are customarily used in the Chinese American community. In the index at the end of the book, we have placed pinyin, Wade-Giles, and English spellings together to help identify those Chinese names, terms, and titles of publication that are spelled differently throughout the Chinese world.

# Foreword

*Him Mark Lai*

Chinese began large-scale immigration to America during the mid-nineteenth century. Like other immigrant groups in the United States, they customarily continued to maintain social, cultural, economic, and even political ties with the ancestral land on both a personal and an institutional level. In the case of the Chinese American community, immigrants continued to be the dominant majority during most of the period from the 1850s to the present, and these ties, as modified over the years, continue to flourish today. Since ties to the ancestral land are affected by the status of U.S.–China relations, Chinese Americans have long been interested parties in the development course and status of this relationship.

At different times up to the present, Chinese Americans individually, institutionally, or as a community have played roles in the evolving relationship. At times, they became involved involuntarily—for instance, when Chinese immigration became a political issue affecting U.S.–China relations in the late nineteenth century—and at other times, they consciously participated in activities affecting developments. During most of the period before World War II, the scope and effect of Chinese American efforts were limited due to the small size of the population and the community's isolation from mainstream America. Since the end of the 1940s, however, the Chinese American population has increased dramatically—mostly due to immigration. Chinese Americans' social, economic, and political status has also improved significantly. Gradually, they have become integrated in mainstream America and growing numbers filled key leadership positions. Today, although still a minority, Chinese Americans are a group that cannot be easily ignored. Increased Chinese American networking with mainstream institutions as well as growing sophistication in the use of these institutions have accompanied socioeconomic developments. These networks and skills often are used to personal and social advantage in a wide variety of activities that affect U.S.–China relations.

The Chinese American role in such transnational activities has been mentioned in passing by historians. Up to now, however, there has been little in-depth research and analysis of its extent and efficacy. Thus, the present collection of essays on topics in this subject area, written by various experts in their fields and edited by Professors Peter H. Koehn and Xiao-huang Yin, is timely. The essays explore various aspects of involvement in U.S.–China relations, with emphasis on recent and contemporary developments, and serve the purpose of helping to fill a long-existing gap in our understanding of the Chinese American experience. The work also is particularly relevant today in view of the general consensus that U.S.–China relations rank among the most important international relationships and are of concern not only for the future course of this country and China, but for the rest of the world as well. The explorations presented herein provide valuable additional information that will enhance understanding of the critical issues involved and, hopefully, will advance prospects for the adoption of rational and constructive policies of benefit for the United States, China, and the global community.

———— Introduction ————

# Chinese American Transnationalism and U.S.–China Relations

## Presence and Promise for the Trans-Pacific Century

*Peter H. Koehn and Xiao-huang Yin*

The late twentieth century witnessed a deepening of U.S.–China relations across cultural, social, economic, and political space on a scale that few imagined would occur. The turn-of-the-century presidential summits awakened many to the growing density of ties between the world's most populous nation and its most influential state.[1] While important diplomatically, strategically, and symbolically,[2] formal state-to-state relations constitute only one part of the exploding network of ties that transcend political and perceptual boundaries.[3] Given today's global emphasis on community identity, moreover, "it now makes less sense to speak of 'U.S.–China relations' than to talk of how one part of the United States (for instance, Chinese Americans . . . ) relates to one part of China. . . ."[4]

At the dawn of the new millennium, the Chinese American population approached 2.8 million persons.[5] While they constitute the largest Asian American community, Chinese Americans are a highly diverse group. This is also predominantly a community of immigrants (some 70 percent), with nearly half of the turn-of-the-century population having arrived since 1970 from the People's Republic of China (PRC), Taiwan, Hong Kong, Southeast Asia, and other parts of the world. Differences in place of origin, socioeconomic status, and political affiliations ensure that members possess divergent outlooks and positions with respect to China–U.S. relations. Given the substantial numbers of recent arrivals, the community's constant replenishment with newcomers from the Chinese world, and the growing practice of transmigration, it is not surprising that most Chinese Americans maintain close contact with their heritage place(s).

### Shifting and Enduring Routes and Linkages

U.S.–China interactions offer particularly vivid illustrations of the increasing influence that nongovernmental actors exert—individually and collectively—over transnational relations[6] and domestic policy. *The Expanding Roles of Chinese Americans in U.S.–China Relations* focuses on one component of the rising stream of global civil-society actions and transactions: the unfolding involvement of Chinese Americans—the vast majority of whom are immigrants and speak both Chinese and English—in distinctive roles that shape official bilateral and people-to-people relations in a rich variety of compelling ways.[7]

The scarcity of reliable sources complicates the task of determining exactly when and where Chinese first settled in North America. Although individual arrivals in the New World can be traced back to the eighteenth century, it was not until the Gold Rush years in the mid-nineteenth century that Chinese immigration reached the scale required to exert a major impact on the receiving society. There were 325 Chinese "forty-niners," [or *Jinshan ke*; *Gam San Hak* in Cantonese dialect, meaning "Gold Mountain Travelers"]. Three years later, their number grew to 20,026. By the time Congress passed the Chinese Exclusion Act in 1882, the Chinese population in the United States had reached about 150,000. If one includes those who returned to China during this period, some 322,000 Chinese took the trip across the Pacific from 1849 to 1882—before the Chinese Exclusion Act prohibited their entry.[8]

Most early Chinese immigrants arrived as unskilled workers. Peasants from rural regions in Guangdong Province (Canton) were strongly influenced by traditional Chinese values, which can be summarized by the dictum "falling leaves settle on their roots"—a person who resides elsewhere finally should return to the ancestral home. Thus, most dreamed of returning to their villages once they gathered enough money in the "Gold Mountain." When they gained little support from the ruling Manchu court in China in their struggle for survival in a strange land, they attributed the hardships—especially the racial discrimination they encountered in U.S. society—to the weakness of their homeland, and they believed that a strong China could help them win acceptance from mainstream society and improve their status in the new country. This explains why, when asked by Chinese American leaders for donations to help China, even immigrants who lived in poverty would respond enthusiastically. As a Chinese American community leader argued emotionally in an interview with New York reporters in 1901: "Why can't you be fair? Would you talk like that if mine was not a weak nation? Would you say it if the Chinese had votes?"⁹ The concerns of early Chinese immigrants for China and U.S.–China relations reflected their strong desire to improve their status in U.S. society.

The early Chinese immigrants included a few intellectuals. Although they only accounted for a tiny fraction of the Chinese American community, these intellectuals made an impact on U.S.–China relations. Among them, Yung Wing, a graduate from Yale College in 1854, stands out as a prominent figure. Brought to the United States in 1847 by missionaries, Yung later became a naturalized citizen. A friend of President Ulysses S. Grant and the writer Mark Twain, he made an important contribution to the development of early U.S.–China relations after his appointment as co-commissioner of the Chinese Educational Mission to the United States in the 1870s.¹⁰ Although a few individuals such as Yung succeeded in promoting mutual understanding between the two nations, early Chinese Americans as a whole failed to achieve much leverage in U.S.–China relations.

Chinese American involvement in U.S.–China relations entered a distinctively different phase during the World War II era. The war brought the United States and China together against a common enemy—Japan. Since China was an ally in the war, Chinese Americans were considered a "loyal minority."¹¹ The government encouraged them to play a prominent role in the U.S. wartime China policy. Wartime opportunities enabled Chinese Americans to emerge as players in U.S.–China relations. For instance, a disproportionately large number of Chinese Americans served as liaison officers or interpreters in the U.S. military or at diplomatic missions in China.¹²

Following the defeat of Japan in 1945 and the emergence of the People's Republic of China in 1949, divisions among Chinese Americans increased. With the enactment of new immigration policies in 1965, more Chinese arrived from the Mainland, Taiwan, Hong Kong, Southeast Asia, and elsewhere. Reflecting the altered population dynamics and the preoccupations of new arrivals, as well as evolving relations between the China Mainland and Taiwan, attempts to influence U.S. policy through the president and Congress expanded and intensified. The existence of two rival governments and Washington's anxiety about communism influenced the character and politics of Chinese communities throughout the United States. In the decades of the Cold War era, the prevailing anti-Communist disposition allowed Chinese American supporters of the Nationalist Party (Kuomintang, KMT) to exert powerful leverage on U.S.–China relations. They affected U.S.–China relations by helping the KMT establish a favored position in the China policy arena and by persuading Washington to maintain close ties with Taiwan.[13] Given the prevailing mood at the time, Chinese Americans who had sympathy for Beijing proved unable to secure a breakthrough in U.S.–PRC relations.

Once mainstream politicians decided that a change in China policy would serve U.S. interests, however, even the influential group of Chinese Americans who strongly opposed the PRC could not reverse the trend. When President Richard Nixon began to explore the normalization of relations with Beijing in the early 1970s, the opinions expressed by Chinese Americans, orchestrated by KMT supporters, were overwhelmingly critical of the new policy. Nevertheless, the Nixon administration continued its new China policy.[14]

During the "honeymoon" period of the 1970s, pro-PRC forces in the Chinese American community, for the first time, began to gain visibility in U.S.–China relations. With the normalization of relations, moreover, Chinese Americans, drawing on their ethnic and cultural identification with China, became actively involved in further developing ties. Throughout the 1970s and 1980s, the PRC government welcomed many Chinese American scholars as distinguished guests and they played an active role in establishing academic-exchange programs.

The shifting, but enduring, transnational routes and linkages that migrants from China built for more than a hundred years became even more important when they coincided with new networks formed in the late twentieth century along functional lines and in response to perceived common identities.[15] Today, the pervasive transboundary presence of Chinese Americans has cast a dense and diverse web of vines possessing varying scope and strength across the folds and crevices in the overall China–U.S. relationship.[16]

## Volatile Reactions

The vast majority of transnational extensions blossom silently and out of public sight. Occasionally, however, connections become glaringly visible on one or both sides of the Pacific. In the wake of the campaign-contribution controversy surrounding John Huang and overseas interests in 1997, for instance, Chinese Americans, in less than a year, went from "being insignificant to [being] a threat to national security."[17] In January 2000, following public protestations and pressure from China scholars and others based primarily in the United States, the PRC government released Dickenson College librarian and Cultural Revolution document collector Song Yongyi after five months of irregular detention on charges of "providing confidential materials to foreigners."[18] Similarly, the New York location of Li Hongzhi, leader of the banned Falun Gong spiritual movement whose protesting members frequently are arrested in Tiananmen Square, is a source of considerable frustration for the PRC government,[19] while U.S. Department of Justice, Energy Department, and Federal Bureau of Investigation suspicions that Wen Ho Lee, a Taiwan-born scientist working at the Los Alamos National Laboratory, had divulged advanced nuclear weapon designs to the PRC received considerable press attention and aroused the ire of Asian Americans. After being held in near solitary confinement for more than nine months, Lee's case ended (1) with U.S. prosecutors dropping fifty-eight of the fifty-nine counts in their indictment while Lee pleaded guilty to one felony count of mishandling nuclear secrets;[20] (2) with a remarkable apology to Dr. Lee issued by Federal District Court Judge James A. Parker "for the unfair manner ["demeaning, unnecessarily punitive conditions"] [in which] you were held in custody by the executive branch"; (3) with Judge Parker's rebuke of top decision makers in the Justice Department and Department of Energy for misleading him about Dr. Lee's supposedly deceptive behavior and for the "embarrassing" way they handled his case[21] along with President Bill Clinton's admission that he was "quite troubled" by the same actions;[22] (4) with an unusual admission by the *New York Times* that, in retrospect, it "found some things we wish we had done differently in the course of the coverage to give Dr. Lee the full benefit of the doubt";[23] and (5) with Attorney General Janet Reno's promise, after meeting with representatives of five Asian American organizations, to seek to make public a classified Justice Department report critical of the investigation and prosecution of Dr. Lee.[24]

Initial government overreactions on both sides of the Pacific to highly charged and publicly exposed situations provide support for Nina Schiller's posited "dialectic between the promotion of identities and relations that span national borders and *renewed efforts* on the part of states to fortify nationalist ideologies."[25] This clash emerges as a recurring theme in the historical and contemporary analyses contributed to this volume.

### Chinese Americans: Core Players in the Contemporary Web of Unofficial Transnational Interactions

Both types of transsovereign civil-society ties—the silent and the piercing—possess ramifications for U.S.–China relations and for the welfare of Chinese Americans. Although they are missing from high-level posts in the foreign-policy establishment,[26] the extensive presence of Chinese Americans in the vital cultural, social, economic, and political interstices that have cemented the interdependent nature of this challenging relationship holds out the promise that informal partnerships will override state-to-state conflicts in the new century. In the process of addressing the explosion of connections with "unofficial China"[27] from a wide variety of perspectives, all of the contributors to this volume assess prospects that the diverse Chinese American community will influence transnational relations in the twenty-first century. On the whole, the evidence and insights they contribute highlight the prominent, albeit understudied and typically unreported, roles that Chinese Americans fill in increasingly powerful transnational civil-society networks—ranging from philanthropy and development to profit-minded business, scientific exchange, and environmental protection. The network builders featured in this book are neither marginalized subjects nor are they on the periphery of China–U.S. relations; their sensibilities are diverse and complex; and their core transnational skills are by no means limited to capabilities possessing value for personal accumulation or other strictly economic transactions.

Compared with the past, today's globally connected society[28] enables Chinese Americans to play a more prominent part in shaping U.S. policy toward China and China's policy toward the United States. At no other time in history have Chinese Americans been so active and articulate concerning relations between their adopted and former countries, so concerned about U.S. policy toward China, and so visible in the mainstream media regarding cultural and political affairs. Their new roles result from improved socioeconomic status,[29] growing ethnic consciousness, the ability to maintain close ties with the Chinese world and concomitantly to stay in touch with both sending and hosting societies,[30] and openings in domestic politics and intercultural appreciation in both countries. Among the factors that have transformed Chinese Americans from passive bystanders to active participants in U.S.–China relations, two stand out: (1) the presence of vast numbers of highly educated immigrants who possess knowledge and expertise in areas that are central to the relationship[31]—many of whom have become U.S. citizens;[32] and (2) the emergence and solidification of extensive trans-Pacific Chinese business, migration, and communication networks. In particular, advances in information technology have instantaneously transplanted the Chinese world within the Chinese American community, created multiple reference points, and transmitted new values, practices, and policies with the potential to transform China from the diaspora. Today, Chinese Americans literally and figuratively are on-line in every independent sphere of activity that promotes denser U.S.–China relations.

**Multiple and Complex Voices**

Given that they constitute such a diverse community—divided by birthplace, language, political experience,[33] and vast disparities in economic status between "downtown" and "uptown" members[34]—it is not surprising that Chinese Americans speak out in multiple voices on China-related issues. For instance, some of those who are active in the dissident movement support a confrontational policy toward China in an effort to topple the ruling PRC government.[35] Others—especially those who work in China-related professions—advocate a constructive relationship. Some prefer not to be involved in foreign-policy making at all. While some Chinese Americans serve as emissaries on behalf of U.S. multinational corporations in the China Mainland or as beachheads for Chinese firms in America,[36] others work to resist the spread of global capitalism.[37] Although the lack of a unified viewpoint substantially reduces their ability to influence the U.S. government's China policy,[38] the diversity of voices heard today accurately reflects the multidimensional Chinese American perspective on U.S.–China relations.

## Cross-national Competency and the Future of China–U.S. Relations

Devoting attention to the ways that migrant and transmigrant[39] connections and flows simultaneously are "embedded in larger, global processes"[40] and bringing about the transformation of what is arguably the world's most important relationship at the start of the trans-Pacific century constitutes an important scholarly undertaking. The contributors to this book explore the immense and diverse involvement of Chinese Americans, acting as skilled individuals and through national and transsovereign nongovernmental collectivities they forge and/or join, in contemporary transboundary relations. Without presuming that all community members possess an inherent competitive advantage in this environment,[41] they consider evidence that Chinese Americans who are cross-nationally competent and "travel" without unwelcome baggage—including certain mainstream American values such as extreme individualism, the arrogance of power, and a missionary complex[42]—are particularly effective in traversing and shaping trans-Pacific interfaces.

Furthermore, *The Expanding Roles of Chinese Americans* moves beyond their current presence along the U.S.–China frontier to consider prospects that members of the Chinese American community will be influential with respect to *future* political, social, cultural, and economic relations between the two countries. The assessments shared by contributors suggest that the nature and scope of their civil-society involvement increasingly will determine the outcome of state-to-state relations between the USA and the PRC. In that event, given the post–Cold War prominence of the United States and China, the actions of Chinese Americans will be of consequence for global politics in the twenty-first century.

## Critical Questions

The questions addressed in *The Expanding Roles of Chinese Americans* bear directly on the changing mix of players involved and on the future impact issue. They include: How, why, and to what extent are Chinese Americans involved in China-related affairs? How have they both been affected by and affected U.S.–China relations? What are the most important changes that have occurred and are occurring in the domestic and international contexts that have heightened Chinese American concerns regarding China-related issues? What is the actual and potential influence of diverse Chinese American interest groups and networks—business, scientific, academic, human rights, philanthropic, development, cultural, American-born Chinese (ABCs), and immigrant communities from the Chinese world (especially the Mainland, Taiwan, and Hong Kong)? Given the diversity of community interests and perspectives, are there grounds for unified action? What are the most promising areas for civil-society cooperation in the coming century? How can and do Chinese Americans promote intercultural appreciation and empathy, mutual learning, and constructive transboundary relations in these areas? What risks and perils are at stake? Does the existence of extensive networks of nonstate ties among Chinese and Chinese Americans effectively limit the scope of policies and actions available to government policymakers and enhance the likelihood that both sides will select constructive approaches over the long term? Shedding scholarly light on these questions takes on growing analytical and practical relevance as U.S. domestic politics and foreign policy become further interwoven and as the China–U.S. relationship becomes even more crucial in global affairs.

## Aim and Arrangement

*The Expanding Roles of Chinese Americans* aims to make a multidisciplinary contribution to understanding the role and promise of Chinese Americans at this critical juncture in transnational relations and to revealing the importance of migrants as transterritorial actors in contemporary global politics. The volume is arranged in three interrelated parts.

### *The Chinese American Presence: Impact and Implications*

In the opening part of the book, the impact of the Chinese American presence is placed in historical perspective and the transnational sensibilities of members are explicated by reference to particularly revealing, albeit rarely cited, diasporic literature. In these chapters, we observe that the presence of Chinese Americans is linked in dynamic fashion to the nature of U.S.–China relations. These complex relationships are revealed most clearly through the changing experiences of Chinese American families and student migrants.

## The Chinese Trans-Pacific Family

Haiming Liu's lead-off discussion establishes the fundamental historical importance of the Chinese family in U.S.–China relations. According to Liu, the most interesting aspect of Chinese American family life is not gradual transformation into a "model minority" institution, but its dynamic development as a transnational network. Typically, Chinese migration involves collective decision making and action that invokes "mutual commitment from parents and children in the interest of collective upward social and economic mobility." Liu's discussion of trans-Pacific family separation (including its origins in racial conflicts in U.S. society and in U.S.–China political relations) from the racist exclusion era through the present time confirms that "Chinese Americans historically have been transnationals."[43] Today, however, bilocality- and multilocality-network-linked immigrant and voluntary transmigrant family members lead a "life that tends to blunt the acute binarism between Asian and American with which earlier generations had to contend strenuously."[44] In spite of the barriers to host-society integration placed in their path, transnational family-migration strategies have empowered many Chinese immigrants.[45]

Of the various social forces that could reshape U.S.–China relations, Chinese American families are among the most established global players. Liu's chapter moves on to consider the current and potential future stabilizing roles in China–U.S. relations filled by unbounded and multicultural Chinese American transterritorial family networks that have been strengthened rather than diminished by migration experiences. He sees trans-Pacific family connections as "the Chinese rim's building blocks" that provide a firm foundation for U.S.–China economic relations in the trans-Pacific century. As a minority both in their place of origin and in the receiving country, however, transmigrants risk acquiring a doubly marginal status. Thus, Chinese American families possess a vital stake in the maintenance of a positive U.S.–China relationship.

## Student Migrants and Transmigrants: Merging Science with Business in the Information Age

Sufei Li documents the role played by PRC and U.S. policies and practices at the nation-state and (in the United States) university level in the expansion of the Chinese American population following the 1979 normalization of U.S.–China diplomatic relations. The official U.S. government response to the Tiananmen crisis in 1989 accounts for much of this mobility. Over 60,000 students took advantage of President George Bush's Executive Order granting Mainland Chinese in the United States between 5 June 1989 and 11 April 1990 permission to remain legally in the United States.[46] More recently, Mainland applicants have secured roughly one out of every ten H-1B (nonimmigrant professional work) visas issued by the U.S. Immigration and Naturalization Service.[47] In some fields (such as information technology), Chinese have been adept at converting H-1B visas, via labor certification, into Green Cards. Li suggests that, with their strong educational credentials, these professionals "have been integrated into mainstream American society to an extent unimaginable among earlier Chinese immigrants who lived and worked inside Chinatowns."

While Chinese authorities consistently intended and expected that students sent abroad, mainly to study science and technology, would return to serve the state after completing their studies, the results often frustrated official intentions since a sizable proportion—particularly among those earning doctoral degrees—opted to stay in the United States. This outcome has helped promote sustained economic expansion in the host country and is increasingly important in terms of U.S. scientific research and technology development. While it generates short-run losses for the PRC, nonreturning U.S.-educated professionals still contribute in important, unanticipated, and ironic (i.e., capitalist) ways to the Mainland's extraordinary economic growth and to U.S.–China relations. For instance, Li reports on the tendency for nonreturning students of physical science and engineering to shift into careers focused on information technology and conducting business with China in order to support themselves in the United States, confirming that, for many "post-Tiananmen Chinese Americans . . . , the finality of their dislocation co-exists with a perpetual turning of one's gaze toward the lost homeland."[48] The growing opportunities to take advantage of China–U.S. trade and business investment, which are likely to expand further as the PRC becomes integrated into the World Trade Organization, certainly will be skewed in favor of Chinese Americans who are "bilingual and bicultural, which means that they are likely to be foreign born and educated, but with U.S. college or postgraduate degrees."[49] Li's data demonstrate conclusively, however, that this is not "only a small group."[50] In addition, her chapter presents evidence of the increasing circular migration of talent;[51] that is, return to the Mainland—particularly Shanghai—by highly qualified Chinese seeking economic opportunities, career advancement, and social recognition that elude them in the United

States.[52] In terms of long-term U.S.–China scholarly network building, one can draw encouragement from data that show Mainland students heading the list of those from abroad studying at U.S. higher-education institutions since 1998 (at slightly more than 10 percent of the total).

## Diasporic Hummingbirds

In contrast to the canonization of English-language Asian American writing in American literature, little attention has been devoted to disaporic writing in Chinese. Out of concern that the neglect of Chinese American literature available in Chinese results in failure to capture the predominant diasporic sensibility, Qian Suoqiao critically examines representative texts drawn from three distinct late-twentieth-century transnational-migration periods in U.S. history. The untranslated works that provide the principal basis for Qian's discussion are particularly revealing because their message is not deflected by a preoccupation with elaborating on Chinese cultural traditions and customs for an uninformed mainstream audience.[53] In these works, he discerns authentic diasporic sensibilities with important implications for present and future U.S.–China relations. For instance, his critical understanding of *Seeing Palm Trees Again* and *Yesterday's Anger*, authored, respectively, by Yu Lihua and Zhang Xiguo—two prolific and accomplished writers who came from Taiwan—highlights the important insight that Chinese American discourses concerning "diasporic patriotism" are less about loyalty as such than they are about the inevitability and fear of assimilation. Qian also considers works by Cao Guilin and Zhou Li that are especially popular with a homeland audience. The images of America presented in these novels have influenced current public perceptions of the United States in the China Mainland. These diasporic authors can be seen as energetic transmigrating hummingbirds whose predominantly "peaceful and fruitful" message traverses the Pacific. As Qian elaborates, "a hummingbird flaps its wings with high frequency, flying from here to there, but it apparently does not have permanent residency and its food-hunting hard work seems to be for its own sake."

## Contemporary Activism

Part II casts a fresh, multidimensional light on contemporary Chinese American involvement in U.S. policymaking and trans-Pacific developments. Although highly diverse in ideological views, cultural identities, and socioeconomic interests, Chinese Americans have expanded their involvement in China-related affairs in comparison with past experience and have become a new force that must be reckoned with. One survey conducted by a

Chinese American newspaper in New York during the 1996 U.S. presidential election, for instance, showed that 78 percent of Chinese American voters regarded candidates' positions on U.S. policy toward China as an important consideration in deciding whom to vote for.[54] In recent years, moreover, Chinese American scholars and activists have participated extensively in debates over human rights in the China Mainland, trade disputes, the U.S. role in China–Taiwan relations, and other transnational issues. Their talks on primetime TV programs and their works written from a Chinese American perspective and published in mainstream newspapers and scholarly presses have helped shape U.S. elite and public opinion.[55]

The chapters included in this section of the volume highlight the activist orientations and behavior concerning issues associated with China that increasingly have been adopted by American-born Chinese and immigrants from the Mainland, Taiwan, and elsewhere. Furthermore, these contributions give voice to important segments of the Chinese American community that do not actively support policies favorable to the PRC regime.[56]

*Interior Political Orientations and Participation*

Yuhang Shi's exploratory study of the political orientations and participation of (primarily first-generation) North Carolina Chinese Americans offers evidence of increasing political activism. If Chinese Americans are to exert a substantial impact on U.S. foreign policy, Shi argues, they must first possess the knowledge, resources, and psychological propensity needed for political participation. His findings show that, in general, interest in politics and participation in various political activities by North Carolina (N.C.) Chinese approaches that of the U.S. population as a whole.

Shi's data also highlight the considerable uniformity that exists among the surveyed N.C. Chinese regarding key China-related issues. For instance, he uncovered virtually no support for measures to contain China and less than 20 percent of his sample favored the idea of helping Taiwan become independent. In general, the mainly immigrant, professional, and "uptown" respondents in Shi's "interior USA" sample evidenced little interest in the traditional security issues involving Taiwan and the China Mainland that preoccupy U.S. foreign-policy makers. Moreover, roughly two-thirds of the N.C. respondents do *not* want the U.S. government to impose sanctions on China for human-rights abuses, to become involved with Taiwan–Mainland reunification, or even to facilitate trade with the PRC.

These suggestive "interior" findings are consistent with preferences for unofficial and less visible bridging roles. They also highlight the challenges involved in consensus-building and in mobilizing traditional forms of political activism on behalf of China-related issues in the face of growing diversity (urban coastal versus interior) within the Chinese American community.[57] Finally, they suggest the intriguing possibility that increasing numbers of politically aware and active Chinese Americans are receptive to becoming politically involved with respect to issues that transcend community and/or homeland interests.[58]

## ABC Involvement

The involvement of American-born Chinese in U.S.–China relations reported by Nancy Yao constitutes one often-overlooked dimension of the broader picture of increasing political activism. Her essay explains the diversity that exists within this community as a function of degree of interest, objectivity, and cross-cultural skills. Yao also shows how the unique cultural position of ABCs serves both as an advantage and as a constraint when it comes to enhancing understanding of China in the United States and promoting positive relations in the future. She concludes that ABC influence on U.S. policy with regard to China-related issues will be exerted by informed individual activists rather than through mass community action. Among other factors, Yao reports that negative media coverage of "Chinese fundraising" for the Clinton campaign and the resulting congressional hearings on possible subversion of U.S. politics by China discouraged ABCs from developing a more vocal and organized voice.

It is important that some American-born Chinese, who in the past have shown little concern for U.S.–China relations, now are expressing interest in the relationship. Their multicultural education and the emergence of trans-Pacific networks have aroused ethnic consciousness and kindled a sense of pride as Americans of Chinese descent. Growing business and professional opportunities in a rapidly expanding China-related field and partisan political manipulation of U.S. policy toward China have served to raise interest levels among ABCs in U.S.–China relations. The changing attitudes, including more favorable sentiments regarding Chinese traditions and practices, are manifest in the large numbers of ABCs majoring in China studies at U.S. colleges and universities in recent decades and by their concentration in China-related professions. As Eric Liu, former foreign-policy speech writer for President Bill Clinton and author of *The Accidental Asian: Notes from a Native Speaker*, noted in an interview with the *Harvard Gazette*, "one way or another, I will stay involved with politics and involved with China and Asia. Those two areas seem really basic to me."[59]

Yao suggests that three developments could generate increased organizational participation and encourage the ABC community to become more active with respect to U.S.–China relations. The future developments she sees as critical are: (1) a higher profile for ABCs in the U.S. foreign-policy establishment; (2) sustained economic growth of the China Mainland and further integration of the PRC into international political and economic regimes—which will continue to heighten the public profile of U.S.–China relations and generate complex, multifaceted challenges that necessitate ABC community involvement; and (3) further expansion of technological and economic ties with the Mainland—which will motivate ABCs and their organizations to act on the understanding that foreign-policy decisions affecting U.S.–China relations ultimately determine personal economic outcomes.

## Legacy of Vulnerability

A powerful legacy of U.S. political history is widespread consciousness among Chinese Americans of their vulnerability to the vagaries of U.S.–China relations and to backlashes directed against those who seek to shape official foreign policy toward China.[60] This legacy enhances the attractiveness of participation in "invisible," or at least less visible, transsovereign civil-society roles. Nevertheless, the widely unappreciated diversity of interests, perspectives, and actions that exists within the Chinese American community includes an important group of players that are intent on influencing U.S. policy toward China through official channels. This type of actor is highlighted in the next two chapters of Part II.

## Intercultural Communicators

James Shen focuses on the strategic intercultural-communication role of Chinese American scholars in building and anchoring positive China–U.S. relations since the early 1970s. He examines the important roles played by these "cultural envoys" as messenger, mediator, consultant, moderator, and opinion leader during periods of conflict and cooperation. Participation in the expansion of cross-cultural communication and understanding among political elites and public-opinion shapers provides a particularly critical outlet for activism in light of Jianwei Wang's finding that "misperceptions, rather than conflict of real interest, could well push U.S.–China relations to the edge."[61] Shen contends that whereas PRC leaders tend to question the political motives of U.S. political leaders, they are open to listening to Chinese American scholars—who share discursive proximity in the high-context culture of China.[62]

*The Powerful Influence of the Taiwan Lobby*

A developing "pan–Asian American consciousness" among some second-generation Chinese Americans[63] provides a fertile foundation for efforts by groups like the 80–20 Initiative to mobilize Asian Americans for block voting and other forms of political participation.[64] Nevertheless, the contemporary Chinese American and Asian American communities are overwhelmingly immigrant, possessing close ties to their homelands and tending to replicate "the divisions and conflicts that beset" their societies of origin.[65] Thus, Paul Watanabe concludes that pan–Asian American unity "is more likely to arise in the domestic arena around distinctly Asian American issues"—such as employment, education, and business opportunities, political representation, and replacing stereotypes with balanced and realistic depictions—rather than around "issues related to U.S. policies toward Asia."[66]

No other "domestic" issue currently arouses deeper concern among the PRC's leadership than the status of what it views as the breakaway province of Taiwan. Across the straits, the China Mainland's rising economic, military, and diplomatic stature, along with the peaceful reintegration of Hong Kong under the "one country, two systems" formula, pose serious challenges for pro-independence sectors of Taiwan's government and population. Given the sensitivity of the "Taiwan issue" in the Mainland, on the island, and for U.S.–China relations,[67] it is not surprising that divisions encountered on the other side of the Pacific also are played out within the Chinese American community.

As Xiaoming Huang points out, Taiwan's leaders have focused efforts to manipulate U.S.–China relations "on influencing U.S. domestic politics by seeking to secure a pro-Taipei lobby in Washington."[68] With reference to pivotal issues in the U.S.–China–Taiwan triangular relationship, Tsung Chi's contribution to this volume demonstrates in vivid detail why, first, the China Lobby and, then, the powerful Taiwan Lobby—led by the highly organized Formosan Association for Public Affairs (FAPA) and its lobby-focused offspring, the Formosan Association for Public Relations (FAPR)—have been so successful throughout the latter half of the twentieth century. The Taiwan Lobby has been particularly effective in mobilizing immigrants from Taiwan to exert political pressure on their members of Congress and through media outlets. In comparison with the pre-2000 election environment, Chi expects the new U.S. political alignment at the national level to be even more favorable for attainment of the Taiwan Lobby's goals—including upgrades in weapons sales and articulation of a new policy that any solution to the Taiwan question must be agreed upon by the people living on the island.

He foresees that the George W. Bush administration will be inclined to pursue "con-gagement" (containment along with engagement) with regard to the Mainland and to play the "Taiwan card" in conflicts with the PRC. At the same time, however, pro-Mainland lobby groups are becoming more influential players in Washington, DC—particularly in terms of aspects of U.S.–China relations that affect trade and investment in the PRC. In any case, the future outcome remains uncertain and anxiety-filled—for major policy victories by the Taiwan Lobby (e.g., advanced-weapons sales) increase the risk that the people of Taiwan will find themselves among the casualties of successful efforts to undermine U.S.–China relations.[69]

*Changing Views on U.S.–China Relations*

In her provocative contribution to this volume, Xiaojian Zhao shows that the ethnic press, which often is overlooked by scholars, plays an important role in the lives of Chinese Americans. Her chapter builds on the premise that through study of the ethnic press, one is able to discern in broad outline the prevailing attitudes of the Chinese American community toward key China-related issues. Among other insights, Zhao's analysis points to an historic shift in prevailing community opinion in a direction that generally is favorable to the PRC and opposed to Taiwan's governing Democratic Progressive Party's pro-independence platform. Most clearly, Zhao finds that Chinese American opinion at the turn of the century, as reflected in Chinese-language newspapers, is preoccupied with avoiding confrontation and conflict over Taiwan.[70] She concludes that if the George W. Bush administration pushes beyond rhetoric and implements drastic measures directed against the Mainland in connection with Taiwan or other volatile issues, it will alienate a large and influential proportion of today's Chinese American community.

**Expanding Networks and Prospects**

The "increased porosity between Asian and Asian American"[71] is facilitated by network expansion and elaboration. Thus, at the same time that the presence of some 2.5 million Chinese Americans can be traced, in part, to changes in China–U.S. relations, the potential for further transformation of the relationship in the trans-Pacific century is enhanced by dynamic population mobility. Part III presents new and detailed investigations of the current and potential scope and impact of Chinese American actions through various transnational civil-society networks that typically receive scant scholarly and public attention. In this section, contributors document the strength, vitality, and importance for future U.S.–China relations of business, philanthropic, Mainland-improvement, scientific, and resource-conservation linkages.

### Transnational Businesspersons: Powerful Brokers or Compradores?

The complex and expanding web of economic contacts among relatives and friends on both sides of the Pacific is at once responsible for and an outgrowth of massively increased trade and financial services involving the China Mainland, Taiwan, Hong Kong, and the United States. Many Chinese transnational businesspersons have successfully foiled nation-state regulations and "enacted their own strategies of accumulation."[72] While Chinese investors from throughout East and Southeast Asia pump increasing amounts of capital into U.S. business ventures and real estate, Chinese Americans and others in the diaspora make massive investments in the country of origin and in training China's managers.[73] In his chapter, Wellington Chan documents the trans-Pacific *modus operandi* of Chinese entrepreneurs and describes the impact of changing immigration patterns on U.S.–Taiwan and U.S.–China economic relations since the 1970s. His analysis highlights the value of transnationally intertwined economic relationships and business networks in terms of the "cross-pollenization" of ideas and innovations and the acquisition of up-to-date knowledge of local conditions. Constantly recharged family, economic, and institutional networks are particularly useful in an emerging era of global entrepreneurship that requires sensitivity and adaptability to different cultural practices and shifting market trends.

Are Chinese Americans engaged in transsovereign business acting as powerful cultural and business brokers in their own right or are they reduced to serving as "*compradores* for non-Asian American global capitalists, who merely use Asian Americans, with their cultural capital, as conduits and instruments to penetrate the Asian market or as subcontractors to manage production and labor relations at the floor level"?[74] According to Chan, who has studied trans-Pacific business networks for the past thirty years, returnees—both to Taiwan and, increasingly, to Shanghai—include many successful Chinese American entrepreneurs (among them, founders, owners, and managers of high-tech Silicon Valley firms) who establish offices and production outlets or are hired to manage existing large-scale enterprises and public corporations.[75] For a number of compelling reasons, moreover, the Chinese American–linked and Taiwan-based computer suppliers that major U.S. firms are heavily dependent upon are moving an increasing share of their production and assembly operations to Shanghai and other Mainland locations.[76] Finally, the core Mainland roles played by

Chinese American transmigrants are likely to be further enhanced as China seeks assistance in its preparation for WTO membership and in implementing required post-accession reforms.[77]

## Transnational Chinese American Philanthropy

While extensive, the involvement of Chinese Americans in transborder philanthropy is arguably the least visible and least appreciated of the community's manifold transnational civil-society activities. John Deeney's chapter fills an important information gap on the impact of giving by Chinese Americans. He first explores the distinctive style—informal, personal and familial, private rather than public, small-scale, and networked—of Chinese American philanthropy. Then, he assesses the impact, particularly on education in the Mainland and on knowledge exchanges between China and the United States, of Chinese American giving—including the contributions of individual Chinese American philanthropists, foundations, associations, and other (including religious) groups. As Deeney demonstrates, Chinese Americans possess the economic resources to make a difference in societal development both in China and in the United States since their median family income is approximately 20 percent higher than the national level. Deeney concludes with a set of recommendations—including streamlined networking through internet communication—aimed both at expanding participation in the community's philanthropic activity and at enabling Chinese Americans, through effective giving, to improve China–U.S. relations and conditions on both sides of the Pacific.

## Chinese American Binational Improvement Associations

The following chapter, by Norton Wheeler, presents a detailed study of four prominent associations recently formed by Chinese American that also are devoted to improving aspects of Mainland society and have not been examined previously under a scholarly lens. Wheeler compares and contrasts these four transnational associations—the 1990 Institute, the Committee of 100, the Association of Chinese Professors of Social Science in the United States, and Human Rights in China—according to membership characteristics, issue orientations, and posture toward the PRC government. His assessment of the diverse contributions each association has made to improving Mainland society and to U.S.–China relations, as well as of their different transnational network strengths and tactics, facilitates understanding of the full panoply of contemporary and potential Chinese American transboundary civil-society involvement.

*Epistemic Communities*

Chinese American scientists have been in the forefront of efforts to develop contacts between China and the United States following President Richard Nixon's visit in 1972. Although diplomatic overtures opened up the opportunity for binational scientific contacts to commence, neither the scale of the subsequent epistemic exchanges nor the enthusiasm of the Chinese and Chinese American participants can be explained in terms of state interests and objectives.

In his chapter, Zuoyue Wang shows how Chinese American scientists engaged in Mainland projects, particularly those of immigrant background, have been able to pursue their own agenda—which simultaneously has involved promoting the advancement of science in the land of origin, improving relations between the two countries, and creating their own distinctive scientific community. Five Chinese American scientists figure prominently in his account of transnational scientific activity: Qian Xuesen (Hsue-shen Tsien), an aerodynamic scientist who arrived in the United States before World War II; C.N. Yang (Chen Ning Yang, or Yang Zhenning) and T.D. Lee (Tsung Dao Lee, or Li Zhengdao), physicists who came in the 1940s and rose to international academic prominence in the 1950s and the 1980s; Chang-Lin Tien, a mechanical engineer who came via Taiwan and gained influence as chancellor of the University of California–Berkeley; and finally, Wen Ho Lee, a computer scientist who arrived in 1965. Although the advice they offered was not always consistent, the prominent role of Chinese American scientists has helped moderate concern in the PRC about the political and cultural values that accompanied scientific exchanges in particular and modernization and globalization in general. At the same time, the identification of Chinese American scientists with Chinese culture and development objectives facilitated the transmission of new values and ideas that have challenged Chinese orthodoxy.

Wang concludes his historical discussion with the observation that exchanges and diplomatic involvements have "transformed Chinese American scientists from a secluded elite group within a marginalized 'model U.S. minority' into agents of transnational technoscience possessing . . . a voice . . . in public-policy making in the United States and China." While his thorough review indicates that the U.S. government's treatment of Wen Ho Lee has had a chilling effect on Chinese American scientists and on the atmosphere for transnational collaboration that they worked hard to create, Wang finds no evidence that the case has caused a Tiananmen-like disruption of U.S.–China scientific exchanges. He expects that collaborative projects outside of sensitive areas will continue to flourish and that the role of Chinese American scientists will be of even greater importance in future U.S.–China relations.

*Sustainable-consumption Advocates for a*
*Natural-resource-scarce Future*

Finally, Peter Koehn demonstrates that Chinese Americans are positioned to transform both U.S. and China Mainland society with respect to critical interdependent environmental-protection and natural-resource-depletion challenges. Koehn's analysis suggests that the turn of the century is graced by the presence of at least one million cross-nationally competent Chinese Americans who are linked to civil-society institutions on both sides of the Pacific that possess the capacity to advance sustainable-development and sustainable-consumption agreements, policies, projects, and values.

Most of the specific nongovernmental roles identified in Koehn's chapter would not be highly visible and would address problems (e.g., limited future fossil-fuel availability) that simultaneously involve the linked destinies of peoples in the China Mainland and the United States. Involvement in these roles is not free of risk. For instance, Chinese Americans actively engaged in advocating curtailed consumption at transnational, national, and/or subnational levels are likely to encounter suspicions of disloyalty both in the PRC[78] and in the United States.[79] Koehn finds room for optimism, however, in certain Mainland practices, preliminary evidence that cross-nationally competent Chinese American actors tend to be sustainable-consumption advocates, and in the multiple transterritorial networks open to strategically prepared and motivated community members from all walks of life for influencing U.S.–China environmental-interdependence challenges.

**Implications and Prospects**

The concluding part of the book considers implications for Asian and Asian American studies and assesses prospects that the expanding involvement of Chinese Americans in U.S., PRC, and transboundary affairs will reinforce a relationship based upon commitment to advancing nongovernmental partnerships in the new century. Our concluding assessment builds on the evidence provided by contributors regarding the individual and collective orientations, networks, and behavior of Chinese Americans acting in diverse civil-society capacities along the U.S.–China frontier. They have shown that devotion to "serving the economic interests of multinational corporations"[80] or to personal/family accumulation and consumption are far from the only motives for participation in transnational capacities that impact China–U.S.

relations.[81] In the trans-Pacific century, there will be even more bridges with China for Chinese Americans to "choose—or choose not—to build."[82]

As a result of increased flexibility in mainstream responses to newcomers and in U.S. foreign-policy orientations and reactions, the expansion of trans-Pacific business and migration networks, growing ethnic consciousness, and improved socioeconomic status, Chinese Americans increasingly are involved in U.S.–China relations. Opportunities for career expansion and to gain social, economic, and political influence have drawn many to China-related affairs. Participation in diverse aspects of U.S.–China relations helps new immigrants and ABCs alike to secure a position in mainstream life.

In analyzing Chinese American involvement, we find it useful to distinguish the informal and nonpolitical from the formal and public. Both types of participation expanded at the end of the twentieth century, but the first grew exponentially while the latter increased incrementally. There are important differences in the nature and implications of the two types of involvement. The informal form is driven mainly by the unbounded movement of information and people and multiplies in response to its own interpersonal, unpredictable, and less-visible dynamic.

Among Chinese Americans, at least, formal political participation in U.S.–China issues responds to quite different, and more predictable, cues. While Chinese Americans have their own reasons to welcome a positive or negative U.S.–China relationship, they tend to become actively involved in a public way only when they find that their interests are not incongruent with those that prevail within mainstream society. They have learned that overt political participation in U.S.–China relations must be deemed consistent with the dominant orientations held among the larger society and/or endorsed by mainstream politicians. That the flows and ebbs in Chinese American political involvement over various historical periods coincide with ups and downs in the volatile formal relationship suggests that activists in the minority community realize that influencing bilateral diplomatic relations requires that their role first fit the domestic and/or international agenda of powerful U.S. political interests.

This distinction further allows us to envision futures where subsurface and publicly observable involvements reinforce one another as well as situations where they move in different directions. Our analysis suggests that, among Chinese Americans, the scope, depth, and momentum established by the unofficial and less-visible interpersonal process is unlikely to be arrested.[83] However, visible involvement in sensitive U.S.–China issues will remain susceptible to changes in mainstream political currents. In the Chinese American case, it is exciting to consider the real prospect that the extent of subsurface transsovereign civil-society networking has become sufficiently deep and interwoven to resist, or even to negate, any substantial cooling of the political winds among state actors.

## Notes

1. See Peter Koehn and Joseph Y.S. Cheng (eds.), *The Outlook for U.S.–China Relations Following the 1997–1998 Summits: Chinese and American Perspectives on Security, Trade, and Cultural Exchange* (Hong Kong: Chinese University Press, 1999).

2. See, for instance, Mark P. Lagon, "The 'Shanghai Coalition': The Chattering Classes and China," *Perspectives on Political Science* 29, No. 1 (2000): 7–16; Xiaoming Huang, "Managing Fluctuations in U.S.–China Relations: World Politics, National Priorities, and Policy Leadership," *Asian Survey* 42, No. 2 (2000): 292–293; Tu Wei-ming, "Cultural China: The Periphery as Center," *Daedalus* 120 (Spring 1991): 16.

3. See Jianwei Wang's interesting study of U.S. and Chinese elite perceptions of the other society and political system. Jianwei Wang, *Limited Adversaries: Post–Cold War Sino-American Mutual Images* (Oxford: Oxford University Press, 2000). One of his many findings is that the sampled business, diplomatic, and intellectual elites in both countries generally "are aware of the interdependence of their respective national interests" (p. 261).

4. Richard Madsen, *China and the American Dream: A Moral Inquiry* (Berkeley: University of California Press, 1995), p. 218.

5. *The Asian Population: Census 2000 Brief* (Washington, D.C.: U.S. Census Bureau, 2002), p. 9.

6. In this chapter, we use "transnational" to refer to issues and interactions that transcend the boundaries of nation-states rather than cut across groups that identify as a nation. Daniel Mato provides a succinct definition of transnational relations as involving "relations between two or more social subjects from two or more state-nations when at least one of these subjects is not an agent of a government or intergovernmental organization. . . ." Daniel Mato, "On Global and Local Agents and the Social Making of Transnational Identities and Related Agendas in 'Latin' America," *Identities* 4, No. 2 (1997): 171. The terms *transsovereign* and *transterritorial* also capture our intended meaning. See Maryann K. Cusimano, "Beyond Sovereignty: The Rise of Transsovereign Problems," in *Beyond Sovereignty: Issues for a Global Agenda* (Boston: Bedford/St. Martin's, 2000), p. 3.

7. Also see David M. Lampton, *Same Bed, Different Dreams: Managing U.S.–China Relations, 1989–2000* (Berkeley: University of California Press, 2001), p. 315.

8. Him Mark Lai, "The Chinese," in *Harvard Encyclopedia of American Ethnic Groups*, ed. by Stephan Thernstrom (Cambridge: Harvard University Press, 1980), p. 218. Other scholars believe that the actual numbers are larger. See Rose Hum Lee, *The Chinese in the United States of America* (Hong Kong: Hong Kong University Press, 1960), pp. 11–13.

9. Wu Ting-feng, *New York Tribune*, 28 November 1901, as cited in Delber L. McKee, *Chinese Exclusion Versus the Open Door Policy, 1900–1906* (Detroit: Wayne State University Press, 1977), p. 51. Born to an immigrant family in Singapore and educated in Hong Kong and Britain, Wu acted as a spokesman for the Chinese American community when he served as China's minister to Washington, D.C., at the turn of the twentieth century.

10. Xiao-huang Yin, *Chinese American Literature Since the 1850s* (Urbana: University of Illinois Press, 2000), pp. 69–84; Peter Wan, "Yung Wing: A Critical Biography" (Unpublished Ph.D. dissertation, Harvard University, 1996).

11. Helen P. Bolman, "Notes: *Father and Glorious Descendant,*" *Library Journal* 68, No. 7 (1 April 1943): 287. For a discussion of changes in attitude on the part of mainstream Americans toward Chinese and Chinese Americans, see Harold R. Isaacs, *Scratches on Our Minds: American Views of China and India* (Armonk, NY: M.E. Sharpe, 1980; reprint), pp. 164–189.

12. For information about the Chinese American involvement in China's anti-Japanese war, see Shih-shan H. Tsai, *The Chinese Experience in America* (Bloomington: Indiana University Press, 1986), pp. 120–142; Ren Guixiang, *Huaqiao dierci aiguo gaochao* (The second patriotic movement of overseas Chinese) (Beijing: Zhonggong dangshi, 1989), pp. 88–128.

13. Xiao-huang Yin and Zhiyong Lan, "Chinese Americans: A Rising Factor in U.S.–China Relations," *Journal of American-East Asian Relations* 6, No. 1 (1997): 35–57.

14. Ibid., pp. 51–54. Also see Xiaojian Zhao's chapter in this volume.

15. Adam McKeown, "Conceptualizing Chinese Diasporas, 1842 to 1949," *Journal of Asian Studies* 58, No. 2 (May 1999): 327–330.

16. This includes criminal networks that trade in drugs, sex, and illegal immigrants. See Ronald Skeldon, "East Asian Migration and the Changing World Order," in *Population, Migration, and the Changing World Order*, ed. by W.T.S. Gould and A.M. Findlay (New York: John Wiley & Sons, 1994), pp. 188–191; Stephen E. Flynn, "Asian Drugs, Crime, and Control: Rethinking the War," in *Fires Across the Water: Transnational Problems in Asia*, ed. by James Shinn (New York: Council on Foreign Relations, 1998), pp. 26–27. Evelyn Hu-DeHart notes that undocumented "Fuzhounese workers were forced into American national consciousness when their overloaded and totally unseaworthy vessel, the infelicitously named *Golden Venture*, ran aground on the New Jersey shore in June 1993." Evelyn Hu-DeHart, "Introduction: Asian American Formations in the Age of Globalization," in *Across the Pacific: Asian Americans and Globalization*, ed. by Evelyn Hu-DeHart (Philadelphia: Temple University Press, 1999), p. 18. Also see Ko-Lin Chin, *Smuggled Chinese: Clandestine Immigration to the United States* (Philadelphia: Temple University Press, 1998).

17. Asia Society, *Bridges with Asia: Asian Americans in the United States*, Summary Report of a 1996 Conference in New York (New York: Asia Society, 1997), pp. 6–7. Also see Taeku Lee, "The Backdoor and the Backlash: Campaign Finance and the Politicization of Chinese Americans," *Asian American Policy Review* 9 (2000): 31–34; Hu-DeHart, "Introduction," pp. 14–16.

18. See Elizabeth Rosenthal, "China Frees Scholar Who Worked in U.S.," *New York Times*, 29 January 2000, p. A3; Erik Eckholm, "China's Arrest of Pennsylvania Librarian Alarms Scholars," *New York Times*, 13 January 2000, p. A10; Elizabeth Rosenthal, "For China-born U.S. Citizens, Visiting Homeland Has Risks," *New York Times*, 1 May 2001, p. A1.

19. See, for instance, Craig S. Smith, "China Attacks the Falun Gong in New Public Relations Effort," *New York Times*, 11 January 2001, p. A8.

20. James Sterngold, "Accused Scientist to Go Free on Bail in Los Alamos Case," *New York Times*, 25 August 2000, p. A1; James Sterngold, "Reno Says She'll Seek Release of U.S. Study on Los Alamos," *New York Times*, 6 October 2000, p. A22.

21. James Sterngold, "Held for Nine Months: Apology from Bench—Case 'Embar-

rassed Our Entire Nation,'" *New York Times*, 14 September 2000, p. A1; "Statement by Judge in Los Alamos Case, with Apology for Abuse of Power," *New York Times*, 14 September 2000, p. A21.

22. David Johnston, "Clinton Criticizes Officials' Actions against Scientist," *New York Times*, 15 September 2000, p. A1; Marc Lacey, "Clinton Doubts Scientist's Race Influenced Case," *New York Times*, 16 September 2000, p. A1.

23. "The Times and Wen Ho Lee," *New York Times*, 26 September 2000, p. A2.

24. Sterngold, "Reno Says," p. A22. While Government prosecutors likely believed that their treatment of Lee protected U.S. interests, their actions damaged the foundation of national security by at least temporarily destroying interest in government laboratory work and confidence in science as a career among some of the country's best and brightest Asian American minds. See Xiao-huang Yin, "The Lee Case Shakes Asian Americans' Faith in Justice System," *Los Angeles Times*, 24 September 2000, p. M1; "Playing Dirty with the China Card," *Nature* 398, No. 6727 (8 April 1999): 445; James Glanz, "Panel Fears Security at Labs Hurts Foreign Hiring," *New York Times*, 16 May 2000, p. A16; James Glanz, "Asian-American Scholars Call for Boycott of Labs," *New York Times*, 31 May 2000, p. A23; Gish Jen, "For Wen Ho Lee, a Tarnished Freedom," *New York Times*, 15 September 2000, p. A25. To offset the "brain drain" that already had occurred by January 2000 in the wake of the firing and arrest of Wen Ho Lee, U.S. Energy Secretary Bill Richardson ordered that clearer policies prohibiting racial profiling be put into effect and reported that he would request an additional $10–$15 million specifically for recruiting more Asian American scientists for national laboratories. "Effort Begun for Asian-American Scientists," *New York Times*, 20 January 2000, p. A11.

25. Nina G. Schiller, "The Situation of Transnational Studies," *Identities* 4, No. 2 (1997): 159 (emphasis ours).

26. Hu-DeHart, "Introduction," p. 20.

27. Madsen, *China and the American Dream*, pp. 202–205.

28. See Manuel Castells, *The Rise of the Networked Society* (Oxford: Blackwell, 1996).

29. Also see Myron Weiner, "Asian Immigrants and U.S. Foreign Policy," in *Immigration and U.S. Foreign Policy*, ed. by Robert W. Tucker, Charles B. Keely, and Linda Wrigley (Boulder, CO: Westview Press, 1990), p. 193.

30. Shigehiko Shiramizu, "Global Migration, Ethnic Media and Ethnic Identity," *Asian and Pacific Migration Journal* 9, No. 3 (August 2000): 273–274.

31. As of 1990, 41 percent of the Chinese American population over twenty-five years of age held a bachelor's or higher degree versus 20 percent for the U.S. population as a whole. The Chinese American working population also was considerably more likely to fill professional positions—especially in medicine, engineering, technology, and education. See Him Mark Lai, "The United States," in *The Encyclopedia of the Chinese Overseas*, ed. by Lynn Pan (Cambridge: Harvard University Press, 1999), p. 271; Franklin Ng, "Chinese Americans: Still the 'Yellow Peril?'" in *Many Americas: Critical Perspectives on Race, Racism, and Ethnicity*, ed. by Gregory R. Campbell (Dubuque: Kendall/Hunt, 1998), pp. 186, 189.

32. Relative to European immigrants, a far higher proportion of eligible immigrants from China have applied for U.S. citizenship. Harry H.L. Kitano and Roger Daniels, *Asian Americans: Emerging Minorities*, 2d ed. (Englewood Cliffs, NJ: Prentice-Hall, 1995), p. 183. Also see Aihwa Ong, "On the Edge of Empires: Flexible Citizenship Among Chinese in Diaspora," *Positions* 1, No. 3 (1993): 753–755, 770.

33. Among Chinese Americans, as well as mainstream Americans, "Tiananmen forces us to see ourselves as a divided 'we' interacting with a multiplex 'they.'" Madsen, *China and the American Dream*, p. 24.

34. While highly educated "uptown" Chinese Americans professionals who reside in suburban communities are well integrated into mainstream society, predominantly working-class "downtown" immigrants struggle to survive in poor urban ghettos. See Xiao-huang Yin, "The Two Sides of America's 'Model Minority,'" *Los Angeles Times*, 7 May 2000; Susumu Awanohara, "Tyros, Triads, Tycoons: Chinatown Ghettos Versus Arriviste Suburbs," *Far Eastern Economic Review* 152, No. 29 (18 July 1991): 50–51; Yin, *Chinese American Literature Since the 1850s*, pp. 194–205; Yen Espiritu and Paul Ong, "Class Constraints on Racial Solidarity Among Asian Americans," in *The New Asian Immigration in Los Angeles and Global Restructuring*, ed. by Paul Ong, Edna Bonacich, and Lucie Cheng (Philadelphia: Temple University Press, 1994), p. 303; Arif Dirlik, "Asians on the Rim: Transnational Capital and Local Community in the Making of Contemporary Asian America," in *Across the Pacific: Asian Americans and Globalization*, ed. by Evelyn Hu-DeHart (Philadelphia: Temple University Press, 1999), p. 45.

35. The spring 2000 debate over permanently granting China normal trade status revealed sharp divisions within the dissident community. See Joseph Kahn, "Conflicting Views Hinder Dissidents on China Trade Vote," *New York Times*, 19 May 2000, p. A12.

36. See Hu-DeHart, "Introduction," p. 9; Dirlik, "Asians on the Rim," p. 45.

37. Lucie Cheng, "Chinese Americans in the Formation of the Pacific Regional Economy," in *Across the Pacific: Asian Americans and Globalization*, ed. by Evelyn Hu-DeHart (Philadelphia: Temple University Press, 1999), p. 75.

38. See Paul Y. Watanabe, "Asian American Activism and U.S. Foreign Policy," in *Across the Pacific: Asian Americans and Globalization*, ed. by Evelyn Hu-DeHart (Philadelphia: Temple University Press, 1999), pp. 110, 121; Walker Connor, "Diasporas and the Formation of Foreign Policy: The U.S. in Comparative Perspective," in *Diasporas in World Politics: The Greeks in Comparative Perspective*, ed. by Dimitri C. Constas and Athanassios G. Platias (Athens: Institute of International Relations, Panteion University, 1993), pp. 174–175.

39. Transmigration refers here to the ceaseless mobility of people between or among nations. See Luis E. Guarnizo, "The Emergence of a Transnational Social Formation and the Mirage of Return Migration Among Dominican Transmigrants," *Identities* 4, No. 2 (1997): 288. Transmigrants qualify diasporic with *multiple* place consciousness and, thus, "feel at home" in the places where they live. On one hand, such consciousness enables "a different kind of politics that grounds transnationalism in the welfare of local communities." Dirlik, "Asians on the Rim," pp. 46, 53; Donald M. Nonini and Aihwa Ong, "Chinese Transnationalism as an Alternative Modernity," in *Ungrounded Empires: The Cultural Politics of Modern Chinese Transnationalism*, ed. by Aihwa Ong and Donald M. Nonini (New York: Routledge, 1997), p. 25. On the other hand, it can diminish the relevance of the local context and reinforce identities that are "at once deterritorialized in relation to a particular country, though highly localized in relation to the family." Ong, "Flexible Citizenship," pp. 771–772. Xin Liu shows that the differential mobility associated with ties to global capitalism has become an important source of power accumulation (independent, but not intrinsically subversive, of the state) in post-reform China—for transmigrants who succeed in securing permanent residence in the United States. See Xin Liu, "Space, Mobility,

and Flexibility: Chinese Villagers and Scholars Negotiate Power at Home and Abroad," in *Ungrounded Empires: The Cultural Politics of Modern Chinese Transnationalism*, ed. by Aihwa Ong and Donald M. Nonini (New York: Routledge, 1997), pp. 107–108, 110–111. Also see Sau-ling Cynthia Wong, "Denationalization Reconsidered: Asian American Cultural Criticism at a Theoretical Crossroads," *Amerasia Journal* 21, Nos. 1 and 2 (1995): 15.

40. McKeown, "Chinese Diasporas," p. 331. For instance, a diasporic perspective is useful in "exploring the role of American foreign policy in shaping global patterns of population movement." Wong, "Denationalization," p. 10. Also see Peter H. Koehn, *Refugees from Revolution: U.S. Policy and Third-world Migration* (Boulder: Westview Press, 1991).

41. As Lucie Cheng ("Chinese Americans," p. 67) points out with reference to U.S.–China business and economic affairs, this "would be tantamount to creating a new myth."

42. Wang, *Limited Adversaries*, p. 265; Setsuko M. Nishi, "Asian Americans at the Intersection of International and Domestic Tensions: An Analysis of Newspaper Coverage," in *Across the Pacific: Asian Americans and Globalization*, ed. by Evelyn Hu-DeHart (Philadelphia: Temple University Press, 1999), p. 183.

43. Cheng, "Chinese Americans," p. 73.

44. Wong, "Denationalization," p. 7. The constant among Chinese transnational families is their bilocal or multilocal focus. What is new are the qualitatively and quantitatively enhanced opportunities "for maintaining regular physical contact" among their split components. Elsie Ho, Manying Ip, and Richard Bedford, "Transnational Hong Kong Chinese Families in the 1990s," *New Zealand Journal of Geography* 111 (April 2001): 25.

45. Ho, Ip, and Bedford, "Transnational Families," p. 29. Indeed, "economic and political vulnerability, magnified by the factor of race, augment the likelihood that immigrants will construct a transnational existence." Linda Basch, Nina G. Schiller, and Cristina S. Blanc, *Nations Unbound: Transnational Projects, Postcolonial Predicaments, and Deterritorialized Nation-States* (Amsterdam: Gordon and Breach, 1994), pp. 26–27; also see pp. 238–242.

46. Haiming Liu's discussion of Chinese migration strategies—particularly husband and wife sponsorship of parents and, later, siblings under the family-preference provisions of U.S. immigration law following the *liusi luka* (June 4th Green Card) awards—reminds us that family ties interwoven with residency decisions of students are responsible in part for the size of the most recent population movement from China to the United States.

47. If this tendency is maintained, Mainland applicants would secure nearly 60,000 new H-1B visas between 2001 and 2004 given that Congress enacted legislation in 2000 that increased the maximum number of H-1B visas that can be issued to 195,000.

48. Wong, "Denationalization," p. 10. The shift to business also reflects awareness of the growing importance of "involvement in economic matters" as a route to political power in the Mainland. Daniel Kane, "The Social and Intellectual Elite" in *China's Quiet Revolution: New Interactions Between State and Society*, ed. by David S.G. Goodman and Beverley Hooper (New York: St. Martin's, 1994), p. 127.

49. Cheng, "Chinese Americans," p. 67. Also see Cindy Sui, "Foreign Workers at Record High: Companies Attracted by Lucrative Mainland Markets Heading for SAR," *South China Morning Post*, 22 March 1998, p. 3.

50. Cheng, "Chinese Americans," p. 67. As David Zweig and Chen Changgui expected, the proportion of nonreturning students with direct business links to China has grown considerably with the sustained expansion of the Mainland economy and dramatically increased opportunities to engage in cross-national business. David Zweig and Chen Changgui, *China's Brain Drain to the United States: Views of Overseas Chinese Students and Scholars in the 1990s* (Berkeley: Institute of East Asian Studies, University of California–Berkeley, 1995), pp. 72–73.

51. T.K. Oommen, "India: 'Brain Drain' or the Migration of Talent?" in *The Sociology of Migration*, ed. by Robin Cohen (Cheltenham: E. Elgar, 1996), pp. 362–364.

52. Also see Li Cheng, "China in 2000: A Year of Strategic Rethinking," *Asian Survey* 41, No. 1 (January/February): 87. One major disincentive is the relative weight placed on age versus professional competence in China. Shuming Zhao reports that "this feature of the value system is one of the factors behind the complaints of young people, especially those who have returned to China after completing their studies abroad, that they were not being used satisfactorily, and that they deserved more advanced positions than they were given when they returned." Shuming Zhao, "Human Resource Management in China," *Asia Pacific Journal of Human Resources* 32, No. 2 (1994): 7. In 2000, however, Jiang Zemin and Zeng Qinghong, head of the CCP's Organization Department, issued statements suggesting that returning students from abroad are deserving of high-level bureaucratic posts in part because they comprise the right age cohort (thirties and early forties) for the newly emphasized recruitment of fifth-generation PRC leaders. See Li Cheng, "China in 2000," p. 88.

On the return of professional talent to Taiwan, see Ng, "Chinese Americans," p. 191; Peter Stalker, *Workers Without Frontiers: The Impact of Globalization on International Migration* (Boulder: Lynne Rienner, 2000), pp. 111–113.

53. Yin, *Chinese American Literature Since the 1850s*, p. 257. Sau-ling C. Wong adds that "fear of exoticization so prevailed (compounded by other obstacles such as English monolingualism among many American-born cultural critics) that literature produced by immigrants in the Asian languages has, for a long time, been neglected. . . ." Wong, "Denationalization," p. 4.

54. In contrast, only 19 percent considered the personal character of the candidates an important factor affecting their decision. *Haojiao* (Herald monthly) 9, No. 8 (August 1996): 1, 4.

55. Yin and Lan, "Chinese Americans," pp. 35–57. In the wake of the 1989 Tiananmen Incident and U.S. media coverage of it, however, it became much more difficult "to say good things about the communist government publicly" in the United States. Wang, *Limited Adversaries*, p. 254.

56. Also see David Palumbo-Liu, *Asian/American: Historical Crossings of a Racial Frontier* (Stanford: Stanford University Press, 1999), p. 387.

57. Myron Weiner ("Asian Immigrants," p. 206) maintains that "the full impact of Asian Americans on the U.S. political system will not be felt until a larger proportion of immigrants become U.S. citizens and second-generation Asian Americans are of voting age." For one indication of growing Asian American influence over local electoral outcomes, see Somini Sengupta, "Political Math in New York Raises Power of Asian Vote," *New York Times*, 25 August 2001, p. A1.

58. See Sanford J. Ungar, "America's New Immigrants: Can 'Fresh Blood' Lead to a Fresh Foreign Policy?" in Asia Society, *Bridges with Asia: Asian Americans in the United States*, Summary Report of a 1996 Conference in New York (New York: Asia Society, 1997), pp. 35–37.

59. *Harvard Gazette*, 2 February 1995, p. 1. On business opportunities for ABCs with U.S. companies operating in Hong Kong and the Mainland, see Stalker, *Workers Without Frontiers*, p. 111.

60. See Watanabe, "Asian American Activism," pp. 111, 114, 118, 120, 123, 125–126.

61. Wang, *Limited Adversaries*, p. 265.

62. Also see Phyllis Bo-yuen Ngai, "Nonverbal Communicative Behavior in Intercultural Negotiations: Insights and Applications Based on Findings from Ethiopia, Tanzania, Hong Kong, and the China Mainland," *World Communication* 29, No. 4 (2000): 18–22.

63. See Nazli Kibria, "The Construction of 'Asian American': Reflections on Intermarriage and Ethnic Identity Among Second-generation Chinese and Korean Americans," *Ethnic and Racial Studies* 20, No. 3 (July 1997): 524, 540.

64. Yin, "Lee Case"; Lee, "Backdoor and the Backlash," p. 38.

65. Dirlik, "Asians on the Rim," p. 42.

66. Watanabe, "Asian American Activism," pp. 121–123; also see Weiner, "Asian Immigrants," p. 206. Such domestic concerns also preoccupy the "uptown" leadership of the nationwide Organization of Chinese Americans and the ABC-centered Chinese American Citizens Alliance. See Awanohara, "Tyros," 50–51. Yen Espiritu and Paul Ong ("Class Constraints," pp. 301–307, 314) further suggest that the unity, legitimacy, and effectiveness of pan–Asian associations are diminished by professional/managerial class dominance. Also see Yin, "Two Sides of America's 'Model Minority.'"

Sau-ling C. Wong contributes a radically different perspective. She finds the status of domestic minorities to raise the most compelling and urgent issues and argues that "coalitions of Asian Americans and other racial/ethnic minorities within the U.S. should take precedence over those formed with Asian peoples in the diaspora." Wong, "Denationalization," 18. Also see Palumbo-Liu, *Asian/American*, p. 391; Dirlik, "Asians on the Rim," pp. 47–48. Among new immigrants, however, "closeness to Asia opens the possibility of distancing themselves from their immediate environments in the United States, especially in their relationships with other minority groups." Dirlik, "Asians on the Rim," p. 42.

67. Peter H. Koehn and Joseph Y.S. Cheng, "The Outlook for U.S.–China Relations in the 21st Century: Regional Security, Trade and Information, and Cultural Exchange," in *The Outlook for U.S.–China Relations Following the 1997–1998 Summits: Chinese and American Perspectives on Security, Trade, and Cultural Exchange*, ed. by Peter Koehn and Joseph Y.S. Cheng (Hong Kong: Chinese University Press, 1999), p. 15; and, in the same volume, Wu Xinbo, "China and the United States: Toward an Understanding on East Asian Security," pp. 74–77. The one-China policy adhered to by the U.S. government did not prevent the sale of an estimated $2 billion of weapons to Taiwan between 1994 and 1998. See Eric Schmitt, "House Approves Expansion of Ties to Taiwan's Army," *New York Times* 2 February 2000, p. A8. On lack of adherence by the U.S. government with the principles set forth in the three Sino-U.S. joint communiqués dealing with Taiwan, see Ren Donglai, "The Taiwan Issue in the Three Joint Sino-U.S. Communiqués and the Taiwan Relations Act," in *The Outlook for U.S.–China Relations Following the 1997–1998 Summits: Chinese and American Perspectives on Security, Trade, and Cultural Exchange*, ed. by Peter Koehn and Joseph Y.S. Cheng (Hong Kong: Chinese University Press, 1999), pp. 171–180; and, in the same volume, Zhang Yebai, "Can a Constructive Strategic Partnership' Be Built Up Between China and the United States?" p. 150.

68. Huang, "Managing Fluctuations," 294. Taiwan's officials are not alone in pursuing this course of action. Yossi Shain reports that "many countries of origin have discovered the critical role of ethnic lobbies in the United States, and these countries' leaders are taking action to build and sustain their U.S.-based compatriots' loyalty and attachment in order to further their own interests." The most successful ethnic lobbies (including the Taiwan Lobby) are predisposed (or learn) "to export and safeguard American values abroad. . . ." Yossi Shain, *Marketing the American Creed Abroad: Diasporas in the U.S. and Their Homelands* (Cambridge: Cambridge University Press, 1999), pp. x–xi.

69. Huang, "Managing Fluctuations," pp. 294–295.

70. These opinion shifts are consistent with (and perhaps reflect) the growing social and economic integration of mainland and island, which renders it increasingly unlikely that either side can afford to antagonize the other. See Craig S. Smith, "Signs in China and Taiwan of Making Money, Not War," *New York Times*, 15 May 2001, p. A1.

71. Wong, "Denationalization," p. 9.

72. Nonini and Ong, "Chinese Transnationalism," p. 20. These strategies include, especially among large Chinese conglomerates, forging multiple linkages of mutual advantage with non-Chinese "actor-networks" associated with international finance and with business media. See Kris Olds and Henry Wai-chung Yeung, "(Re)shaping 'Chinese' Business Networks in a Globalising Era," *Environment and Planning D: Society and Space* 17 (1999): 535–551.

73. Also see Murray Weidenbaum and Samuel Hughes, *The Bamboo Network: How Expatriate Chinese Entrepreneurs Are Creating a New Economic Superpower in Asia* (New York: Free Press, 1996), pp. 5–6.

74. Hu-DeHart, "Introduction," p. 19. Also see Ong, "Flexible Citizenship," pp. 768–769.

75. Also see Smith, "China and Taiwan," p. A10.

76. See Mark Lander, "These Days 'Made in Taiwan' Often Means 'Made in China,'" *New York Times*, 29 May 2001, pp. A1, C2.

77. For a discussion of bureaucratic dispositions in Shanghai that are related to implementing post-accession reforms, see Peter H. Koehn, "The Shanghai Outlook on China's WTO Accession: Middle-Management Orientations Toward Selected Institutional Distributional Reforms and Human-Resource Enhancements" (Paper presented at the 2001 Western Conference of the Association for Asian Studies, Missoula, 19 October 2001).

78. As Merle Goldman and Roderick MacFarquhar point out with respect to the PRC, for instance, "the ordinary person increasingly defines the public good less in terms of public spiritedness and nationalism than in terms of material well-being and consumerism." Merle Goldman and Roderick MacFarquhar, "Dynamic Economy, Declining Party-State," in *The Paradox of China's Post-Mao Reforms*, ed. by Merle Goldman and Roderick MacFarquhar (Cambridge: Harvard University Press, 1999), p. 24.

79. On the significance of transformative struggles by Asian Americans against dominant paradigms, see Gary Y. Okihiro, *Margins and Mainstreams: Asians in American History and Culture* (Seattle: University of Washington Press, 1994), pp. 155, 174–175.

80. Wong, "Denationalization," p. 13.

81. In addition to the importance of transnational resource-conservation activities, treated in Koehn's chapter in this volume, Ong and Nonini argue for strengthening

transnational linkages built upon "a cosmopolitan sense of social justice. . . ." In particular, they suggest "we need to counter capital's mobility by forming transnational linkages between persons and groups disempowered by globalization, whatever their ethnic or national affiliations." Aihwa Ong and Donald M. Nonini, "Toward a Cultural Politics of Diaspora and Transnationalism," in *Ungrounded Empires: The Cultural Politics of Modern Chinese Transnationalism*, ed. by Aihwa Ong and Donald M. Nonini (New York: Routledge, 1997), p. 330.

    82. Cheng, "Chinese Americans," p. 75.

    83. Relevant in regard to informal interpersonal relationships is Jianwei Wang's research finding that U.S. and China Mainland elites "held quite positive attitudes toward each other as individuals . . ." at the same time that "both sides perceived a higher incompatibility level between the two societies." In addition, a majority of the sampled elites from both countries "regarded personal contact as the most important source for their image of the target country." Wang, *Limited Adversaries*, pp. 244–245, 251. Kimberly Maynard also concludes that "unofficial contacts" increasingly influence "individual and national attitudes toward other countries." Kimberly A. Maynard, *Healing Communities in Conflict: International Assistance in Complex Emergencies* (New York: Columbia University Press, 1999), p. 4.

# Part I

# The Chinese American Presence: Impact and Implications

# —— 1 ——

# Historical Connections Between the Chinese Trans-Pacific Family and U.S.–China Relations

*Haiming Liu*

## Transnational Separation and Networks

Conventional studies of Chinese immigrant families in the United States often focus on comparing the dominant social values and systems of the sending country with those developed in the adopted country and emphasize the changes experienced in adapting to U.S. life.[1] However, the Chinese experience is more complex than conventional studies suggest. The Chinese migrant family has invoked expressions of ethnic resilience, provided the basis for a culture of resistance in a racist environment, and functioned as a social institution that transcends the borders and boundaries of the nation-state. The most interesting aspect of Chinese American family life is not gradual transformation into a "model minority" institution, but its dynamic development as a transnational network.

Family separation, involving the presence of siblings, children, parents, and even husbands and wives on both sides of the Pacific for a prolonged period of time, has long shaped the Chinese American experience. During the exclusion era (1882–1943), family reunion was nearly impossible. Split households prevailed until the termination of all Chinese exclusion laws in 1943. Although the Chinese population in the United States began to grow dramatically once the Immigration Act of 1965 removed the national-origin system from U.S. immigration policy, trans-Pacific families still are commonly encountered.

While the trans-Pacific Chinese family pattern is relatively well documented, its origins in U.S. racial conflicts and in U.S.–China political relations are less thoroughly studied.[2] This chapter assesses the development of such families as an important dimension of the Chinese American experience and documents how the evolving U.S.–China relationship has shaped the environment in which transnational family networks have arisen. It also examines the use of family networks as a creative and adaptive strategy for overcoming legal barriers to immigration and analyzes the importance of family networks in terms of current and future U.S.–China relations.

## Exclusion Laws, U.S.–China Relations, and the Chinese Transnational Family

The majority of Chinese who began to arrive in the United States in the early 1850s were young, able-bodied males. Although roughly half of them were married, most came without their wives and children.[3] Jobs in mining, farming, and railroad construction often required Chinese laborers to move from place to place. While some immigrants saw their life in the United States as transitory and intended to return after a short period of stay, others found it unrealistic to envision a family life in the new land. Nevertheless, the immigrants' initial response to the frontier life-style did not mean that they did not intend to send for their families later—as emigration essentially involves family-oriented decisions.

Discrimination against Chinese immigrants reflected China's international standing as well as the ups and downs in U.S.–China relations that began with anxious efforts by American merchants to open China's market.[4] In 1858, Britain and France launched the second Opium War, forcing China to open eleven additional treaty ports, to lower further its tariffs on Western imports, and to lift the immigration ban in Guangdong Province. Sharing the fruits of the war, the United States obtained its second unequal treaty with China—the Tientsin (Tianjin) Treaty—which specified that Americans should receive all the privileges that the Chinese government had granted or would grant to any other country.[5]

In 1861, Anson Burlingame, the first U.S. minister plenipotentiary, arrived in Beijing. When the Tientsin Treaty expired, his mission led to a new treaty—the 1868 Burlingame Treaty. This treaty recognized free immigration between the two nations, provided expanded opportunities and protection to U.S. merchants and missionaries, and guaranteed most-favored-nation treatment to each other's immigrants as well as the right of permanent residency in each other's country.[6] Under the Burlingame Treaty, China became more open and the Chinese government began to use diplomatic missions to speak for Chinese immigrants.

Shortly after negotiation of the Burlingame Treaty, however, California experienced an economic recession. In battles between organized labor and the business class, Chinese immigrants served as scapegoats and were blamed for unemployment, low wages, and poor working conditions. White labor took out their frustration and anger against the Chinese. Union leaders launched anti-Chinese mass meetings. California journals and newspapers began to carry inflammatory articles about the Chinese threat to American life. "Chinese must go!" became a common slogan in political campaigns. Hostility sometimes grew into violent riots. In October 1871, after a white man was accidentally killed in a feud between two Chinese clans in Los Angeles, a mob of several hundred surrounded Chinatown, blocked every exit, and began to burn, loot, and kill, hanging nineteen Chinese. In 1877, during another outbreak in Chico, a small city in the Sacramento Valley, mobs tied up four Chinese, set them on fire, and burned them to death.[7]

The Qing government established a Chinese embassy in Washington, D.C., and a consulate office in San Francisco in 1878. When Chen Lanping, the first Chinese minister plenipotentiary, arrived, one of his major tasks involved heading off a Chinese exclusion law being debated in Congress. Chen and Yung Wing, a Yale graduate, visited Secretary of State William Evarts and pointed out that such a law would violate the Burlingame Treaty. Many U.S. merchants and missionaries joined Chen in opposing the proposed law. Although President Rutherford Hayes vetoed the bill, he sent James Angell, president of the University of Michigan, to negotiate a new treaty with China in June 1880.[8]

While Angell negotiated for restrictions on Chinese labor immigration with the Chinese representative, Li Hongzao,[9] another riot broke out in the United States. In October 1880, about 400 whites attacked a group of Chinese without any provocation in Denver, Colorado. The mob killed one Chinese and brutally beat many others. Minister Chen immediately sent an investigation team and demanded compensation as the Burlingame Treaty held the U.S. government liable for such an incident. However, U.S. officials defined the incident as a local issue and refused Chen's compensation request.[10]

During the negotiations with Angell, China was preoccupied with a number of troubling domestic and international issues. Thus, the government signed the 1880 Angell Treaty at the expense of Chinese immigrant interests. The 1880 treaty allowed the U.S. government to regulate, limit, and suspend Chinese labor immigration, although it could not absolutely prohibit such and still guaranteed most-favored-nation treatment to Chinese immigrants— including protecting them from harassment and physical assault.[11]

The Angell Treaty marked a turning point in the U.S.–China immigration relationship. First, it ended open Chinese immigration and delinked U.S. trade interests from the immigration issue. Second, it opened the door for anti-Chinese lobbyists to push for an exclusion law as U.S. politicians realized that immigrants were not a priority consideration in the Qing government's diplomacy. Third, the protection of Chinese immigrants only existed on paper as U.S. public opinion perceived China to be a weak nation that had no military strength to back up any demands.[12]

Within two years of the signing of the Angell Treaty, Republican senator John F. Miller from California proposed an immigration bill that involved suspending Chinese immigration for twenty years, establishing a certification and registration system with deportation and imprisonment penalties, and forbidding state and federal courts from naturalizing Chinese. After both the Senate and the House passed the bill, Zheng Zaoru, a successor of Chen Lanping, immediately protested to Secretary of State Frederick T. Frelinghuysen.[13] However, the Chinese government did not have much bargaining power as it was again beset with a number of international disputes. President Chester Arthur vetoed the bill only because the twenty-year suspension seemed too harsh. Congress quickly adjusted that provision to ten years and passed the bill again. On 6 May 1882, President Arthur signed it into law.[14]

The Chinese Exclusion Act of 1882 resulted in severe and enduring damage to Chinese family life. Between 1882 and 1891, petitioners filed more than seven thousand *habeas corpus* cases in the district court for northern California as the federal collector of San Francisco's port detained numerous Chinese passengers—including women.[15] Two cases illustrate how exclusion laws stopped the entry of Chinese women. In *Chew Heong vs. United States* (1884), the U.S. Supreme Court decided that Chinese laborers who had lived in the United States before 1880 could enter. However, the Court denied them the right to bring in a spouse who had not legally lived in the United States before 1880.[16] In another case in the same year, Judge Sawyer of the Circuit Court for the District of California allowed the entry of a Chinese laborer who possessed a return certificate, but denied the entry of his wife, Ah Quang, who did not have such a certificate. Sawyer based his decision on the premise that the wife of a laborer acquired her husband's occupational status upon marriage. Thus, without a return certificate, she could not enter.[17]

The Chinese Exclusion Act of 1882 further inflamed anti-Chinese hysteria.[18] Violence and mass expulsion reached a peak in 1885. In November of that year, anti-Chinese mobs rioted and threatened to drive away by force every Chinese person in Seattle until the state government sent troops to quiet the agitation. The worst riot occurred in September 1885. When Chinese workers refused to join a strike in Rock Springs, Wyoming, a violent mob of several hundred whites attacked their labor quarters, killing twenty-eight Chinese, wounding fifteen, and destroying property worth $140,000.[19] After this riot, the Qing government's only retaliation involved blocking a newly appointed U.S. ambassador who vehemently advocated exclusion of Chinese laborers.[20]

In September 1888, the U.S. Congress passed the Scott Act, which forbade the entry of Chinese holding a valid return certificate—including over 20,000 Chinese who temporarily had visited their families in China. Both the U.S. Circuit Court in California and the U.S. Supreme Court upheld the constitutionality of the Scott Act in 1889.[21] The Geary Act of 1892 extended the Chinese Exclusion Act of 1882 for another ten years and the Chinese Exclusion Act of 1904 made Chinese exclusion indefinite.[22] Out of frustration over the Qing government's repeated diplomatic failures in dealing with the United States, Chinese people began to boycott U.S. goods in May 1905. Although the boycott did not result in a more favorable treaty, it linked the treatment of Chinese overseas to nationalist sentiment across China.

The Chinese exclusion laws further exacerbated the lopsided gender ratio that existed within the Chinese American community and promoted a population decline from over 100,000 in 1882 to around 85,000 in 1920.[23] In 1890, gender imbalance within the Chinese immigrant community reached its highest point at 27:1.[24] Nevertheless, an 1880 California state law forbade marriages between Chinese and Caucasians. Other western states enforced similar laws. In 1907, white women would lose their U.S. citizenship if they married aliens ineligible for citizenship.[25] During this period, therefore, family life for most Chinese immigrants involved split households. While husbands worked in the United States, wives and children remained in China. For a long time, Chinatown was known as a "bachelor society."

## Trans-Pacific Family Networks as Mobility and Survival Strategies

During the exclusion period, Chinese immigrants in the United States fought many legal battles and even won a number of cases concerning family-reunification rights. In the 1899 *Wong Kim Ark vs. U.S.* case, the Supreme Court ruled that American-born Chinese could become citizens and had the right to enter and re-enter. Children of an American-born Chinese father also were eligible for entry whether they were born in China or the United States.[26] In *Gue Lim vs. U.S.*, the Supreme Court in 1900 affirmed the right of Chinese merchants to bring their wives to the United States as an exempt class. Subsequently, many laboring-class Chinese converted their status to merchants by setting up small businesses.[27]

## *"Paper Sons" and Transnational Households*

The *Wong Kim Ark* case had an unexpected consequence when the 1906 earthquake in San Francisco destroyed all immigration records. Many Chinese took the opportunity to claim American birth. Then, they visited China, reported the birth of a child, and, thus, created an entry slot. The slot could be used to sponsor one's own child, or sold to a potential immigrant who would become the sponsor's "paper son." The discriminatory restrictions affecting other U.S. immigration laws and the weakness of the Qing government meant that many Chinese had no alternative but to approach their immediate social circles, create fraudulent family ties, and use "paper son" schemes to gain entry to the United States.

To enforce the exclusion laws, the U.S. Immigration Service established the notorious Angel Island Detention Center in the middle of San Francisco Bay in 1910 and subjected arriving Chinese to rigorous interrogation. Nevertheless, thousands of Chinese managed to enter the United States during this period. Between 1910 and 1940, the Angel Island Center processed 175,000 Chinese entries and deported about 10 percent of the detainees.[28] The majority of those entering were men without families, and about two-fifths of the Chinese American community at this time consisted of married men living apart from their wives and children.[29] With their wives and children left behind and permanent settlement made difficult by the hostile racial environment they encountered in the United States, Chinese men became perpetual sojourners and the trans-Pacific family became a way of life for many Chinese immigrants during the exclusion period.[30]

While the Immigration Act of 1924 had treated Chinese as aliens ineligible for citizenship, Congress modified the law in 1930 to allow for the entry of a Chinese merchant's wife and of Chinese women married to U.S. citizens before 1924.[31] Between 1910 and 1930, the ratio of Chinese men to women fell from 14:1 to 4:1 due to increases in the U.S.-born Chinese population. The percentage of children (14 and under) rose from 3.4 percent in 1900 to 20.4 percent by 1930.[32] Thus, in spite of racist laws that created obstacles to family formation, the number of Chinese families and American-born Chinese began to grow.

## *Employment Opportunities and Chinese-language Schools*

During the exclusion period, many American-born Chinese discovered that even a college education did not facilitate social mobility in U.S. society. Due to racial prejudice, they could not gain access to professional jobs. According to a 1938 report prepared by the Oriental Division of the U.S. Employment Service in San Francisco, 90 percent of the Chinese youth worked in menial services such as laundries, restaurants, curio shops, or grocery stores.[33] The prevailing racial environment made Chinese language and culture training a must for second-generation Chinese. As the number of children increased, Chinese communities throughout the country gradually established Chinese-language schools where children attended a few more hours of class on Chinese culture following the end of their public-school day. The best-known schools were Daqing shuyuan (Chinese Central High School) in San Francisco, the New York Chinese Public School, and Minglun School in Hawaii. In the late 1930s, the San Francisco Chinese community enrolled over two thousand students in ten schools—seven of which had a junior-high section.[34] The functions of the early Chinese schools were not linguistic and cultural in the sense of preserving an ethnic culture. Instead, as Sauling C. Wong points out, "at the turn of the century, under Exclusion, the Chinese in America had no chance for integration into American life and were therefore seen as logical candidates for contributing to the development of China."[35]

### Return Migration

To avoid being trapped in the segmented labor market, many Chinese youth returned to China to pursue educational and/or job opportunities. In 1933, the San Francisco Chinese-language newspaper *Chung Sai Yat Po* (China-West Daily) strongly advised Chinese youth to return to China, where opportunities were "unlimited" and they would not be denied jobs because of their race.[36]

In 1936, the Ging Hawk Club of New York sponsored a national essay contest for Chinese American youth on the theme "Does My Future Lie in China or America?" Robert Dunn, a Harvard University student who won the contest, concluded that his future lay in the United States because he was as much indebted to America as he was to China, and he was culturally American. Nevertheless, Dunn returned to China after graduation. Kaye Hong, winner of the second prize, firmly believed that China was a land of opportunity for overseas Chinese with U.S. backgrounds.[37] Between 1927 and 1932, about 741 U.S. citizens of Chinese ancestry in Hawaii returned to live in China—including more than a hundred who returned to teach.[38] As Western enterprises and missionary-established educational institutions offered employment opportunities for overseas Chinese, many children of Chinese immigrants in America joined youth from Australia, Cuba, Southeast Asia, and other parts of the world in returning to China.[39]

## From Exclusion to Quotas

Following extensive lobbying by the Citizen Committee to Repeal Chinese Exclusion headed by Richard J. Walsh, an influential New York publisher and husband of Pearl Buck, Congress finally repealed the Chinese exclusion laws in December 1943. The token immigration quota of 105 provided in the new law included Chinese born anywhere in the world. In the War Brides Act of 1946, however, the Chinese wives of U.S. citizens (both native-born and naturalized) could be admitted on a nonquota basis. Between 1948 and 1952, adult women (around 10,000) joining their husbands in the United States comprised 90 percent of all Chinese immigrants. By 1950, the gender ratio among Chinese Americans had reached the level that prevailed among the general population[40] and family separation had been greatly reduced.

## Post-1965 Immigrants

Pushed first by President John F. Kennedy, and signed into law by President Lyndon B. Johnson, the Immigration Act of 1965 removed racial criteria from immigration policy for the first time in U.S. history. A new wave of Asian immigrants began to arrive in large numbers. As the new law provided an equal allotment to each nation-state, the annual quota of 105 jumped to 20,000 for China. In the next fifteen years, approximately a quarter of a million Chinese entered the United States.[41] By 1990, the Chinese community had been transformed from 61 percent American-born in the 1960s to a 70 percent immigrant community.[42]

Ironically, the authors of the 1965 law did not intend to promote Asian immigration. Congressman Emanuel Celler of New York, a major sponsor of the bill, assured his congressional colleagues that few Asians possessed the requisite family networks to enter as immigrants since the entire Asian population in the United States comprised less than 0.5 percent of the total U.S. population. Moreover, Asian immigrants in 1965—approximately 20,683—represented only 5 percent of the total immigrant population.[43] Thus, U.S. politicians believed that the family-reunification principle would primarily benefit European immigrants. Indeed, Italians, Greeks, and Portuguese dominated immigration flows in the first decade following the 1965 reform.[44]

The 1965 law favored family reunification by allocating 80 percent of the available visas to the extended-family members of U.S. citizens and to the immediate-family members of permanent residents. The spouses, minor children, and parents of U.S. citizens do not count against the quota. Chinese immigrants quickly took advantage of these provisions. In 1969, for instance, about 61 percent entered in the family categories.[45] By the mid-1970s, Chinese had overtaken Italians in the quota-exempt categories such as spouse and minor children of U.S. citizens.[46]

This unexpected result reflects, in part, the failure of U.S. politicians to understand Asian American history and culture. The Chinese were one of the pioneer immigrant groups in the American west. As early as the 1860s, Chinese constituted about 10 percent of California's population. Regardless of the small size of the Chinese population in the 1960s, these residents possessed long historical roots in the United States while, at the same time, they maintained kinship relations in Guangdong (Kwangtung)—where migration abroad had become a way of life. Once the opportunity arose, kinship relationships helped many Chinese come to America quickly.

Post-1965 Chinese immigration also reflects U.S.–China relations. To support noncommunist regimes in Korea, Vietnam, and Taiwan, the United States sent troops, built military bases, provided massive financial aid, and opened its domestic market for merchandise produced in these areas. Between 1953 and 1964, the United States injected an average of $100 million a year into the Taiwanese economy.[47] From 1950 to 1974, a total of 30,765 students from Taiwan came to the United States.[48] Most of these students readjusted their legal status through jobs or marriage to American-born Chinese.

After settling down in the United States, professional/student immigrants began to invite their family members to join them. Thus, the new student immigrants became the base for an extended-family immigration network. After obtaining permanent residency through work or marriage to a U.S. citizen, they would become citizens themselves. As citizens, they then could bring in not only quota-exempt parents, but brothers and sisters under Preference 5 in the Immigration Act of 1965. In fact, Preference 5 is the most widely used and most popular preference. By 1985, 81 percent of the Chinese immigrants entered in the family categories, while occupational immigrants dropped to 16 percent.[49] Post-1965 immigration demonstrates that once family networks become the driving force in the chain-migration process, family movements expand and develop their own momentum.

Until 1979, most Chinese immigrants came from Taiwan and Hong Kong since the People's Republic of China (PRC) did not maintain diplomatic relations with the United States. The 1965 Act included a refugee preference to benefit Chinese who had fled China in 1949. Before 1968, non-native persons (mainly refugees from China) comprised over 40 percent (1.5 million) of Hong Kong's total population.[50] They could either enter the United States as refugees, or by using family preferences.[51]

As a British colony, moreover, Hong Kong had a quota of its own. The Immigration Reform and Control Act of 1986 expanded the quota for Hong

Kong to 5,000. When China began to negotiate with Britain about resuming sovereign responsibility for Hong Kong in 1997, Congress enlarged the quota—first to 10,000 in 1990, and then to 20,000 in 1995.[52]

The quota set for Taiwan is linked to U.S. foreign policy in Asia as well. As China stepped up its reunification campaign, Congress quietly granted a separate 20,000 quota in a 1981 defense bill that provided Taiwan with U.S. protection from China.[53] In sum, the total annual quota of 60,000 for Chinese from the PRC, Taiwan, and Hong Kong is not only a result of immigration reform, but a consequence of international politics, especially U.S.-China relations.

The normalization of relations between the United States and China in 1979 occurred almost simultaneously with reforms in the People's Republic of China. As part of China's reforms, the government relaxed its emigration restrictions. At the same time, normalization made it possible for Chinese to enter the United States directly from China. Thus, China issued 1,346,909 exit permits between 1979 and 1990, and 700,000 persons actually obtained visas to enter or immigrate to another country. The United States quickly became the largest receiving country of Chinese emigration.[54]

Reform and normalization also encouraged cultural-exchange activities between the two countries and allowed Chinese students to study in the United States. The PRC government required graduate students to return to China after they completed their studies. To ensure their return, China requested that the United States issue J-1 (exchange) rather than F-1 visas to Chinese students. According to U.S. immigration rules, J-1 visa holders should return to their home country for at least two years before they are allowed to apply for permanent residency in the United States. Unwilling to damage the newly normalized Sino-U.S. reconciliation, the U.S. government cooperated. As graduate studies, especially doctoral programs, take a long time to complete, the PRC government also often allowed the spouse to join a married graduate student under the *peidu* (student-dependent) policy.[55]

To protest the actions taken by the Chinese government in the Tiananmen Incident in 1989, and as a gesture of sympathy with the student victims, President George Bush announced on 2 December 1989 that 80,000 Chinese students and their families would be allowed to stay in the United States. Furthermore, the policy permitted all Mainland Chinese who had arrived before the end of 1989 to apply for permanent residency if they wished. The *liusi luka* (June 4th Green Card) provided numerous Chinese students and scholars with a shortcut to permanent residency.[56] As many eligible students already had their spouses and children with them because of the *peidu* policy, both husband and wife could sponsor their parents separately—allowing them to obtain permanent residency and citizenship within a few years. Then, other siblings in the family could join them by using family preferences in the immigration law. Between 1991 and 1998, 350,000 Mainland Chinese immigrated to the United States.[57] Thus, like traditional Chinese immigrants before them, the "June 4th Green Card" students and scholars functioned as the nucleus for an extended-kin migration network. President Bush's action also made the Chinese American community even more diverse, as eligible Chinese students and visiting scholars came from all over China.

Whether they came from China, Taiwan, or Hong Kong, post-1965 Chinese immigrants belong to a truly trans-Pacific community. Many of them maintain close kinship, social, and cultural ties with their home areas through letters, phone calls, e-mail, and other forms of communication. In their daily life, they eat Chinese food, speak Mandarin or a Chinese dialect at home,[58] listen to Chinese-language radio stations, watch Chinese-language television channels, and/or read Chinese-language newspapers. In 1995, the southern California Chinese community supported at least 23 different daily and weekly Chinese language newspapers and there were seven daily Chinese-language newspapers and three television stations in the San Francisco area.[59] These media outlets keep the Chinese American community attuned to developments in Hong Kong, Taiwan, and the China Mainland. Thus, the lives of contemporary Chinese immigrant families are shaped by their transnational links as well as by adaptation to U.S. situations.

### Three Types of Contemporary Trans-Pacific Chinese Families

The members of today's mobile Chinese families are not uprooted individuals, but participants in a socially connected migrant network that spans national boundaries. Return migration and remigration are part of the continuous flow of people within these transnational networks.

As immigration to the United States often involves downward mobility, especially for educated Chinese, the trans-Pacific family remains a viable strategy for contemporary Chinese immigrants concerned with maximizing resources and opportunities. Many contemporary Chinese immigrants are highly educated and worked as business executives, educators, or other professionals in their place of origin. Although the U.S. racial environment has improved, language barriers, the "glass ceiling," and lack of a U.S. college diploma or professional license remain major obstacles to career success for new immigrants. Consequently, many educated Chinese immigrants who pursue jobs locally are employed in the service sector—restaurants, businesses, bakeries, beauty shops, gift shops, and so forth. As vibrant Asian economies grow further and become increasingly integrated into global capitalism, U.S. business and employment prospects become increasingly uninviting and reverse and circular migration take on greater appeal among professionals and entrepreneurs.

Circular and reverse migration rarely involve the entire family, however. Three types of trans-Pacific Chinese families are common today. In one version, the family emigrates to the United States, but the chief breadwinner, usually the husband, returns to work in the place of origin shortly after obtaining permanent residency. He periodically flies back to the States to visit his family. Such frequent air travelers are referred to as "astronauts." Their commuting is facilitated by the dozens of daily flights that link major U.S. metropolitan areas to Hong Kong, Taiwan, and major cities in the Mainland. In 1993, the *Los Angeles Times* reported that David Wong, a typical "astronaut," made the twelve-hour flight between Hong Kong and Los Angeles twelve times a year. He usually vacationed in the United States for one or two weeks, while he mostly worked in Asia. One anecdote about such "astronauts" involves the commuter who reported his permanent address on the landing card as "Seat 1A, First Class, Cathay Pacific."[60] Returning to high-paying jobs or lucrative businesses in the place of origin allows trans-Pacific families to minimize the economic sacrifices involved in migration to the United States.

In the second type of trans-Pacific Chinese family, both husband and wife return to work in Asia—leaving their children by themselves in the United States as "latch-key" or "parachute" kids. Although such physical separation involves hardships and can have adverse psychological effects on children, the intense competition in college-entrance exams that exists in China, Hong Kong, and Taiwan, the more flexible and less demanding nature of the U.S. K–12 school system, and the greater marketability of degrees from U.S. universities, explains why upper- and middle-class families choose this trans-Pacific family-migration strategy. My May/June 2000 in-person and telephone survey of fifty youth from Taiwan and Hong Kong living in southern California revealed that half of them had parents or siblings commuting across the Pacific to work in the place of origin. Most of those interviewed confirmed that their parents came here so that the children might benefit from the U.S. educational system.[61]

In the third type of trans-Pacific Chinese family, all nuclear family members are based in the United States. However, they maintain extensive transnational kinship networks and close ties with their place of origin. In 1990, the *Los Angeles Times* reported about a Chinese family with relatives in more than three nations. A U.S. citizen in Orange County, California, Victor Chung came from China as a former Red Guard and graduated from U.C.–Berkeley. He managed a company that assembled components exported to the China Mainland. Typically, Chung made ten or more trips across the

Pacific a year to confer in Thailand with his grandfather—who directed family business operations in Hong Kong, Taiwan, China, and Vancouver. His grandfather's six sons and seven daughters had produced the third generation that spanned the Pacific Ocean.[62] Just as the nuclear Chung family in California is part of a Chung clan that stretches across the Pacific, many other Chinese American families are connected with a global family network and are not just part of the Asian American community.[63]

The three types of contemporary Chinese American trans-Pacific families demonstrate that migration typically has not been an individual adventure; it has been a collective action, with the family and kinship relationship as its central organizing unit. Instead of family collectivism giving way to individualism, there has been a compromise between personal goals and the greater good of the family and lineage. Migration often is a family decision involving mutual commitment from parents and children in the interest of collective upward social and economic mobility.

The contemporary trans-Pacific family pattern also demonstrates that immigration does not mean a complete break from the past as much as the beginning of a new life that transcends national boundaries. Instead of a unidirectional trip from Asia to America, the Chinese trans-Pacific family experience involves prolonged, complicated, transnational circular migration. During this ongoing process, family members continuously consider and reconsider various factors that might affect their lives and the strategies they should adopt in the best interest of their collective future.

## Trans-Pacific Families and the Future of U.S.–China Relations

The trans-Pacific family pattern demonstrates a complexity that the classical assimilationist model is unable to account for. One obvious divergence from the classical model is the strengthening rather than weakening of family and kinship ties in the migration process. During the chain-migration process, family and kinship networks are dislocated and reorganized, but not disrupted. Social instability and political weakness in China and the racial environment in the United States prevented family members from developing a sense of community attached to place rooted on either side of the Pacific. Instead, the family itself became the focal point of social existence. In a circular manner, members of Chinese immigrant families traveled back and forth across the Pacific and maintained involvement in both societies for decades.

Although separation has been a painful experience, the history of the Chinese trans-Pacific family is replete with evidence of resilience and adaptability when confronted with immigration restrictions and racial discrimination.

Thanks to their creative coping strategies, family members have succeeded in defying nation-state territorial boundaries and maneuvering around spatial barriers. As a minority both in their place of origin and in the receiving country, however, transmigrants risk acquiring a doubly marginal status. The historical experience reviewed here suggests that Chinese American families have an important stake in a healthy U.S.–China relationship in the new century.

Among the various social forces that could re-shape U.S.–China relations, Chinese American families are among the most established global players. Chinese-immigrant entrepreneurs not only have transplanted their family networks, they also have expanded Chinese-owned trans-Pacific trade, transportation businesses, and banks. The third type of trans-Pacific family, in particular, illustrates how Chinese Americans who maintain borderless family networks act to strengthen U.S.–China economic relations—one critically important aspect of the overall relationship. Businesses on both sides need a gateway to help penetrate each other's market. Trans-Pacific family networks of all three types can provide such a gateway.[64] Family and kinship connections are the Chinese rim's building blocks. Given their global family networks and economic power,[65] Chinese Americans have profoundly shaped and will continue to influence U.S.–China relations.

## Notes

1. See Francis Hsu, *The Challenge of the American Dream: The Chinese in the United States* (Belmont, CA: Wadsworth, 1971); Shien-woo Kung, *Chinese in American Life: Some Aspects of Their History, Status, Problems, and Contributions* (Seattle: University of Washington Press, 1962); Melford Weiss, *Valley City: A Chinese Community in America* (Cambridge: Schenkman, 1974); Shih-shan Henry Tsai, *The Chinese Experience in America* (Bloomington: Indiana University Press, 1986); Betty Lee Sung, *The Adjustment Experience of Chinese Immigrant Children in New York City* (New York: Center for Migration Studies, 1987).

2. On Chinese transnational family networks, see Haiming Liu, "The Trans-Pacific Family: A Case Study of Sam Chang's Family History," *Amerasia Journal* 18, No. 2 (1992): 1–34; James T. Fawcett and Fred Arnold, "Explaining Diversity: Asian and Pacific Immigration Systems," in *Pacific Bridges: The New Immigration from Asia and the Pacific Islands*, ed. by James T. Fawcett and Benjamin V. Cariono (New York: Center for Migration Studies, 1987), pp. 453–473; Choi Kwai Keong, "Overseas Chinese Family," in *The Encyclopedia of the Chinese Overseas*, ed. by Lynn Pan (Cambridge: Harvard University Press, 1999), pp. 77–80.

3. Mary Coolidge, *Chinese Immigration* (New York: Henry Holt and Company, 1909), p. 18; Roger Daniels, *Asian America: Chinese and Japanese in the United States Since 1850* (Seattle: University of Washington Press, 1988), p. 16.

4. Li Chunhui, Yang Shengmao, Sha Ding, Li Chaozeng, Liang Zuosheng, and Lu Guojun, *Meizhou huaqiao huaren shi* (A history of Chinese immigration to North and South America) (Beijing: Dongfang, 1990), p. 229.

5. Liu Pei-chi (Liu Baiji), *Meizhou huaqiao yishi* (A history of the Chinese in America) (Taipei: Liming, 1976), pp. 557–558.

6. On the Burlingame Treaty of 1868 and various exclusion laws, see *Racism, Dissent, and Asian Americans from 1850 to the Present: A Documentary History*, ed. by Philip S. Foner and Daniel Rosenberg (Westport: Greenwood Press, 1993), pp. 22–23; and Appendix C in Bill Ong Hing, *Making Asian America Through Immigration Policy, 1850–1990* (Stanford: Stanford University Press, 1993).

7. Sucheng Chan, *Asian Americans: An Interpretive History* (Boston: Twayne, 1991), p. 49.

8. Tsai, *Chinese Experience*, p. 60.

9. Ibid., pp. 60–62; and Liu, *A History of the Chinese in America*, pp. 565–566.

10. Li et al., *Chinese Immigration*, p. 229.

11. Tsai, *Chinese Experience*, pp. 61–63.

12. Foner and Rosenberg, *Racism*, p. 107.

13. Tsai, *Chinese Experience*, p. 64.

14. For a detailed discussion regarding the passage of the Chinese Exclusion Act of 1882, see Shirley Hune, "Politics of Chinese Exclusion: Legislative Executive Conflict 1876–1882," *Amerasia Journal* 9, No. 1 (1982): 5–27.

15. Christian G. Fritz, "Due Process, Treaty Rights, and Chinese Exclusion, 1882–1891," in *Entry Denied: Exclusion and the Chinese Community in America, 1882–1943*, ed. by Sucheng Chan (Philadelphia: Temple University Press, 1991), p. 28.

16. Hing, *Asian America*, p. 24.

17. Sucheng Chan, "The Exclusion of Chinese Women," in *Entry Denied: Exclusion and the Chinese Community in America, 1882–1943*, ed. by Sucheng Chan (Philadelphia: Temple University Press, 1991), p. 110.

18. Tsai, *Chinese Experience*, p. 67.

19. Li et al., *Chinese Immigration*, p. 210; and Tsai, *Chinese Experience*, p. 70.

20. Joanna Waley-Cohen, *The Sextants of Beijing: Global Currents in Chinese History* (New York: W.W. Norton, 1999), p. 177.

21. Charles J. McClain and Laurene Wu McClain, "The Chinese Contribution to the Development of American Law," in *Entry Denied: Exclusion and the Chinese Community in America, 1882–1943*, ed. by Sucheng Chan (Philadelphia: Temple University Press, 1991), pp. 17–20.

22. Stanford Lyman, *Chinese Americans* (New York: Random House, 1974), pp. 55–85.

23. Hing, *Asian America*, p. 47.

24. Timothy P. Fong, "The History of Asians in America," in *Asian Americans: Experiences and Perspectives*, ed. by Timothy P. Fong and Larry H. Shinagawa (Upper Saddle River, NJ: Prentice Hall, 2000), pp. 13–14; and Chan, "Exclusion of Chinese Women," p. 94.

25. Hing, *Asian America*, p. 45.

26. McClain and McClain, "Chinese Contribution," pp. 20–21.

27. Chan, "Exclusion of Chinese Women," pp. 94–146.

28. Tsai, *Chinese Experience*, p. 100.

29. Madeline Y. Hsu, *Dreaming of Gold, Dreaming of Home: Transnationalism and Migration Between the United States and South China, 1882–1943* (Stanford: Stanford University Press, 2000), p. 99.

30. In one extreme case, three generations of men in a Chinese family worked over sixty years before being able to bring a female member of the family to the United States. The grandfather arrived in 1890, worked and sojourned for twenty years until he retired in China in the 1910s—when his son came to take over his small business. The son continued to work alone until he sent for his own son in the 1940s. The third-generation immigrant finally managed to bring his wife over in the 1950s, although this family did not have their first U.S.-born child until the 1960s. Evelyn Nakano Glenn, "Split Household, Small Producer and Dual Wage Earner: An Analysis of Chinese-American Family Strategies," *Journal of Marriage and the Family* 45 (February 1983): 35–46.

31. Him Mark Lai and Philip P. Choy, *Outlines: History of the Chinese in America* (San Francisco: Chinese American Studies Planning Group, 1972), p. 53.

32. Evelyn Nakano Glenn with Stacey G.H. Yap, "Chinese American Families," in *Asian Americans: Experiences and Perspectives*, ed. by Timothy P. Fong and Larry H. Shinagawa (Upper Saddle River, NJ: Prentice Hall, 2000), p. 279.

33. See Carey McWilliams, *Brothers Under the Skin* (Boston: Little, Brown and Company, 1942), p. 111.

34. Li et al., *Chinese Immigration*, pp. 240–242; Liu Baiji and K. Tom, "Functions of the Chinese Language Schools," *Sociology and Social Research* 25 (1941): 557–561; *Chongshan ribao* (Zhongshan daily) cited in Yong Chen, *Chinese San Francisco 1850–1943: A Trans-Pacific Community* (Stanford: Stanford University Press, 2000), p. 230.

35. Sauling C. Wong, "The Language Situation of Chinese Americans," in *Language Diversity: Problem or Resource*, ed. by Sandra Lee McKay and Sauling C. Wong (New York: Newbury House, 1988), p. 213.

36. Ronald Takaki, *Strangers from a Different Shore: A History of Asian Americans* (Boston: Little, Brown, 1989), p. 267.

37. For contest essays, see *Chinese America: History and Perspectives (1992)* (San Francisco: Chinese American Historical Society, 1992), pp. 148–176.

38. In addition, several pioneering Chinese pilots in Hawaii returned to China in the 1910s and started aviation enterprises. Tsai, *Chinese Experience*, p. 112.

39. See John King Fairbank and Edwin Reischauer, *China: Tradition and Transformation* (Boston: Houghton Mifflin, 1989), p. 393; John King Fairbank, ed., *The Missionary Enterprise in China and America* (Cambridge: Harvard University Press, 1974); William P. Fenn, *Christian Higher Education in Changing China, 1880–1950* (Grand Rapids, MI: Eerdmans, 1976); Jessie G. Lutz, *China and the Christian Colleges, 1850–1950* (Ithaca, NY: Cornell University Press, 1971); and Philip West, *Yenching University and Sino-Western Relations, 1916–1952* (Cambridge: Harvard University Press, 1976).

40. David Reimers, *Still the Golden Door: The Third World Comes to America* (New York: Columbia University Press, 1992), p. 27; and Hing, *Asian America*, p. 49.

41. Reimers, *Golden Door*, p. 103.

42. Takaki, *Strangers from a Different Shore*, p. 421.

43. Reimers, *Golden Door*, p. 92.

44. Ibid., p. 89.

45. Hing, *Asian America*, p. 81.

46. Reimers, *Golden Door*, p. 103. Between 1961 and 1970, the number of Chinese immigrants admitted to the United States reached 109,771—four times greater than the number for the previous decade. Min Zhou, *Chinatown: The Socioeconomic Potential of an Urban Enclave* (Philadelphia: Temple University Press, 1992), p. 45.

47. John Liu and Lucie Cheng, "Pacific Rim Development and the Duality of Post-1965 Asian Immigration to the United States," in *The New Asian Immigration in Los Angeles and Global Restructuring*, ed. by Paul Ong, Edna Bonacich, and Lucie Cheng (Philadelphia: Temple University Press, 1994), p. 76.

48. Huping Ling, *Surviving on the Gold Mountain: A History of Chinese American Women and Their Lives* (Albany: State University of New York Press, 1998), p. 150.

49. Hing, *Asian America*, p. 81.

50. Ibid., pp. 250–251, note 214.

51. Most non-Chinese filed immigration petitions with documents such as a birth certificate, marriage certificate, or family registry. Chinese needed to provide a long list of secondary evidence, such as photographs, old correspondence, school records, money receipts, affidavits, blood tests, and old Hong Kong documents. Immigration officials sometimes trusted these documents and sometimes did not. Ibid., p. 116.

52. Reimers, *Golden Door*, p. 103.

53. Hing, *Asian America*, p. 82.

54. Zhou, *Chinatown*, p. 57.

55. See Leo Orleans, *Chinese Students in America: Policies, Issues, and Numbers* (Washington, D.C.: National Academy Press, 1988), pp. 4–9, 114–122.

56. See David Zweig and Changgui Chen, *China's Brain Drain to the United States: Views of Overseas Chinese Students and Scholars in the 1990s* (Berkeley: University of California, Institute of East Asia Studies, 1995); Jianji Huang, *Chinese Students and Scholars in American Higher Education* (Westport: Greenwood, 1997), pp. 185–205; and Xiao-huang Yin, *Chinese American Literature Since the 1850s*, (Urbana: University of Illinois Press, 2000), pp. 185–205.

57. Evelyn Iritani, "Chinese in U.S. Shape Economy," *Los Angeles Times*, 17 October 1999, p. A1.

58. The *Los Angeles Times* 1997 survey indicated that 79 percent of the Chinese in southern California spoke Chinese at home. K. Connie Kang, "Chinese in the Southland: A Changing Picture," *Los Angeles Times*, 27 June 1997, p. A1.

59. Joe Chung Fong, "Transnational Newspapers: The Making of the Post-1965 Globlized/Localized San Gabriel Valley Chinese Community," *Amerasia Journal* 22, No. 3 (1996): 65–77; Mary Curtius, "A Coming of Age for S.F. Chinese," *Los Angeles Times*, 11 October 1999, p. A1.

60. Daniela Deane, "Have Job, Will Travel," *Los Angeles Times*, 31 March 1993, p. E1.

61. Also see Nancy Cleeland, "Irvine Grows as Chinese Gateway: Schools, High-Tech Jobs Are Magnets Creating a Demographic Shift," *Los Angeles Times*, 7 December 1998, p. B1.

62. Robert W. Gibson, "Networks of Chinese Rim Pacific," *Los Angeles Times*, 22 July 1990, p. A1.

63. In Southeast Asia, there are nearly six thousand family clan networks like the Chung clan—many of which are involved in global business activities. John Naisbitt, *Megatrends Asia: Eight Asian Megatrends That Are Reshaping Our World* (New York: Simon & Schuster, 1996).

64. Ibid., pp. 47–49.

65. See Robert W. Gibson, "Networks of Chinese Rim Pacific," p. A1; and J.A.C. Mackie, "Chinese Business Organizations," in *The Encyclopedia of the Chinese Overseas*, ed. by Lynn Pan (Cambridge: Harvard University Press, 1999), pp. 91–93.

# 2

# Navigating U.S.–China Waters

## The Experience of Chinese Students and Professionals in Science, Technology, and Business

### Sufei Li

After the normalization of U.S.–China diplomatic relations in 1979, large numbers of Chinese, mostly young graduate students, began to come to the United States for advanced education and training—especially in science and technology. The wave reached its peak at the end of the 1980s and remained stable in the 1990s. Why does this population movement deserve special attention? What impact has it had and is it likely to have on U.S.–China relations?

Encouraging students to study in the United States is not a new phenomenon in Chinese history. The Chinese government also sent students abroad to study science and technology during two earlier periods. The first period commenced in 1870 and ended with the Chinese Exclusion Act of 1882. Although a relatively small number of students arrived during the short initial period, this pioneering development set the stage for the future movements.[1]

The Boxer Rebellion Indemnity scholarships established in the early twentieth century for the education of Chinese students in the United States provided the impetus for the second period, which lasted approximately thirty years. The government of China used this program for the training of Chinese professionals in the United States in order to strengthen the country's economic development. A number of Chinese educated at U.S. universities during this period later became well-known scientists in their fields and made important contributions to China and the United States. For instance, the first group of scholarship recipients included Bing Zhi (Ph.D., Cornell, 1918), the founder of the first biological institute in China; Zhu Kezhen (Ph.D., Harvard, 1918), later president of Zhejiang University; and Hu Shi (Ph.D., Columbia, 1917), later the president of Beijing University and ambassador to the United States.[2]

Over these three periods, which span more than a century and vastly different political systems, Chinese authorities held consistent intentions and expectations with respect to students sent to the United States; that is, governments expected them to learn science and technology and, after completing their studies abroad, to return to serve the state. However, the results, especially during the third period, have frustrated official intentions. In particular, many of those sent to the United States chose to stay instead of going back to China immediately. While the PRC experienced a short-run loss from the draining out of their intelligent minds, these U.S.-educated professionals still have contributed in important ways to China's modernization and to U.S.–China relations.

This chapter is devoted, first, to analyzing the educational backgrounds of students and professionals from the People's Republic of China who arrived in and, in many cases, have settled in the United States over the past two decades. The terms *student* and *professional* are used to distinguish those who are studying in universities and colleges abroad from those who have graduated and are working in professional jobs.[3] The issue of brain drain versus brain gain presents the central focus for discussion. Recent data regarding the academic fields of study of Chinese students, their personal interests and career development, as well as their present and future prospects provide the basis for evaluation. Based on the results of this assessment, I will consider the likely future impact of immigrants in science, technology, and business on China and on U.S.–China relations.

## Government Policies and Student Flows: The Interaction of PRC Policies and Individual Interests and Decisions

In 1978, the government of the People's Republic of China introduced a series of major reforms that included the education sector. After being isolated from the outside world for more than a decade, Deng Xiaoping emphasized the importance of sending students to study abroad in order to expedite the development and modernization of the country so that China could catch up with the rest of the world in the shortest possible time. In June 1978, during a meeting with the governing body of Qinghua University, Deng maintained that China should send large numbers of students to study other countries' advanced science and technology as soon as possible. This speech later became the basis for the new national policy on sending students abroad.[4]

Between the time of Deng Xiaoping's 1978 speech and 1999, according to statistics issued by the PRC's Ministry of Education, about 320,000 Mainland students and scholars studied in approximately 103 countries.[5] This number is more than twice as many as the total number of students/scholars who studied abroad during the two earlier sending periods in Chinese history. The recent group includes roughly 150,000 students funded by Chinese authorities (50,000 with government sponsorship and 100,000 sponsored by Mainland institutions they were affiliated with) and 170,000 self-sponsored students. More than 160,000 of the total have studied in the United States. The Ministry contends that, as of 1998, 96,000 U.S.-educated students, and 60 percent of all students who studied abroad, had returned to China.[6] However, figures released by the Education Section of the Embassy of the People's Republic of China in the United States in 1999 indicate that only 30,000 of the U.S. group (19 percent) had returned as of 1998.[7]

The PRC government has adjusted the policies that govern sending students abroad several times over the past twenty years. From 1978 to 1983, the government mainly allowed advanced-study students and visiting scholars to leave for the United States. For instance, the Nobel Prize winner, T.D. Lee (Tsung Dao Lee, or Li Zhengdao), established the China-U.S. Physics Examination and Applications (CUSPEA) program in 1980. Each year, from 1980 to 1988, the program supported 100 top Chinese physics students for graduate studies at elite U.S. universities or research institutions.[8]

From 1983 to 1986, additional educational reforms granted Chinese universities greater autonomy from the central government. At the same time, the government encouraged universities to establish academic-exchange programs with their own overseas counterparts. The availability of financial assistance from U.S. universities enabled many who did not qualify for Chinese government funding to study in the United States. Thus, between 1984 and 1987, more than half of all Mainland students who went abroad attended U.S. universities[9] and the total number of graduate students from the PRC in the United States increased dramatically. Institute of International Education (IIE) statistics show that the number of PRC students in the United States doubled in 1986 (20,030) over the 1984 number (10,100).[10]

Between 1986 and 1989, China's policy returned to favoring advanced-study students and visiting scholars and excluded undergraduate students— who had a poor record of returning from the United States after completing their studies. The government also realized that sending undergraduate students abroad did not constitute the most efficient way to meet the nation's advanced science and technology needs. Although it imposed more restrictions on those who applied after 1989 (including the requirement that college graduates must complete five years of public service, or pay 10,000 RMB for each year short of five, before leaving the country for further studies), the number of graduate students coming to the United States still increased—even though the five-year requirement prevented some from studying abroad immediately after graduation. Many received scholarships or financial support from U.S. universities or through overseas ties.[11]

Table 2.1

**Chinese Students Studying in the United States, 1979–2000**

| Year | Total Number | Year | Total Number |
|------|------|------|------|
| 1979–80 | 1,000 | 1989–90 | 33,390 |
| 1980–81 | 2,770 | 1990–91 | 39,600 |
| 1981–82 | 4,350 | 1991–92 | 42,940 |
| 1982–83 | 6,230 | 1992–93 | 45,126 |
| 1983–84 | 8,140 | 1993–94 | 44,381 |
| 1984–85 | 10,100 | 1994–95 | 39,403 |
| 1985–86 | 13,980 | 1995–96 | 39,613 |
| 1986–87 | 20,030 | 1996–97 | 42,503 |
| 1987–88 | 25,170 | 1997–98 | 46,958 |
| 1988–89 | 29,040 | 1998–99 | 51,001 |
|  |  | 1999–00 | 54,466 |

*Source:* Compiled by the author from the Institute of International Education's *50 Years of Open Doors*, CD-ROM disk (New York: IIE, 2000), and from the *Open Doors* website at www.iie.org.

The 1989 Tiananmen Incident did not stop Mainland students from coming to the United States either. Table 2.1 clearly shows a steady increase in Chinese students studying here in the post-Tiananmen period. By 1997–1998, only students from Japan outnumbered those from the PRC. Since 1998, students from the China Mainland have been at the top of the list. Year 2000 figures indicate that PRC students comprise 10.5 percent of all international students studying in the United States.[12]

The Chinese government refers to those who receive financial support from outside the country as *self-financed* students. Self-financed study, one of the channels encouraged by the government for study abroad, increased dramatically in the mid to late 1980s.[13] Over the past two decades, more than 120,000 self-financed students went abroad. According to Ministry of Public Security statistics, between 20,000 and 30,000 students apply annually for self-financed study. In Beijing alone, over 5,000 applicants with university degrees in 1997 (and more than 6,000 in 1998) applied. Most of the successful applicants came to the United States.[14]

Unlike other Western countries such as France, Germany, and the United Kingdom, where the return rate exceeded 50 percent, the rate of return among those who studied in the United States did not even reach 20 percent.[15] One reason for such a wide gap is that many graduates found jobs in the United States after completing their studies. Thus, the PRC's policy adjustments proved to be no match for individual interests and diligence in finding ways to stay in the United States.

## Chinese Students on U.S. Campuses: Destinations, Academic Levels, Fields of Study, and Future Careers

### Destinations

Since 1985, when PRC nationals became one of the largest foreign-student populations, almost every major U.S. university has enrolled Chinese students. However, the majority went to a few big states. Data show that California, New York, Texas, Massachusetts, and Illinois are the five states enrolling the most international students. They also indicate that among the top ten institutions hosting the largest numbers of Chinese students, six are found in those states.[16]

### Academic Levels

Starting in 1989, the PRC adjusted its policy by no longer sponsoring students for undergraduate studies. Since then, private sponsors, like relatives, supported the majority of undergraduates who came to the United States. Visa figures from the University of Minnesota illustrate the dramatic changes that occurred at the beginning of the 1990s in the type of PRC student enrollment (see Table 2.2). The decline in J-1 student visa numbers at the University of Minnesota shows that fewer and fewer students received government sponsorship by 1991.

During 1990–1991, graduate students comprised the largest percentage of new arrivals. Those arriving as J-1 visiting scholars remained relatively steady in their numbers. As part of its tighter controls, the PRC had required that all junior faculty at Mainland universities apply for J-1 visas because J-1 scholars are limited to a maximum of three years in the United States. J-1 scholars are also required to return home for at least two years before changing to work visas. These requirements made it almost impossible for PRC scholars to stay in the United States at that time.[17]

By 1997–1998, China ranked as the number one country on the enrollment list for U.S. research and doctoral institutions. Among the total of 46,958 Chinese students, 25,835 enrolled in research institutions, 7,270 in doctoral institutions, and 10,642 in master's institutions. Only 7 percent of all PRC students attended liberal arts colleges, community colleges, and other specialized institutions.[18] In 1998–1999, 12.9 percent of all students from the Mainland participated in undergraduate programs and 80.9 percent in graduate programs; another 6.3 percent attended other institutions.[19]

Table 2.2

**Visa Type Held by Chinese Students: University of Minnesota, 1988–1991**

|         | Scholars J-1 | Students J-1 | Students F-1 |
|---------|--------------|--------------|--------------|
| 1988–89 | 64           | 40           | 50           |
| 1989–90 | 49           | 15           | 106          |
| 1990–91 | 41           | 3            | 69           |

*Source:* Adapted from M.P. Needle, "A University of Minnesota Report," *China Exchange News* 19, No. 1 (Spring 1991): 18.

## Fields of Study

We can see from Table 2.3 that 41 percent of the 44,318 Chinese students in the United States during the 1993–1994 academic year (the last breakdown available from IIE) studied engineering, math and computer science, physical and life sciences. Another 10 percent engaged in business studies. In 1997, 88 percent of the doctoral students from China studied physical sciences, engineering, or life sciences, and less than 5 percent studied social sciences.[20]

In contrast, the percentage of undergraduate students majoring in business (23 percent) was higher than those in engineering (16 percent) and the physical/life sciences (11 percent). The choice of major usually is an individual decision among undergraduate students since they are privately (family) funded and do not face any government restrictions. These findings suggest an interesting change in the traditional view that natural science is more important than any other field. Among most family-funded undergraduates, the choice of major is primarily shaped by the U.S. job market; many later become involved in international business—especially with China.

## Career Pursuits

Chinese students who studied in the United States during the past two decades have received financial support from the PRC government, U.S.–China exchange programs, U.S. university scholarships and assistantships, and overseas relatives. Of these, U.S. academic institutions have provided the largest portion of financial support for Chinese students and scholars—approximately $200 million annually—mainly in the form of teaching and research assistantships.[21] In the case of visiting scholars, financial support came from mixed sources, including the Chinese government, U.S. universities, international organizations, and private funds. In particular, many universities hired visiting scholars for laboratory research.

University authorities generally found Chinese graduate students and schol-

Table 2.3

**Chinese Students by Field of Study, 1993–1994** (in percent)

| Field | Total | Graduate | Undergraduate |
|---|---|---|---|
| Agriculture | 2.4 | 2.8 | 1.0 |
| Business | 10.8 | 8.7 | 22.7 |
| Education | 2.5 | 2.5 | 1.5 |
| Engineering | 22.0 | 23.9 | 15.8 |
| Fine and applied arts | 2.6 | 2.0 | 4.5 |
| Health science | 4.1 | 3.5 | 7.0 |
| Humanities | 2.3 | 2.6 | 1.2 |
| Math and computer science | 12.1 | 12.0 | 14.7 |
| Physical and life science | 26.9 | 31.5 | 10.8 |
| Social science | 6.6 | 6.3 | 3.4 |
| Other | 3.8 | 3.2 | 6.9 |
| IEP | 0.8 | 0.1 | 3.6 |
| Undeclared | 3.1 | 1.2 | 7.0 |
| Total | 44,318 | 8,418 | 3,854 |

*Source:* Adapted from Todd Davis, ed., *Open Doors 1994–1995, Report on International Educational Exchange* (New York: Institute of International Education, 1995), pp. 52–53.

ars to be academically competitive, hard-working assistants, and capable of adapting to the U.S. university scene.[22] Furthermore, most universities use GRE scores as one of the criteria in evaluating applicants for financial support. Mainland students receive strong preparation in mathematics and, therefore, often score high on the GRE quantitative examination. Moreover, most Chinese graduate students applied in the physical sciences, engineering, biological sciences, and health sciences—fields that typically secure industrial or government funding for long- or short-term research projects. Faculty with this type of funding need to hire graduate assistants to work on various projects. Given their reputation for being hard-working, many labs hired Chinese graduate students.[23]

After Chinese students graduated and completed their post-doctoral training, however, they often encountered employment difficulties. Some of those who came to train in occupations desperately needed in China had difficulty finding employment in their field in the United States in cases where demand for such occupations was low (e.g., animal science, economics, English).[24] Thus, even some doctoral-degree holders opted to change their careers, often at their own expense, to occupations (such as computer science) in which they had no former training, but which held out bright U.S. employment prospects and promised higher salaries. David Zweig and Chan Changgui's mid-1990 study confirms that in order to stay in the United States, many Mainland graduates switched to applied sciences (including computer science) as an immigration strategy. This development raises two possibilities: either China is experiencing a severe loss of trained minds in sorely needed fields, or these newly skilled technical personnel still will play an important role in helping China.[25] We shall return to this issue later in the chapter.

### Residency Trends Among Ph.D. Recipients and Other PRC Students and Professionals

The 1989 Tiananmen Incident convinced most Chinese students in the United States that they should not return home immediately. The political climate in China and economic conditions in the United States presented a sharp contrast. In addition to the relative political freedom available, most Chinese students opted to remain in the United States due to superior current and future employment opportunities and working conditions.[26]

However, many of those who desired to remain here held either J-1 or J-2 visas, which required that after completing the study program one must return to one's home country for at least two years before being eligible to come back to the United States. President George Bush's Executive Order 12711—granting Mainland Chinese in the United States between 5 June 1989 and 11 April 1990 permission to stay—provided the opportunity to remain legally.[27] As a result, over 60,000 Chinese students, not including family members, are estimated to have remained in the United States.[28] Highly educated in both China and the United States, these professional immigrants have been integrated into mainstream society to an extent unimaginable among earlier Chinese immigrants who lived and worked inside Chinatowns.

Students from the PRC comprise the largest group of foreigners who earn doctoral degrees in the United States. Table 2.4 shows that 2,408 students from China earned doctorates in 1997—mainly in science and engineering. Among these graduates, fully 95 percent stayed in the United States.[29] In general, graduates of physical science and engineering programs record the highest stay rates.[30] These are vital fields for China's development. However, when the students graduate with the needed skills and knowledge, they realize that the PRC's existing technological capacity will not meet their high expectations and that what they learn in the United States cannot be applied in China immediately. In order to use their advanced knowledge, they choose to remain.

President Bush's Executive Order enabled a large proportion of Mainland students to remain in the United States without worrying about their visa status. By the end of 1993, 49,000 out of the 53,000 who applied for a Green

Table 2.4

**Nationality of Non-U.S. Citizens Earning Most U.S. Doctoral Degrees in 1997**

| Country | Total | Physical Sciences % | Engineering % | Life Sciences % | Social Sciences % | Other % |
|---|---|---|---|---|---|---|
| China | 2,408 | 29.5 | 25.7 | 33.6 | 4.8 | 6.4 |
| India | 1,368 | 20.8 | 42.3 | 18.2 | 7.3 | 11.3 |
| Taiwan | 1,209 | 18.2 | 34.5 | 24.3 | 8.7 | 14.4 |
| Korea | 1,071 | 17.7 | 27.2 | 15.4 | 15.2 | 24.6 |
| Canada | 403 | 14.9 | 10.8 | 22.4 | 16.9 | 35.0 |

*Source:* Calculated from reports by National Opinion Research Center at the University of Chicago, *Washington Post*, 25 November 1999, p. G14.

Card had secured permanent-resident status.[31] However, students who arrived after 11 April 1990 and were not covered by the Executive Order still faced challenges finding legal employment and gaining permanent-residency status.

One available option is the H-1B visa—a nonimmigrant-professional work visa. If the applicant holds at least a bachelor's degree or its equivalent, the proposed job position is in a specialty occupation, and the salary is at the prevailing wage, the Immigration and Naturalization Service (INS) can issue an H-1B visa.[32] The INS increased the global quota for the H-1B visa from 65,000 to 115,000 in 1998. In 2000, the U.S. Congress enacted legislation that increased the maximum number of H-1B visas that can be issued to 195,000 for the following three years.[33]

The Green Card application process associated with professional jobs is demanding and complicated. Before applying, one first must obtain labor certification from the Department of Labor. To succeed, an employer needs to prove that no qualified American worker applied for the particular job held by the applicant. The application process can last as long as two or three years—depending on the area where the applicant resides and on employer policies and practices.[34] Once the labor certificate is pending, applicants usually remain at the same job because changing one's position would require starting the whole process over.

Nevertheless, many Mainland professionals who arrived after 11 April 1990 have successfully used the H-1B visa as a bridge to obtain a Green Card—the permanent-resident permit. Since most Chinese students come here for graduate studies, and a large percentage complete Ph.D. degrees, they are quite competitive for H-1B visas. Many Mainland nonreturnees obtain professional jobs related to their field of study. However, some switch career paths—often to the computer field, where they find more U.S. employment opportunities and much higher salaries. The Immigration and Naturalization Service (INS) issued 4,377 H-1B visas to PRC citizens during the 1996 fiscal year, and the number reached 7,987 during the five months from October 1999 through February 2000.[35] If Mainland applicants continue to secure roughly 10 percent percent of all H-1B visas, that would amount to nearly 60,000 new grantees over the next three years.

In sum, increasing numbers of PRC students are arriving for studies in the United States. A sizable number of graduates remain after completing their studies by successfully navigating the H-1B visa process. At the same time, more and more students and former students are looking at the Mainland market when planning for their future.

## Impact on China and the United States: Brain Drain, Brain Gain, or Migration of Talent?

Without question, a large number of highly educated China Mainland citizens who studied abroad have not returned home in recent decades. The United States, in particular, has gained from this late-twentieth-century development. Foreign students, of whom the largest contingent are from the China Mainland, currently receive more than half of the doctoral degrees in engineering granted by U.S. universities and are becoming increasingly prominent in physics, chemistry, mathematics, and computer science in the United States.[36] Top officials at the Los Alamos National Laboratory realized their dependence on foreign scientists when they advertised for a post-doctoral fellow to conduct unclassified research in nuclear materials and had twenty-four applicants—none of whom were U.S.-born citizens.[37] These are indications that, in terms of scientific research and technology development, the United States relies heavily on foreign scientists—especially Chinese and Asian American scientists.

At the same time, changes in career and migration patterns have occurred in recent years that carry important implications for U.S.–China relations. In the early 1990s, for instance, in order to exchange information with their colleagues in the China Mainland, Chinese students and scholars in the United States formed a number of professional associations in specific disciplines—such as economics, history, political science, international studies, agriculture, and ecology. Examples include the Center for Asian Studies (University of Georgia), the Chinese Academy of Sciences' Department of Systems Ecology, and the Chinese Scholars of Political Science and International Studies.[38] The main purposes of such associations are (1) to promote the exchange of ideas, knowledge, and information among Chinese scientists overseas as well as between scientists overseas and those in China; and (2) to provide a channel between Chinese and foreign scientists through which mutual understanding and cooperation can be achieved.

In addition, many Chinese alumni associations have sprung up in the United States during the past decade. The main purposes of these new organizations are to communicate and exchange information among Chinese from the same university or college, or from the same local area (city or province) in China, and to convey opinions and concerns regarding U.S. national and local issues—including educational issues such as adding Chinese to the available SAT foreign-language tests.[39] Some alumni organize and/or attend international conferences held in the China Mainland or in the United States.[40] The information exchanged at such conferences not only is valuable for Chinese American students and professionals, it also is of value to mainstream Americans interested in Chinese culture and the Mainland market.

Furthermore, many of the migrants who have settled in the United States are increasingly attracted by the China Mainland market. Current opportunities in China are especially promising for professionals in business, financial services, and information technology. Thus, a number of former students have started to engage in trade between the United States and China, using their knowledge of both countries and available networks.[41]

While young Chinese continue to arrive in the United States for education, a return wave has caught up U.S.-based Chinese immigrant professionals —particularly those in academic and corporate settings who have experienced racial discrimination in career mobility.[42] One reason is the lower social status revealed by comparisons with one's counterparts in China. Many Chinese immigrants discover that former colleagues and classmates in China have been promoted to high management and administrative levels. Although the U.S.-based professionals possess much higher salaries than their counterparts in China, they do not have equivalent social status. Another reason for the growing appeal of China is that some Chinese immigrant professionals see no future in mainstream U.S. society because of the language barrier. They are looking for a place where their knowledge and the advantages their skills provide would be recognized by career advancement. In 1999, for instance, more than half of the Harvard Business School MBA-program graduates from the PRC chose to return to the China Mainland based on career advancement considerations.[43]

Recently, moreover, the PRC government has instituted policies intended to attract Chinese students abroad to return to work in China, or to establish businesses in China. For instance, the central government established over 32 Career Development Centers around the country to help returned professionals start up new businesses and to attract more people from overseas to return.[44] Local governments in nearly all major Mainland cities have sent delegations to the United States and have promised special tax advantages in an effort to entice professionals living there to return to work in their former hometowns.[45] According to official PRC statistics, the return rate has increased by 13 percent every year, starting in 1995. About 5,000 students returned in 1995; 6,000 in 1996; and over 7,000 in 1997.[46] By 2000, the number reached 7,379—five times as many as the total number of returned students from 1990 to 1995.[47] Most returnees studied finance, business administration, and communications networking in the United States, Japan, Canada, or the United Kingdom. Many of them are entrepreneurs who have established businesses in China and are profiting from the knowledge they gained in the United States.[48]

Over the past five years, Shanghai has become the most attractive city for Chinese students and professionals abroad. Since 1993, Shanghai received 18,000 returning professionals. Most of them were under age thirty-five and had returned from the United States, Japan, United Kingdom, France, and Canada. Over 80 percent returned with doctoral degrees. Their specializations are in fields needed in China: electronic information, biological and medical sciences, international finance, and so forth. By the end of May 2000, according to government statistics, returned professionals established 900 business companies and enterprises with a total investment of 2 billion U.S. dollars. The Shanghai Municipal government reported that most of those enterprises are high-tech companies—including 150 in information technology, 80 in bioengineering, and 20 in new materials. In order to encourage increasing numbers of Chinese students and professionals abroad to come to Shanghai, the municipal government has established five career-development centers for entrepreneurs from abroad that offer advantageous office rental, venture capital, and tax breaks.[49]

Other Chinese American graduates represent U.S. companies in the China Mainland. While unanticipated by the government of the PRC, the bilateral trade and business initiatives launched by former Chinese students have contributed to the economic boom experienced by the two complementary economies.[50]

On the whole, the recent U.S. experience of Chinese students and scholars suggests that a long-term pattern of two-way "migration of talent"[51] will prevail over the brain drain from China to the United States. To date, the individual participants in study-abroad programs have been the principal beneficiaries of student migration outcomes. However, the prospective future benefits for the sending country are promising as increasing numbers of Chinese immigrants in America value opportunities to contribute to and gain from homeland involvements. Although the migration of professionals to developed countries involves both short-term economic and "opportunity" loss for poor sending countries, in the long run such losses can be offset by the reverse migration of talented professionals trained abroad.[52]

In the case of Chinese Americans, return migration requires the presence of certain home-country conditions—including jobs that pay competitive salaries, choice of employment, favorable working conditions, high social status, personal freedom, political stability, and a highly regarded educational system for one's children. We can expect to find an increase in both the migration of trained talent and in return professional migration as these attractive factors become more widespread in China.

## Conclusion

The new generation of Chinese immigrant professionals is playing an increasingly important role both in U.S. society and in the China Mainland. The United States relies heavily on foreign scientists, many of whom are from the PRC. Chinese professionals who arrived in the middle and late 1980s have finished their studies, found jobs, and settled in the United States. With their deep roots in China, many Chinese professionals, even after becoming naturalized U.S. citizens, tend to see their future connected to China. These professionals, many of whom spend substantial amounts of time in both China and the United States, play important roles in improving and promoting relations between the two countries. Chinese immigrants familiar with both Chinese and U.S. cultures are in an excellent position to conduct international business transactions in China. There are also Chinese professionals who are sought by U.S. companies to head business offices in China because of their knowledge of the culture and the language, as well as their other talents. Twenty years ago, when the PRC began to send many students to study abroad, business was not on the list of sponsored fields. However, many individual Chinese foresaw the future potential of international business and trade with China. Their contributions to U.S. economic expansion and to the modernization of China's economy and society are of great value to both countries.[53]

The U.S.–China relationship has been greatly strengthened by the cross-national movement of PRC students and scholars. Through success in science, technology, and business, they have become nongovernmental diplomats promoting dense ties and friendship between the United States and China. In the twenty-first century, Chinese student and professional immigrants, along with their children, who painlessly can merge into mainstream U.S. society, are poised to become an even wider bridge between the two countries.

# Notes

1. See Shi-shan Henry Tsai, *China and the Overseas Chinese in the United States 1868–1911* (Fayetteville: University of Arkansas Press, 1983), p. 40; Xiao-huang Yin, *Chinese American Literature Since the 1850s* (Urbana: University of Illinois Press, 2000), pp. 69–78.

2. Iris Chang, *Thread of the Silkworm* (New York: HarperCollins, 1995), p. 36.

3. Many Chinese American graduates took professional jobs after completing their studies in the U.S. In this chapter, therefore, the term *professional* refers to those on H-1B visas, Green Card holders, or naturalized citizens who are not (no longer are) students. Although data are available regarding the number of Chinese who receive H-1B visas, we do not know how many actually arrive with this status.

4. Kemiao Chen, "Sending Students in the Past Twenty Years," in *Shenzhou xueren* (Chinese scholars abroad), (June 1998): 7.

5. Ibid., pp. 7–8.

6. Ibid., p. 7.

7. "Zhongguo dalu zhuoshou wenzhu huiliu renxin" (Mainland China started new policies to keep overseas returnees), *Shijie ribao* (World journal), 29 August 1999, p. 2.

8. Huanxian Wang, "From Stream to Flood—An Overview of Sending Chinese Students to Study Abroad in the Past Twenty Years," in *Shenzhou xueren* (Chinese scholars abroad), (June 1998): 5. Also see Zuoyue Wang's chapter in this volume.

9. Chen, "Sending Students," p. 9.

10. Data compiled by the author from *50 Years of Open Doors*, a CD-ROM published by the Institute of International Education (New York, 2000).

11. See David Zweig and Chen Changgui, *China's Brain Drain to the United States: Views of Overseas Chinese Students and Scholars in the 1990s* (Berkeley: Institute of East Asian Studies, University of California, 1995), p. 22.

12. *Open Doors 2000* on IIE's website at www.opendoorsweb.org.

13. Qian Ning, *Liuxu meiguo* (Studying in the USA) (Nanjing: Jiangsu wenyi, 1996), pp. 177–210.

14. "Making More Progress in the Future," *Special Report on Sending Students Abroad for the Tenth Anniversary of the Establishment of the Service Center for Chinese Scholars*, Vol. 2 (Beijing: Zhongguo liuxue fuwu zhongxin [CSCSE], 1999), p. 31.

15. "Mainland China Started New Policies to Keep Overseas Returnees," p. 2.

16. Todd Davis, ed., *Open Doors 1998–1999, Report on International Educational Exchange* (New York: Institute of International Education, 2000), p. 12.

17. See Zweig and Chen, *China's Brain Drain*, pp. 21–22.

18. Todd Davis, ed., *Open Doors 1997–1998, Report on International Educational Exchange* (New York: Institute of International Education, 1998), p. 47.

19. Davis, *Open Doors 1998–1999*, p. 30.

20. National Opinion Research Center data cited in Vernon Loeb, "Espionage Stir Alienating Foreign Scientists in the U.S.," *Washington Post*, 25 November 1999, p. G14.

21. Carol Strevy, *Chinese Students/Scholar Needs* (New York: Institute of International Education Clearinghouse, 1990), p. 46.

22. Jianyi Huang, *Chinese Students and Scholars in American Higher Education* (Westport: Greenwood, 1997), pp. 49–50. Also see Leo A. Orleans, *Chinese Students*

*in America: Policies, Issues, and Numbers* (Washington, D.C.: National Academy Press, 1988), pp. 117–118.

23. See, for instance, Huang, *Chinese Students*, pp. 98–100.

24. M.P. Needle, "A University of Minnesota Report," *China Exchange News* 19, No. 1 (Spring 1991): 19.

25. Zweig and Chen's study showed that 43 percent of the survey group leaning toward staying were not China-trained Ph.D.s., and that 59 percent of the visiting scholars in whom China had invested a great deal were likely to return. Zweig and Chen, *China's Brain Drain*, pp. 67–68.

26. Ibid., pp. 50–53. The presence of family members constitutes another important factor affecting residency intentions. When the spouses and/or children of Chinese scholars joined them, graduates with terminal degrees were likely to choose the privileged material conditions of life available in the United States. Ibid., pp. 47–48. Although more and more Chinese immigrants are becoming involved in business dealings in China or with China, most of them continue to reside in the United States. Traditional Chinese culture places great emphasis on the younger generation's education. Thus, for the future of their children, many parents decide to live in the United States even though they realize that this decision means that their U.S.-educated and raised children will consider themselves American rather than Chinese.

27. *Interpreter Releases: Report and Analysis of Immigration and Nationality Law* 67, No.15 (16 April 1990): 447–448.

28. Zweig and Chen, *China's Brain Drain*, pp. 7, 23, 118, 120.

29. National Opinion Research Center data found in Loeb, "Foreign Scientists," p. G14.

30. Todd Davis, ed., *Open Doors 1995–1996, Report on International Educational Exchange* (New York: Institute of International Education, 1996), pp. 108–109.

31. Zweig and Chen, *China's Brain Drain*, pp. 7–8. Also see Kyna Rubin, "Fifty Thousand Individual Decisions," *NAFSA Newsletter* 45 (March 1994): 5.

32. See INS regulations in *8 CFR Section 214.2*, pp. 185–187.

33. *The American Competitiveness in the Twenty-First Century Act (AC21)*, INS website at www.ins.usdoj.gov.

34. In theory, one can apply for labor certification three months after obtaining the H-1B. However, conversations with employees at large consulting firms confirm that each firm has internal policies for H-1B holders such as "the two-year waiting period before submitting a labor-certification petition." In some regions, moreover, INS backlog for awarding the labor certification is as long as four to five years. Austin T. Fragomen, Jr., and Steven C. Bell, *Labor Certification Handbook*, 2000 edition (Washington, D.C.: West Group, 2000), pp. 1–33.

35. U.S. Immigration and Naturalization Service, *Statistical Yearbook of the Immigration and Naturalization Service, 1996* (Washington D.C.: U.S. GPO, 1997), p. 122. For 2000 data, see www.ins.usdoj.gov/graphics/services.

36. Loeb, "Foreign Scientists," pp. G1, G14.

37. Ibid., p. G14.

38. The latter has received support from the Rockefeller Foundation, the Rockefeller Brothers Fund, the Ford Foundation, the Asia Foundation, and the Embassy of the PRC. Its purpose is to develop and strengthen members' relations with corresponding institutions and colleagues in China as well as with international academics, and to coordinate members' collective or individual research focused on important Chinese issues. There are similar organizations like the Chinese Young Economist Society

and the Chinese Agricultural Association of Students and Scholars. See "Chinese Academic Associations in the U.S: Bridges for Scholarly Discourse," *China Exchange News* 19 (Spring 1991): 8–15.

39. This occurred in 1994. See www.collegeboard.org/sat.

40. For instance, the Nanjing University Alumni organized a delegation in June 2000 to attend the Symposium on the 21st Century's High-tech Personnel held at Nanjing University. As a delegation member, I presented a paper about U.S. immigration policy and its impact on development of the Chinese high-tech market. The presentation provided information on U.S. high-tech markets and how Americans deal with high-tech personnel. The audience included the personnel departments of various local communities in Jiangsu Province. Also, the First North America Business and Overseas Chinese Exchanges Conference held in November 2000 provided an environment for Chinese professionals in the United States and companies in China to exchange professional opinions and make contacts for mutual benefit. For more information see *New World Times*, 20 October 2000, p. 26.

41. Qian, *Studying in the USA*, pp. 277–295.

42. Yin, *Chinese American Literature*, pp. 185–194.

43. "Chinese Students in the United States Chose to Return for Career Development," *A. & C. Business News* (Meihua shangbao), 28 July 2000. p. 4. Also see Wen Pan, "From Studying Abroad Wave to Return Wave," *Renmin ribao* (People's daily, overseas edition) 16 December 2000, p. 4.

44. "It Is the Golden Time for Overseas Students Coming Back for Career Development," *People's Daily* (overseas edition), 8 July 2000, p. 3.

45. *People's Daily* (overseas edition), 8 February 1999, p. 3; 27 December 1999, p. 3; and 27 June 2000, p. 3.

46. *People's Daily* (overseas edition), 8 February 1999, p. 3.

47. "Chinese Students," p. 4.

48. *People's Daily* (overseas edition), 27 June 2000, p. 3.

49. Ibid.

50. See Zhao Haiying, "Sino-U.S. Economic Relations across Time and Space," in *The Outlook for U.S.–China Relations Following the 1997–1998 Summits: Chinese and American Perspectives on Security, Trade, and Cultural Exchange*, ed. by Peter H. Koehn and Joseph Y.S. Cheng (Hong Kong: Chinese University Press, 1999), pp. 216–220.

51. T.K. Oommen, "India: 'Brain Drain' or the Migration of Talent?" in *The Sociology of Migration*, ed. by Robin Cohen (Cheltenham: Edward Elgar, 1996), pp. 362–364.

52. Zweig and Chen, *China's Brain Drain*, pp. 45–49, 67–68, 74–78.

53. Furthermore, expanding business and professional opportunities in China-related fields have increased the interest of ABCs in U.S.–China relations. See Xiaohuang Yin, "The Growing Influence of Chinese Americans on U.S.–China Relations," in *The Outlook for U.S.–China Relations Following the 1997–1998 Summits*, pp. 331–349.

# 3

# Transnational Sensibilities in Chinese American Diasporic Literature

*Qian Suoqiao*

## Naturalization—A Scene at INS

Sitting Stiffly
His rough hands, of February peach-red but rather dull
Many years of dishwashing work
Lying on his spiffy suit
His English vocabulary as barren as his bank account
Already fully alert
The Examiner smiles and begins to attack
Yes or No, never, never make a mistake
The American lawyer, hired to be there for $450
Hinting with his eye, and sometimes with his foot

"Do you love the United States of America?"
"Yes."
The Examiner extends his hand
With a formal congratulation
At last—Naturalized
He uttered a long sigh
Wiping off the sweat wrapped up by the tie
Suddenly, he turned around and began to cry

This surgeon from a big hospital of a provincial capital
Will raise his peach-red but dull, rough hand
And swear to the Star-Spangled Banner

(Though he didn't know how to sing the anthem yet)
All his friends and relatives joyfully congratulating his
    good luck
(He spent ten months remembering and reciting the
    questions)
But he cried, rather embarrassingly
Crying for himself
Crying for his old country he will always be tied up with
Crying for the joy of his children and grandchildren on
    the other side of the Pacific
(They will soon reach their American Dream)

The rootless man, generation after generation—Naturalized

    —Liu Huangtian, *Beimeizhou de tiankong* (North American sky)[1]

Most studies of U.S.–China relations focus on political, economic, and social aspects of the United States or China, and how they affect each other. Another fruitful way to examine this relationship is to look at migrants who cross the borders of China or the United States to reside in the other land. Compared to the American community in China, the Chinese community in the United States, given its long continuous history and its current magnitude, certainly plays a more important role in U.S.–China relations.[2] This chapter attempts to shed light on the nature of this role by interpreting the sensibilities of the Chinese American diaspora through a reading of major motifs in Chinese American diasporic literature.

There is no homogeneous Chinese community in the United States of America. Thus, any generalization runs the risk of misrepresentation. First, there are the historical differences—the Chinese communities of the exclusion era and of the post-war era are markedly dissimilar, for instance. Moreover, all kinds of variations exist with regard to point of origin and dialect —American-born, Cantonese-speaking, from the Mainland, Taiwan, Hong Kong, and so forth. Equally dangerous, however, is willful overemphasis on difference among the diverse communities of Chinese America. It is true, for instance, that American-born Chinese and immigrants have quite distinct sensibilities, but even that is by no means incommensurate, as the majority of the immigrant Chinese and American-born today live under the same family roof.[3] My examination will focus on the contemporary period and, given their predominance within Chinese America today, my analysis will tilt toward the *modus vivendi* of the Chinese-speaking immigrant community.

By "Chinese American diasporic sensibilities," I mean the cluster of sentiments and attitudes associated with and circumscribed by the *modus viv-*

*endi* of the Chinese-speaking world of Chinese America. I will approach such sensibilities through a critical reading of Chinese American diasporic literature; that is, Chinese American writings in Chinese as well as those in English that are usually not included in the canon of Asian American literature. In contrast to the canonization of Chinese American writing in English in American literature, little critical attention has been paid to Chinese American diasporic writings in Chinese, even though the two share the same ethnocultural space. When Asian American literary studies build upon the premise of a "native" sensibility rooted in the boundary of the U.S. nation-state, immigrant writings in Chinese are somehow excluded as "other" on grounds of both language and nativity.[4]

Although Chinese American diasporic literature started as soon as Chinese immigrants embarked on their journey to America, the majority of works did not appear until the latter half of this century. This body of literature can be treated according to three basic chronological phases: *first*, from the 1950s to the 1960s, led by refugee writers from Mainland/Taiwan; *second*, from the 1960s to the 1980s, with a new generation of educated youth from Taiwan in the forefront; and, *third*, from the 1980s onward, inspired by immigrants from post-Mao Mainland China.[5]

To account for "Chinese American diasporic sensibilities," I will offer a close reading of certain representative texts in all three phases of contemporary Chinese American diasporic literature and explore major motifs therein. The argument developed here is that Chinese American diasporic sensibilities, first and foremost, are transnational and the major motifs are threefold: *xiangjia* (home-longing), *aiguo* (diasporic patriotism), and *facai* (realizing the American Dream). Precisely because of their transnational nature, such sensibilities both affect and are affected by U.S.–China relations.[6] Although these sensibilities are interrelated and crisscrossed, and each literary text is not necessarily restricted to one theme, I will examine aspects of the threefold sensibilities in relation to the literary texts in which certain themes stand out.

### Where Is Home? China as Home Lost

It is almost universally acknowledged that a diasporic longing for home begins as soon as one embarks on the journey to the "new world." This sentiment is most acute at the beginning stage of the diasporic experience, although it can last for a lifetime. Once in the diaspora, "home" is in some way remembered and identified by Chinese in America as "China." Thus, it is no coincidence that China-writing is a major obsession in Chinese American diasporic literature. *The Eavesdropper*, written in English by Lin Taiyi and published in 1959, stands out as a unique work in this respect.[7] The novel captures the sense of loss of home for her generation of refugee intellectuals. Written in the first person, *The Eavesdropper* recounts the trans-Pacific journey of the protagonist, Liang Shutung, a self-made novelist of national esteem, back and forth between China and the United States during the first half of the twentieth century. It begins and ends with Shutung's last displacement from China to the United States. Having just escaped from the imminent takeover of China by the Communist Army, Shutung finds himself "beginning to achieve a complete objectiveness about [himself] and the world around [him]";[8] that is, it is as if he were another person eavesdropping upon himself. Here appears the sign of a schizophrenic split personality so artistically dramatized in a later classic of Chinese American diasporic literature—*Sangqing yu taohong* (Mulberry and peach) by Nie Hualing—in which the trauma of modern China is most dramatically narrated with artistic sophistication.[9]

However, the actual schizophrenia never occurs in Lin's novel. In fact, the narratives in the last chapter show some quite promising and positive signs of Shutung's new beginning. As Henry Yee, Shutung's father-in-law, tries to persuade his son to treat Shutung as a family business partner instead of a mere employee, Henry confides to Shutung:

> I came here with empty pockets just like Shutung here. . . . And now I will never go back again. But suddenly you have come to me instead. You know, Shutung, what you and your children mean to me. It's as if I were young again, and through you, come closer again to home.[10]

Shutung reflects, in response, as if in a moment of revelation:

> I looked at the back of the old man's head. The heritage of four thousand years must be all there, in his bones and blood, a heritage which had survived as many disasters, man-made or natural, as in all the white men's histories put together. He was passing it all on to me—I must carry on.
>
> And then, for the first time since I arrived in America, the deep blue sea seemed to recede around me, and a meaning of why I was here seemed to emerge.

It is logical for the diasporic to want to make the current place of abode his/her new home, and it is natural for the new immigrant to continue the Chinese American tradition. However, will Shutung carry on "the heritage of four thousand years" passed on by Henry Yee and finally make peace with himself and find "home" at last in America? The narrative stops short of offering any definitive answer to Shutung's problematic of "home." The narrator only suggests that, "perhaps, I might find that I was like a cicada which could get out from under its skin when cold weather came on and leave the shell of itself completely intact."[11] The reason that "*jinchan tuoqiao*," or the cicada shaking off its shell to emerge as a new being, is only a theoretical possibility is because the "shell" proves to be too heavy. For a "*youzi*," or Chinese diasporic, like Shutung, the primary and most immediate concern is to avoid being schizophrenic out of displacement, to prevent himself from becoming an invisible object. In order to achieve that, you need to put your *self* together, you need to look back at the "deep blue sea" and begin a process of healing in order to retrieve your subjectivity. That goal is achieved in this case through the writing of the novel itself, cast as the narrator's autobiography, which largely consists of "remembrance of things past"—in other words, a literary representation of modern Chinese history, a presencing of a Chinese diasporic subjectivity into wholeness.

The narrative act of remembrance of the past, a motif recurrent in many diasporic literary works, is engendered by the Chinese American diasporic sensibility itself. For diasporics, their History stems from across the Pacific and there is a transnational journey in between. Recounting this History usually becomes a first priority for diasporic writers in order to make sense of the diasporic state of being they now find themselves in. Therefore, when Asian American literary study imagines and redefines its own History as originating from early Asian immigrant settlement in and contributions to America, such as Chinese contributions to the building of the transcontinental railroad, it simultaneously deprives immigrants of their own History, and creates a dichotomy of "native Chinese American" versus "overseas-born Chinese American."

In *The Eavesdropper*, diasporic historical subjectivity is represented and problematized through the portrayal of Shutung's two failed love relationships. Instead of an Orientalized static and stereotypical image of "China," the historical China in which Shutung was born and grew up is shown to be one of hybridity and con/fusion. As the narrator tells us, in Shanghai "everything had a duplicity of meaning and a hybrid quality. . . . Shanghai was divided in those days into French, English, Japanese, and International Concessions, and the European metropolis rose from the heart of the city like a great white mountain, awful in its power and beauty,"[12] surrounded by a crowded and jammed "Chinese city" on its edge. Accordingly, the psyche of contemporary intellectuals also was divided and split between a blind worship of the West and a deep hatred of its imperialism. Not surprisingly, Mr. Wu, Shutung's patron, has a double self: "a domestic Wu" and "an aesthetic Wu." As Wu explains, "We're caught in between times and in between worlds. That's why you see a spectacle like myself. There are no uncomplicated Chinese left any more."[13]

While Mr. Wu is split between a utilitarian Chinese wife and an ideal American mistress, both of Shutung's love relationships are highly symbolic of the traumatic historical encounter of modern China and the West. During his first journey to the United States, as a poor graduate student of English literature at Yale, Shutung makes his living as a waiter at the Pagoda Restaurant where he meets co-worker Elizabeth, a Eurasian who grew up in America. Shutung falls in love for the first time in his life with Elizabeth, as she somehow embodies his imagined American dream. Bound together at the Pagoda, Shutung thinks he has much in common with Elizabeth. He comes to think that they even share the same dream, as Elizabeth draws a mountain and confides in Shutung: "See? There we are, on top of the world. Let's make a pact. We'll meet up there one day, but whoever gets there first has to wait for the other. Okay?"[14] However, as Shutung tries his best to climb up that mountain and urges Elizabeth to join him "body and soul" (meaning to be sexually involved) in their quest, Elizabeth hesitates, recedes, and encloses herself, claiming she has to be "sensible." It later turns out that Elizabeth's idea of the mountain top is totally different from Shutung's, as one day she suddenly elopes with Dick Miller, a trombone player in a dance band, leaving Shutung to return to a wartime China.

What Shutung finds in wartime China is rampant corruption, as well as doomed love. Lin casts an alternative symbolic relationship between Shutung and Feina. An elegant but sickly beauty, the character of Feina immediately reminds one of Lin Daiyu, the classical type of beauty celebrated in *The Dream of Red Mansion*. Intelligent and educated, Feina fully appreciates the work of Shutung. The otherworldliness of Feina represents a kind of purity desperately needed for Shutung to maintain his sanity in a corrupt world. Yet Shatung's dream of marriage with Feina is only an illusion. The emplotment of the novel is deployed as such that Feina is the wife of Shutung's brother, a fate decided before their first meeting. Moreover, Feina is an eternal invalid destined to die. Indeed, Shutung is not so much attracted to Feina as to "that mysterious and complicated body of hers,"[15] a sick body soon to vanish, as Feina symbolizes the classical order China no longer embodies.

At one level, Shutung's displacement is a result of the political turmoil of modern China. However, his political ill fate took place in a complex cultural context of con/fusion between East and West as well. The loss of home for Shutung's generation is a consequence of the political and cultural incapacity of modern China to synthesize coherently the myriad forces of hybridization. The United States of America already is part of the history of this loss. After all, the America Shutung finds himself in again at the end of his journey is the America of Elizabeth, who has once rejected him. It also is important to note that it is only America that Shutung could escape to. While

Shutung's two love relationships both failed, it is his marriage without love to Lilien Yee that sustained him and brought him to the United States, due to the Yee family's established history in America. It also is upon Shutung's new arrival, the narrator tells us, that Henry Yee, after forty years of stay in America, finally decides to become a U.S. citizen and makes peace with his soul.

We do not know if or how Shutung will follow the path of Henry Yee, but we do know that, by the end of the novel, Shutung has achieved a level of self-understanding through his remembrance of the past, by coming to terms with his own History. Only through such remembrance and reconciliation could he begin to make sense of his present being in America. In this respect, *xiangjia*, or home-longing, is not a negative sentiment of mere nostalgia, but rather an indispensable part and parcel of diasporic sensibility.

### Diasporic Patriotism, or Anxieties of American Settlement?

The history of Chinese American diasporic experience shows that China as "home lost" is seldom regained, as those who stay, especially in the contemporary period, far outnumber those who have returned. Beyond and besides the sentiment of longing, a diasporic can develop three attitudes toward China: love, hate, or disinterest. In the general experience of U.S. immigration, the immigrant's attachment toward his/her sending country usually is predominantly one of disinterest. However, the general attitude regarding China for the majority of Chinese immigrants can still be characterized as one of "love," or *aiguo*—that is, diasporic patriotism, where "loyalty" is directed toward China, even though such sentiment can involve a mixture of love and hate. In fact, it is important for diasporic Chinese writers to maintain "native" sentiment in the diaspora—"nativism overseas" is considered an extension of "native Chinese" sentiment.[16]

In the Chinese American experience, "diasporic patriotism" has less to do with loyalty to China as such than with the precarious in-between-ness of diasporic existence. "Diasporic patriotism" is possible precisely because the "patriots" are in the diaspora (United States). Caught up in transnational power relations between China and the United States, a Chinese diasporic's attitude toward the United States is indeed subtle and complex. What underlines and translates such complexity usually is enthusiasm toward "homeland politics." However, "homeland politics" cannot be understood within the critical framework of cultural nationalism, as it is always a transnational phenomenon. The issue of "diasporic patriotism" opens up, rather than closes, meaningful examination of the literary discourses of Chinese American diasporic writing.

"Diasporic patriotism" is an ongoing phenomenon in the history of Chinese

American experience. Perhaps no event in modern history has surpassed the intensity and scale of diasporic involvement than the *Baodiao* (Defending Diaoyutai Islands) Movement of the early 1970s, when almost the entire Chinese immigrant community rose up and publicly gathered to protest against the U.S. and Japanese infringement of Chinese sovereignty over the Diaoyutai Islands. The ironies of the Baodiao Movement in the diasporic context provide the subject matter of *Zuori zhinu* (Yesterday's anger), a novel by Zhang Xiguo, one of the most prolific and accomplished diasporic writers in America.

Yesterday's Anger is meant to be a historical fictional account of the Baodiao Movement. The authorial intention to interpret History is so intense that we are urged not to take it as a "literary work." As Zhang tells us in an "Afterword" to the novel:

> *Yesterday's Anger* is only my personal interpretation on the political movement by Chinese youth. It does not have any artistic value, and perhaps does not fit into any artistic line or camp. The only significance is to account for ourselves, for myself and my fellow friends who once worked together for the Movement but who are now dispersed in Africa, America, Taipei, Wuhan, Beijing and other parts of the world. . . . History will prove that we were innocent. We tried our best.[17]

Thanks to the author's personal involvement in and testimony about the Baodiao Movement, and also to his sharp and sophisticated artistic perception, we are presented in the narratives of the novel not merely with the emotional intensity of the movement itself, but also with the intellectual background of his generation and the diasporic foreground to their political outburst.

The activists in the Baodiao Movement featured in the novel, among them the leading hero Ge Rixin, all grew up in and came from Taiwan. During their college years in Taiwan—most of them attended Taida (Taiwan University)—they were young and idealistic cultural rebels against the Kuomintang ideology enforced by the Republic of China government on Taiwan. Gathered around their mentor, a certain Professor Ying, they went on outings together, attended lectures on the latest (counter-)cultural trends in the West and America, and spent every night at Mingxing (Star) Café engaged in endless philosophical debate.[18] While the always melancholy, rich, and dandyish Hu Weikang would quote Sartre, Heidegger, and Jaspers, Ge Rixin would counter with Russell, Whitehead, and Wittgenstein. However, "when the pretty maid of the Hu family, coming from the path of the garden, brought them hot and delicious food, everybody jumped on it and forgot all about the absurdity of Being."[19]

Once they come to the United States, however, subtle and significant changes occur. The melancholy philosopher Hu, for instance, becomes truly melancholy. Previously given to philosophizing and talk, he becomes rather silent. Hu discovers a big gap between his imagined West, of which he considered himself a staunch follower, and the reality of the America in which he is now a graduate student in philosophy. He finds the hippie counterculture, which he worshiped in Taipei, quite superficial and boring. He finds the rigor of U.S. academia, especially in the humanities, intolerable—for one thing, his English can never catch up with American students. He finds the Anglo emphasis on logic in U.S. philosophy departments stifling. He even starts to wash dishes. Most importantly, all of them find themselves "Chinese."

In Taipei, their mentor, Professor Ying, once confessed to them that he had begun to read Chinese books. Ge Rixin flatly countered that Professor Ying was wrong in taking such a regressive move. When Ge is at Berkeley, however, all he reads are Chinese books. He proudly confesses: "the Chinese books I have read during this past half year since I am at Berkeley amount to much more than all the Chinese books I read during my four years at Taiwan University."[20] Instead of a (Western) philosophical salon, he organizes a "Study Group of Modern Chinese History" at Berkeley that discusses such issues as modern Chinese youth movements and the Nanjing Massacre.

Such diasporic "Chinese" rediscovery is, in fact, a reflection of the characters' American entrance, or rather of their American otherness. This can be seen in two ways. The 1960s and early 1970s were a period of hyper political activism in the United States. Such political activism stood in sharp contrast to the political inactivity of their fellow Chinese students on U.S. campuses—especially at Berkeley, where two of the chief characters, Ge Rixin and Shi Ping, are situated. Observing and joining the student rallies there prompts a questioning of self-consciousness. At the climax of a student rally at Sproul Plaza, Shi Ping remarks to Ge Rixin:

> "It's a pity I forgot to bring my camera with me. We should take some pictures and send them back to our friends in Taiwan."
> "Shi Ping, in witnessing such American student demonstrations, is all you can think of to take some pictures?"
> Shi Ping was stunned for a minute, and said,
> "This is their country. They do not want to fight wars overseas, hence these demonstrations; it's their business. And we . . ."
> "But what about us?" Ge Rixin suddenly became emotional, which gave Shi Ping a real shock. "Shi Ping, so what about us? All we know is to study, study and study. . . . Why couldn't we create our own fate? Why couldn't we be just like these American students, boldly claiming what they want and do not want?"

"We are different. We are not Americans after all," replies Shi Ping, "on another note, nobody forces you to come abroad. You came abroad of your own will, isn't that so?"

"But you can't put it that way. . . ."

Ge proceeds to give Shi a lecture on how they should become politically potent as Chinese at Berkeley, and, in the end, declares:

"Is it that the heart of our generation is all dead? Is it that we can't do anything but spend the rest of life peacefully as a wanderer abroad? I don't believe it! So long as we are given a chance, we shall prove that the youth of our generation are not cold-blooded."[21]

Another factor that pushes their "Chinese" self-consciousness is fear of and instinctive resistance to the prospect of assimilation. When Mimi claims that she wants to finish her master's degree as soon as possible so that she can apply for a Green Card, and argues that being a permanent resident would in no way deny her of being "Chinese," Ge Rixin bursts into a rage:

"I will never do such a thing. Coming to their country to study is already a big shame. Now you want to apply for their permanent residency? Never!"[22]

This is certainly a big change—from taking it as axiomatic to study abroad to considering one's present status as shameful.

Then Ge mentions a visit that he and Shi Ping paid to a certain Professor Gong who had been teaching at Berkeley for more than twenty years. Professor Gong's diasporic sense of loss of China left a deep impression on them. When Gong played a Chinese record they had brought him, his eight-year-old son came out to ask him in English what kind of music it was:

Professor Gong touches the head of his son, and remarks to them apologetically (in classical Chinese poetic diction):
"First time my foreign son hears Chinese sound."[23]

Given this psychological diasporic foreground, when an actual opportunity arrives in the form of the *Baodiao* Movement, it is no wonder that all of the characters become enthusiastic "patriotic" activists. Although diasporic patriotism, and only such patriotism, can unite and bring the diaspora together for a political cause, it is, nevertheless, a momentary illusion as diasporic politics does not operate in a vacuum either. The short-lived *Baodiao* Movement is soon overtaken—by a combination of factional political feuds brought over and extended from the "homeland" and whimsical foreign-policy shifts toward the "homeland" on the part of the government of their country of residence. We are told, for instance, that right after President Richard Nixon's visit to the People's Republic of China, many *Baodiao* activists swung to the left, and that pro-PRC leftists suddenly dominated a "patriotic" meeting at the University of Michigan. The aftermath of the *Baodiao* Movement is the norm of diasporic patriotism—actual political impotence due to historical legacies, factions, and feuds as well as contemporary transnational power politics.

While diasporic patriotism can never materialize politically, it survives as an important sentiment in the diaspora because it helps to comfort and rationalize many contradictions of diasporic existence and serves as a defense mechanism for holding on to as much as possible against the inevitable prospect of assimilation. After the *Baodiao* Movement dies out, Shi Ping leaves Berkeley for New York and finds a job as an editor with the Chinese-language newspaper *Chinese American Daily*. While the newspaper is oriented toward reporting news on China and Asia, Shi knows that the future of the newspaper will have to be reoriented toward community issues in Chinatown. Shi admires and joins American-born Chinese youth in their struggle for equal rights in the United States and for a better community environment in Chinatown. Yet even though the younger generation of Chinatown does not reject his participation, Shi cannot bring himself wholeheartedly to join in such an exclusively Chinatown-oriented cause. For one thing, he feels that working for the benefit of Chinatown, such as by teaching Chinese to American-born youth, is a rather depressing task. More importantly, by fully devoting himself to the cause of Chinatown, a cause embraced by American-born Chinese who no longer share deep emotional ties with China, Shi feels he would become a "Chinese American." At the same time, it is impossible to unite the immigrant generation given their deep-rooted political differences and internal hatreds. The only hope of unity for the overseas Chinese community lies in the younger generation—who are free from those feuds, but no longer care that much for China:

> Every time Shi Ping tries to think of these issues, he is always trapped into a contradictory conclusion: this generation of overseas Chinese cannot be united, and unity only resides in the next generation. But the younger generation has already become Chinese American. He cannot devote himself to becoming Chinese American, he still wants to be a Chinese. . . . Again and again, Shi Ping comes to such dead knot in thought. Chinese, American, Chinese, American . . . what on earth is he?[24]

In the final analysis, diasporic patriotism can only be understood as a sentimental attachment and allegiance to a "homeland" to which the diasporics know they will not return. By the end of the novel, we find Shi Ping in Taipei, pondering and hesitating over where his home is: China or America. While everything he sees in Taipei is intimate and positive, and there are always women offering their love and expecting his, the protagonist, of course, will eventually return to the United States. Yet, diasporic patriotism allows our diasporic hero to declare to his new girlfriend/motherland/Chinese-reading audience, "Hui Mei, you must wait for me. I will come back, I will surely come back!"[25]

If "diasporic patriotism" is only an illusion in the diaspora and if U.S. experience prompts the uneasy, intense ethnic consciousness of being Chinese, the logical solution for diasporics seems to lie in return to the "homeland," where they need be neither "ethnic" nor "patriotic." From this perspective, Shi Ping's mere yearning for homeland seems disingenuous. However, diasporic life is never logical. Sometimes, in fact, the depth of their American entanglement is beyond the control of diasporics themselves.

The problematics of diasporic settlement in the United States provide the central focus of *Youjian zonglu, youjian zonglu* (Seeing palm trees again), a novel set ironically, exclusively in Taiwan. Published in 1967, this novel by Yu Lihua was an instant success and enormously popular in the diasporic Chinese communities.[26] With its publication, Yu established herself as a spokesperson for the "rootless generation." One reviewer regards *Seeing Palm Trees Again* as a "song of exile" that offers "a panoramic picture of the Chinese intellectual in exile on the American continent" from the 1960s onward.[27]

The novel begins with the protagonist Mou Tianlei arriving at Taipei Airport after ten years in the United States—first, as a student of English literature, and then as a professor of Chinese language at an obscure college. The story takes place in Taipei during Tianlei's vacation "home." The supposed purpose for his visit is to marry Yishan, whom he has not yet met, but with whom he has corresponded for over a year—a modern version of the "picture bride." While his fiancée stands firm in her condition for their marriage —that is, they must go to America—Tianlei dreads returning. All he wants is a peaceful "break" at "home"—if not staying permanently in Taipei. After ten years of solitary sojourn in the United States, Tianlei has truly become a wandering character with no warmth and no resolution. When he meets his correspondence fiancée, his family, and her family, and visits his former schoolmates, his former university, and Taipei streets, Tianlei hesitates and vacillates at every turn of action on the Hamlet-like question: To return or not to return to America?

Tianlei's crisis of "home" results from a huge gap between his own experience in the United States and his "hometown" imagination of America. At the root of this conflict is the power of "America" transnationally imagined, experienced, and exercised. Tianlei represents a "rootless generation" in the sense that, first of all, he can no longer find root in Taiwan because, wherever he goes, he is now identified as "America." To his parents, he is the glory of the family, being a *yang boshi*, or "American Ph.D." and a professor at a U.S. university. His father informs him that his picture with a doctoral cap is hung on the family wall and, thanks to that achievement, his mother has sustained hope for her own life. The news of his "homecoming" attracts local media attention. He is invited by the government in Taiwan to attend an official banquet as an honorable "overseas scholar." Even the neighborhood snack-bar owner requests that Tianlei sponsor him to go to the United States and open a restaurant there. Then, there is the fact that his fiancée is interested in him because he is an "American Ph.D." and their marriage promises her exit from Taiwan and the fulfillment of *her* golden American Dream.

Tianlei now resents his American identification, however. After spending ten years there, he has experienced a totally different America. He cannot help throwing out negative remarks about America to anyone around—his family, relatives, media, and fiancée. His cold and negative remarks are not only irritating, but rude and offensive to his hometown people. However, all Tianlei can think of concerning the past ten years is "the inevitable experience of racism, his own hard and bitter work, the incredible difficulties he had to overcome as a humanities major foreign student, as well as that endless loneliness thicker than the fog, deeper than the sea and colder than the ice. Such a sense of emptiness he could not explain to anybody, and nobody would understand."[28] This terrible loneliness, which is at the heart of Tianlei's gloomy disillusionment with America, results from the realization that he would be a perpetual stranger/outsider in U.S. society. There are many reasons why Tianlei feels disillusioned about the United States (he could not find a job that his English literature degree entitled him to, could not find a wife in the marriage market there, and so forth), but the nature of his disillusionment is captured in the metaphor of the palm tree. When he revisits his alma mater and sees again the tall and firm palm trees standing high into the sky, he yearns to be what he was ten years ago: youthful, ambitious, and courageous. When everyone was trying hard to go abroad for studies, he took the challenge and sailed across the Pacific to conquer the world. Now, America has belittled him. He is a mere pitiful shadow under the palm tree.

What is even more tragic, perhaps against authorial recognition, is that Tianlei is helplessly caught between the power relations of the transnational representation of America. On the one hand, he has no reason to deny his fiancée's right to experience her own American Dream. More importantly, however, the knot of Tianlei's homelessness crisis resides in himself. As he confesses to his sister:

> "Yes, you guessed it right, I'll go back, not entirely for my parents . . . not for my fiancée. . . . I'll go back ultimately for myself. Although there is no root there for me, I have become used to it, reconciled my fate to it. I have become accustomed to a life with a sentiment of nostalgia. . . . Most importantly, I can have a pleasant hope that every several years I could come back . . . like now, having a chat with you."[29]

This actually is a rather vague understatement. What is unsaid in the authorial voice is that Tianlei, in fact, takes pleasure in the only thing he can relish: being a transnational diasporic. Although he resents his hometown's exhilaration regarding America, he cannot challenge the power of the imagined America. After all, it is because of that power that he can afford to take a wife. Puzzled by Tianlei's constant negative comments on America, his fiancée once asks him: "Do you dislike Americans?" "No," he replies, "Americans are my food providers. How could I dislike them?"[30]

For Tianlei, his sentiment toward the United States cannot be simply expressed by an innocent "like" or "dislike." Moreover, he cannot admit that the desire for America that prompted him to embark on the exodus in the first place is at the core of his current crisis, as that would mean too fundamental a negation of himself. Tianlei, our diasporic hero, is already too deeply involved in the transnational power play of "America."

## American Dream—By the Chinese, for the Chinese, and Through the Chinese

In the preface to *Beijingren zai niuyue* (Beijinger in New York) by Cao Guilin (Glen Cao), the author acknowledges an intertextual link between his work and Yu Lihua's *Seeing Palm Trees Again*. Compared to Yu's confession that her ten years in America have left her with nothing but loads of book drafts, Cao thinks he is worse off; he does not even have a book draft and spiritually he is zero, even though he has amassed considerable material wealth.[31] This is an interesting and telling comparison. Along with the post-Mao waves of Chinese student-immigrants from the PRC to the United States, there also emerged, especially in the 1990s, a new group of immigrant writers.[32] In comparison with the earlier diasporic writing by authors from Taiwan, one finds that the dominant theme in their works is concern with *facai*, or realizing the American Dream, although sentiments of home-longing and diasporic patriotism are also always intertwined. This emphasis is attributable to a number of factors. One could argue that these writers are simply less intellectual than their predecessors from Taiwan, as the former grew up during the Cultural Revolution in China (1966–1976). I tend to think it is mostly due to the huge disparity between the Maoist indoctrination of Chinese superiority over the "American imperialists" and the humiliating realization of China's extreme poverty once one is in the "land of the gold."

Whatever the case, the overwhelming focus on their U.S. experience, including the vicissitudes of the American Dream, reflects a close Chinese relevance. First, that which engenders their American experience bears deep Chinese background. In addition, their written work in the diaspora also is largely directed toward a Chinese readership at home. As such, the images of the United States portrayed in the work of recent immigrant writers certainly exert tremendous influence upon contemporary Chinese understanding of and sentiment toward "America." New student-abroad/immigrant literary works have been so popular in China recently that, according to one Chinese critic, "anyone who reads must have read a couple of works of new immigrant literature."[33]

In this genre, *Beijinger in New York* by Glen Cao and *Manhadun de zhongguo nuren* (Manhattan's China lady) by Zhou Li (Julia Zhou Fochler) are two of the most popular and influential pioneering works. However, even though these are typical immigrant stories about the U.S. experience, neither work has attracted much attention from the mainstream American audience. Cao's book has been translated into English, but has a rather limited circulation. I expect that Zhou's book will never be translated into English. The issue here is not language accessibility. Unlike Amy Tan or Gish Jen, who skillfully narrate Chinese American stories to the U.S. audience, both Cao's and Zhou's works are unquestionably meant for the Chinese audience in that the discursive values enveloped in their narratives strike a much more direct echo with Chinese readers undergoing rapid social changes at home.

At first glance, Cao and Zhou seem to project two rather different images of America in telling their stories—Cao's being "bitter" and Zhou's "rosy." *Beijinger in New York* tells of the rise and fall of Wang Qiming and his family in the United States. Starting from scratch as a "fresh-off-boat" (FOB), Wang first finds a typical job for a new Chinese immigrant—dishwashing in a Chinese restaurant in Chinatown. Later, aided by two of his women—his wife, Yan, and his mistress, Ah Chun, Wang is able to own and run successfully a garment workshop in Chinatown. Just as he is achieving his American Dream, however, Wang runs into conflicts with his daughter, who has adjusted poorly to U.S. public-school life, and he mismanages his investment. In the end, he loses his daughter and family and almost gambles away his hard-earned fortune. He summarizes his U.S. experience as *neishang*—he is psychologically hurt.

By contrast, Zhou offers an upbeat autobiographical account of how she starts out as a poor student with $50 in her pocket upon arrival in the United States and becomes a successful businesswoman in New York, running a multimillion-dollar import/export business between China and the United States. Zhou contrasts her growing-up years during the Cultural Revolution in China to her U.S. years of second growth, and demonstrates that the latter offer not only far more opportunities for material success but enchanting fulfillment in terms of personal happiness. A major motif in Zhou's book involves a eulogy to her white husband and to the bliss of their marriage, which contributes to making her accepted, and even a darling, in the New York business world.[34]

When Cao's novel was made into an extremely popular television drama—the first series shot in the United States by a Chinese TV crew—he was rather uneasy about its success. Cao felt his message was somehow misunderstood. That is, while he intended to reveal the hardships and pitfalls of his U.S. experience, the audience was attracted to the glamorous scenes of New York and to how the hero *makes it* there.[35] In other words, Cao's sense of "internal hurt" was not taken seriously by the Chinese audience. In their Chinese reception, the U.S. adventures of Wang Qiming are still uplifting and inspirational because they offer the possibility of an American Dream—and Chinese readers in the 1990s need such a dream, whether "American" or not. When Zhou portrays herself as a "weak little woman" from China, darting along the Avenue of Americas on a bike and eventually becoming part of the elite business world of New York, that certainly arouses admiration from her Chinese readers. However, even the scenes of Wang Qiming dishwashing in the restaurant, or buried under loads of clothing in his own apartment-turned-workshop, do not constitute negative images of the United States. Rather, they demonstrate that, given hard work and self-struggle, you can make it there.

Thus, the end results of both Cao's and Zhou's representations of "America" are the same. They promote a cluster of classic American values —such as adventurism, individualism, entrepreneurship, self-struggle, self-promotion, competition, hard work, and risk-taking—that are most welcome in 1990s China. "America" never loses. Neither Zhou's "rosy" picture nor Cao's "bitter America" in any way challenge the powerful influence of America on the Chinese imagination.

The promotion of American values does not mean, however, that the U.S. public will have a particular liking for such Chinese American stories. While these immigrant values run deep in the national psyche and new immigrants continue to boost the American project, the mainstream U.S. cultural taste has long surpassed such clichés of the American Dream. The popular way of narrating Chinese American stories seems to be represented by Maxine Hong Kingston, Amy Tan, and Gish Jen—who understand the current taste of the mainstream reading public—and not by such diasporic writers as Cao and Zhou. The images portrayed by such diasporic narratives reflect Chinese appropriations of America. Their appropriations are engaging rather than confrontational. Yet "America" is engaged for the sake of self-empowerment. The link between the American Dream and Chinese empowerment is underscored.

In addition to the fact that diasporic works such as those authored by Cao and Zhou are written for home consumption, the ways in which the protagonists achieve their American Dream also bear direct connection to China. Wang Qiming makes it by running a sweatshop in Chinatown while the "I" in Zhou's work succeeds through international trade with China.[36] In another diasporic novel, *Luoshanji de fengniao* (A hummingbird in Los Angeles) by Xiao Yang, this connection between the American Dream and China takes an explicit and ironic turn.[37]

In the very first chapter of *A Hummingbird in Los Angeles*, the I-narrator relates a funny tale of how he chased after a limousine in order to see a Hollywood actress to no avail. Chinese diasporic writers like Xiao Yang understand that Chinese immigrants live at the margin in American society—their diasporic terrain in Los Angeles does not include Hollywood. What makes the Chinese diaspora different from an ethnic ghetto is, after all, the connection to China. However, this connection also is an American connection. The protagonists in the novel are able to realize their American Dream by running a travel agency dealing with clientele from China. In other words, they achieve their American success by acting as salesmen of "America" for Chinese visitors. This requires a diasporic repositioning that can be rather ironic. For immigrants in general, but especially for recent immigrants from Mainland China, "America" means, above all, freedom from the repressive political culture in the sending country. For the I-narrator and his business partner, Qian Daming, however, their first major business deal involved entertaining and showing around a group of Communist Party bureaucrats from China headed by the old-fashioned, career-oriented party chief, Lao Zhao. When the I-narrator appears a bit cocky in his manner toward Lao Zhao, Qian Daming gives him a serious lecture:

> Ever since you met Lao Zhao, you haven't spoken a word of respect, only showing off your bits of snotty wits. Let me warn you: shake up and serve Lao Zhou the best you can. I don't believe back in China you haven't

curried favor with party leaders. Pamper Lao Zhao the way you pamper your old leader! Don't take this as a joke. Don't you ever think you're now in America and nobody is your boss. Let me tell you: in America, money is your boss, and you be respectful.[38]

## Surround Sound of the Hummingbird

In a moment of self-reflection, Xiao Yang's I-narrator compares himself to a hummingbird.[39] A hummingbird flaps its wings with high frequency, flying from here to there, but it apparently does not have permanent residency and its food-hunting hard work seems to be for its own sake. The diasporic poet Liu Huangtian also captures this paradox in Chinese diasporic existence when he observes an Immigration and Naturalization Service scene: "The rootless man, generation after generation/Naturalized." Generation after generation of Chinese have come to the land of the Gold Mountain and adapted to the new land. To be naturalized, however, does not necessarily mean to be rooted. They strive hard to be naturalized, but the moment they attain that goal, they turn around and cry for their "motherland" over the Pacific.

Of course, new flocks of hummingbirds striving for the same goal will continue to arrive. However, hummingbirds are native to the New World. They may be small, but they are certainly full of energy.

Wherever they go, moreover, they make their humming sound heard. If Chinese Americans are a new breed of hummingbird that migrates seasonally across the Pacific, the message of their humming sound must be to wish for a peaceful and fruitful migrating path so that there will be food to gather on both ends of their journey.

## Notes

1. Liu Huangtian, *Beimeizhou de tiankong* (North American sky) (Chengdu: Sichuan wenyi, 1990), pp. 18–19. All translations in this chapter are mine unless otherwise noted.

2. This statement is not meant to underestimate the impact of the American community in China. Historically, for instance, U.S. missionary communities exerted considerable influence in shaping U.S.–China relations. At present, there is a growing U.S. business community in China, and some of their children are attending local schools. When they come of age, they will certainly have a unique perspective on U.S.–China relations. See Harold R. Isaacs, *Scratches on Our Minds: American Views of China and India* (Armonk, NY: M.E. Sharpe, 1980; reprint), pp. 126–148.

3. A striking example is the changing attitude of Frank Chin, who first polarized the "native" and China-born sensibilities. See Qian Suoqiao, "'China' in the Diaspora: Re-linked and Legitimized," in Marc Shell, ed., *Babel in America: Essays on Language, Immigration, and Ethnicity* (Cambridge: Harvard University

Press, 2002); Xiao-huang Yin, *Chinese American Literature Since the 1850s* (Urbana: University of Illinois Press, 2000), pp. 240–246.

4. While much of the critical emphasis of Asian American literary studies has been targeted at mainstream America's exclusion of Asian American writing on the ground of race and ethnicity, the establishment of Asian American literary studies has simultaneously exercised its own disciplinary exclusionary act in its canon-making. Since the political agenda of the discipline has been to ground Asian American writing as legitimate U.S. minority writers in American literature—with race, ethnicity, and English language as its identifying criteria—it is understandable that the bulk of Asian immigrant writings are deemed as an embarrassing "other." The exclusionary criteria of language and nativity work together in intricate ways, for, while Chinese-language writings are certainly not considered as canonical Asian American literature, certain English-language writings also can be sidelined if the author and authorial discourses are considered as not denoting a "native" sensibility. The consequences are rather perplexing. While Asian American literary studies in the main are positioned in a politically progressive and leftist discourse, they also tacitly confirm some of the most conservative agendas of narrow mainstream American nationalism, such as the English-only campaign and anti-immigrant sentiments.

5. For a pioneering critical work in English of Chinese-language writings, see Yin, *Chinese American Literature*, chapters 5 and 6. Also see Kao Hsin-sheng, ed., *Nativism Overseas: Contemporary Chinese Women Writers* (Albany: State University of New York Press, 1993).

6. U.S.–China relations are treated here primarily in cultural aspects. While not overtly political by itself, the cross-cultural trafficking of images, ideas and (mis)understandings, generated by the agency of Chinese American diasporic sensibilities, nevertheless, exerts a huge impact on U.S.–China relations as a whole.

7. Lin Taiyi, *The Eavesdropper* (Cleveland, OH: World Publishing Company, 1959). Growing up in both China and America following the erratic life of her well-known father Lin Yutang, Lin Taiyi became an accomplished writer in her own right who was quite active in New York Chinese-exile literary circles in the 1950s.

8. Ibid., p. 16.

9. Nie Hualing, *Sangqing yu taohong* (Mulberry and peach) (Taipei: Hanyi seyan, 1988; reprint).

10. Lin, *The Eavesdropper*, p. 247.

11. Ibid., p. 22.

12. Ibid., p. 23.

13. Ibid., p. 50.

14. Ibid., p. 67.

15. Ibid., p. 185.

16. See Kao, *Nativism Overseas*, p. 13.

17. Zhang Xiguo, *Zuori zhinu* (Yesterday's anger) (Taipei: Hongfan, 1978), p. 300.

18. "Professor Ying" here refers to Professor Ying Haiguang, an actual figure noted for his liberal and Westernized posture in Taiwan at the time. Mingxing Café is also an actual locale where elite youth gathered in Taipei at the time. In fact, most of the characters in the novel have actual references. For a detailed account regarding Ying and his disciples in Taiwan, see Liu Daren, *Fuyou qunluo* (Floating tribes) (Taipei: Huangguan, 1997).

19. Zhang, *Yesterday's Anger*, p. 97.

20. Ibid., p. 103.
21. Ibid., pp. 107–109.
22. Ibid., p. 125.
23. Ibid., p. 126.
24. Ibid., pp. 77–78.
25. Ibid., p. 294.
26. Yu Lihua, *Youjian zonglu, youjian zonglu* (Seeing palm trees again) (Taipei: Huangguan, 1989; reprint). Together with Zhang Xiguo, Yu is one of the most prolific and accomplished diasporic writers in Chinese in America. See Yin, *Chinese American Literature*, chapter 6.
27. See Pai Hsien-yung, "The Wandering Chinese: The Theme of Exile in Taiwan Fiction," *Iowa Review* 7, No. 2–3 (Spring–Summer 1976): 208.
28. Yu, *Palm Trees*, p. 91.
29. Ibid., p. 159.
30. Ibid., p. 141.
31. Cao Guilin, *Beijingren zai niuyue* (Beijinger in New York) (Beijing: Zhongguo wenlian, 1991), p. 2.
32. For an overview of new Chinese immigrant writing, not only in the United States, but also in other countries, see Chen Xianmao, ed., *Haiwai huawen wenxue shi* (A history of overseas Chinese literature), vol. 4 (Xiamen: Lujiang, 1999), chapter 7.
33. Wu Yiqi, "Xinyiming wenxue" (New immigrant literature), in ibid., p. 639.
34. Zhou Li, *Manhadun de zhongguo nuren* (Manhattan's China lady) (Beijing: Beijing chubanshe, 1996). I have elsewhere discussed Zhou's book in greater detail. See Qian, "'China' in the Diaspora."
35. Cao Guilin, *Luka* (Green card) (Beijing: Xinshijie, 1993), preface.
36. How much is fiction and how much is fact in such autobiographical works by Cao and Zhou remain a question. In any case, publication in China of their works about the "American Dream" brought them handsome royalties. Some observers allege that Zhou Li never made as much money through international trade as she brags about in her book, as she did through sales of her book in China.
37. Xiao Yang, *Luoshanji de fengniao* (A hummingbird in Los Angeles) (Beijing: Zuojia, 1997).
38. Ibid., p. 106.
39. Ibid., p. 214.

# Part II

# Contemporary Activism: Changing Orientations and Participation in Shaping U.S. Policy Toward China

# 4

# The Involvement of Chinese Americans in China-related Issues

## Implications of a North Carolina Study of Current Political Orientations and Future Expectations

*Yuhang Shi*

In recent years, ethnic groups that rarely have been involved in the articulation of U.S. foreign policy increasingly have focused on transnational interests.[1] One such group is Chinese Americans.[2] During the past two decades, Chinese American scholars have published important contributions related to U.S.–China relations in professional journals and books. Chinese American scientists have served as go-betweens for Washington and Beijing. Supporters of Taiwan have organized powerful lobbying campaigns. Chinese students, community activists, and representatives of the dissident movement have appeared frequently on prime-time TV programs to offer their views concerning China-related issues. Organizations such as the Committee of 100 (C-100), formed in 1990 by a group of prominent Chinese Americans striving to help improve U.S.–China relations,[3] have been active in speaking out on issues of concern to Chinese Americans and in endeavoring to promote mutual understanding between the two countries.

However, like other racial minority groups, Chinese Americans are confronted with enormous barriers in their attempt to join the forces that shape U.S. foreign policy. In spite of extraordinary population growth and remarkable achievements in education and socioeconomic status, Chinese Americans remain largely outside the mainstream political processes and social institutions that shape public policy and opinion. Few U.S. elections at any level feature Chinese American candidates and, among those rare candidates, few have been successful—even in areas with a high concentration of Chinese American residents.[4] In the past two decades, many

Chinese community activists have worked hard to raise voter turnout and political contributions, but few organizations have succeeded in attracting and maintaining a large number of followers, let alone serving as representatives and advocates of the community.[5] The event that is most revealing of the Chinese American community's political impotency is the 1996 fund-raising controversy. During that episode, the media and members of Congress often portrayed Chinese Americans (and other Asians as well) as a threateningly hostile force.[6] The major political parties purged their names from donor rosters and returned their contributions. After the 1996 election, Chinese Americans could not even approach Clinton administration officials, let alone persuade them to accord desired treatment to issues of concern to the Chinese community.

This chapter describes the results of a study designed to investigate the dynamics of political orientations and expectations among ordinary Chinese Americans in light of their life experience in the United States. The goal is not to explain the observed disparity in political status between the Chinese community and other ethnic groups, but to assess the prospect of more active involvement by Chinese Americans in the political process with respect to U.S.–China relations.

If Chinese Americans are to have an impact on domestic and foreign policies, they must first possess the knowledge, resources, and psychological propensity needed for political participation.[7] Successful ethnic involvement in U.S. foreign policy requires an effective lobbying apparatus along with concerted action by members of the group who are respected players in the policymaking process. A recurrent observation by students of U.S. foreign policymaking is that ethnic groups that have been influential in this area tend to be well established in the mainstream political process and in influential social institutions.[8]

The chapter begins with an elaboration of the central concepts that form the theoretical foundation for the author's research and analysis. Then, based on survey data, I describe how Chinese Americans perceive their relations with the U.S. political system and how they view U.S.–China relations. The following analysis explores the relationship between respondent political orientations and expectations and (1) their life experiences in the United States—including acculturation and assimilation, socioeconomic status, and race relations—as well as (2) the nature of their ties to the China Mainland, Hong Kong, Taiwan, and/or other places. The chapter concludes with a discussion of the role that Chinese Americans are likely to play in shaping the future relationship between the United States and China—considered one of the most important in the new century.

## Theoretical Foundation and Hypotheses

Two concepts lie at the core of the research reported here: political orientations and expectations. Whether an ethnic group becomes an issue-advocacy force in the foreign-policy arena is largely a function of individual political orientations and expectations. The concept of orientations refers to a person's disposition toward political objects and relationships—such as the governmental system; political leaders, parties, and events; public policies; and the person himself/herself as a member of the polity. Orientations are important because they determine how a person views himself or herself in relation to the political system and they predispose one to act in certain ways regarding political matters. For instance, a person who feels positively about political rights enjoyed as a citizen, or has a strong sense of civic duty, is more likely to engage in such forms of political participation as voting. Likewise, a person with a solid understanding of politics and government and a high level of confidence in the capability and responsiveness of government is likely to consider politics to be a useful vehicle for personal action. A person without these psychological dispositions is likely to stay out of politics.

Expectation implies a clearly articulated preference and is a prerequisite for issue-specific political action. Like orientations, expectations determine the extent and mode of individual political involvement. Participation occurs when a person feels dissatisfied with the status quo and looks forward to a preferred change, or conversely, when s/he anticipates something undesirable emerging and wants to forestall it. A person who feels intensely or passionately about an issue (e.g., gun control) is more likely to act upon it.

Recognizing the importance of political orientations and expectations in political behavior, social scientists have developed a variety of theoretical models to account for their formation. One model centers on explanations based on socioeconomic status (SES)—education and wealth in particular—and predicts that socioeconomic progress will result in a participatory orientation and generate a different set of preferences.[9] Education frames a person's views on various political objects and relationships by instilling democratic values and knowledge of government and politics, cultivating skills for political involvement, and expanding opportunities for interacting with the political elite. Wealth becomes relevant by offering a person expanded resources with which to exert political influence. Wealth also provides a person with more educational opportunities.

The SES model has received some support in the literature on Chinese (and Asian) Americans. There is evidence, for instance, that many Chinese came to the United States with scant financial resources and that, out of economic necessity, they have set economic security as the priority, shunning anything political except for activities organized by local labor unions.[10] Since Chinese tend to rely on themselves to achieve economic success, heightened socioeconomic status may not be accompanied by increased political activism.[11] A self-reliant and successful person could have fewer reasons to turn to government and politics for help.[12] Another mitigating factor is that many Chinese Americans have pursued careers in scientific and technological areas. While promising a great deal of economic security and status, such career choices have the potential to limit the development of political consciousness. What Moon Jo has noted about Asian Americans could apply among Chinese Americans. By concentrating in science and technology, Jo argues, Asians have limited their opportunity to develop an awareness of the intricacy of human relations and sensitivity to social and political issues involving the Asian American population—particularly relationships between Asian American minority groups and the mainstream society.[13]

In contrast to the SES model, the structural model stresses the importance of social forces—most notably, race relations. Designed mainly to explain the pattern of political involvement of African Americans, this model assumes that the formation of psychological properties is internal rather than external to organized social life, and holds that the history and state of race relations have an important effect on the formation of political orientations and expectations. However, researchers who subscribe to this model disagree on the nature of that effect. One hypothesis is that, due to its coercive nature, discrimination and violence against people of color instills a sense of powerlessness or fear among victims, thereby undermining their trust in the political system and their self-confidence as a member of the polity. This can be the case even after overt discrimination is removed from the political and legal systems.[14] Another hypothesis claims that because racial discrimination entails a feeling of relative deprivation or unfairness, members of disadvantaged groups will develop a strong sense of internal "us" versus external "them" and rely on their common identity as a source of mutual support. This, in turn, will galvanize group solidarity and political assertiveness.[15] Thus far, empirical evidence from studies on African Americans favors the latter hypothesis.[16]

The structural model possesses enormous appeal among researchers who study Chinese Americans. For a long time, U.S. laws barred Chinese from giving testimony against Caucasians in court and from applying for naturalization, denied them the right to vote and the protection of habeas corpus, and required that they obtain a certificate to remain in the United States. When anti-Chinese prejudice approached its climax in 1882, Congress passed the Chinese Exclusion Act. Although the restrictive legislation that denied Chinese Americans political and civil rights had been removed from the legal system by the mid-1960s, de facto anti-Chinese discrimination remains a significant part of racial antagonism. To many observers, this situation is responsible for the fact that Chinese Americans, in general, continue to evidence a low level of political awareness and involvement.[17]

The suppressing effect of racism on political participation is not absolute, however. In 1996, for instance, Asian American activists, in coalition with African Americans and Hispanic Americans, launched a massive voter-registration campaign and educational effort in opposition to California's Proposition 209—an initiative intended to thwart various affirmative-action programs. After the 1996 fund-raising controversy erupted, they continued that political momentum.[18] This suggests that, in the face of racial discrimination, Chinese Americans might develop the kind of political activism observed among African Americans.

Another model that has been popular among students of Chinese (and Asian) American behavior emphasizes cultural explanations. Many ethnic groups in America have maintained values, rituals, customs, religion, languages, and art that they and/or their ancestors brought from the native or ancestral land. In many cases, such ethnic subcultures define how members of a group view and deal with political matters in the receiving society and set them apart from the rest of the population.[19] This point is especially relevant here because traditional Chinese culture differs from mainstream U.S. culture in that it sanctions obedience, resignation, reverence for authority, and passivity. It is possible that these cultural characteristics not only have influenced the behavior of early Chinese immigrants, but also continue to influence Chinese Americans today.[20] In addition, because many first-generation Chinese Americans were born and raised in a society governed by an authoritarian regime, they might have developed a political orientation incompatible with democratic politics.[21]

Of course, one's ethnic heritage may fade away over time in a different cultural environment, and experience in the homeland can be modified or even displaced by life in the new country. Thus, we might expect that American-born Chinese or Chinese immigrants who have lived in the United States for a long period of time and/or have had extensive interaction with the larger society would demonstrate two distinct psychological tendencies compared to those who just came or have remained relatively isolated. First, they would have a better understanding of the U.S. political system and develop more interest in U.S. political issues. Second, they would retain less traditional behavior and, hence, possess less emotional attachment to their native or ancestral land.[22] The first tendency would motivate Chinese Americans to become more involved in the political process, while the second might diminish their interest in China-related issues.

While all three of these explanations—socioeconomic status, social and political structure, and culture—have influenced previous studies on Chinese Americans, they have not been tested in a way that allows us to determine the relative importance of each set of variables in shaping their political orientations and expectations. It is hoped that the research reported here will begin to fill this gap and, thereby, enhance understanding of the future role that Chinese Americans are likely to play in the articulation of U.S. policy toward China.

## Methods and Data

Political orientations and expectations are individual psychological properties assessable by standardized surveys. As far as Chinese Americans are concerned, limited information is available from two previous surveys, both conducted in Southern California. In August 1992, the Republican National Committee (RNC) compiled a sampling frame of 5,000 adult Asian Americans by selecting names from the membership directories of major Asian ethnic organizations and an ethnic-surname database of registered voters.[23] Of the 1,149 respondents who completed the subsequent RNC survey, about 482 are Chinese. The RNC survey investigates respondents' attitudes toward political institutions, policies, and events. It also covers respondent participation in election-related activities. The second survey is based on telephone interviews conducted by the *Los Angeles Times* (LAT) in May 1997 with 773 Chinese Americans.[24] The LAT designed this survey to gauge the assimilation experiences of Chinese Americans and their reaction to the anticipated handover of Hong Kong to China on 1 July 1997. The following analysis draws upon some of the findings from these two surveys. However, both studies are deficient in critical respects in terms of the issues addressed in this chapter. For the RNC survey, only aggregated results are available. The LAT survey included only a few questions related to political orientations and participation.

The main source of the data used in the analysis presented here is a survey conducted by the author in the summer of 2000 through two Chinese nondenominational Christian churches in Raleigh and Durham, North Carolina.[25] The questionnaire consisted of thirty-six items, half of which concerned political characteristics; the other half dealt with nonpolitical characteristics. The author selected and worded questions in a way that would make the results comparable to those from surveys of the general public. Three sets of questions (about a dozen items) are used to measure political orientations— each corresponding to a type of political orientation as defined by Gabriel Almond and Sidney Verba in their classic *Civic Culture*. Items that ask respondents to identify the contents of the Bill of Rights, key elected officials, and the majority party in the U.S. House of Representatives and the U.S. Senate are designed to tap cognitive orientations, or knowledge about the political system and process. Items dealing with the attention a person pays to political and policy matters and about participation in various political activities measure affective orientations, or feelings about being a member of the polity. Items about party identification and policy preferences on various domestic-policy issues measure evaluative orientations, or judgments and opinions about political objects and policy issues.[26]

Several questions tap expectations concerning key China-related issues: relations between the China Mainland and Taiwan; human rights in China; U.S.–China trade; democratization in China; and overall U.S.–China relations. Questions about what the U.S. government should do about these issues measure the relative cohesiveness of preferences among respondents. Questions about how important these issues are to one's decisions regarding party identification and electoral choice, as well as in conversations with family members and friends, are intended to discover the saliency of China-related issues.

The most relevant nonpolitical characteristics for this discussion are respondent perceptions of race relations in the United States, access to the Internet, socioeconomic status, assimilation experience, and selected demographic traits—age, gender, and marital status. Indicators of assimilation experience include language spoken at home, ethnic characteristics of one's neighborhood, citizenship, and length of residence in the United States.[27] Socioeconomic status is measured by family income, educational attainment, and occupation.

While sampling confined to Chinese in North Carolina limits the scope of analysis, the findings still are interesting because North Carolina Chinese represent an emerging, yet understudied, segment of the Chinese population in America—those living outside coastal metropolitan areas. For much of the last 150 years, Chinese have concentrated in metropolitan areas in California, New York, Hawaii, Illinois, and Texas. Until the 1960s, the 1,200 Chinese living in the Mississippi Delta constituted the largest Chinese American population in the South.[28] Beginning in the 1980s, however, a large number of newcomers—particularly students—have settled in areas, including North Carolina, that are not traditional destinations for Chinese immigrants. Although the precise extent of this development is not yet known, we can discern the changing settlement pattern in the preliminary report of the 2000 census. From 1990 to 1999, the number of Asians and Pacific Islanders grew by 36.8 percent in California, 44.5 percent in New York, 42.3 percent in Illinois, and 8.4 percent in Hawaii. Twenty-five other states experienced percentage increases that ranged from 50 percent to the high seventies. North Carolina's growth rate of 99 percent was surpassed only by Nevada (123.7 percent) and Georgia (109 percent).[29]

As shown in Table 4.1, where the Raleigh and Durham survey data are compared with those from the LAT survey, North Carolina Chinese have several things in common with other Chinese Americans. Most are married and most of their spouses are ethnic Chinese. The primary language spoken at home is Chinese. A large majority of them are content with the state of race relations.[30] However, the North Carolina group possesses more resources of value for political involvement. First, they have benefited from the restructuring of the U.S. economy over the past two decades that has created career opportunities in academia and high-tech industry for educated immigrants.[31] Second, they resemble the so-called "uptown" Chinese in terms of income and education level,[32] but they differ from those middle- or upper-middle-class Chinese who live, for example, in Monterey Park, California, in the sense that they have fewer opportunities to be exposed to activities organized by Chinese or Asian American organizations.[33] Third, they have lived in this country for a somewhat longer period of time and, therefore, are likely to have been more assimilated where they live and work.

The next three sections describe the political characteristics of this group of Chinese Americans. We will see how they differ from other Americans in terms of political participation, their understanding of politics, and their views on various policy issues. Their positions on policy issues concerning U.S.–China relations will be examined. We also will explore how upward mobility, cultural heritage, race relations, and assimilation experiences affect the development of their political orientations and expectations. These questions will be addressed in order to assess the prospect that Chinese Americans will become more actively involved in the foreign-policy-making process.

**Chinese Americans and U.S. Politics**

Nearly twenty years ago, Vincent Parrillo observed that the power of the ballot box and of ethnic politics had not yet become evident among Chinese Americans—except in Hawaii—and predicted that, given demographic and social changes, the remaining two decades of the twentieth century would be a different story.[34] Parrillo's predictions have been partially borne out. As early as 1984, voter turnout among Chinese Americans approached that of non-Hispanic whites.[35] There also is evidence that, together with other Asian Americans, Chinese have made substantial contributions to political parties and candidates in recent election cycles.[36] These developments are not surprising given the socioeconomic changes that have occurred in the Chinese

Table 4.1

**Nonpolitical Characteristics of Chinese Americans** (in percent)

| | North Carolina survey | Los Angeles Times survey |
|---|---|---|
| Education | | |
| College degree | 17.5 | 31.3 |
| Post-college | 82.5 | 15.5 |
| Family income | | |
| $10,000 or less | 5.6 | 5.0 |
| $10,000 to $20,000 | 0.0 | 11.0 |
| $20,001 to $30,000 | 0.0 | 12.3 |
| $30,001 to $40,000 | 0.0 | 11.5 |
| $40,001 to $50,000 | 8.3 | 8.9 |
| Above $50,000 | 86.1 | 51.3 |
| Occupation | | |
| Professional (e.g., medical doctor) | 15.4 | n/a |
| Engineer | 35.9 | n/a |
| College professor | 12.8 | n/a |
| Businessperson | 5.1 | n/a |
| House worker | 12.8 | n/a |
| Government employee | 5.1 | n/a |
| Student | 7.7 | n/a |
| Self-employed | 2.6 | n/a |
| Other | 2.6 | n/a |
| Age | | |
| 18–30 | 7.5 | 28.4 |
| 31–40 | 25.0 | 25.0 |
| 41–50 | 35.0 | 18.6 |
| Above 50 | 32.5 | 29.0 |
| Gender | | |
| Male | 62.5 | 47.9 |
| Female | 37.5 | 52.1 |
| Marital status | | |
| Married (or cohabiting) | 95.0 | 66.4 |
| Single (or divorced/separated) | 5.0 | 33.6 |
| Ethnicity of spouse | | |
| Chinese | 97.4 | 93.8 |
| Other | 2.6 | 6.2 |
| Length of residence in the U.S. | | |
| Mean (years) | 18.9 | 15.4 |
| Language spoken at home | | |
| English | 7.5 | 18.4 |
| Chinese | 87.5 | 78.8 |
| Other | 5.0 | 2.8 |
| Characteristics of neighborhood | | |
| Racially mixed | 20.0 | n/a |
| Predominantly white | 80.0 | n/a |

*(continued)*

Table 4.1 *(continued)*

| | North Carolina survey | *Los Angeles Times* survey |
|---|---|---|
| Ancestral land(s) | | |
| Mainland | 44.7 | n/a |
| Taiwan | 23.7 | n/a |
| Hong Kong | 2.6 | n/a |
| Mainland and Taiwan | 18.4 | n/a |
| Mainland and Hong Kong | 7.9 | n/a |
| Other | 2.6 | n/a |
| Residency status | | |
| Citizen | 62.5 | 72.4 |
| Permanent resident | 17.5 | n/a |
| Other | 20.0 | 27.4 |
| Perception of race relations | | |
| Generally good | 61.0 | 76.0 |
| Generally bad | 19.5 | 14.0 |
| Don't know | 19.5 | 10.0 |

*Source:* North Carolina survey conducted by the author in summer 2000; LAT survey conducted by the *Los Angeles Times* in May 1997.

American community. By the time of the 1990 census, 46.7 percent of Chinese males and 35 percent of Chinese females held a college degree or higher. Both figures are above the national average. The per capita income of Chinese Americans now approaches that of whites.[37]

The increased participation of Chinese in the political process is evident in North Carolina as well as in states with larger Chinese populations—California and New York, in particular. As shown in Table 4.2, the overall level of interest in politics and participation in various political activities by North Carolina Chinese compares favorably to that of the general population of the United States. Among citizens, 62 percent reported voting in an election; 18 percent have contributed to a candidate for public office; and 9 percent have attended a campaign rally. Among those who have voted, 43 percent have signed a petition; 22 percent have written to a government official; and 6 percent have attended a fund raiser. The only figure that is lower among North Carolina Chinese than the general public relates to attending a public meeting. Signs of increased political activism among this well-educated group of Chinese Americans also are encountered in another survey item: an overwhelming majority of the respondents reported that they follow what is going on in government and politics most or some of the time. On the other hand, few respondents had heard of politically oriented ethnic organizations and only one respondent reported being a member of a civic organization.

However, increased participation is only part of the story. Favorable comparisons disappear when we turn to cognitive orientations. Table 4.3 shows the percentage of North Carolina Chinese able to tell what the Bill of Rights is, who key elected officials are, and which party is in control of the two

Table 4.2

**Affective Orientations of Chinese Americans** (in percent)

|  | North Carolina Chinese | U.S. population |
|---|---|---|
| 1. Follow politics and government policies |  |  |
| Most of the time | 15.4 | 23.0 |
| Some of the time | 56.4 | 40.0 |
| Only now and then | 25.6 | 26.0 |
| Never | 2.6 | 12.0 |
| 2. Have ever voted in election | 62.5 | 54.2 |
| 3. Have ever made political contribution | 18.7 | 9.0 |
| 4. Have ever attended a campaign rally | 9.4 | 6.0 |
| 5. Have ever attended a fund raiser | 10.0 | n/a |
| 6. Have ever attended a public meeting | 15.0 | 25.2 |
| 7. Have ever signed a petition | 45.0 | 13.0 |
| 8. Have ever written to a government official | 35.0 | 21.6 |
| 9. Have ever written to newspapers, etc. | 10.0 | 4.7 |
| 10. Have ever participated in protest, etc. | 10.0 | 1.7 |
| 11. Have ever run for public office | 0.0 | n/a |

*Source:* Data for North Carolina Chinese are from the survey conducted by the author in 2000. For question 1, data for the U.S. population are from National Election Study (NES) of 1996; for questions 2, 3, and 4, from the 1996 Census; and for questions 6 through 10, from NES of 1976. These aggregate results can be found in M. Margaret Conway, *Political Participation in the United States* (Washington, D.C.: C.Q. Press, 2000), pp. 7, 8, 50, and 144.

*Note:* For questions 2, 3, and 4, the data for North Carolina Chinese are confined to those who are U.S. citizens. For questions 5 through 10, the data for North Carolina Chinese are for those who have voted.

houses of the U.S. Congress. Only one in four of the respondents, as compared to almost half of the general public, correctly identified the Bill of Rights as the first ten amendments to the U.S. Constitution that protect individual rights. Asked to name political leaders at the national level, North Carolina Chinese also scored consistently lower than the general public—with the exception of knowing Vice President Al Gore. The most glaring gap is with regard to knowledge of political parties. Only about one-third of the North Carolina Chinese could identify the party that controls the U.S. House of Representatives and Senate. This compares to 68 percent and 55 percent, respectively, among the general public. These findings suggest that Chinese Americans resemble other newly arrived immigrant communities in terms of basic political knowledge.

In terms of evaluative orientations, North Carolina Chinese differ from the general population in some respects, while showing similarity in others. As we find in Table 4.4, almost half of the respondents identified themselves

Table 4.3

**Cognitive Orientations of Chinese Americans** (in percent)

|  | North Carolina Chinese | U.S. population |
|---|---|---|
| 1. What is the Bill of Rights? | | |
| Correct | 12.5 | 46 |
| Partially correct | 12.5 | n/a |
| 2. Name government officials and parties | | |
| President | 87.5 | 96 |
| Vice president | 82.5 | 74 |
| Senators of your state (at least one) | 52.5 | 55 |
| Congressman of your district | 27.5 | 29 |
| Governor of your state | 57.5 | 74 |
| Majority party in the U.S. House of Representatives | 35.0 | 68 |
| Majority party in the U.S. Senate | 37.5 | 55 |

*Source:* Data for North Carolina Chinese are from the survey conducted by the author from April to June of 2000. Data for the U.S. population are from Michael X. Delli Carpini and Scott Keeter, "Stability and Change in the U.S. Public's Knowledge of Politics," *Public Opinion Quarterly* 55 (Winter 1991): 583–612.

with the GOP, compared to only 27 percent of the U.S. public. Consistent with this party identification, North Carolina Chinese also lean to the conservative side on welfare issues—only about one in three supports government programs that would provide aid to the poor, while almost half of the general public does so. Other issues on which North Carolina Chinese differ from the general public involve abortion, health care, and legal immigration. The vast majority (75 percent) hold a liberal stance regarding abortion; an equally large majority want government to provide health care; and only 5 percent agreed that legal immigration should be reduced. The views of North Carolina Chinese resemble those of the general public with regard to gun control, the government's role in job creation, stopping illegal immigration, race relations, and homosexuality.

What is particularly interesting in the Table 4.4 data is the finding that, perhaps due to their religious background and/or due to the South being more conservative, North Carolina Chinese are more Republican-leaning than other Chinese Americans.[38] In California and New York, for example, voter registration and exit polls show that Chinese voters are heavily Democratic.[39] Another example of this difference can be illustrated by comparing the N.C. survey data with the RNC survey data. Of the Chinese respondents in the RNC survey, 44.6 percent identified themselves as very or somewhat conservative, 30.2 percent as middle of the road, and 24.8 percent as some-

Table 4.4

**Evaluative Orientations of Chinese Americans** (in percent)

|  | North Carolina Chinese | U.S. population |
|---|---|---|
| 1. Identify with a party | | |
| Republican | 50.0 | 27.4 |
| Democratic | 30.0 | 38.5 |
| Independent | 17.5 | 25.9 |
| Others | 2.5 | 8.0 |
| 2. Agree that government should do more to | | |
| Help the poor | 35.0 | 45.8 |
| Provide jobs | 37.5 | 26.0 |
| Provide health care | 75.0 | 38.7 |
| Restrict abortion | 25.0 | 56.6 |
| Restrict gun ownership | 50.0 | 46.4 |
| Stop illegal immigration | 52.5 | 64.7 |
| 3. Agree that government should do more to | | |
| Reduce legal immigration | 5.0 | 51.0 |
| Discourage homosexuality | 40.0 | 43.0 |
| Help minorities | 40.0 | 40+ |
| Promote racial harmony | 60.0 | n/a |

*Source:* Data for Chinese Americans are from the survey conducted by the author in 2000. For the U.S. population, the figures for questions 1 and 2 are calculated from 1996 National Election Study (NES) data. See Steven J. Rosenstone, Donald R. Kinder, and Warren E. Miller, *American National Election Study, 1996: Pre- and Post-election Survey* (www.icpsr.umich.edu), ICPSR #6896. Figures for question 3 are drawn from Mark Gillespie, "U.S. Public Changing Views on Immigration," Gallup News Service [online], 16 March 1999 (www.gallup.com/poll/releases/pr990316.asp); Frank Newport, "Some Change over Time in American Attitudes towards Homosexuality, but Negativity Remains," Gallup News Service [online], 1 March 1999 (www.gallup.com/polls/releases/pr990301b.asp); the NES data.

what or very liberal. Even among this relatively conservative group, only about one-third identified themselves as Republicans; the rest are evenly divided between Democrats and Independents. The different take on political-party affiliation evidenced by North Carolina Chinese suggests the difficulty of bringing all Chinese together to form a unified and respectable force in U.S. politics.

Table 4.5 reports the attitudes of North Carolina Chinese regarding some key China-related issues.[40] In the first section of the table, we observe considerable homogeneity in respondent preferences. Virtually none of the North Carolina Chinese support measures to contain China. Only 17.5 percent support the idea of helping Taiwan become independent—in sharp contrast to the 56 percent in the LAT survey who favored the establishment of full diplomatic relations with Taiwan by the U.S. government.[41] About two-thirds of

Table 4.5

**Expectations of North Carolina Chinese on China-related Issues**
(in percent)

|  | All (N = 33 ) | Citizens (N = 9) |
|---|---|---|
| 1. Government should do more to |  |  |
| Help Mainland and Taiwan reunite | 30.0 | 25.0 |
| Help Taiwan become independent | 17.5 | 18.7 |
| Impose sanctions on China for human rights abuse | 32.5 | 31.2 |
| Promote trade with China | 37.5 | 37.5 |
| Improve relations with China | 50.0 | 46.9 |
| Contain China | 2.5 | 3.1 |
| Promote democracy in China | 72.5 | 75.0 |
| 2. Importance of China policy to party identification |  |  |
| Very important | 20.0 | 12.5 |
| Somewhat important | 45.0 | 56.2 |
| Not important | 25.0 | 25.0 |
| Not important at all | 5.0 | 6.2 |
| 3. Importance of China policy to vote choice |  |  |
| Very important | 12.5 | 9.4 |
| Somewhat important | 45.0 | 50.0 |
| Not important | 15.0 | 21.9 |
| Not important at all | 10.0 | 9.4 |
| 4. Talk about events related to U.S.–China relations |  |  |
| All the time | 17.9 | 21.9 |
| Sometimes | 76.9 | 71.9 |
| Never | 5.1 | 6.2 |

*Source:* Survey conducted by the author in 2000.

the N.C. respondents support measures to promote democracy in China, but do *not* want the United States to impose sanctions on China for human-rights abuses, to become involved with the reunification of the Mainland and Taiwan, or to promote trade with China. When asked whether the U.S. government should do more to improve overall relations with China, the N.C. respondents are evenly split.

The Table 4.5 data also show a low level of intensity on China-related issues. Almost everyone talks about China-related issues with family members or friends at least some of the time, but, contrary to the speculation we often see in the literature, these are not pivotal issues when it comes to party identification and voting. Less than 20 percent of the North Carolina Chinese Americans report that a party's or candidate's stance on China is *very* important to their decision regarding which party to support or which candidate to vote for. Nearly half regard China policy as somewhat important. For about one-quarter of the respondents, it is not an important factor. This finding is surprising given that virtually all the respondents are first-generation immigrants. Moreover, their observed lack of passion regarding candidate/party positions toward China suggests that North Carolina Chinese are unlikely to be involved actively in China-related issues.

## The Dynamics of Political Orientations and Expectations

In this section, an empirical model of political orientations and expectations is applied to the N.C. survey data in order to ascertain the factors that have contributed to the orientations and expectations described above. Given the nonscientific basis of the survey, the results of this analysis must be interpreted in suggestive rather than conclusive terms.

Table 4.6 lists the dependent and independent variables in the model and how they are operationalized. There are four separate dependent variables. *Affective orientation* is a composite scale that sums a respondent's responses to the items in Table 4.2. The scale is constructed as follows. First, we assign a respondent a score of 3 if he or she follows politics and government policies most of the time, 2 if some of the time, 1 if only now and then, and 0 if never. Next, we assign a respondent a score of 1 every time he or she responds positively to questions about participation in political activities, and 0 if he or she responds negatively. The summation of these scores constitutes the scale, which has a maximum value of 13 and a minimum value of 0. The higher a respondent is on this scale, the more participatory that respondent is.

*Cognitive orientation* also is a composite scale, but constructed with the data reported in Table 4.3. This scale measures a respondent's knowledge about the Bill of Rights, government officials, and parties. Again, we assign a respondent a score for each question depending on his or her response, and then sum the scores.[42] The range of the composite scale is from 0 to 10, where 0 means a respondent fails to answer any questions correctly and 10 means a perfect response.

The two other dependent variables pertain to expectations concerning China-related issues. *Preference* is derived from question 1 in Table 4.5, using a dimension-reduction technique known as factor analysis. The question asks about a respondent's positions on seven key issues involved in U.S.–China relations. Preference is one of the two major factors with a significant eigen value. It is chosen to be a dependent variable because it accounts for 75 percent of the variance and has a positive loading with the statements favoring a more cooperative relationship with China and a negative loading with the statements favoring a more antagonistic relationship.[43]

Table 4.6

**Variable Definition and Operationalization**

| Name | Property | Range of value |
|---|---|---|
| *Dependent variables* | | |
| Affective orientation | Composite scale | 0 (apathic) to 13 (participatory) |
| Cognitive orientation | Composite scale | 0 (little interest and knowledge of politics) to 10 (extensive interest and knowledge) |
| Preference | Binary | 1 (expect government to do more to improve relations with China); 0 (otherwise) |
| Intensity | Composite scale | 0 (indifferent to Chinese-related issues) to 10 (highly concerned) |
| *Independent variables* | | |
| Education | Binary | 0 (college or less); 1 (post-college) |
| Family income | Scale | 1 ($10,000 or less) to 8 (above $100,000) |
| Age | Scale | 1 (under 18) to 5 (above 50) |
| Gender | Binary | 0 (female); 1 (male) |
| Marital status | Binary | 0 (single/divorced/separated); 1 (married/cohabiting) |
| Length of residence | Year | number of years in the United States |
| Language spoken at home | Binary | 0 (non-English); 1 (English) |
| Neighborhood | Binary | 0 (racially mixed); 1 (predominantly white) |
| Nature of China ties | | Self or ancestors come from a place: |
| Mainland | Binary | 0 (other than Mainland China); 1 (Mainland) |
| Taiwan | Binary | 0 (other than Taiwan); 1 (Taiwan) |
| Hong Kong | Binary | 0 (other than Hong Kong); 1 (Hong Kong) |
| Mainland and Taiwan | Binary | 0 (other than China and Taiwan); 1 (China and Taiwan) |
| Mainland and Hong Kong | Binary | 0 (other than China and Hong Kong); 1 (China and Hong Kong) |
| Citizenship | Binary | 0 (non-U.S. citizen); 1 (U.S. citizen) |
| Perception of race relations | Binary | 0 (bad or don't know); 1 (good) |

Thus, a person with a lower value on this variable is more in favor of a confrontational policy than a person with a higher value.

*Intensity* is a composite scale that sums the answers to questions 2, 3, and 4 in Table 4.5. A respondent is assigned a value of 3 if he or she considers China-related issues very important to his or her decision on party identification, 2 if somewhat important, 1 if not important, and 0 if not important at all or no opinion. The same procedure is applied to the question about the importance of China-related issues in voting. The value assigned on question 4 is 2 if a respondent talks about China-related issues with family members or friends all the time, 1 if some of the time, or 0 if never. The Intensity scale has a maximum value of 10 and a minimum value of 0.

The independent variables in our model focus on a person's socioeconomic status, demographic characteristics, assimilation experience, Chinese ties, and perception of race relations. The respondents in the N.C. survey are relatively homogeneous in terms of some of these characteristics. As seen in Table 4.1, most of them report a post-college degree, family income above $50,000, and are married. This homogeneity has affected how the related variables are operationalized. Moreover, Table 4.6 does not include independent variables dropped during the course of analysis—such as access to the Internet, ethnicity of spouse, and two binary variables indicating whether a respondent or his or her ancestors came from Taiwan and Hong Kong or other places. These variables tended to have little variance.

The model is estimated with the regression technique of ordinary least square. The results are displayed in Table 4.7, with each column corresponding to one of the four dependent variables. Several interesting relationships emerge.

First, income level has a systematic effect on a respondent's interest in and knowledge about politics, but in a way that distinguishes between affective and cognitive orientations. Respondents with a higher level of income are likely to know more about the political system, but are less active in politics at the same time. This paradox is consistent with the notion that while economic success can help a person understand politics and public policies better, it might have induced some Chinese Americans to become less interested in government and less sensitive to political issues. It also is worth noting that another socioeconomic indicator—education—exerts no effect at all. This could be due to the fact that almost every respondent in our survey has completed a college education.

Second, length of residence has an important impact on orientations and, to a lesser degree, on intensity. The signs of the regression coefficient associated with this variable suggest that respondents who have lived in the United States for a long period of time are more participatory and knowledgeable than are those who came recently and that they are less likely to

Table 4.7

## Regression Coefficients of Political Orientations and Expectations

| Independent variables | Dependent variables | | | |
| --- | --- | --- | --- | --- |
| | Affective orientation | Cognitive orientation | Preference | Intensity |
| Intercept | 3.39 | 2.89 | −.31 | 2.56 |
| | (1.85) | (.8) | (−.21) | (.93) |
| Education | 1.01 | −.21 | .01 | −1.52 |
| | (1.35) | (−.14) | (.01) | (−1.35) |
| Family income | −.46** | 1.18** | .25 | .08 |
| | (−2.64) | (3.43) | (1.79) | (.32) |
| Age | −.40 | −1.28* | .18 | −.17 |
| | (−1.23) | (−1.99) | (.69) | (−.34) |
| Gender | −.31 | 2.61** | .20 | −.78 |
| | (−.66) | (2.75) | (.51) | (−1.08) |
| Marital status | 1.59 | −5.73** | −1.12 | 1.62 |
| | (1.32) | (−2.41) | (−1.16) | (.89) |
| Length of residence | .12** | .20** | .00 | −.09* |
| | (3.89) | (3.32) | (.16) | (−2.05) |
| Language spoken at home | .35 | .98 | −.39 | .41 |
| | (.32) | (.45) | (−.44) | (.25) |
| Neighborhood | .98 | −.48 | .31 | .56 |
| | (1.51) | (−.37) | (.59) | (.57) |
| Nature of China ties | | | | |
| Mainland | −1.16 | −.03 | −.43 | 2.59* |
| | (−1.36) | (−.02) | (−.63) | (2.01) |
| Taiwan | −1.24 | −.45 | −1.13 | 3.51** |
| | (−1.34) | (−.25) | (−1.52) | (2.52) |
| Hong Kong | −.64 | −1.65 | −2.11** | 5.91** |
| | (−.53) | (−.69) | (−2.16) | (3.24) |
| Mainland and Taiwan | −.62 | .96 | −.37 | 3.34** |
| | (−.67) | (.52) | (−.50) | (2.38) |
| Mainland and Hong Kong | .19 | 2.34 | −.55 | 2.93 |
| | (.15) | (.92) | (−53) | (1.51) |
| Citizenship | .48 | −.46 | −1.05 | .12 |
| | (.9) | (.44) | (−2.47) | (.15) |
| Perception of race relations | −.99* | −.86 | −.08 | −.55 |
| | (−2.01) | (−.89) | (−.21) | (−74) |
| Adjusted R-square | .59 | .61 | .26 | .41 |
| N | 31 | 31 | 31 | 31 |

*Note:* Figures in parentheses are T-values. ** significant at .05 level and * significant at .10 level.

associate their party identification and vote choice with a party's or candidate's stance on China-related issues. This important finding underscores the role of assimilation or acculturation experience in the development of political orientations and expectations. However, it is intriguing to discover that being a U.S. citizen, speaking English at home, and living in a predominantly white neighborhood all exert little impact on the formation of political orientations and expectations. The modal distribution of these three variables (62.5 percent of the respondents are U.S. citizens, 87.5 percent speak Chinese at home, and 80 percent live in predominantly white neighborhoods) partly accounts for this finding. Another possible reason is confounding effects since length of residence, citizenship, language spoken at home, and other variables measure more or less the same assimilation process. A person who has been here for a longer period of time is more likely to obtain citizenship (the correlation coefficient is .59). The same effect applies to the language one speaks at home (length of residence has a correlation coefficient of .38 with speaking English at home). In fact, if we drop length of residence from the estimation, the chance for citizenship and speaking English at home to exert a positive impact on political knowledge increases—although it is still short of statistical significance.

Third, a respondent's perception of race relations in the United States does not affect how s/he understands the working of political system and feels about China-related issues—although it is associated in a statistically significant way with his or her affective orientation (i.e., interest in political matters and participation in various political activities). The regression coefficient associated with the perception of race relations has a negative sign, suggesting that a respondent who feels content with the state of race relations is politically less active. This is consistent with the hypothesis that members of a disadvantaged ethnic group may develop a participatory orientation due to a feeling of relative deprivation or unfairness, and seek redress of grievances through the political process.[44] Since only a small minority of Chinese Americans currently characterize race relations in negative terms,[45] however, it is not likely that much political activism will result from experiences with racial discrimination.

Fourth, after controlling for education and income, a respondent's knowledge of political matters is closely related to his or her age, gender, and marital status. Young people scored better than their older counterparts in identifying the Bill of Rights, political leaders, and parties. In the North Carolina survey, male respondents performed better than female respondents did. Other things being equal, married respondents scored almost six points lower than the unmarried in terms of political knowledge.[46]

## Prospects for Chinese American Involvement in Foreign Policy Issues Related to China

Much of the Chinese American involvement in U.S.–China relations to date has not been directly related to foreign-policy making. To change that, Chinese Americans as a whole must first raise their status in mainstream social institutions and political processes. On an exploratory basis, the preceding sections have considered the political orientations and expectations of a growing segment of Chinese population in the United States—those residing in areas that most Chinese immigrants have not selected in the past (specifically, those living in North Carolina, a state with one of the fastest-growing Chinese populations). This group of Chinese Americans is typical of those who have attained high socioeconomic status. Although the environment they live in is less multicultural than that found in a major coastal metropolis such as the San Francisco Bay Area or the New York Metropolitan Area, these first-generation immigrants have no memory of the exclusion period and personally have encountered little racial discrimination.

From the analysis reported above, we can conclude that the development of the political orientations and expectations of North Carolina Chinese Americans follows the SES and cultural models. This group of primarily first-generation immigrants is less familiar with politics than the native-born population, but the gap should narrow with increased length of U.S. residence and further integration into mainstream society. Concomitantly, these same factors are likely to result in higher rates of participation in electoral politics. It is doubtful, however, that high socioeconomic status and assimilation will be sufficient by themselves to motivate many North Carolina Chinese to join in efforts to influence policies directly connected to U.S.–China relations. The exploratory findings presented in this chapter suggest that increased economic security and societal assimilation are likely to diminish interest in China-related issues among Chinese Americans similarly situated to those in the N.C. survey. Since these two trends are not uncommon, Chinese American activists and community leaders must find ways to cultivate and maintain a high level of political and ethnic consciousness regarding the importance of issues affecting relations between the country of origin and the country of choice.

Meeting this challenge will not be an easy task. The results of this study suggest that it will become increasingly difficult to maintain group unity in the face of growing diversity within the Chinese American community. One indication of this development is lack of common political-party affiliation. While half of the sampled North Carolina Chinese Americans are Republican, only one-third of all Chinese Americans in California identify as Republicans.[47] Another complicating factor is lack of exposure to ethnically oriented political mobilization among Chinese Americans who do not live in California and New York. Few of the N.C. respondents had heard of any major Chinese American political organizations and no one was a member of such an organization.[48] Therefore, they lack access to an institutional base and to leaders capable of articulating a common goal for members of the community and mobilizing them to become involved in foreign-policy shaping.

The positions respondents take on foreign-policy issues involving U.S.–China relations constitute another constraint. With the exception of promoting democracy in China, these North Carolina Chinese Americans demonstrated little interest in a proactive U.S. posture toward the Mainland or Taiwan. Less than 40 percent even supported U.S. government activities aimed at promoting trade with China. It is possible that the complications and contradictions involved in foreign-policy issues affecting U.S.–China relations (e.g., trade versus human rights) produce ambivalence and diminished interest in seeing the U.S government become involved.[49] An alternative explanation is that, with enhanced socioeconomic status and assimilation, Chinese Americans become less concerned with foreign-policy issues that are exclusively related to U.S.–China affairs—in contrast, for instance, to global issues that are of consequence for the China Mainland, the United States, and their long-term relationship.[50]

In conclusion, future prospects for more active involvement by Chinese Americans in U.S.–China relations depend on overcoming obstacles arising from past experience and the current situation, and from both inside and outside the community. It is likely to be a long journey.

## Notes

1. Others, including those of Irish, Jewish, and Cuban descent, have played high-profile roles in the formation of U.S. policy toward the country or region of their origin. See Mohammed E. Ahrari, ed., *Ethnic Groups and U.S. Foreign Policy* (Westport: Greenwood Press, 1987); Louis L. Gerson, *The Hyphenate in Recent American Politics and Diplomacy* (Lawrence: University Press of Kansas, 1964); Abdul Aziz Said, ed., *Ethnicity and U.S. Foreign Policy* (New York: Praeger, 1977).

2. For a detailed description, see Xiao-huang Yin, "The Growing Influence of Chinese Americans on U.S.–China Relations," in *The Outlook for U.S.–China Relations Following the 1997–1998 Summits: Chinese and American Perspectives on Security, Trade and Cultural Exchange*, ed. by Peter H. Koehn and Joseph Y.S. Cheng (Hong Kong: The Chinese University Press, 1999), pp. 331–350. For research purposes, I define Chinese Americans as those who (or whose ancestors) migrated from the Mainland, Taiwan, or Hong Kong and either are U.S. citizens or have legal resi-

dence status in the United States. The survey analysis presented later in the chapter includes a few Chinese who are not yet U.S. citizens or permanent residents, but are in the process of becoming permanent residents.

3. Individuals who lend their prestige to C-100 include Yo-Yo Ma, I.M. Pei, Chang-lin Tien, Oscar Tang, Shirley Young, Henry Tang, and others. For the organization's mission statement, visit its website at www.committee100.org/aboutus/default.htm. Organized efforts by Chinese Americans to influence the China policy of the United States did not start with C-100. Those who established the National Association of Chinese Americans in 1977, for instance, did so for the purpose of advocating normalization of U.S.–China relations and, before that, groups favoring Taiwan had successfully lobbied Congress and the administration.

4. Aside from a few well-known cases, such as Gary Locke, David Wu, S.B. Woo, Michael Woo, March Fong Eu, Lily Lee Chen, Judy Chu, Matt Fong, and so on, data on officeholders of Chinese origin are not available. Nevertheless, one can gauge the paucity of Chinese American politicians by looking at the data for Asian Americans. The 1990 Civilian Labor Force Survey conducted by the U.S. Bureau of the Census shows that only 1.4 percent of all legislators in the nation were Asians. The 1987 Census of Government reports that .07 percent of all local elected officials were Asians; this percentage rose to .13 percent in 1992. Similarly, an analysis using the 1991 Form of Government Survey found that only .2 percent of the nation's city council members or mayors were of Asian ethnicity. See the discussion in Pei-te Lien, *The Political Participation of Asian Americans* (New York: Garland Publishing, 1997), pp. 6–7.

5. One exception is the newly created 80/20 Initiative—a pan-Asian organization with a majority of ethnic Chinese members. Led by the former lieutenant governor of Delaware, S.B. Woo, the organization registered 130,000 e-mail accounts in the summer of 2000 and expected the number to reach between 300,000 and 400,000 by the end of the year. See the organization's website at www.80–20Initiative.net/table.html. Although engaged in an aggressive recruitment campaign, the organization has yet to develop a coherent policy agenda.

6. Paul Watanabe recorded another case that illustrates the foreignness associated with Asian Americans. When a high State Department official was asked why no Asian American had been appointed to a major Asian country, the response was "It would be a conflict of interest." In reaction to this widespread perception, some activists in the Asian American community have urged their constituencies to distance themselves from foreign-policy issues in order to maintain their "American" credentials. See Watanabe, "Asian American Activism and U.S. Foreign Policy," in *Across the Pacific: Asian Americans and Globalization*, ed. by Evelyn Hu-DeHart (Philadelphia: Temple University Press, 1999), p. 120.

7. For a theoretical and empirical treatment of this approach, see M. Margaret Conway, *Political Participation in the United States*, 3d ed. (Washington, D.C.: CQ Press, 2000), chapter 3. On the relationship between political orientations and conventional forms of participation, see Gabriel Almond and Sidney Verba, *Civic Culture* (Boston: Little, Brown, 1963). On the relationship between political orientations and nonconventional forms of participation, see M. Kent Jennings et al., *Continuities in Political Action* (Berlin: Walter de Gruyter, 1989).

8. See Ahrari, *Ethnic Groups and U.S. Foreign Policy*, chapters 1, 4, 5, 6, and 7; Gerson, *The Hyphenate*, chapters 2, 3, 6; Said, *Ethnicity and U.S. Foreign Policy*, chapters 2, 4–7; Rene Lemarchand, ed., *American Policy in Southern Africa* (Washington, D.C.: University Press of America, 1978), pp. 313–340.

9. See Sidney Verba and Norman H. Nie, *Participation in America: Political Democracy and Social Equality* (New York: Harper & Row, 1972); Sidney Verba, Kay L. Scholzman, Henry Brady, and Norman H. Nie, "Race, Ethnicity and Political Resources: Participation in the United States," *British Journal of Political Science* 23, No. 4 (1993): 453–497.

10. Xiao-huang Yin, *Chinese American Literature Since the 1850s* (Urbana: University of Illinois Press, 2000), pp. 194–205.

11. Socioeconomic status has been found to play a relatively small role in the electoral participation of Asian Americans. Lien, *Political Participation of Asian Americans*, p. 130.

12. For more discussion on this revisionist view, see Felix Huenks, "From Personal to Political," in *Continuities in Political Action*, ed. by M. Kent Jennings et al. (Berlin: Walter de Gruyter, 1989), pp. 135–160.

13. Moon H. Jo, "The Putative Political Complacency of Asian Americans," *Political Psychology* 5, No. 4 (1984): 600.

14. See Lester M. Salamon and Stephen Van Evera, "Fear, Apathy, and Discrimination: A Test of Three Explanations of Political Participation," *American Political Science Review* 67, No. 4 (1973): 1288–1306; Joel D. Aberbach, "Power Consciousness: A Comparative Analysis," *American Political Science Review* 71, No. 4 (1977): 1544–1560. For a more general discussion of this hypothesis, see Edgar Litt, *Ethnic Politics in America: Beyond Pluralism* (Glenview: Scott, Foreman, 1970); and M. Kent Jennings, "Perception of Social Injustice," in *Continuities in Political Action*, ed. by M. Kent Jennings et al. (Berlin: Walter de Gruyter, 1989), pp. 161–199.

15. Marvin Olsen, "Social and Political Participation of Blacks," *American Sociological Review* 35, No. 2 (1970): 682–697; Sidney Verba and Norman H. Nie, *Participation in America*; Arthur H. Miller, Patricia Gurin, Gerald Gurin, and Oksana Mulanchuk, "Group Consciousness and Political Participation," *American Journal of Political Science* 25, No. 3 (1981): 494–511; Richard D. Shingles, "Black Consciousness and Political Participation: The Missing Link," *American Political Science Review* 75, No. 1 (1981): 76–91.

16. Olsen, "Political Participation of Blacks," 682–697; Miller et al., "Political Participation," 494–511; Shingles, "Black Consciousness and Political Participation," 76–91.

17. Jo, "Asian Americans," pp. 583–605; James Loewen, *The Mississippi Chinese: Between Black and White* (Cambridge: Harvard University Press, 1971), pp. 164–165; Ling-chi Wang, "The Politics of Ethnic Identity and Empowerment: The Asian American Community Since the 1960s," *Asian American Policy Review* 2, No. 1 (Spring 1991): 43–56; Watanabe, "Asian American Activism and U.S. Foreign Policy," pp. 109–128.

18. Don Nakanishi, "Drive-by Victims of DNC Greed," in *1998–99 National Asian Pacific American Political Almanac*, ed. by James Lai (Los Angeles: University of California at Los Angeles, Asian American Studies Center, 1999), pp. 34–35.

19. Henry Brady and Paul Sniderman, "Attitude Attribution: A Group Basis for Political Reasoning," *American Political Science Review* 79, No. 4 (1985): 1061–1087; Aaron Wildavsky, "Choosing Preferences by Constructing Institutions: A Cultural Theory of Preference Formation," *American Political Science Review* 81, No. 1 (1987): 3–22.

20. See Stanley Sue and Derald W. Sue, "Chinese-American Personality and Mental Health," *Amerasia* 1, No. 1 (1971): 36–49; W.L. Li, "Chinese Americans:

Exclusion from the Melting Pot," in *The Minority Report: An Introduction to Racial, Ethnic, and Gender Relations*, 2d ed., ed. by Anthony G. Dworkin and Rosalind J. Dworkin (New York: Holt, Rinehart and Winston, 1981); Aihwa Ong, "On the Edge of Empires: Flexible Citizenship Among Chinese in Diaspora," *Positions* 1, No. 3 (1993): 745–778. A study by Loretta Bass and Lynne Casper is enlightening in this regard. They found that, other things being equal, naturalized citizens are less likely to register and vote than are native-born citizens. Another important finding is that, among naturalized citizens, those who have been in the United States for a long time are more likely to register and vote. See Loretta E. Bass and Lynne M. Casper, "Are There Differences in Registration and Voting Behavior Between Naturalized and Native-born Americans?" (Paper presented at the Annual Meeting of the American Sociological Association, San Francisco, August 1998).

21. William Wei, *The Asian American Movement* (Philadelphia: Temple University Press, 1993), p. 245.

22. In her *Ethnic Options: Choosing Identities in America* (Berkeley: University of California Press, 1990), Mary Waters documents many cases of ambivalent ethnic identity among assimilating Irish and Italian Americans. Similarly, James Loewen found that many second- and third-generation Mississippi Chinese felt alienated from Chinese culture. In contrast to the Irish and Italian case, however, he attributes cultural alienation among Mississippi Chinese to "Chinese inferiority complex" rather than to assimilation. Loewen, *Mississippi Chinese*, chapter 7.

23. Susan Gall and Timothy Gall, *Statistical Record of Asian Americans* (Detroit: Gale Research, Inc., 1993), pp. 16–31.

24. The data set for the LAT survey can be acquired through the Ropercenter. The reference code is USLAT1997–396.

25. The author distributed one hundred copies of the questionnaire in both Chinese and English to adult members of the two churches. Some respondents completed the questionnaire right after the church service. Most did so at home and returned the instrument through mail. The return rate is 41 percent. Additional survey data are available from the author upon request.

26. Almond and Verba, *Civic Culture*, chapter 1. Others define these phrases slightly differently. See Margaret Conway, *Political Participation*, chapter 3.

27. Outgroup marriage, another indicator of assimilation experience, is not used because only one person is married to a non-Chinese spouse.

28. James Loewen, *Mississippi Chinese*, pp. 1–2.

29. CNN, "State-by-State Breakdown of Population Estimates," CNN.Com (www.cnn.com/2000/US/08/29/minority.growth.glance.ap/index.html).

30. The question on race relations is worded slightly differently in the two surveys. In the LAT survey, it reads, "Thinking of the Chinese people who live in Southern California and their ability to get adequate housing, and education, and job opportunities and social acceptance by whites, and things like that, generally speaking, do you think conditions for the Chinese people in Southern California are very good, or good, or bad, or very bad?"

31. In the LAT survey, the question on occupation uses different categories. However, the percentage choosing professional, engineering, and higher education is lower than in the North Carolina survey.

32. Peter Kwong is among the first to divide Chinese Americans into downtown and uptown groups. The former tend to enter the United States under family reunifi-

cation provisions or with refugee status, speak little English, work at low wages in manual or service jobs, and live in urban ghettos. The latter tend to be more affluent and educated before coming to the States and have fared much better in U.S. society. Uptown Chinese include those stranded after 1949, wealthy individuals coming from Taiwan and Hong Kong, and second- or third-generation downtown Chinese who have received college education and advanced up the economic ladder. See Peter Kwong, *New Chinatown* (New York: Hill and Wang, 1996).

33. One sociological treatment of uptown Chinese is Timothy Fong, *The First Suburban Chinatown: The Remaking of Monterey Park, California* (Philadelphia: Temple University Press, 1994).

34. Vincent N. Parrillo, "Asian Americans in American Politics," in *America's Ethnic Politics*, ed. by Joseph Roucek and Bernard Eisenberg (Westport: Greenwood, 1982), p. 94.

35. See Carole Uhlaner, Bruce Cain, and Roderick Kiewiet, "Political Participation of Ethnic Minorities in the 1980s," *Political Behavior* 11, No. 3 (1989): 195–231. Also see Gall and Gall, *Asian Americans*, pp. 16–31. For conflicting evidence, see Don Nakanishi, "The Next Swing Vote? Asian Pacific Americans and California Politics," in *Racial and Ethnic Politics in California*, ed. by Byran Jackson and Michael Preston (Berkeley: Institute of Government Studies, 1991), pp. 25–34.

36. Nakanishi, "Drive-by Victims of DNC Greed," pp. 34–35. Also see the discussion in Lien, *Political Participation of Asian Americans*, p. 9.

37. Edno Paisano, *We the Americans: Asians*, WE-3 (Washington, D.C.: Bureau of the Census, 1993), Tables 4 and 7.

38. Like many other southern states, North Carolina has been a Republican stronghold in national elections since 1968.

39. See National Asian Pacific American Legal Consortium, "The 1996 National Asian Pacific American Legal Consortium Exit Polls: New York City, S.F. Bay Area, and Los Angeles," in *1998–99 National Asian Pacific American Political Almanac*, ed. by James Lai (Los Angeles: University of California at Los Angeles, Asian American Studies Center, 1999), pp. 36–41; Connie Kang, "Poll Says Democrats Gained Among Asian Americans," *Los Angeles Times*, 10 March 2000 (www.latimes.com/news/politics/elect2000/congress/cal20000310/t000023147.html) and "Asian Americans Lean to Democrats, Poll Says," *Los Angeles Times*, 10 November 2000, p. B7. Although the polls reported in these publications target Asian Americans, they were conducted in areas possessing large Chinese American populations.

40. The list of key U.S–China relationship issues presented to respondents is by no means complete. In particular, it would have been valuable to assess the degree of consensus that exists among respondents with respect to the important dimension of "promoting educational and cultural exchanges with the Mainland."

41. In terms of their origins (and possible loyalties), 22 percent of the LAT respondents and 24 percent of the N.C. respondents claim Taiwan as their ancestral land; the figures for Mainland heritage are 33 percent and 45 percent, respectively.

42. For the question regarding the Bill of Rights, the values assigned are 0 (wrong), 1 (partially correct), or 2 (correct). For the question about U.S. senators, the value assigned is 2 if a respondent knows both senators from his or her state, 1 if the respondent knows one of them, or 0 if neither is known. For the questions on other officials and parties, the score assigned is either 1 (correct) or 0 (wrong).

43. The following factor pattern is generated by SAS Proc Factors with Harris method and varimax rotation options.

|  | Factor 1 | Factor 2 |
|---|---|---|
| Helping the Mainland and Taiwan reunite | 0.61365 | 0.36752 |
| Helping Taiwan become independent | -0.35594 | -0.05161 |
| Imposing sanction on China for human rights violation | -0.18986 | 0.36612 |
| Promoting trade with China | 0.61667 | 0.05696 |
| Improving relations with China | 0.73852 | -0.16227 |
| Containing China | -0.05276 | 0.45453 |
| Promoting democracy in China | -0.16780 | 0.53188 |

44. Circumstantial evidence also supports this point. See Don Nakanishi, "When the 'Spin' Is Out of Control: Asian Pacific Americans After the November 1996 Elections," in *1998–99 National Asian Pacific American Political Almanac*, ed. by James Lai (Los Angeles: UCLA Asian American Studies Center, 1999), p. 9.

45. See findings reported in Table 4.1.

46. Since 95 percent of these respondents are married, this study cannot be used to determine why such a marriage gap exists.

47. For California party-affiliation data, see Gall and Gall, *Statistical Record*, Table 41. For additional information regarding intra-group diversity, see Peter Kwong's discussion of downtown Chinese and uptown Chinese in his *New Chinatown*, pp. 58–62; and Xiao-huang Yin, "The Two Sides of America's Model Minority," *Los Angeles Times*, 7 May 2000, p. M1.

48. For information on ethnic organizations in the Chinese community, see Wei, *Asian American Movement*, chapters 6–8; Kwong, *New Chinatown*, Chapter 7; Wang, "Ethnic Identity," 43–56. Most Chinese American political organizations have only existed since the 1970s or 1980s and have failed to attract a large number of followers.

49. According Irving Horowitz, contradictions like these account for one of the principal reasons that most ethnic groups in the United States do not pay attention to foreign-policy issues. Irving L. Horowitz, "Ethnic Politics and U.S. Foreign Policy," in *Ethnicity and U.S. Foreign Policy*, ed. by Abdul Aziz Said (New York: Praeger, 1977), pp. 175–180.

50. It also is possible that sampling bias (e.g., sampling through churches) accounts for the low level of observed interest in proactive U.S. policies toward China.

# 5

# From Apathy to Inquiry and Activism

## The Changing Role of American-born Chinese in U.S.–China Relations

*Nancy Yao*

American-born Chinese (ABCs) are important, but underexamined, actors in U.S.–China relations. This essay explores critical dimensions of ABC involvement in shaping U.S. foreign policy, including the group's unique, advantaged cultural position to contribute to improved understanding of China by the American public and its important role as a link between Chinese immigrant communities and mainstream society in terms of U.S.–China relations.

The first section of the chapter provides a theoretical backdrop to this discussion. As a domestic (albeit fragmented) interest group, ABCs are relevant actors in the foreign-policy-shaping process from the perspective of international relations theory. The following section examines the formation of the ABC community and its attributes. Section three analyzes ABC attitudes toward China-related issues by dividing the community into three subgroups based on their level of activism and understanding of U.S. foreign policy and relations with China.

The conclusion considers possible future roles for ABCs in U.S.–China relations. It suggests that the group's degree of influence primarily will be determined by the degree of cohesion within the ABC community itself and that ABC influence in the political process most likely will be effectuated through interested individuals rather than through mass community action.

### Theoretical Perspective

With the transition away from state-centric models of explaining international interaction, an examination of ABC involvement in U.S.–China bilateral relations is particularly relevant from an international relations theory perspective. The opening of the "black box" of the state has resulted in an examination of international relations as a function of domestic politics, domestic and international public-interest groups, and economic actors in the political process. This "inside-out" approach to understanding international politics has gained weight with increased economic globalization and interdependence (and the resultant focus on economic actors) at the expense of traditional power politics.[1]

For interdependence theorists, there are multiple channels of international interaction: interstate, transgovernmental, and transnational.[2] According to Peter Gourevitch, interdependence empowers various interest groups, altering policy direction. Specifically, "complex interdependence alters domestic structures because it entails shifts in power . . . outside the government to private actors, or to international actors, or other foreign actors."[3] Helen Milner also suggests that the key agents of interdependence are domestic actors within states rather than states themselves.[4] An "inside-out" perspective sheds light on the "black box" of the state and the internal processes of interdependence that influence foreign-policy formation. At the same time, theories of collective action suggest that the formation of strong groups of American-born Chinese focused on influencing the China policy of the United States will be difficult given the lack of group cohesion and the perceived absence of rewards for cooperative interaction.[5]

The economic wealth of the overseas Chinese community already has been translated into political power in Asia. Overseas Chinese living and/or working in Southeast Asia have gained political clout throughout the region based on their economic strength. Their influence on local political systems has been carefully studied. Aihwa Ong and Donald Nonini, for instance, take a dark view of the apparent extraterritoriality of overseas Chinese in the Pacific Rim, describing it as an "ungrounded empire" formed for the purpose of economic accumulation and ultimately subverting the nation-state:

> The potential of wild and dangerously innovative powers associated with Chinese diasporic mobility has now therefore been incorporated into the open-ended logics of flexible capitalism itself. Thus, for instance, the commercial and real-estate holdings of Liem Sioe Leong conform to, yet transcend, the postcolonial orderings of the Indonesian state and of ASEAN; Taiwanese investors in Guangdong form new links with local officials that explicitly repudiate the older Cold War divisions between the People's Republic of China and Taiwan. . . . In these and a multitude of other examples, Chinese transnational practices represent forms of power that collude with the contemporary regimes of truth and power organizing the

new flexible capitalisms and modern nation states, but also act obliquely to them, and systematically set out to transgress the shifting boundaries set by both.[6]

Since the 1980s, China's economic development has been spurred by the investment of overseas Chinese communities, and the PRC government has offered preferential treatment (both de jure and de facto policies) for entrepreneurs from the Chinese world—including Taiwan, Hong Kong, Singapore, and Chinese communities elsewhere in Southeast Asia. Lee Kuan Yew, former prime minister of Singapore, has become a spokesperson for the importance of the overseas Chinese in China's economic development. He articulates a view of a transnational community in Asia that is based on shared ethnicity:

> People feel a natural empathy with those who share their physical attributes. This sense of closeness is reinforced when they also share basic culture and language. It makes for easy rapport and the trust that is the foundation of all business relations.[7]

The perceived opportunities offered by the Mainland market in the context of greater openness have encouraged a more accommodating foreign policy toward China in the region.[8]

The ABC interest group includes actors with domestic and international reach. They constitute a subset of the overseas Chinese, or *huaqiao* community, with the potential to expand its transnational presence. However, the role of ABCs in U.S. foreign policy has been relatively unexamined in comparison with the international involvement of the group's Asia-based peers. Hence, a focus on ABCs as a nonstate actor is particularly timely. The history of involvement by the Chinese diaspora (of which ABCs constitute an integral part) in transnational economic and foreign relations through trade and investment and its frequent transcendence of the political and territorial confines of the modern nation-state, adds weight to this emphasis. Nevertheless, this essay also will identify critical differences in terms of involvement in international relations that exist between ABCs and overseas Chinese communities in Asia.

## Defining the ABC Community

Group labels, such as Chinese Americans and American-born Chinese, surfaced with the increasing recognition of Chinese individuals as vital members of U.S. communities and with the gradual increase in cultural self-awareness that has occurred over the past four decades. Congress passed a new immigration act in 1965, ending the country-specific quota system. The 1965 act permits the immigration of up to 20,000 individuals per year from every country outside of the Western Hemisphere. It resulted in a dramatic shift in the composition of the Chinese population in the United States and promoted the formation of a diverse Chinese American community. From the 1940s through the mid-1960s, the majority of Chinese in the United States were native-born. As more family members from the Mainland, Taiwan, Hong Kong, and Southeast Asia emigrated to the United States, a domino effect occurred. A family member who remained abroad would begin the emigration process as soon as his or her relative had settled in the United States. Hence, by 1970, the majority of Chinese Americans were born overseas (mainly in the China Mainland) and, in 1990, 63 percent were first-generation immigrants.[9] In contrast to the earlier immigrants, moreover, the new entrants from the Chinese world were of diverse socioeconomic status and included many highly skilled and highly educated professionals.[10] Chinese Americans also tended to live in urban areas—especially in the three metropolises of New York, Los Angeles, and San Francisco.[11]

## The ABC Label

In this discussion, the ABC descriptor refers primarily to individuals born to parents who immigrated to the United States since the 1960s. By permitting a more dynamic, diversified flow of Chinese immigrants, the 1965 act led to the formation of a larger, flourishing subculture.

Development of the "ABC" label is difficult to trace. It was not common until the mid-1970s. At that time, where one was born, whether the Chinese-looking individual could speak Chinese, and explanations for poor Chinese-language abilities assumed greater relevance in light of the changing composition of the Chinese American community. In addition, Chinese children who immigrated to the states before attending formal schooling—the 1.5 generation—identified more with ABCs than with immigrants who have greater native-language ability and more extensive homeland-culture exposure.

In U.S. society today, the Chinese label is more a symbol of cultural self-perception and identity than a designation of citizenship. Tu Wei-ming characterizes the Chinese people as inhabiting three symbolic universes: first, there are those in China, Taiwan, and Hong Kong (the region commonly referred to as Greater China); second, overseas Chinese, or *haiwai huaren* (or *huaqiao*) for those living outside Greater China; and third, those with an interest in China (economists, journalists, missionaries).[12]

While ABCs fit within the second universe of overseas Chinese, many lack a defined Chinese-ness beyond their external features; culturally, they are more "American" than "Chinese." In general, ABCs, particularly those with many siblings who resist parental pressure to retain their ancestral identity, lean more toward a state-centric identification (i.e., U.S. American) and deemphasize the Chinese part of their label.[13] In contrast, most immigrant parents of ABCs preserve their birth nationality as a central part of their identity.

## ABC Political Organization

Within the ABC community, organized political activity remains low—even when compared to other minority groups in U.S. society. This is due, in part, to the fact that the vast majority of ABCs are the children of Chinese immigrants who arrived in the United States since the 1960s in search of economic opportunities not available in their countries of origin. The ABC descendents of this subgroup of Chinese immigrants typically come from families that focused on achieving economic stability and success rather than on becoming active members of the U.S. political system.

## Domestic Politics

Chinese American social and political organizations typically have formed in response to domestic issues that directly impact the community rather than in reaction to international relations. For instance, the Chinese Progressive Association has worked for the rights of new immigrants and bilingual education. In New York and San Francisco, the Chinatown Planning Association and Chinese for Affirmative Action combat poverty and provide social services for the local Chinese community. In response to outbreaks of violence against Asian Americans in the early 1980s, the Committee Against Anti-Asian Violence helped to strengthen the legal response of Asian American victims of racially motivated violence. In addition, the Washington, D.C.–based Organization of Chinese Americans has endeavored to improve the political representation of the community; it organized a response to recent campaign-financing scandals in order to help preserve the right of Chinese Americans to participate in the political process through political donations. The Chinese American Voters Association (CAVA) attempts to mobilize the community to participate in electoral politics.[14]

Organizations like the 80–20 Initiative seek to create a bloc vote for political candidates that support an Asian American agenda—that is, the opportunity to advance to the top of one's profession and to enjoy equal political representation. The group's primary concerns are with the perceived "glass ceiling" for Asian Americans in the workplace and with underrepresentation in influential political and corporate positions. They note that while Asian Americans constitute around 4 percent of the current population of the United States, only 7 of the 875 active federal judges are Asian Americans, and Asian Americans held only two of the 250-plus cabinet and subcabinet positions in President Bill Clinton's Administration in 1998. Although the 80–20 Initiative is targeted to Asian Americans, its founders are predominantly Chinese Americans—notably Michael Lin, former national president of the Organization of Chinese Americans; Henry Tang, chair of the Committee of 100; Chang-Lin Tien, former chancellor of the University of California–Berkeley; and S.B. Woo, former lieutenant governor of Delaware.[15] Visible participation by Chinese Americans in the 80–20 Initiative creates a precedent for more Chinese Americans, including ABCs, to become active in U.S. politics in the future.

*Foreign-policy Involvement*

Until most recently, only a few Chinese American political organizations catered specifically to the foreign-policy interests of ABCs, and individual involvement in this realm also has been limited. One of the more prominent organizations is the Committee of 100—a nonpartisan group that attempts "to bring an Asian American perspective to U.S. relations with the largest continent in the world and to address the concerns of Americans of Chinese/ Asian heritage."[16] Its founders established the organization shortly after the 1989 Tiananmen Incident on the basis of deliberate, long-term strategic thinking. The group summarizes its current role in the foreign-policy arena as "seeking common ground, while respecting difference."[17] The Committee includes a number of active and influential ABC participants, such as Alice Young (lawyer), Nancy Young (lawyer), Michael Woo (former Los Angeles city councilman), and Eric Liu (former foreign-policy speechwriter for President Bill Clinton).

Larger numbers of ABCs express foreign-policy opinions through public demonstrations and rallies. They have joined with Chinese immigrants in meetings and demonstrations over political situations in and/or affecting the latter's place of origin, including the 1999 Taiwan presidential elections, the 7 May 1999 bombing of the Chinese mission in Belgrade, and the 1989 Tiananmen Square Incident.

*Constraints on Development of an ABC*
*Foreign-policy Community*

Chief among the necessary attributes for participation in formulating policy is a level of expertise regarding key policy issues. Competition over which subgroup has a greater understanding of U.S.–China relations is intense as ABCs function within academic communities that are saturated with immigrant scholars from the Chinese world who often challenge their "understanding" of critical issues in U.S.–China relations. Moreover, the voice of the ABC community can be drowned out by the more passionate opinions of immigrant groups.[18]

While the number of organizations that have surfaced in the United States to coordinate ABC political action and representation is impressive, they continue to lack much weight and influence in policy-making realms. In spite of their participation in U.S. politics, they have not succeeded in generating a voice in China-related issues. What accounts for their lack of influence on U.S.–China relations? The following sections explore one possible explanation: that the absence of a cohesive ABC identity has diminished interest among ABCs in involvement in the bilateral relationship and, hence, limits prospects that an identifiable and active voice will surface.

## From Apathy to Individual Activism and Inquiry

ABCs typically assume one of three distinguishable roles in U.S.–China relations: (1) naïve and disinterested observer; (2) biased, yet interested, participant; and (3) informed and objective activist.[19] The three categories reflect the conflicted identities of the ABC community that lie at the core of these different approaches to U.S. foreign-policy formulation. The majority of the ABC community falls into the first two categories; only a small number of individuals have developed the necessary academic and professional knowledge base to approach issues in U.S.–China relations objectively.

From a psychological perspective, sociologists Stanley Sue and Nathaniel Wagner have delineated three possible attitudes that ABCs might hold toward traditional Chinese culture.[20] These distinctions are helpful for understanding the range of their responses to U.S.–China relations. The first type of ABCs, who typically have been fully assimilated into mainstream culture, manifest a "reactionary" attitude—indiscriminately rejecting Chinese culture. For this group, "China" is not a major part of their conscious adult life. Many ABCs of this type intermarry with non-Chinese and perceive little need for the Chinese community/world. The second type of ABCs find it difficult to examine U.S.–China issues dispassionately. These ABCs typically rely on family background and passed-on perspectives, and/or respond to events in a "reactionary" and defensive manner. The third type of ABCs possess a "traditional" orientation and are comfortable with Chinese language and culture. They are likely to have traveled to China or have studied there.

## Naïve and Disinterested Observers

The first category of ABC views the issues involved in U.S.–China relations as unimportant and nondistinct; they often are unable to identify critical issues. These individuals tend to have assimilated completely into U.S. society and identify more with mainstream culture than with the Chinese community. A key similarity among these individuals is their upbringing—typically in suburban or rural America. With few other ABCs or Chinese Americans in their surrounding communities, this group does not have the opportunity to create a distinct Chinese-based identity. Instead, they do not distinguish themselves from their non-Chinese or non-Asian peers. Although in many cases the parents of these individuals attempted to encourage the maintenance of Chinese language and culture, the lack of an exterior environment to stimulate interest and hone abilities on a daily basis inspired little curiosity with regard to complex U.S.–China relations.[21]

For most adult ABCs, the mainstream mass media has only shown extensive interest in China since the Tiananmen Incident in 1989. During most of the 1960–1980 period (i.e., the formative educational and awareness-raising years for the majority of adult ABCs today), the media and public devoted minuscule attention to U.S.–China relations. China was "Red," closed to the Western world, and U.S. foreign policy centered on Cold War concerns and on Europe rather than on the PRC or the broader Asian region. The dearth of positive exposure limited awareness among this group. Given greater media attention to China and increased public interest in Asia in recent years—not only in the foreign-policy arena, but also in film, media, medicine, sports, and literature—the "naïve and disinterested" group of ABCs is slowly decreasing. They have become more inclined to discuss and become involved in aspects of U.S.–China relations that are sanctioned by the mass media and popular culture.

## Biased, Yet Interested, Participants

The second group of ABCs reacts with curiosity when headline events such as China's entry into the World Trade Organization (WTO) or the bombing of the Chinese Embassy in Belgrade surface. Many of these individuals have been raised in areas that have a large Chinese American population, and they have been exposed to immigrants from China through various community organizations or formal schooling. Given the opportunity to participate in an environment possessing a distinct Chinese American identity, the individuals in this second category form more solidified opinions on topics such as Taiwan's presidential elections, or China's human-rights record.

Although they tend to be viewed as experts by default due to their cultural standing, members of this group have difficulty examining U.S.–China issues objectively. Frequently, as pressure to express a position emerges both from external and internal forces, these ABCs dismiss formal examination of the issues involved and fall back on familial and cultural assumptions for an "informed" opinion. At other times, the pressure to appear informed and to become involved in China-related affairs creates a "reactionary" and defensive response. A case in point is the issue of Taiwan's status. An ABC or ABT (American-born Taiwanese) raised in a household with firm pro-independence parents may never have the opportunity to hear a balanced discussion of the independence question. As a result of hearing only the perspective of one's parents, he or she comes to believe that the issue truly is one-sided. If that individual does not study the topic from an academic or a balanced standpoint, he/she also is likely to be defensive when discussing the issue. The same tendencies occur among ABCs raised in a family where parents are strongly disposed in favor of China–Taiwan reunification.

## Informed and Objective Activists

The third category of ABC is composed of informed and objective activists. These individuals possess the language and cultural skills as well as the requisite depth of study and interest needed to examine current issues in U.S.–China relations with objectivity. They rely on information gathered from primary sources and distinguish key concerns without allowing particular cultural or national affinities to interfere with reasoned analysis. Eric Liu, Iris Chang (author of two bestsellers, *Threads of the Silkworm* and *Rape of Nanking*), and Helen Zia (community activist and author of *Asian American Dreams*) provide a few outstanding examples of this group.

In general, the third group is well educated, Chinese-speaking, possesses formal and/or informal exposure to bilateral relations, and is able to leverage —without relying solely on—cross-cultural experiences.[22] The challenge for the group of informed and objective activists rests in presenting themselves, first, as foreign-policy experts; second, as Americans; and, third, as individuals who possess valuable Chinese cultural exposure. This subgroup is relatively small and faces steep hurdles to entering the U.S. policy-making arena at high levels.

## Changing Orientations and Involvement

The opening of the China Mainland in the late 1970s and the rise of the East Asia economic "miracle" spurred the emergence of overseas Chinese activism in economic and political relations. As an ABC scholar points out, the capitalist Chinese diaspora in the Pacific Rim has strongly influenced the region's domestic politics—creating and manipulating political arrangements to support its economic interests.[23] Their influence is apparent in the statements of local political leaders who praise the Confucian model of political and economic organization.[24] The attraction of Mainland economic opportunities, which, to date, primarily have been exploited by overseas Chinese, also has influenced the foreign policies of regional actors.

Why have ABCs not played a role similar to the Chinese diaspora in Asia when, as a group, they potentially would benefit from a constructive relationship with China? One barrier is the conflicted public perception of Chinese activism in U.S. politics. Negative media coverage of "Chinese fund-raising" for the Clinton campaign and the resulting congressional hearings on possible subversion of U.S. politics by China have discouraged ABCs from creating a more vocal and organized voice.[25]

Other micro and macro factors have limited the development of more active ABC contributions to U.S.–China relations. On the micro level, the ABC who has assimilated into mainstream culture often views herself/himself only as "American"—with little interest in China-related affairs. A focus on financial security, often learned from one's immigrant parents, preoccupies many talented ABCs with pursuit of high-income professions—such as those in the medical and private-finance sectors. The lack of role models in the U.S. public sector also has discouraged ABCs from pursuing careers in foreign policy.

On the macro level, the U.S. government's persistent suspicions of PRC intentions over the last half-century—from the McCarthy Era to the Wen Ho Lee prosecution—has deterred ABCs from joining the ranks of policymakers in U.S.–China relations. This is a problem that some other ethnic groups, including Irish, Jewish, and Cuban Americans, do not face. The tepid response of the ABC community on most critical Greater China foreign-policy issues underlines the limited prospects for organized involvement in the near future.

Given the macro and micro constraints that confront organizational involvement, the participation of ABCs in U.S.–China relations is likely to remain centered on key individuals from the third category who possess the knowledge, skills, and self-awareness needed to exploit their comparative advantage. Although their critical contributions provide a potential basis for extending this group's role into the realm of ABC political mobilization, concerted *mass* political action has been confounded by issues that typically hinder collective action—conflicted identities, divided political loyalties, and widespread apathy. Hence, if ABCs are to play an influential role in the U.S.

foreign-policy-making process, this development is likely to evolve less like the collective voice of Jewish Americans on Middle East issues and more like that of the individual (typically nonethnic Chinese) "China hands" who have helped shape policy based on intimate knowledge of the country's history and politics and expertise in Chinese language and/or culture.

Nevertheless, developments in three areas could generate increased organizational participation and allow the ABC community to play important roles in promoting overseas Chinese business networks and in advancing U.S.–China relations. First, a higher profile for ABCs in the U.S. foreign-policy establishment could encourage the development of larger and more powerful interest groups.

In addition, China's development and its integration into international political and economic regimes would continue to heighten the profile of U.S.–China relations. The issues will become more complex, multifaceted, and normalized rather than focused on the simplistic dichotomies that have characterized treatment of the relationship in the past. Increased complexity and relevance open the door for a more involved ABC community.

Finally, the expanded flow of information through technological developments in the context of a more open China would lead to greater contact and communication with the PRC across all U.S. communities. This could well inspire assimilated ABCs and their organizations to take greater interest in issues affecting U.S.–China relations—considering that foreign policy ultimately structures the nature of personal and economic relations at the local level.

## Notes

1. Peter Gourevitch, "The Second Image Reversed: The International Sources of Domestic Politics," *International Organization* 32, No. 4 (Autumn 1978): 881–911.

2. Robert Keohane and Joseph Nye, *Power and Interdependence: World Politics in Transition* (Boston: Little, Brown, 1977).

3. Gourevitch, "Second Image," p. 893.

4. Helen Milner, *Resisting Protectionism: Global Industries and the Politics of International Trade* (Princeton: Princeton University Press, 1988).

5. Mancur Olson, *The Logic of Collective Action: Public Goods and the Theory of Groups* (Cambridge: Harvard University Press, 1965).

6. Aihwa Ong and Donald Nonini, *Ungrounded Empires: The Cultural Politics of Modern Chinese Transnationalism* (New York: Routledge, 1997), p. 20.

7. Lee Kuan Yew, interview with Hong Kong television, cited in Ong and Nonini, *Ungrounded Empires*, p. 181.

8. See, for instance, Amitav Acharya, "ASEAN and Conditional Engagement," in *Weaving the Net: Conditional Engagement with China*, ed. by James Shinn (New York: Council on Foreign Relations, 1996), p. 221.

9. U.S. Census Bureau, Washington, D.C., 1970 and 1990 surveys.

10. A greater percentage of Asian Pacific Americans (APAs) also fall into higher income brackets compared to non-Hispanic whites. U.S. Census Bureau, 1990 survey.

11. U.S. Census Bureau, Washington D.C., 1990 survey.

12. Tu Wei-ming, *The Living Tree: The Changing Meaning of Being Chinese Today* (Stanford: Stanford University Press, 1994), pp. 18–25.

13. Simon H. Cheng and Wen H. Kuo, "Family Socialization of Ethnic Identity Among Chinese American Pre-adolescents," *Journal of Comparative Family Studies* 31, No. 4 (2000): 477.

14. *AsianWeek* 27, No. 46 (19–25 July 1996).

15. www.80–20.net website on 16 February 2001.

16. From the Committee of 100 website (www.committeeof100.org) as of 15 October 2000.

17. Committee of 100 website; see note 16.

18. Qian Ning, a faculty member of the University of Michigan and son of PRC's Vice Premier Qian Qichen, describes the activism and patriotism of Chinese students studying in America in Qian Ning, *Liuxu meiguo* (Studying in the USA), (Nanjing: Jiangsu wenyi, 1996).

19. The three categories and the following discussion are based on the author's conversations with a wide range of ABCs conducted from 1999 to 2001 in Flushing, New York; San Francisco, California; and Hong Kong.

20. Stanley Sue and Nathaniel N. Wagner, "Division and Unity: Social Process in a Chinese-American Community," from the website of *A Guide to Asian American Empowerment* (www.modelminority.com/identity/personality.htm).

21. Also see Cheng and Kuo, "Family Socialization," p. 478.

22. See, for instance, Eric Liu, *The Accidental Asian: Notes from a Native Speaker* (New York: Random House, 1998).

23. Ong and Nonini, *Ungrounded Empires*, pp. 19–20.

24. See Kishore Mahbubani's discussion of Asian values in the foreign-policy literature—including *Foreign Affairs*. Kishore Mahbubani, "The United States: 'Go East, Young Man,'" *Washington Quarterly* 17, No. 2 (Winter 1994): 5–23.

25. Phil Tajitsu Nash and Frank Wu, "Asian Americans Under Glass," *The Nation*, 31 March 1997.

# 6

# Communicating Through Conflict, Compromise, and Cooperation

## The Strategic Role of Chinese American Scholars in the U.S.–China Relationship

*James Jinguo Shen*

The U.S.–China relationship is one of the most important and complicated of the late twentieth and early twenty-first centuries. Media coverage of U.S.–China affairs tends to focus on U.S. politicians and the political stands they take in congressional debates and presidential campaigns, and research emphasizes public policies and the diplomatic performance of government actors. The important mediation role of Chinese American scholars in this volatile bilateral relationship is yet to be explored systematically.

This chapter examines the strategic role of Chinese American scholars in building and maintaining the U.S.–China relationship since the early 1970s. Based on literature review and historical research, the essay investigates how Chinese American scholars differ from U.S. politicians and businesspeople in their communication strategies, and how they act as a subgroup of the multicultural nation in dealing with Sino-American conflicts and cooperation.

Three aspects of this issue are explored here. First, the chapter addresses the characteristics and strengths of the subgroup, analyzing how their cross-cultural education and bilingual capability has helped Chinese American scholars gain entry to political negotiations between the two countries. It explores how, in the cultural domain of political interpretation, they serve as the missing link between the U.S. low-context culture and the Chinese high-context culture.[1] It also examines their unique understanding and interpretation of the meaning of democracy and modernization—through which they helped Chinese leaders and academicians foresee the full benefits of economic and political reforms and reinforced *kaifang* (open-door) policies and strategies.

Second, the chapter offers an explicit analysis of the multilevel communication roles of Chinese American scholars. It scrutinizes the individual roles of these "cultural envoys" as messenger, mediator, consultant, moderator, as well as opinion leader throughout the recurrent political clashes and collaborations. These sections explicate the significance of *guanxi* (connections), "insider," and "expert" in U.S.–China cross-cultural communication. Furthermore, I analyze the strategic influence of prominent scholars in promoting cultural exchange and in reducing misunderstanding between the two nations.

Finally, the chapter highlights how the growing presence and strategic position of Chinese American scholars constitutes a dynamic persuasive force between the two countries, and how their communication practices and intentionality can impact the policymaking process in the United States and the PRC. These scholars have established an alternative channel that bridges an important gap. They are likely to extend their influence over the U.S.–China relationship in the next century.

### The Gap that Chinese American Scholars Bridge

The disparate political and cultural conditions that exist in the two countries present a major challenge for the U.S.–China relationship. As former Secretary of State Henry Kissinger put it, "The scope of developing Sino-American exchanges was all the more remarkable because of the vast gulf in the history, culture, ideology, and economic development separating the two societies."[2] Many prominent U.S. politicians, such as Richard Nixon, helped increase ties with China after negotiating with Chinese leaders on numerous occasions. However, the PRC counterparts of these hardliners typically rejected both their political assumptions/viewpoints and their hardball approach.[3]

After the China Mainland opened its doors to the rest of the world in the late 1970s, U.S. entrepreneurs played a critical opinion-forming role in Sino-American affairs. However, their focus on the Chinese market and trade profit-taking diminishes their strategic role in the political relationship. While sizable investments in the largest overseas market facilitated China's drive for modernization and globalization, the impact of business entrepreneurs on political reform in the Mainland is not as noticeable.

Although largely unappreciated, Chinese American scholars have made a substantial narrowing impact on the vast cross-national gap over the past two decades through cultural and political exchanges. The role of Chinese American scholars cannot be overemphasized. They serve as a unique bridge by participating in bilateral "talks" without the paranoia or profit-centered burden of the politicians and entrepreneurs.

## The Critical Subgroup of Chinese American Scholars

Chinese American scholars have become a distinct and influential subgroup in the multicultural U.S. society.[4] In terms of time, age, and geographic origins, members of this subgroup can be separated into three major constituent parts. The first group came to the United States from the China Mainland in the 1930s and 1940s.[5] They stayed on and became U.S. scholars after receiving terminal degrees. Many of them are now respected professors at U.S. universities or professional experts in their chosen field.

The second set of Chinese American scholars consists of the former students from Taiwan and Hong Kong who arrived in the United States from the 1950s to the 1990s. They established a strong foothold in U.S. academia through outstanding research and teaching accomplishments.

Scholars from the Mainland who have arrived since the early 1980s constitute the third part of the subgroup. They are mostly masters and doctoral degree holders with little experience of the notorious Cultural Revolution. This third group is the youngest; it includes newly arrived scholars and professionals and recently tenured professors.

The entire subgroup of Chinese American scholars is likely to have received some U.S. higher education and to have experienced life in the United States. Unlike earlier local-dialect-speaking Chinese immigrants, most scholars are urbanities who typically spoke Mandarin—considered a marker of respectability.[6] By drawing on their unique cultural backgrounds and academic strengths, many of them reached the apex of their careers in the United States. The Nobel laureates C.N. Yang (Chen Ning Yang, Yang Zhenning), T.D. Lee (Tsung Dao Lee, Li Zhengdao), Samuel Chao Chung (Ding Zhaozhong), and Yuan Tze Lee (Li Yuanzhe) not only are prominent scientists in North America, but also well-known figures in the China Mainland, Taiwan, and Hong Kong.

Chinese American scholars constitute a sizable part of the membership of new Chinese American associations, such as the Committee of 100, which possess a broad vision of improving relations between the United States and the Greater China region.[7] While they strive to strengthen sociopolitical relations with the mainstream society on the home front, they aim to enhance mutual understanding between the United States and China and other Asian countries on the international front. Many retain a strong affinity with both Chinese and American cultures and desire to see an improved U.S.–China relationship. For instance, C.N. Yang, a 1957 Nobel laureate in physics and emeritus Albert Einstein professor at the State University of New York, Stony Brook, is said to have been "deeply hurt by the separation from his family in China, and the political separation between the United States and China, which are two sides of a tragedy."[8]

On visits back to the China Mainland, Chinese American scholars typically are received as Chinese compatriots (*huaqiao*) by the people and government, and are likely to become celebrities. Those who return home to Taiwan and Hong Kong also enjoy special attention due to their kinship networks, shared ethnic values, and sociopolitical preferences.[9]

Unlike politicians or businessmen, Chinese American scholars tend to be perceived as a marginal and loosely organized intellectual group. Their potential to promote cross-cultural communication and negotiation is virtually ignored by the mainstream media. Yet this group constantly is seeking out novel ways to promote U.S.–China relations and to contribute to political and intercultural understanding between the two countries. Since many current PRC officials possess backgrounds in science or engineering, they tend to pay attention to the interpretations of issues affecting U.S.–China relations expressed by prominent Chinese American scientists. Moreover, Premier Zhu Rongji, Vice Premier Wu Bangguo, and C.N. Yang all are alumni of Tsinghua University in Beijing. This facilitates political communication in the Chinese context by providing "ice-breaker" topics that set a friendly tone before sensitive issues are broached.

## An Intercultural-communication Link Between Low-context and High-context Cultures

Given the historical animosity and cultural/political gaps that exist between the PRC and the United States, it is difficult to establish successful communication channels on such sensitive issues as human rights and nuclear proliferation. At present, since there only are a handful of Chinese American politicians on the national scene—such as Washington State governor Gary Locke and Oregon congressman David Wu—they can hardly play a pivotal role in resolving possible U.S.–China conflicts. Without the political masks of Western diplomats, Chinese American scholars find it easier to mediate between U.S. and Chinese cultures and to communicate with Mainland Chinese on substantive issues.

### Gaining Entry and Trust

Historically, Chinese political systems and cultural traditions have prescribed respect for renowned scholars, elite scientists, and scholar politicians. "Good government" practices often are adopted and implemented based on the advice of experts. When the Chinese media cover a politician or visitor, they invariably highlight his/her scholarly titles first. This is the way the official Xinhua (New China) News Agency would report an informal meeting between Dr. C.N. Yang and a Chinese official, for instance. This communication ritual can be traced back to the way the Mainland media treated Dr. Kissinger during his meetings with the late Chinese leaders in the early 1970s.

Almost half a century ago, Yale researchers pointed out that credibility of any source is tied to "trust and confidence" attributes. Trust involves receivers analyzing a speaker's motives or hidden agenda. A person's motivation offers a key to his or her sincerity.[10] After accepting Deng Xiaoping's reform dictum to find the practical way to cross the river, the PRC leadership needs technical advice related to implementing the experimental socialist market economy. While they tend to question the political motives of Western politicians regarding their national reforms, PRC leaders are open to listening to Chinese American scholars—who share discursive proximity in the high-context culture. In light of this advantage, coupled with their knowledge of both cultures, Chinese American scholars are able to enter into dialogue with Chinese leaders.[11]

### Cultural Ambassadors

Seasoned U.S. diplomat Henry Kissinger maintains that, due to the particularly volatile nature of the U.S.–China relationship, the best way to coordinate policies, deter conflict, and reach compromises and cooperation between the two countries is through accurate understanding of each other's strategies.[12] Such understanding is often achieved with the assistance of a third party outside official channels. The bicultural and bilingual background of Chinese American scholars has afforded them the prestige and position to act as cultural bridges between the two nations.[13] Both domestically and internationally, they are recognized field experts and academic leaders. In the fluctuating political clashes and collaborations between the United States and the PRC, their minor and major multilevel communication roles in cultural and political negotiation include those of messenger, mediator, consultant, moderator, and opinion leader.

The influence of prominent Chinese American scholars in promoting cross-national understanding can be illustrated on one level by the linkages they possess (academic and semi-official positions in the United States and China), as well as by their lectures, books, and personal contacts with college students and local and central government officials in the PRC. For instance, C.N. Yang—international member of the Chinese Academy of Sciences, distinguished professor-at-large at the Chinese University of Hong Kong, and professor at Tsinghua University in Beijing—established an exchange link between the State University of New York at Stony Brook and Fudan University in Shanghai.[14] The Shanghai-born University of California–Berkeley professor T.D. Lee, who shared the Nobel Prize in Physics with Yang in 1957, has lectured frequently in China. Chang-Lin Tien (Tian Changlin), former chancellor of U.C. Berkeley and professor of mechanical engineering, also lectures in the PRC. In 1999, he was chairman of both the Asia Foundation and the Chief Executive's Commission on Innovation and Technology in Hong Kong. In 2000, the Clinton administration named him to the U.S. National Science Board and the U.S. National Commission on Mathematics and Science Teaching for the Twenty-first Century. Samuel Ting, 1976 Nobel Prize winner in physics and MIT professor, is also well received on both sides of the Taiwan Straits.

When China increased its opening to the world in the 1990s, many younger and less famous Chinese American scholars frequented China for various academic activities—including guest teaching and conference participation. For instance, members of the Association of Chinese Communication Studies, an affiliate of the National Communication Association, are actively engaged in Mainland discussions regarding the role of the media.[15] At both technical and political levels, such scholars have demonstrated their rewarding experiences in the United States to Chinese nationals, who are looking for expanded human networks and career prospects in the age of globalization. To their audience of liberal-minded reform officials and the next generation of Chinese policymakers, Chinese American scholars disseminate a variety of ways of understanding and interpreting the meaning of democracy and modernization. In so doing, they help Chinese leaders and academicians foresee the full benefits of economic and political reform and encourage them to reinforce open-door policies and strategies.

Moreover, shared life experiences help the visiting scholars find the exact subject to start dialogues with Chinese counterparts. In the Chinese high-context culture, implicit agreement in the codified communication environment is conducive to in-depth conversations.

### Guanxi

Chinese American scholars are experts at using their ethnic background and intercultural affinity to forge strategic personal relationships (*guanxi*) with Chinese leaders. As bicultural "insiders," they maximize their communicative power by applying "situational dialects" in specific contexts.[16] If *guanxi* is solidified by rounds of friendly interpersonal communication, even the most sensitive topics find their way into political communication.

One of the intractable issues in U.S.–China relations involves Taiwan. The PRC will never give up its plan for the reunification of China, while the United States opposes any military solution by the Chinese side. Over the past decade, support for the pro-independence movement in Taiwan has surged. Given these circumstances, Yuan Tze Lee's visits to China have become even more important.

Before Lee, a Taiwan-born professor of chemistry at U.C. Berkeley and a 1986 Nobel Prize winner, assumed his current position as president of Taiwan's Academia Sinica, he traveled back and forth between the China Mainland and Taiwan as a Chinese American scholar and special envoy across the Straits. With his distinctive cross-cultural background and personality, he impressed many top Chinese government officials, who considered him to possess "the heart and soul of China."[17] In 2000, Lee reflected on a 1987 visit to China:

> Deng Xiaoping asked me at dinner why the DPP (Democratic Progressive Party) wants to be independent. I told him the Taiwan history and explained why. Having heard my explanations, Deng said, "Professor Lee, I think the Taiwan problem will have to be left for the next generation to solve. Let's eat."[18]

In this case, *guanxi* paved the way for straightforward conversation. The polarized political point of view of a Taiwan/American scholar and a Chinese politician dissolved into a temporary compromise.

Under certain situations when Chinese American scholars engage in consensual discourse with Chinese counterparts, *guanxi* is more important than language itself in establishing dialogic relationships. Many ABCs (American-born Chinese) or second-generation scholars also have demonstrated an ability to advance U.S.–China relations even though they may not speak Mandarin well. For instance, Iris Chang, a second-generation Chinese American author, secured full cooperation from local government officials and historians when she conducted interviews for her widely acclaimed book *The Rape of Nanking*.[19]

## Intermediation

In the face of bilateral conflicts on sensitive issues, such as human rights and media censorship, Chinese American scholars normally avoid confronting their "obstinate audience"—who are inclined to resist the dominant Western discourse. Instead, from their personal and, frequently, technical perspective, they interpret the meaning of U.S. policies and responses as members of the Chinese American community. They use their own mode of reading to explain the denotative and connotative meanings of the crucial issues involved, thus creating a new episteme for their dialogic partners to re-examine the Chinese Self and the Western Other. For instance, one of the organizational goals of the Committee of 100 with respect to U.S.–China relations is to "seek common ground while respecting differences." When a delegation from C-100 met with Jiang Zemin and Li Ruihuan in 1994, they presented research findings from the Wirthlin survey of U.S. attitudes toward China that they had commissioned in the context of recommended ways in which the PRC could improve its international image as well as relations with the foreign press.[20]

Intermediation by Chinese American scholars exerts considerable impact on the U.S.–China relationship. In order to promote mutual understanding and deter potential conflicts, they have participated in conferences on bilateral relations held in the United States and China. Such conferences, including the closed symposiums sponsored by the Foreign Relations Association and the U.S.–China Policy Foundation's annual roundtable discussion, provide valuable negotiation forums for leading scholars from the United States, China, Taiwan, and Hong Kong.[21] The mediated communication that occurs at these meetings facilitates understanding of the participants' political stands and enhances prospects for international cooperation. While it is difficult to identify specific immediate results, the policy decisions of the current PRC leaders generally are influenced by the expert opinions of their think-tank representatives who interact with Chinese American scholars at such meetings.

*Persuasive Intentionality*

The growing presence of Chinese American scholars at strategic points in the political relationship constitutes a persuasive force. When Chinese American scholars meet Chinese officials, they easily move beyond obligatory statements of Sino-American goodwill, and each side can enunciate its immediate concerns on bilateral issues. As they attempt to reconcile the sharp differences that exist between the two ideological rivals, their persuasive influence trickles up to top PRC policymakers.

Moreover, while engaging Chinese leaders at different levels in constructive dialogues, Chinese American scholars instill U.S. values of efficiency, practicality, and pragmatism through the persuasive process.[22] For instance, forensic scientist Henry Lee (Li Changyu), professor at the University of New Haven and former Commissioner of Public Safety in Connecticut, has trained police officers in both the Mainland and Taiwan. A celebrated speaker across the Taiwan Straits, he has offered lectures at the prestigious Beijing University and holds an honorary title in Chongqing, a major city in central China. Lee's expertise and pragmatism has changed the vision of officials at local levels in ways that facilitated unprecedented cooperation in forensic science and criminology between the United States and China.[23]

In China, many people reject radical changes in existing systems and approaches out of deference to the historical accomplishments in the country's past. They yearn for a "return to the mythical time of their 'Great Time.' "[24] In contrast, Chinese Americans are prone to provide reflections and recommendations regarding concrete and pragmatic solutions to contemporary Chinese problems.

## Wen Ho Lee Syndrome

The mediating role of Chinese American scholars can be seriously constrained by the volatile context of U.S.–China relations. After being fired from the Los Alamos National Research Lab, the Taiwanese-American scientist Wen Ho Lee was indicted in December 1999 on fifty-nine counts of mishandling nuclear secrets and held in solitary confinement, at times shackled, for nine months. Lee's detention drew increasing criticism from Asian American scholars and Chinese American organizations, such as the Committee of 100 and the 80/20 Committee. Even though the courts eventually released Lee and dismissed most of the charges against him, many Chinese Americans believe that Wen Ho Lee was a victim of racial profiling. In spite of the apology the presiding federal judge made for Lee's unfair detention, the repercussions caused by the incident run far and deep among Chinese American scholars. Henry Tang, chairman of the Committee of 100, predicted that it will take years to repair the damage caused by the Wen Ho Lee fiasco.[25] In the short run, at least, the strong feelings of unfair treatment that the Lee case evoked among Chinese American scholars has undermined the commitment of many to act as neutral mediators and facilitators in the U.S.–China relationship.

Lee's treatment also suggests that when Chinese American scholars are caught up in a major domestic political controversy involving U.S.–China conflicts, they are "a bit of each but not a lot of either."[26] In spite of the ever-increasing communication and movement between Asia and the United States, the "model minority" still can be projected as alien and foreign, and their persuasive power drastically reduced. Thus, at the same time that their transnational perspective is a source of communicative strength and, thereby, provides them with an advantage in cross-cultural negotiations, independence from the U.S. government's position means that Chinese American scholars are vulnerable to charges that they constitute national-security risks—particularly at times of rising conflict or competition between the two countries.

## Conclusion

Chinese American scholars play important strategic roles in many aspects of the bilateral U.S.–China dialogue. Although not heralded as it deserves, this subgroup has established an effective mediation channel that effectively bridges the enormous gap between the two countries. The subgroup is likely to continue to grow in the future. Promoting and facilitating the constructive roles of Chinese American scholars is in the interest of both China and the United States. Among other benefits, by reinterpreting controversial policies and finding a common ground for new approaches, their "shuttle diplomacy" offers one viable means to avoid the civilizational conflict envisioned by Samuel Huntington.[27]

As an underreported but growing group, Chinese American scholars cannot replace the role of politicians in bilateral diplomacy, and their communicative potential is not yet fully reflected in the international policymaking process. However, as more young professionals join the persuasive force in cross-cultural communication, Chinese American scholars can be expected to extend their influence over the U.S.–China relationship in the next century.

## Notes

1. A high-context communication or message is one in which most of the information is either in the physical context or internalized in the person, while little is in the coded, explicit, transmitted part of the message. China's complex culture is on the high-context end of the scale. For details, see Edward Hall, *Beyond Culture* (New York: Anchor, 1976), pp. 90–91.

2. Henry Kissinger, *Years of Renewal* (New York: Simon & Schuster, 1999), p. 138.

3. Chris Matthews, *Hardball: How Politics Is Played—Told by One Who Knows the Game* (New York: Simon & Schuster, 1999), p. 13.

4. This chapter's discussion is restricted to immigrant scholars and students from the Chinese world.

5. A typical example is the world-famous architect I.M. Pei. Pei was born in Shanghai and came to the United States in 1935. After graduating from the Massachusetts Institute of Technology in 1940, he received a master's degree from Harvard University in 1946.

6. Benson Tong, *The Chinese Americans* (Westport: Greenwood, 2000), p. 82.

7. The Committee of 100 is a national nonpartisan organization composed of U.S. citizens of Chinese descent. Members have achieved positions of leadership in the United States in a broad range of professions. They collectively pool their strengths and experience to address important issues concerning the Chinese American community. See the chapter by Norton Wheeler in this volume.

8. Freeman Dyson, "C.N. Yang: A Conservative Revolutionary," *Twenty-First Century* 54 (August 1999): 93.

9. Tong, *Chinese Americans*, pp. xi, 83.

10. Charles Larson, *Persuasion: Reception and Responsibility*, 9th ed. (Belmont, CA: Wadsworth, 2001), p. 207.

11. See, for instance, the talks that scholars belonging to the Committee of 100 have held with Vice Premier Li Ruihuan in China and their luncheon and "fireside chat" with President Jiang Zemin during his U.S. visit in October 1997. Committee of

100, "Issues & Activities," 10 December 1999, at http://www.committee100.org/issues/default.html (16 December 1999).

12. Kissinger, *Years of Renewal*, p. 874.

13. Gloria Heyung Chun, *Of Orphans and Warriors: Inventing Chinese American Culture and Identity* (New Brunswick, NJ: Rutgers University Press, 2000), p. 41.

14. C.N. Yang, "Vitae," 15 December 2000, at http://www.physics.sunysb/~yang/Vitae.html (17 January 2001).

15. In the late 1990s, Ringo Ma of the State University of New York, Fredonia, offered guest lectures on Western media theories and practices in the context of China's reforms at universities in Wuhan and Qiangdao. Personal communication with the author, 6 November 1999. The author lectured on the U.S. media and educational system to interested and responsive audiences at Tsinghua University and Luwan District College (Shanghai) in 1998.

16. Hall, *Beyond Culture*, p. 132.

17. Qingfeng Tong, "The Political Addition to the Nobel Laureate," *The International Chinese Newsweekly*, 6 March 1999, p. 19.

18. This quote appears in *Open Magazine*, March 2000, p. 5.

19. Chinese News Digest, "Interview with Iris Chang," 3 February 1998, htttp://www.cnd.org/CND-Global.98.1st/CND-Global.98–02–23.html (1 December 2000).

20. Committee of 100, "Issues and Activities."

21. USCPF, "Annual USCPF Roundtable Discussion Proves Fruitful," *U.S.–China Policy Foundation Newsletter* (Spring 2000) at http://www.uscpf.org/newsletter/2000/Spring/v4-1roundtable.html (21 December 2000).

22. Larson, *Persuasion*, p. 211.

23. Myrna Watanabe, "Forensic Scientist Henry Chang-Yu Lee," *The Scientist* 14, No. 7 (2000):10.

24. Larson, *Persuasion*, p. 198.

25. Lucinda Fleeson, "Rush to Judgment," *American Journalism Review: AJR News Link*, 5–11 December 2000, http://ajr.newslink.org/ajrfleenov00.html (6 December 2000).

26. Eric Liu, *The Accidental Asian: Notes of a Native Speaker* (New York: Random House, 1998), pp. 134–135, 138.

27. Huntington maintains that the West will find itself more and more at odds with non-Western civilizations, including China. For details, see Samuel Huntington, *The Clash of Civilization and the Remaking of World Order* (New York: Simon & Schuster, 1997).

# 7

# From the China Lobby to the Taiwan Lobby

## Movers and Shakers of the U.S.–China–Taiwan Triangular Relationship

### Tsung Chi

Throughout the second half of the twentieth century, Taiwan's people and government, with help from their U.S. supporters, have attempted to influence the China policy of the United States in order to promote Taiwan's interests. This chapter highlights the influential positions regarding U.S.–China relations advocated by immigrants from Taiwan and contrasts them with other Chinese American views.

Although loosely organized, the China Lobby proved effective in opposing the People's Republic of China's entry to the United Nations and in preventing diplomatic recognition of the PRC by the United States in the 1950s and 1960s. Even after President Richard Nixon's trip to China in 1972, remnants of the China Lobby remained influential throughout the 1970s. In subsequent years, however, the China Lobby aged and its influence drastically weakened. In the meantime, as the community of the Taiwanese Americans grew, more Taiwanese organizations, many of which had a clear political agenda, formed in the congenial environment of the United States. As a result, the 1980s witnessed the rise of an organized Taiwan Lobby. Instead of striving to damage the PRC's image, the Taiwan Lobby and officials from Taiwan positively portrayed Taiwan as an economic miracle and an emerging democracy as a strategy aimed at countering the growing influence of pro-Mainland groups in the United States.

This chapter explores the distinctive lobbying practices of the China Lobby and the Taiwan Lobby and analyzes their outcomes in terms of the triangular relationship. It first raises and addresses descriptive questions regarding various lobbying activities by the two groups—including their memberships, organizations, incentives, strategies, and goals. Then, it explores similarities and differences between the two groups. Following this important background discussion, several crucial historical cases in the U.S.–China–Taiwan relationship—including China's entry to the United Nations, recognition of the PRC by the United States, Taiwan's participation in international organizations, and passage of the Taiwan Security Enhancement Act in the U.S. House of Representatives in February 2000—are examined in an effort to evaluate how the lobbying activities of the two groups have affected the push-pull nature of the U.S.–China–Taiwan triangular relationship.

### China Lobby: The Committee of One Million

Although it exerted substantial influence on the China policy of the United States, the term "China Lobby" did not appear until the end of the 1940s. The "Program for Action on China Policy," issued by the Communist Party of New York State on 1 March 1949, first used the term in print.[1] Subsequently, "China Lobby" referred to a broad coalition, both foreign and domestic, that included Chinese agents of the Nationalist government (Kuomintang, KMT) in Taiwan, Chinese Americans, paid U.S. lobbyists, U.S. politicians, scholars, businesspersons with financial stakes, missionaries expelled from the newly founded People's Republic of China, and military leaders frustrated by the "loss of China" after World War II who strived to keep alive Taiwan's Nationalist government and to demolish Chinese communism.[2] Basically, these activists can be divided into two categories: Chinese and Americans who were materially motivated, and those who were politically or ideologically motivated.[3]

While loosely organized, the China Lobby established a formal organization in 1953 known as the Committee for One Million Against the Admission of Communist China to the United Nations. The Committee and its successor, the Committee of One Million, constituted the core of the China Lobby from the 1950s to the 1970s.[4] Throughout those years, China Lobby activists principally were concerned with representation in the United Nations, opposing recognition of and trade with the PRC, and securing U.S. economic and military aid for Taiwan. Most essentially, the Committee endeavored to keep the survival of Taiwan's Nationalist government in the minds of the U.S. public.[5] Since Taiwan's international status greatly depended on the United States, the Nationalist government funded many of the Committee's activities indirectly—through donations (including funds for social and travel amenities) to its secretary, Marvin Liebman.[6]

The Committee carefully formulated strategies to pursue its goals. Utilizing the anti-Communist mentality of the Cold War era, it portrayed Taiwan's Nationalist regime as a bulwark against Asian communism and equated support for this regime to loyalty to the United States. The fear that prevailed among the U.S. public at the time concerning the threat of communist takeovers made the task of the Committee, and the China Lobby in general, easier.

Members of the Committee pursued their goals through newspaper columns, radio broadcasts, petition drives, newsletters, letter-writing campaigns, campaign contributions, and congressional hearings. They aimed to influence public opinion, members of Congress, scholars, and officials in the U.S. government, especially those in the Department of State and Department of Defense.[7] The success of the Committee's activities is exemplified by the case of China's representation in the United Nations. Year after year, it succeeded in securing congressional resolutions opposing the PRC's membership. To assist in this effort, the Committee, as suggested by its name, successfully collected one million signatures on petitions supporting its cause.[8] In addition, it succeeded in ensuring the continuation of aid to the Nationalist government by holding hostage Marshall Plan funds and the Military Assistance Program.[9] The fact that a handful of Committee of One Million members also were congressional leaders, part of the so-called "China bloc" in Congress, and acted as an insider-type lobby from their own congressional offices, greatly facilitated its efforts.[10]

In sum, the success of the Committee of One Million is attributable to three factors: (1) the anti-Communist sentiment that prevailed in the United States during the Cold War period; (2) encouragement, advice, and financial support from Taiwan's Nationalist government; and (3) lobbying by insiders. By 1968, however, majorities sympathetic to the China Lobby's mission had vanished in both houses of the U.S. Congress.[11] Its influence was further weakened after China's admission to the United Nations in 1971 and President Nixon's historic visit to Beijing in 1972. Although remnants persisted throughout the 1970s, the China Lobby lost its last battle in 1979 when the United States recognized the PRC as the only legitimate government of China.

## The Taiwan Lobby

While the influence of the China Lobby faded away in the 1970s, the 1980s witnessed the rise of a better-organized Taiwan Lobby. With rapid growth in the population of immigrants from Taiwan—including many professionals, intellectuals, and scholars—Taiwanese Americans have created new organizations. Many of these organizations possess political agendas that focus on Taiwan's internal politics, security, and international status rather than on U.S. politics. Aimed at terminating the half-century control of the KMT in

Taiwan and promoting Taiwan's de facto status as an island nation independent from the China Mainland, these Taiwanese political organizations, which together comprise the Taiwan Lobby, have labored to influence Congress and the White House at the national level, and state and local governments at grass-roots levels.

While the Committee of One Million conducted most of the lobbying activities of the China Lobby, the core of the newly formed Taiwan Lobby is the highly organized Formosan Association for Public Affairs (FAPA). Other organizations that are influential, but less active than FAPA, include the Taiwanese Chamber of Commerce of North America (TCCNA), the Center for Taiwanese International Relations (CTIR), World United Formosans for Independence (WUFI), the Democratic Progressive Party's Mission in the United States, and the Taipei Economic and Cultural Representative Office (TECRO).

## TCCNA

In 1988, Guei-Ron Wang and a few other business leaders from the Taiwanese American community established the Taiwanese Chamber of Commerce of North America (TCCNA) as a nonprofit organization. Wang, TCCNA's first president,[12] has long supported the movement in opposition to KMT rule. By 2000, thirty-two local chambers of commerce located in major metropolitan areas throughout North America belonged to the TCCNA and the organization boasted more than 3,500 individual members—primarily immigrants from Taiwan. Its president in 2000, Chang Chiu-hsiung, was a commissioner in the Taiwan government's ministry-level Overseas Chinese Affairs Commission.[13] Even though the TCCNA's primary mission is to promote business interests through collaboration and networking among its members, similar to the American Chamber of Commerce in Taipei, it also works to increase ties between Taiwan and the United States. Since many members of its local chapters have maintained good relations with local politicians over years, this general goal frequently is approached in a less visible way at state and local levels.

## CTIR

The Center for Taiwan International Relations (CTIR), formed in Washington, D.C., in 1988, is a research-oriented lobbying organization. It has asserted that the sovereignty of Taiwan (including the Pescadores) belongs to no one else but the people of Taiwan. To advance this mission, CTIR conducts research and policy analyses, develops contacts with government cials, provides speakers, seminar leaders, and expert congressional testimony, and disseminates information about Taiwan to members of Congress, the media, and the U.S. public.[14] It also has a branch office in the Empire State Building in New York to deal with issues related to the United Nations—especially Taiwan's entry.[15] Members of the CTIR, including its director in 2001, Tsai Wuhsiung, have been strong supporters of Taiwan's pro-independence Democratic Progressive Party.[16]

## WUFI

World United Formosans for Independence (WUFI) is one of the oldest Taiwanese political organizations in the United States. Chang Tzenhung (who later became mayor of Tainan in southern Taiwan), along with a small group of pro-independence activists who were active in other Taiwanese American associations, formed WUFI-USA in Los Angeles. In 1970, a number of Taiwan independence movement organizations in Japan, Europe, Canada, and the United States joined forces under the WUFI umbrella. In 2000, Hsu Simou, a medical doctor, headed the organization and it was headquartered in Dallas, Texas, with branches elsewhere in the United States and in Taiwan, Japan, Europe, Canada, and South America.

As its name suggests, the main purpose of WUFI is to promote Taiwan as an independent country free from China. To further this goal, it organizes talks and meetings and publishes the *Taiwan Tribune*.[17] Published twice a week, the *Tribune* was popular and influential in Taiwanese American circles and on university campuses in the 1970s and the 1980s before Taiwan embarked on the process of democratization. During those years of political repression, the *Tribune* carried pro-independence articles that were too sensitive to be published inside Taiwan. As Taiwan became more open and democratic, this newspaper's importance diminished; its circulation has shrunk to between 2,000 and 3,000.[18]

## DPP Mission in the United States

The pro-independence Democratic Progressive Party (DDP) provided the main opposition in Taiwan from the time of its founding in 1986 until the May 2000 elections when its presidential candidate, Chen Shuibian, won and it thus became Taiwan's ruling party. The DPP established its Washington, D.C., Mission in 1995 for the primary purpose of explaining its positions—especially concerning Taiwan's international status—to U.S. policymakers and the international community.[19] It attempted to further this goal by bringing key DPP figures on visits to the United States. While here, they lobbied members of Congress, visited think-tanks, met with scholars and the media, and interacted with the expanding Taiwanese American communities.

At the time of the organization's abolition in November 2000, Yichung Lai, a physicist who received his Ph.D. from Cornell University, headed the DPP Mission. Given the DPP's status as the ruling party in Taiwan, members decided to disband the Mission since their positions could be officially expressed and pursued through Taiwan's diplomatic corps in Washington, D.C.

## TECRO

The Taipei Economic and Cultural Representative Office (TECRO), Taiwan's de facto embassy in Washington, D.C., has been ambivalent about the lobbying activities of the other Taiwanese groups. While they promoted the interests of Taiwan as a whole, these groups also advocated an independent Taiwan and opposed the rule of the Nationalist government.

TECRO and its branch offices throughout the United States have maintained good relations with many members of Congress and have established strong ties with state and local governments. Although the Office also has engaged in a variety of lobbying activities, it generally has kept a low profile and proceeded in a cautious and indirect manner in order not to irritate the U.S. government or, in some cases, the PRC government. TECRO's indirect methods have been influential in the past. In the most notable case, the Nationalist government paid the Washington, D.C., firm of Cassidy & Associates (C&A) $1.5 million for a successful effort to lobby the U.S. government to grant President Lee Teng-hui a visa to make an unprecedented visit to the United States.[20]

The DPP government that assumed power in May 2000 continued to hire C&A to work with the press and Congress. Under the name Taiwan Study Institute, its financial backers signed a $2 million per year contract with the lobbying firm in July 2000. While TECRO aims to avoid offending the U.S. State Department, it relies on C&A to play the role of the heavy.[21]

## FAPA

The backbone of the Taiwan Lobby is the Formosan Association for Public Affairs (FAPA). The most active Taiwanese lobbying group, FAPA is a nationwide organization that wields enormous influence. Founded in Los Angeles in 1982 by Trong R. Chai, a political science professor who later became a DPP member of Congress in Taiwan, FAPA is modeled after the American Israel Public Affairs Committee (AIPAC).[22] Its headquarters is located in the nation's capital and it had forty local chapters scattered throughout the United States in 1999.[23] In that year, FAPA headquarters received about $520,000 from donations and membership dues, and it employed five full-time workers.[24] One of its goals for 2000 was to increase membership to 2,000 families.[25] With an estimated population of half a million Taiwanese Americans,[26] FAPA possesses the potential to raise sizable amounts of funding and to increase its membership substantially. In FAPA's 1999 Headquarters Work Report, its president, Wen-yen Chen, expressed his intention eventually to assist the Taiwanese American community by establishing a Taiwanese American Political Action Committee (PAC).[27]

This well-organized lobbying network has two main goals: (1) "promotion of international support for the right of the people of Taiwan to establish an independent and democratic country, and to join the international community"; and (2) "promotion of peace and security of Taiwan."[28] To further these goals, it provides policymakers, the media, scholars, and the U.S. public with information on Taiwan-related issues. More importantly, it works diligently at national, state, and grass-roots levels to inform and update members of Congress and their staffers on issues concerning Taiwan.

Throughout the 1980s and 1990s, FAPA not only monitored all legislation related to Taiwan. It actively pushed for the passage of legislation favorable to Taiwan, including:

- *H.Con.Res.148*, passed 369–14 on 19 March 1996, deploring China's missile tests and military exercises; also passed 97–0 in the Senate two days later;
- *H.Con.Res.212*, passed by a voice vote on 24 September 1996, supporting Taiwan's effort to join the United Nations;
- *H.R.2386*, passed 301–116 on 6 November 1997, directing the Secretary of Defense to study the establishment of a Theatre Missile Defense (TMD) system that would incorporate Taiwan; and
- *H.Con.Res.334*, passed by unanimous consent on 7 October 1998, supporting Taiwan's participation in the World Health Organization (WHO).[29]

Due in part to FAPA's lobbying efforts, Congress approved all of these resolutions in the face of strong opposition from the executive branch and harsh criticism by the PRC government. The case of *H.Con.Res.212* illustrates FAPA's congressional influence. On 19 September 1996, five days prior to passage of the resolution, Representatives Tom Lantos (D-CA), Christopher Cox (R-CA), Nancy Pelosi (D-CA), Peter Deutsch (D-FL), and Steven Chabot (R-OH) expressed support for the measure at a FAPA-sponsored luncheon.[30]

In 1999, FAPA's legislative priorities were the Taiwan Security Enhancement Act (TSEA), participation in the World Health Organization (WHO) and other international organizations, and reevaluation of the Clinton administration's "One-China Policy." FAPA made progress with its two top priorities (TSEA and WHO). Close examination of FAPA's lobbying efforts to push for passage of legislation related to WHO and TSEA reveals the extent of the organization's influence. In general, FAPA members and staff pursue their goals simultaneously at both national and grass-roots levels. At the grassroots, local FAPA chapters around the United States receive information about targeted legislation from the Washington, D.C., headquarters. Then, they ask their members of Congress to support the legislation. Petition letters drafted by FAPA headquarters are distributed, collected, and mailed back to Washington, D.C. These letters are delivered personally to congresspeople by FAPA staff.[31] Local members also are encouraged to turn materials supplied by headquarters into op-ed pieces, letters to the editor, or longer articles for publication in local newspapers. For instance, FAPA board member Song Y. Lee used the "Democracy Is No Joke, Premier Zhu" article that originally appeared in FAPA's June 2000 *Newsletter* as background for the op-ed piece titled "Election Was for Real, and Democracy Is No Joke" he submitted to the *South Florida Sun-Sentinel*.[32]

At the national level, regular communication with members of Congress and the executive branch is conducted through faxed and e-mailed press releases, reports, and commentary on specific legislation. Special meetings are organized with selected politicians to press for concrete legislative actions. Press conferences are also held.[33] FAPA staff also send letters and op-ed pieces to the editors of major newspapers and magazines—such as the *New York Times*, *Washington Post*, *Los Angeles Times*, and *Foreign Affairs*. For instance, on 29 January 1998 the *New York Times* published a letter from FAPA's headquarters urging the newly elected director general of the World Health Organization to "do what lies in her capability to see to it that Taiwan be admitted to the WHO."[34] In another case, the president of FAPA's Washington, D.C., chapter F. Chung Fan wrote an op-ed piece titled "What Taiwan Problem?" that the *Washington Post* ran on 7 November 1997. In this piece, Fan maintained that "it should be clear that there is no 'Taiwan problem.' China is the problem. . . . Taiwan is . . . a de facto independent democracy eager to join the international community as a full member."[35]

Specifically, in the case of WHO legislation, the lobbying effort began in Cleveland, Ohio. Since Taiwan is not a WHO member out of deference to the PRC's insistence on a one-China policy, the president of FAPA's Cleveland chapter approached his good friend Representative Sherrod Brown with a request to do something to change the prevailing situation. In February

1999, Brown introduced a House resolution in support of Taiwan's participation in WHO. In the meantime, FAPA headquarters encouraged its members all over the United States to contact their own representatives and ask
them to co-sponsor Brown's resolution. Headquarters staff also kept in close
contact with members of Congress who were on the Foreign Relations Committee and continuously updated them on new developments. For instance, a
virus broke out in Taiwan that summer, killing over fifty children. Since it
might have been prevented if Taiwan had had access to the WHO, FAPA
Executive Director Coen Blaauw wrote an article about it that promoted
Taiwan's WHO membership. Brown put this article on his letterhead and
forwarded it to the *Washington Post*. After it was printed in the *Post*, FAPA
sent a copy to all congressional staff with a cover note detailing the importance of Taiwan's entry to the WHO. The House passed Brown's resolution
(H.R.1794) that summer and the Senate later followed suit.[36]

FAPA worked even more aggressively on the TSEA. In July 2000, *Los
Angeles Times* commentator Jim Mann concluded that when the Taiwan Security Enhancement Act passed the House, "the most active organization
was not Cassidy but a non-profit grass-roots group called the Formosan Association for Public Affairs."[37]

Drafted by the House Majority Whip Tom DeLay, TSEA would allow
senior U.S. military officials to coordinate with Taiwanese military officers,
establish secure communication links between the two nations' militaries,
and require the administration to report on both Taiwan's security needs and
the U.S. ability to respond to an attack against Taiwan. Compared to the
lobbying efforts in the case of the WHO, FAPA's TSEA campaign was more
organized and much larger in size. It mobilized not only its own members,
who sent over 2,000 letters to their congressmen and congresswomen in support of the bill,[38] but members of other Taiwanese American organizations
throughout the United States.

The TSEA Grassroots Educational Workshops constituted another element
added to FAPA's lobbying efforts. FAPA held the first workshop in Maryland
from 11 to 14 June 1999. Several members of Congress were present. Each
workshop attendee received a package of documents dealing with pending
legislation on Taiwan's security along with instructions regarding how to contact the offices of their own congressional delegation and sample letters to be
sent to them.[39] In addition, FAPA headquarters had produced detailed guidelines on "how to visit," "how to write a letter to," and "how to phone" congressional offices.[40] A total of seventy FAPA activists attended the three-day
workshop and lobbied their members of Congress directly on Capitol Hill.[41] A
member of FAPA's North Carolina chapter reported that participants visited
staffers of one senator and five representatives from that state in one day.

The workshop, along with other lobbying efforts,[42] proved quite success-ful. On 26 October 1999, the House International Relations Committee passed TSEA by a vote of 32–6 and sent it to the House floor. On 1 February 2000, the bill was approved by a bipartisan vote of 341 (140 Democrats, 200 Re-publicans, and 1 independent) to 70. A *New York Times* reporter described the Taiwan Lobby that pushed to pass the bill as "formidable."[43]

After the House passed TSEA, FAPA immediately concentrated on the Senate. FAPA headquarters hosted another Grassroots Campaign Workshop during the week of 10 June 2000. About thirty representatives of the Taiwan-ese Association of America (TAA)—a nationwide organization with sixty-six local branches under six regional councils in 1996[44] that used to focus more on Taiwan's internal politics—along with twenty FAPA members joined together to participate in intensive lobbying training. On 12 June, the group split into teams by state of residency to lobby their respective senators. They visited a total of nine offices.[45]

In the summer of 2000, FAPA organized a lobby-oriented sister organiza-tion, the Formosan Association for Public Relations (FAPR). As a nonprofit, tax-deductible organization, FAPA is restricted to a maximum 20 percent of a given year's expenses for lobbying purposes. FAPR, which shares offices and personnel with FAPA, focuses entirely on lobbying issues. As an I.R.S.-designated 501(c)(4) organization, FAPR can conduct unlimited lobbying without jeopardizing its tax-exempt status as long as the legislation that it attempts to influence pertains to the purpose for which it was formed.[46]

Given its strong ties to the Democratic Progressive Party (DPP) and the potential lobbying power of its newly formed sister organization FAPR, FAPA is likely to be even more active and effective in its future lobbying activities on Capitol Hill. The changed national political situation following the 2000 elections also has enhanced both organizations' short-term prospects for suc-cess as they now can expect support from the administration of George W. Bush for TSEA and other issues of concern to Taiwan.

## Comparative Analysis

While the China Lobby was most active in the 1950s, the Taiwan Lobby came to maturity in the 1990s. Moreover, important differences between the two groups in many aspects of their lobbying activities have affected the ways they have influenced the China policy of the United States.

### Memberships

The China Lobby's members consisted of mainly non-Chinese Americans who were politically and professionally diverse—including journalists, scholars, businessmen, missionaries, and military leaders. In contrast, the Taiwan Lobby is comprised exclusively of Taiwanese Americans, especially immigrant professionals from Taiwan. Unlike the China Lobby, which even counted some "insider" congressional leaders—mostly Republicans—among its members, the Taiwan Lobby has had to work much harder to garner support from members of Congress.

*Organizations*

Compared with the Taiwan Lobby, the China Lobby was rather loosely organized. It consisted of only one formal organization—the Committee of One Million—under the leadership of one man (Marvin Liebman). The Taiwan Lobby is composed of several large-scale, grass-roots organizations with local chapters in many metropolitan areas. FAPA, the locomotive of the Taiwan Lobby, is well organized and capable of mobilizing members across the United States.

*Finances*

The China Lobby possessed an indirect financial relationship with the Nationalist government and it cooperated closely with Taiwan's embassy in Washington, D.C. In contrast, the Taiwan Lobby (with the exception of TECRO, which the other groups sometimes worked against), primarily has relied upon private donations and membership dues instead of receiving money from the Nationalist government because the participating Taiwanese American political organizations opposed the Kuomintang regime and typically were allied with the DPP. Since the DPP has become Taiwan's ruling party, there could be a shift in funding practices regarding the Taiwan Lobby toward the pattern that prevailed during the China Lobby period.

*Goals*

While both the China Lobby and the Taiwan Lobby shared the general goal of promoting Taiwan's interests, their specific aims did not exactly coincide. The China Lobby invariably pursued two goals: opposing China's membership in the United Nations, and supporting the continuation of U.S. aid to the Nationalist government. In contrast, as Taiwanese society became more democratic in the 1990s, the Taiwan Lobby shifted its primary goals from improving Taiwan's human-rights conditions and democracy in opposition to the Nationalist government to enhancing Taiwan's security and promoting its international status. Although both campaigned for Taiwan's membership in the United Nations, the Taiwan Lobby pushed for a new membership, separate from that of China; that is, for Taiwan under the name of "Taiwan" or "Republic of Taiwan," whereas the China Lobby tried to keep Taiwan's U.N. seat under the name of "Republic of China" by opposing China's entry to the United Nations.

*Strategies*

The China Lobby's campaigns were far more negative than those of the Taiwan Lobby. Even though both the China Lobby and the Taiwan Lobby utilized the anti-Communist mentality of U.S. society during the Cold War era and after the 1989 Tiananmen Incident, the former negatively portrayed China as a threat to the free world, while the latter positively presented Taiwan as an economic miracle and emerging democracy instead of always vigorously attempting to tarnish China's international image.

*Activities*

Both the China Lobby and the Taiwan Lobby pursued their goals through newspaper columns, letters to the editor, op-ed pieces, petition drives, newsletters, letter-writing campaigns, all-expenses-paid trips to Taiwan arranged by Taiwan's embassy and later by its successor, TECRO, and testimony at congressional hearings aimed at influencing public opinion, members of Congress, scholars, and officials in the Departments of State and Defense. However, while contributing to political campaigns constituted one of the China Lobby's activities, FAPA is prohibited from engaging in political campaigning. Thus, making campaign contributions is absent from FAPA's list of lobbying activities although its members (as well as the members of other Taiwanese American organizations) contribute on an individual basis.

Another conspicuous difference in the two groups' lobbying activities is that the Taiwan Lobby is more grass-roots oriented than was the China Lobby (whose activities mainly occurred in Washington, D.C.). With the aid of modern technologies such as faxes, e-mail, and Internet sources, the Taiwan Lobby has been able to run successful grass-roots campaigns.

## Recent and Likely Future Impact of the Taiwan Lobby on U.S. China Policy

From PRC and U.S. perspectives, the Taiwan issue presented a major obstacle to the improvement of U.S.–China relations throughout the Cold War era. The issue became even more problematic as the momentum built up for Taiwan's independence in the early 1990s under President Lee Teng-hui's leadership eventually led to a military showdown during the Taiwan Straits crisis in the spring of 1996. In the late 1990s, from the PRC's perspective, "the Taiwan question constituted the chief obstacle to the building of a strategic partnership between Beijing and Washington."[47]

Has the Taiwan Lobby destabilized U.S.–Mainland relations? Its efforts certainly have been aimed at undermining the long-standing "one-China" policy that both the United States and China at least nominally have agreed to respect.[48] From the point of view of pro-independence Taiwanese, however, the Taiwan Lobby is not a "troublemaker," but merely is striving to protect the interests of a small island country that seeks a complete international personality in order to be an accepted member of the global community. Whether one views Taiwan's actions as "destabilizing" or not, the Taiwan Lobby has been an effective force in moving and shaking U.S. China policy in recent years. While it did not achieve all of its goals, its prospects for even greater future influence are bright given the post-2000 makeup of the U.S. Congress and replacement of the Clinton administration with an executive branch selected and guided by President George W. Bush.

Prior to 2001, the Taiwan Lobby proved to be far more influential with powerful members of Congress who represent districts with sizable Taiwanese American constituencies than with the White House. Thus, while it played an instrumental role in the passage of legislation that favored Taiwan over the past decade, it failed to prevent the chief executive from embracing policies deemed detrimental to Taiwan's interests—most notably, President Bill Clinton's "three no's" statement during the 1998 Summit with Chinese President Jiang Zemin,[49] refusal to sell certain advanced-weapon systems highly desired by Taiwan, and denial of official visits to the United States by Taiwan's top leaders. While TECRO endeavored to improve its semi-official working relationship with the administration, the rest of the Taiwan Lobby, cognizant of its limited influence with the White House, urged Congress to pass binding legislation, such as the Taiwan Security Enhancement Act, rather than congressional resolutions of a nonbinding nature.

In the new millennium, the Taiwan Lobby is likely to work assiduously for the following: (1) addition of a "fourth no" to the "three no's" policy stating that no solution to the Taiwan issue should be adopted unless agreed upon by the 23 million people of Taiwan; (2) enactment of the Taiwan Security Enhancement Act accompanied by upgrades in arms sales; (3) Taiwan's entry to international organizations—such as the United Nations and the World Health Organization; and (4) officially recognized visits by Taiwanese leaders to the United States. The Lobby's future influence with respect to these objectives depends on at least three critical factors: the orientation of the Bush administration toward China; the dynamics of Taiwanese domestic politics; and the impact of the new pro-Mainland Lobby.

In view of the orientations of President Bush's national-security team, including Secretary of State Colin Powell, Secretary of Defense Donald Rumsfeld, and National Security Advisor Condoleezza Rice, along with the possibility of an official shift from viewing the PRC as a strategic partner to a competitor, the Bush administration is more likely than the past administration to adopt a policy of "con-gagement" (containment and engagement) toward China. In that case, the U.S. government might decide to play the so-called "Taiwan card" when dealing with the Mainland. This scenario would make the political environment in Washington, D.C., more conducive for attainment of the Taiwan Lobby's goals.

Although Taiwan's four major political parties all endorse the major issues targeted by the Taiwan Lobby, they differ in prioritizing among these objectives, over long-term goals, and over when and how to negotiate with the United States and with the China Mainland. As long as the DPP does not hold a majority of the seats in Taiwan's Congress, President Chen Shuibian will not be able fully to support the activities of the pro-independence Taiwan Lobby. Therefore, the nature and extent of the Lobby's future influence in Washington, D.C., also depends on whether or not Chen's DPP government is able to consolidate and broaden its political-power base.

Finally, the influence over U.S. China policy exercised by the Taiwan Lobby in the future is likely to be counterbalanced to some extent by groups that have a favorable image of the PRC. While the latter include mainstream scholars and businesspeople engaged in trade and/or investment in the Mainland, the pro-PRC lobby still is in its infancy because, unlike their Taiwanese counterparts, most Mainland immigrants are recent arrivals who are still preoccupied with making a living in their new country. Thus, even though the majority of immigrants from the PRC share the view that Taiwan is part of China and should never become independent, they have lacked comparable time and energy as well as the requisite organizational/financial resources for participation in shaping U.S.–China relations.[50] On the other hand, according to FAPA sources, China's diplomatic team in Washington, D.C., began to hire lobbying firms to work with Congress after the Taiwan Straits crisis in 1996.[51] Over time, China's diplomatic team is likely to work more aggressively. Moreover, the more numerous immigrants from the Mainland are likely to jettison their nonparticipation attitudes and challenge the influence of the Taiwan Lobby.

## Conclusion

Both the China Lobby and the Taiwan Lobby have been influential in shaping U.S.–China–Taiwan triangular relations in the second half of the twentieth century. While the similarities between the two groups demonstrate the un-changing nature of the confrontation between China and Taiwan, their many differences reflect changes over the past decades in the larger international environment as well as in Taiwan's internal politics. As the China Lobby succeeded in helping Taiwan block China's entry to the United Nations and U.S. recognition of the PRC government during the Cold War era, the Taiwan Lobby promoted Taiwan's security and international visibility in the face of the Mainland's strong opposition in 1990s.

In the 1980s, the PRC acted in a somewhat ambivalent manner toward the activities of the Taiwan Lobby, primarily because the Lobby's principal target was KMT rule. While it promoted Taiwanese independence, the Taiwan Lobby also used the U.S. media and congressional hearings as a vehicle for calling attention to Taiwan's human-rights conditions and lack of democracy and for undermining the image of the KMT government in the eyes of the U.S. public. Although the PRC did not object to these efforts, it still viewed the competition between the China Mainland and Taiwan for U.S. support as nearly a zero-sum game in which one's gain is the other's loss. As Taiwanese society became more democratic in the 1990s, the Taiwan Lobby gradually shifted its goals to the enhancement of Taiwan's security and promotion of its international status. Meanwhile, the PRC became increasingly concerned as the DPP and its pro-independence platform gained popular support. PRC leaders also became more antagonistic toward the Taiwan Lobby whose lobbying activities increasingly concentrated on promoting Taiwan's independence.

Ever since the KMT's defeat on the Mainland, the issue of Taiwan has posed a major obstacle to improved U.S.–PRC relations. Like the China Lobby before it, the Taiwan Lobby has been instrumental in the entrenchment of that obstacle. The Taiwan Lobby can be expected to remain influential in moving and shaking the U.S.–China–Taiwan triangular relationship. However, the extent of its influence will be determined in large measure by the dynamics of U.S. and Taiwanese domestic politics and by the growing impact of pro-Mainland lobby groups.

## Notes

1. Joseph Keeley, *The China Lobby Man* (New Rochelle, NY: Arlington House, 1969), p. 114.

2. Ross Y. Koen, *The China Lobby in American Politics* (New York: Octagon Books, 1974), pp. xx, 212; Nancy B. Tucker, *Taiwan, Hong Kong, and the United States, 1945–1992* (New York: Twayne Publishers, 1994), p. 21.

3. Stanley D. Bachrack, *The Committee of One Million* (New York: Columbia University Press, 1976), p. 8.

4. Ibid., pp. 3–4.

5. Tucker, *Taiwan*, pp. 21, 46.

6. For instance, Taiwan's ambassador Tsiang Tingfu made out checks to the travel agency, booking Liebman's trip to Taiwan in 1961. On 13 November 1961, to cite another example, Liebman wrote a letter to the ambassador requesting $1,750 for prints of the film *Red China-Outlaw*. Ibid., p. 46; and Bachrack, *Committee*, pp. 191–95.

7. Tucker, *Taiwan*, pp. 22, 46.

8. Ibid., p. 48.

9. Ibid., p. 22.

10. These members included Representatives Walter Judd and John Vorys, and Senators Williams Knowland, Styles Bridges, Kenneth Wherry, and Pat McCarran. Bachrack, *Committee*, pp. 4, 36–40.

11. Tucker, *Taiwan*, p. 122.

12. Taiwanese Chamber of Commerce of North America, *Yearbook, 1998–1999* (Markham, Ontario: TCCNA, 1999), p. 9.

13. www.wtcc.net.

14. www.taiwandc.org.

15. Franklin Ng, *The Taiwanese Americans* (Westport: Greenwood Press, 1998), p. 68.

16. In fact, both CTIR and FAPA share a website with the DPP Mission in the United States: www.taiwandc.org.

17. Ng, *The Taiwanese Americans*, p. 67.

18. Telephone interview by the author with a former *Taiwan Tribune* employee in Los Angeles, 26 December 2000. In December 1998, WUFI moved its headquarters from Los Angeles to San Diego.

19. www.dppmission.org.

20. Jim Mann, "Taiwan's New Era Looks a Lot Like Old One," *Los Angeles Times*, 12 July 2000, p. A5.

21. Ibid.

22. www.fapa.org.

23. Wen-yen Chen, "FAPA Headquarters Work Report, 1999," *FAPA Newsletter*, November 1999, p. 2.

24. Ibid.

25. *FAPA Action Plan 2000* at www.fapa.org.

26. Tucker, *Taiwan*, p. 182.

27. Chen, "Work Report," p. 2.

28. www.fapa.org.

29. Ibid.

30. *FAPA Newsletter*, September/October 1996, pp. 16–17.

31. For sample letters, see "Letter Campaign Drive" at www.fapa.org.

32. The *Sun-Sentinel* published the piece. See *FAPR News*, Vol. 1, No. 1 (July 2000): 9.

33. *FAPA Action Plan 2000* at www.fapa.org.

34. *FAPA Newsletter*, January/February 1998, p. 3.

35. *FAPA Newsletter*, December 1997, p. 13.

36. Jerry Chou, "How Taiwanese Americans Influence American Foreign Policy on U.S., China, and Taiwan Relations" (unpublished manuscript, Occidental College, Los Angeles, 1999), p. 13.

37. Mann, "Taiwan's New Era," p. A5.

38. Wen-yen Chen, "A Major Victory for Taiwan," *FAPA News*, October 1999, p. 1.

39. Chou, "Influence," pp. 13–14.

40. www.fapa.org.

41. Chen, "Major Victory," p. 1.

42. Headquarters staff also did the daily work of contacting congressional offices, pressing for co-sponsorship of the bill, writing opinion pieces, and working with congressional staffers on details and negotiations. Ibid.

43. Eric Schmitt, "House Approves Expansion of Ties to Taiwan's Army," *New York Times*, 2 February 2000, p. A1. Also see Representative Louise M. Slaughter's statement regarding the interest in passage expressed by Taiwanese Americans in her New York constituency. *Central News Agency*, 1 February 2000, at www.fapa.org.

44. Ng, *Taiwanese Americans*, p. 57.

45. *FAPA Newsletter*, June 2000, p. 6.

46. *FAPA Newsletter*, June 2000, p. 31; *FAPR News* 1, No. 1 (July 2000): 8.

47. Wu Xinbo, "China and the United States: Toward an Understanding on East Asian Security," in *U.S.–China Relations Following the 1997–1998 Summits: Chinese and American Perspectives on Security, Trade, and Cultural Exchange*, ed. by Peter H. Koehn and Joseph Y.S. Cheng (Hong Kong: Chinese University Press, 1999), p. 75. Also see Zhang Yebai, "Can a 'Constructive Strategic Partnership' Be Built Up Between China and the United States?" in *U.S.–China Relations Following the 1997–1998 Summits: Chinese and American Perspectives on Security, Trade, and Cultural Exchange*, ed. by Peter H. Koehn and Joseph Y.S. Cheng (Hong Kong: Chinese University Press, 1999), pp. 146, 149.

48. See Ren Donglai, "The Taiwan Issue in the Three Joint Sino–U.S. Communiqués and the Taiwan Relations Act," in *U.S.–China Relations Following the 1997–1998 Summits: Chinese and American Perspectives on Security, Trade, and Cultural Exchange*, ed. by Peter H. Koehn and Joseph Y.S. Cheng (Hong Kong: Chinese University Press, 1999), pp. 171–180; Wu, "China and the United States," pp. 75–76.

49. The "three no's" articulated by Clinton involved verbal confirmation that the United States does not support "one China, one Taiwan" or "two Chinas"; nor independence for Taiwan; nor Taiwan's admission to international organizations that require that members be states. See Harry Harding, "The Clinton–Jiang Summits: An American Perspective," in *U.S.–China Relations Following the 1997–1998 Summits: Chinese and American Perspectives on Security, Trade, and Cultural Exchange*, ed. by Peter H. Koehn and Joseph Y.S. Cheng (Hong Kong: Chinese University Press, 1999), p. 34.

50. Xiao-huang Yin, "The Growing Influence of Chinese Americans on U.S.–China Relations," in *U.S.–China Relations Following the 1997–1998 Summits: Chinese and American Perspectives on Security, Trade, and Cultural Exchange*, ed. by Peter H. Koehn and Joseph Y.S. Cheng (Hong Kong: Chinese University Press, 1999), p. 344.

51. Interview by the author with a FAPA worker at Washington, D.C., 24 August 2000.

# 8

# Chinese Americans' Views on U.S.–China Relations

## An Analysis Based on Chinese-community Newspapers Published in the United States

*Xiaojian Zhao*

Like other ethnic groups in the United States, Chinese Americans have a long history of publishing their own newspapers. Since the 1850s, they have published more than 100 newspapers and journals—most of which have been written in Chinese.[1] The existence of a large number of community newspapers over such a long period of time suggests the ongoing importance of the ethnic press in the lives of Chinese Americans. This rich mine of primary sources, however, has been largely overlooked by scholars—especially in the study of U.S.–China relations.

This chapter analyzes Chinese American views on U.S.–China relations through the lens of Chinese-community newspapers published (mainly in Chinese) in the United States. Historically, ethnic newspapers have kept Chinese Americans informed of affairs in China and in mainstream U.S. society. Since the enactment of the 1965 Immigration Act, the number of Chinese immigrants has increased drastically.[2] More than two-thirds of the Chinese American population today were born outside the United States. In recent years, as economic, cultural, and educational exchange across national boundaries have become more frequent, Chinese American newspapers have worked to put Chinese Americans in touch with policymakers in Washington, D.C., Beijing, and Taipei. During the 2000 U.S. presidential election, these newspapers informed presidential candidates of Chinese Americans' concerns and circulated information regarding each candidate's position on U.S.–China relations.

### Ethnic Press, Chinese Language, and the Formation
### of the Chinese American Community

Chinese has been the primary language used in Chinatowns and in Chinese American newspapers. After the 1920s, Chinese Americans born and educated in the United States became more familiar with English, although few attempts to publish English newspapers have been successful. The first all-English weekly, the *Chinese Digest*, lasted only for five years, and its circulation never exceeded 500. The *Chinese Press*, another English-language newspaper, managed to survive from 1940 to 1952; it recorded a peak circulation of about 2,500.[3] These early English-language community newspapers presented the ideas of second-generation Chinese Americans who saw themselves as different from their parents. By privileging a community subgroup, the papers alienated immigrants and, therefore, failed to promote ethnic solidarity. Consequently, they received little support from ethnic enterprises that aimed at appealing to all Chinese Americans; such enterprises preferred placing advertisements in newspapers with large circulations.[4]

Competition from mainstream newspapers presented another challenge. With limited funding and few trained staff writers, community-based English-language newspapers did not have the capacity to cover national and international news in a timely and sophisticated fashion. Thus, English-speaking Chinese Americans were more likely to subscribe to mainstream U.S. newspapers.[5] Not until the 1960s did a few new English-language community newspapers begin to enjoy some success. To reach a larger audience, some of them, such as *AsianWeek*, expanded to include other Asian American groups.

Recent studies of ethnic identity, influenced in particular by the theoretical work of Benedict Anderson, have emphasized the role and significance of ethnic language and the ethnic press in identity formation.[6] Chinese immigrants came from many regions of China. They brought with them different regional cultures and many dialects. Different dialects made it difficult for one group of Chinese to communicate orally with another, but all Chinese share a common written language, which provided a basis for ethnic solidarity. After World War II, Chinatowns in large cities became less cohesive as a growing number of Chinese Americans moved to the sprawling suburbs of large cities and relocated in different parts of the country. Community newspapers responded to these changes and kept all the Chinese in the United States connected. These papers helped maintain an informed community, identify issues of special concern, and create a forum for public discussion. After 1949, as conflict intensified among community groups over politics in China, the ethnic press urged Chinese Americans to sever their ties with political parties in China and to focus their energy on building their own community in the United States.[7]

Over the past few decades, as new waves of Chinese immigrants arrived from China, Hong Kong, Taiwan, and Southeast Asia, the Chinese American community has become increasingly diverse. The number of Chinese-language newspapers also increased. In 1995, there were at least twenty-three Chinese-language newspapers and periodicals published in Southern California.[8] Seven Chinese newspapers and over a dozen weeklies are now distributed in Los Angeles's Chinatowns.[9] Most established newspapers long supported the government in Taiwan, but they gradually began to acknowledge improvements in China. Newspapers that have sided with one government against the other have a narrow audience.

The largest Chinese-language daily newspaper in the United States, the *World Journal* (*Shijie ribao*, formerly *Chinese World*), has established itself as a transnational media network. In North America, the paper has branch offices in New York, Los Angeles, San Francisco, Vancouver, and Toronto. More than a thousand journalists employed by the paper are stationed in Hong Kong, Taiwan, China, Singapore, Japan, Thailand, the United States, Canada, and Europe. The paper provides the most comprehensive coverage of the Chinese experience from a global perspective, and its readers include Chinese Americans originating from China, Hong Kong, Taiwan, and Southeast Asia. The Southern California Corporation Center of the *World Journal* in Los Angeles claims to have reached an estimated 200,000 readers.[10] In the 1970s and 1980s, the newspaper clearly supported the Kuomintang (KMT) in Taiwan. In recent years, however, it has distanced itself from the government in Taiwan and become critical of both Taipei's and Beijing's policies.

Ethnic newspapers continue to attract Chinese Americans because they provide information that is unavailable elsewhere. It is only from these newspapers that one can learn in detail about the lives of Chinese people all over the world and about the issues and developments that are critical to their lives. In 1996, for example, Chinese living everywhere were concerned about the China–Japan disputes over Diaoyutai Islands. Ethnic newspapers kept their readers informed, created a forum for public debate, and promoted the cooperative spirit of the *Baodiao* (Defending Diaoyutai Islands) Movement.[11] Mainstream newspapers such as the *New York Times*, in contrast, paid little attention to the issues involved.

As Chinese Americans appeared more frequently in Hollywood movies, more Chinese films entered the international market, and Chinese and Chinese American athletes became visible in international sport events, the entertainment sections of ethnic newspapers assumed special appeal among readers of all ages. During the season of Olympic games, copies of the *World*

*Journal* sold out immediately at bookstores and vending stands, and one could hardly find an unoccupied copy of the paper in college libraries and Chinese business establishments. Besides turning to ethnic papers for popular Chinese and Chinese American culture, many Chinese Americans also rely on these papers' classified sections for advertised services. Mandarin- and Cantonese-speaking babysitters, immigration-related legal assistance, and traditional Chinese medicine or medical practices are among the most demanded services for Chinese Americans—including those born in the United States—while employment information is especially critical for new immigrants.

Ethnic newspapers not only provide entertainment and service information; they also guard against racism. Chinese Americans often receive biased treatment from the mainstream media. Some mainstream journalists still portray all Asian Americans as foreigners, or reduce them to sources for sensational stories of atypical achievement or notoriety. Frustrated by the way the establishment network media treated Wen Ho Lee's case, the large group of Chinese Americans who gathered in Palo Alto on 20 September 1999 to support the effort of Lee's daughter and friends only invited Chinese American newspapers.[12] Their reports enabled ethnic newspapers to represent the voices of Chinese Americans and stand in the forefront of the struggle against racial discrimination.[13] Moreover, some Chinese Americans are more willing to participate in public debates hosted by ethnic newspapers. Although not every Chinese American agrees with everything printed in every ethnic paper, reports and discussions found in these papers illuminate the ways the community is presented to itself.

### The Ethnic Press and U.S.–China Relations

Chinese American newspapers exerted limited direct impact on U.S.–China relations until recently. Since only a fraction of Chinese Americans could vote before World War II, few politicians took them seriously. The situation began to change after Chinese immigrants became eligible for naturalization in 1943. Since then, it has been common to see political candidates visiting Chinatowns or placing campaign advertisements in Chinese American newspapers. The Communist victory in the Chinese Civil War in 1949, followed by the U.S.–China conflict in Korea, however, turned the People's Republic of China into an archenemy of the United States. Caught in the middle of a war between the land of their ancestors and the country of their residence, many Chinese immigrants became subjects of political accusations and government investigation—which also intensified internal conflict among Chinese Americans. Newspapers that were sympathetic to the PRC went out of business one after another. Under the circumstances, there was little room for Chinese Americans to voice opinions on foreign policies.[14]

After France recognized the PRC, many Chinese Americans hoped that China soon would be accepted by the international community. However, by seeking normalization of U.S.–China relations during the Cold War period, private citizens risked raising questions about their loyalty to the United States. Under these circumstances, several independent community newspapers— including *Chinese American Weekly* (Zhongmei zhoubao) and *Chinese Pacific Weekly* (Taipingyang zhoubao), for example—suggested that their readers sever their ties with the ancestral homeland and not become involved in discussions about China. They encouraged Chinese Americans to study the laws and political system of the United States, to secure rights promised by the U.S. constitution, and to create a united front to carry out their political agendas.[15]

The only group that influenced U.S. policies toward China in the Cold War era was the China Lobby—which tried to secure support to aid Taipei against Beijing.[16] Although the number of Chinese Americans who supported the PRC was relatively small, most readers and journalists (except for those strictly controlled by the Kuomintang) also questioned lobby activities that would further escalate hostilities between China and Taiwan, or between the United States and China. In 1954, Lin Yutang, a prominent writer living in the United States, took a job in Singapore as chancellor of Nanyang University, the first major university outside China for overseas Chinese. Lin resigned from the post several months later, however, due to financial disputes with the university board. Back in the United States, he told *Life* magazine that Nanyang was run by Chinese Communists. This provocative accusation, with the potential to incriminate those who supported the founding of the university, angered many Chinese Americans. In spite of Lin's reputation as a scholar, he was publicly denounced in the Chinese-language press. Wu Jinfu, the editor of the *United Daily News* (*Lianhe ribao*), a paper originally affiliated with the Kuomintang, wrote in the *Chinese American Weekly* that Lin's unsubstantiated charges, which made him out to be an "anticommunist hero," would jeopardize Chinese living outside of China and further damage the relationship between the PRC and the West.[17]

As an outcome of secret diplomacy between top officials of the two governments, contact resumed between the United States and China in the early 1970s. Although this dramatic development surprised citizens and scholars, many Chinese Americans found the reconciliation encouraging. Gilbert Woo, editor of the *Chinese Pacific Weekly*, described Chinese Americans as children with two sets of parents. They suffered when their "adopted parents" fought against their "birth parents," and they were greatly relieved when both sets of parents started to talking to one another.[18]

Once the United States and China began to normalize diplomatic relations, it became possible for Chinese Americans openly to express a wider range of opinions and feelings concerning the PRC. A number of the newspapers that appeared in the 1970s and 1980s reflected such changes.[19] The voices of Chinese Americans, especially on issues of trade, cultural and educational exchange, human rights in China, and China–Taiwan relations, began to impact U.S.–China relations in the 1980s and 1990s. Thousands of Chinese Americans protested against the government of China's treatment of student demonstrators in Tiananmen Square in 1989, and almost all of their newspapers denounced the government's brutality. The administration of President George Bush responded to the domestic pressure by reducing the level and frequency of official U.S. contact with China, and the administration of President Bill Clinton later threatened to terminate China's most-favored-nation (MFN) status unless its human rights record improved.

The early 1990s witnessed considerable tension between the United States and China. After the collapse of the Soviet Union in 1991, and partially because of the wide U.S.–China trade imbalance, Washington showed reluctance to cooperate with Beijing. The involvement of the United States in China–Taiwan conflicts further escalated tensions. The sale of F-16 jets to Taiwan in 1992, and especially the permission granted Taiwanese president Lee Teng-hui to visit Cornell University in 1995, caused China to suspect that the United States was encouraging *taidu* (Taiwan independence movement) tendencies on Taiwan.

For most of the 1990s, Chinese Americans held divided opinions. Some worried that China would become the next enemy of the United States. This group urged the American government to avoid antagonizing the PRC and to lift the sanctions imposed after the 1989 Tiananmen crisis. Dissidents and human rights groups, on the other hand, raised audible voices against Beijing. Given that large numbers of Chinese Americans now are involved in business, cultural, and intellectual exchanges with the China Mainland and/or Taiwan and that many Chinese Americans have family members and relatives living on one side of the Taiwan Straits or the other, few would like to see a war between China and Taiwan with U.S. involvement.

While the voice of Chinese Americans advocating pressure on China reflected in ethnic newspapers was loud from time to time throughout most of the 1990s, by the turn of the century, the voice promoting a friendly and stable relationship with the PRC became dominant. News analyses and editorials suggested that most Chinese Americans wanted the United States to endorse the eventual reunification of China and Taiwan. To understand this important shift, it is necessary to examine developments in the last few years of the twentieth century and their impact on Chinese American newspapers.

## China–Taiwan and U.S.–China Relations: A New Perspective

Several developments helped reshape Chinese American views about U.S.–China relations. The first noticeable development was the reduction in tension between China and the United States during the second term of the Clinton administration. In 1997, President Jiang Zemin visited the United States. President Clinton's visit to China followed a year later. The summits produced few substantial concrete results, but the extensive dialogue between the two leaders on friendly terms suggested that both governments were interested in the possibility of establishing a partnership. The top leaders of the two nations acknowledged that the United States and China share vital interests in the growing global political economy, and that peace and stability would protect such interests.[20] By the end of 2000, the United States had separated trade from human rights issues and granted China permanent MFN status. A trade agreement reached on 15 November 2000 had paved the way for China's accession to the World Trade Organization (WTO). To Chinese Americans, these changes not only signaled significant improvements in U.S.–China relations; they also would ameliorate China–Taiwan relations.[21]

In addition, the image of PRC leaders has improved. The whole world watched a rather stiff Jiang Zemin attending the historic ceremony in which the British handed back Hong Kong to China in 1997. However, the Western media noticed that President Jiang has been more relaxed in his subsequent international appearances. After the Beijing summit in 1998, Clinton praised Jiang as a "man of extraordinary intellect" who "has vision" and "can imagine a future that is different from the present."[22] During his visit to the United Nations in September 2000, Jiang delivered a public speech in English at a luncheon in New York that received high marks from the U.S. media—even though it offered few new insights. The *World Journal* reported that Jiang spoke with ease, showing that the leader of China is "mature." Quoting several China specialists who heard the speech, the report said that the Chinese president impressed his U.S. audience and that he handled important and sensitive issues with wisdom and skill. While the paper gave positive and lengthy coverage to his appearance, it paid limited attention to the protests against Jiang that occurred in New York City.[23] Two weeks later, a reporter praised Jiang for creating the image of an open-minded, pragmatic, well-educated, and pro-Western Chinese leader.[24]

China's economic progress also has helped to change Chinese American orientations. The year 2000 saw the slowing of the U.S. economy, with the stock market and high-tech companies ending on a dismal note. The impact of the U.S. economic shock wave was felt in Asia as well—especially in countries that depend heavily on exports of technology. In contrast, China's economy, which is not dependent on Western technology, enjoyed an 8 percent growth rate in 2000, according to statistics released by the Chinese government.[25] Even more impressive, the Chinese stock market shot up 30 percent. *AsianWeek* noted that China was "making great leaps" and saw the country's strong economic performance as an indication of its sound reform policy.[26] Citing the opinions of economic specialists, the newspaper suggested that China was becoming the best place in the world to invest for long-term growth and security.[27]

Meanwhile, Taiwan showed signs of instability. On 18 March 2000, voters elected Chen Shuibian, the leader of the Democratic Progressive Party (DPP), as Taiwan's new president. The outcome of this election turned the island's political order upside down. The Kuomintang, which fled to Taiwan after its defeat by the Communists in 1949, had been the ruling party for fifty-one years. However, its candidate received only 23 percent of the votes. Within days after the election, former party president Lee Teng-hui was forced to step down.[28]

Beijing expressed concern over the outcome of the election because the new president and the DPP historically had advocated independence. A week before the election, Chinese premier Zhu Rongji suggested that if voters made the wrong choice and selected a *taidu* president, they would regret it later. To Chinese living all over the world, the most pressing question was whether Chen's victory would undermine or advance peace and stability on both sides of the Taiwan Straits.[29]

Since Chen Shuibian took power, his administration has been occupied with domestic crises. The new president does not have the support of the former Kuomintang affiliates, and his determination to make drastic changes in the government has encountered strong opposition. Many of his decisions— including a call for slowing down business investment in the China Mainland, the termination of a nuclear power plant already under construction, and appointment of a group of young and inexperienced cabinet members—have encountered extensive criticism. When Taiwan's stock market took a dive, hundreds of small- and medium-sized enterprises folded and the unemployment rate increased dramatically. With the economy showing no sign of recovery, many people in Taiwan have little confidence in Chen's government.

Although Chen Shuibian does not want people to pour money into business ventures in the Mainland, the economic opportunities available in China increasingly appeal to Taiwanese entrepreneurs. A number of business leaders who agreed with him at first have changed their positions. Wang Yongzai, vice president of Taiwan's plastic-production corporation, had been a strong supporter of Chen's economic policy. After he visited the Mainland, however, Wang acknowledged in public that he was wrong.[30] Zhang Zhongmo, known as the "Godfather" of Taiwan's semiconductor industry, had said earlier that he would not invest in China for several years because he considered China's semiconductor technology to be ten years behind that in Taiwan. Speaking at a conference in late October of 2000, however, Zhang maintained, in opposition to the government's investment policy, that "if we don't try to expand the China market, the chance of survival for our enterprises would be smothered." He added that the future of Taiwan's economy required a stable relationship with China.[31]

Zhang's argument coincides with views expressed in Chinese American newspapers in late 2000 and early 2001. In a public forum published in the *World Journal* in September 2000, Gu Xin, a postdoctoral fellow at the John King Fairbank Center for East Asian Research at Harvard University, contended that if Taiwan had the ambition to create another "miracle," it must see China as its "development opportunity." Another writer argued that the Mainland would become an important factor in determining Taiwan's fate, and that the latter should seriously reevaluate China and approach its relations with the PRC from the perspective of worldwide trade and economic development.[32] Six months after Chen Shuibian took office, the *World Journal* published an editorial entitled "One, Two, Three, Save Taiwan." The editorial suggested that Taiwan was in dire straits and urged leaders on the island to deal with its political, economic, social, and diplomatic crises with determination. It further exhorted the DPP government to give up its dream for independence and reestablish the traditional concept of "one China" in recognition that the people residing on both sides of the Straits are Chinese. The editorial reasoned that taking such a step would by no means indicate that Taiwan was weaker; it only would imply that the Chinese people on the island had the ability and the wisdom to cooperate with Chinese in the Mainland. President Chen, the editorial argued, "should walk out of the shadow of independence and open the door for negotiation with China under the 'one China' premise."[33]

The "one China" concept is by no means new. What has changed is the perception of China in relation to Taiwan. Instead of looking at the United States as the only source of power that could lend a hand to Taiwan when needed, Chinese American newspapers now argue that a working relationship with China is crucial for Taiwan's future. *Taidu* sentiment is not likely to disappear overnight, but it is clear that not many Chinese Americans want to see a military confrontation between China and Taiwan. In November 2000, the *World Journal* published a number of essays, surveys, and special interviews. None supported the idea of *taidu*. At the same time, a public-opinion survey concluded that the views of the U.S. public toward Taiwan and China also had changed. Whereas about 43 percent of those surveyed agreed that their government should provide Taiwan with military protection in 1996, only 37 percent held the same opinion four years later.[34] An essay on government policies argued that the Clinton administration lost many supporters because of its pro-Taiwan policies.[35]

As soon as he won the presidency, Chen Shuibian adopted a cautious approach. He immediately announced that he would like to hold a "peace summit" with Beijing—provided the latter treated Taiwan as its equal. He even proposed to revise the provocative provision in his party's platform regarding independence. After Chen's victory became a reality, Chinese president Jiang Zemin announced that he would welcome talks with the new leader of Taiwan—as long as Chen accepted the concept that the island is part of China. Chinese American newspapers carefully examined such rhetoric and concluded, with a sense of relief, that neither China nor Taiwan wanted a military confrontation. People in Taiwan, however, demanded more. Since March 2000, Chen Shuibian's Democratic Progressive Party has been under pressure to abandon its pro-independence position. In late November, leaders of all political parties in Taiwan, except for the DPP, rallied to urge Chen to return to the "one China" concept.[36]

Chinese Americans have contributed their part to promoting stable relations between China and Taiwan. Their newspapers interviewed government officials from both sides. Most papers praised prospects for peaceful unification and criticized military exercises.[37] Through editorials and public forums, ethnic newspapers repeatedly expressed Chinese Americans' desire for unification and hoped that China and Taiwan would "break the ice" and start negotiating.[38] "This is a time for new ideas," argued an editorial in the *United Daily News*; "both sides of the Taiwan Straits should cooperate and compete in the new global economic structure."[39]

In a public speech reported in the *World Journal*, Chinese American Nobel laureate Yuan Tze Lee said that since Chinese living on both sides of the Taiwan Straits shared the same desire for freedom, peace, and prosperity, there is no reason for them to fight against each other.[40] Lee later asserted that helping to establish a positive relationship between China and Taiwan is an important mission for all ethnic Chinese.[41]

Whereas a few years earlier ethnic newspapers were preoccupied with the possibility of China attacking Taiwan, they now seemed to presume that China would not attack provided that *taidu* is abandoned.[42] Every attempt made by the Taiwan government to separate from China drew criticism. When Chen Shuibian's officials announced their intention to adopt a new *pinyin* (romanization) system that would phoneticize the Chinese language in a different way from that used in the China Mainland, they argued that in doing so the native Taiwanese dialect could be incorporated. However, most Chinese American newspapers viewed the idea as a further effort to alienate the island from China.[43] The *United Daily News* criticized Taiwan for politicizing an academic issue—arguing that adopting a different *pinyin* system would bar people in Taiwan from the system accepted by the international community.[44]

On 1 October 2000, nine days before the annual celebration of Taiwan's national holiday, the leaders of many Chinese American organizations attended parties celebrating the founding of the PRC in Chinatowns throughout the United States. The *World Journal* invited readers to express their opinions on whether this was a proper thing to do. Most of the eleven people who responded acknowledged that they had previously supported the Taiwan government. However, nine of them now agreed that political disputes between the PRC and Taiwan should be a thing of the past and that Chinese Americans no longer should favor one government over another.[45] These published views reflect a monumental change that has taken place over the past two decades. Many Chinese American businessmen, who used to belong to the staunch anti-Communist camp, have cut lucrative business deals with enterprises in the Mainland. A large number of Chinese Americans from all walks of life have visited the PRC; they are now able to see China in a new light. As one scholar pointed out in a letter to the *World Journal*, China and Taiwan no longer are enemies; the differences between the two are "internal conflicts among our own people" (*renmin neibu maodun*).[46] Following South Korean president Kim Dae Jung's conciliatory approach to North Korea and televised images of South and North Korean athletes marching together into the Olympic Stadium in Sydney, an editorial in the *World Journal* cried out that the leaders of China and Taiwan should "not let Kim Dae Jung steal the show," but "should give full play to your wisdom and make the best decision toward unification."[47]

## The Press, the Voters, and the 2000 Presidential Election

In 2000, Asian Americans increased their involvement in local and national elections. First, they organized a political action committee—the 80–20 Initiative—in an effort to convince 80 percent of all Asian Americans to vote as a bloc and elect a president deemed most attuned to their concerns. Led by S.B. Woo, former lieutenant governor of Delaware, and Chang-Lin Tien, former chancellor of the University of California at Berkeley, the group together mobilized an estimated membership of 350,000. A bipartisan endorsement committee met in late August 2000 in Los Angeles and decided to endorse Al Gore for president. The committee then vowed that it would deliver 80 percent of the Asian American vote for Gore in the November election. In its endorsement, the committee noted that neither political party had treated Asian Americans well, but between the two, the Democrats seemed to have done more than the Republicans.[48]

Before the 80–20 Initiative met to discuss the endorsement, members sent letters to the presidential nominees, asking them to address the specific concerns of Asian and Pacific Island Americans. These included immigration issues, racial profiling, the treatment of Wen Ho Lee, hate-crime legislation, affirmative action, and trade with China. The fact that U.S.–China trade, rather than general foreign policy toward Asian countries, made the list of concerns suggests that the U.S.–China relationship is important not only to Chinese Americans, but to Asian Americans in general. When the presidential candidates responded, their comments were published in English- and Asian-language Asian American newspapers and aired on ethnic television and radio stations. Neither Gore nor Bush gave satisfactory responses, but Gore made some promises while Bush avoided direct answers.[49] Even if Gore ultimately lost the presidential race, the 80–20 Initiative wanted to make politicians in Washington aware of the interests of Asian Americans.[50]

The English-language Asian American newspaper *AsianWeek* endorsed Gore as well, arguing that he would do more to "recognize, promote, and preserve the voice of Asian America."[51] However, while most Chinese American newspapers supported the formation of the 80–20 Initiative, they opted not to endorse a specific presidential candidate in the close race. Instead, they asked voters to wait and see and make a wise choice by "supporting a candidate who will help us." Political columnist Chen Shiyao of the *World Journal* pointed out that, overall, Democrats had a better record than Republicans on issues of affirmative action, immigration, and supporting the poor. However, he added, Chinese Americans should keep in mind that the Wen Ho Lee incident occurred during the Clinton administration, and that Gore mistreated and abandoned Chinese Americans when fund-raising scandals caught the spotlight.[52] The newspaper was especially disappointed that Gore did not make a public statement regarding Wen Ho Lee's case.[53] Between August and November, the *World Journal* published dozens of editorials, news analyses, and responses from specialists and readers in order to provide more in-depth perspective on each presidential candidate.

The *World Journal* perceived the close race between Gore and Bush as a great opportunity for a minority group to exercise power because both candidates were obliged to "please undetermined voters." "If one candidate were in a dominant position," said an editorial, it would be possible for him not to pay any attention to Asian American voters. "Only when the race is close could the relatively few minority votes have the decisive impact."[54]

U.S.–China policy has been one of the most important issues for Chinese

American voters since the early 1990s. A survey conducted during the 1996 presidential election showed that 78 percent of Chinese American voters regarded U.S. policy toward China as a significant factor in their choice of a candidate.[55] At that time, however, voters' opinions were divided, and Chinese American newspapers from time to time called for economic and strategic containment of China by the United States. Kuomintang supporters, PRC dissidents, human rights groups, and *taidu* sympathizers joined together in opposing close ties between Washington and Beijing. Another matter of concern was the security of Taiwan. Chinese military exercises in the Taiwan Straits and the U.S. response—dispatching two carrier-battle groups—suggested the possibility of war.

During the 2000 presidential election, however, the Chinese-language press made it clear that most Chinese Americans favored the policy that had developed during the last few years of the Clinton administration. This policy is centered around treating China as a strategic partner of the United States. Discussions in the editorial and opinions sections of Chinese-language newspapers indicated that most Chinese Americans wanted to see a positive and stable U.S.–China relationship, with normal and regular cultural and economic exchanges.[56] In order to make the presidential candidates aware of these opinions, Chinese-language newspapers worked to foster a dialogue between the candidates and Chinese American voters. Three days before the election, the *World Journal* asked both Gore and Bush to address five issues: immigration, U.S.–China relations, China–Taiwan disputes, national missile defense, and the case of Wen Ho Lee. The second, third, and fourth questions all pertained to U.S.–China relations. Based on the responses of the candidates, the newspaper pointed out that Gore and Bush had taken similar positions regarding U.S.–China relations. While it seemed that the vice president was most likely to continue Clinton's China policy if elected, Bush was cited as saying that he hoped that Taiwan would not announce independence and that China would not attack the island.[57] Without publicly endorsing a particular candidate, the paper urged Chinese Americans to vote. Overall, the readers seemed to agree with the paper that it was unwise to endorse a particular candidate. "What if the person we supported lost in the race?" one reader asked. "How could Chinese Americans ask for support from a President whom we did not support in the election?"[58]

The *World Journal* also analyzed the past performance of Chinese American incumbents who ran for U.S. Congress seats. In most of the 1990s, the newspaper had been an advocate for human rights in China. During the 2000 election, however, it reminded readers that some Chinese American candidates had supported sanctions against China or had voted against the renewal of China's MFN status—implying that, once elected, these candidates might not promote U.S.–China relations in positive ways.[59]

If the relationship between China and Taiwan is hostile, an equally hostile relationship between the United States and China would make the situation worse. One Chinese American reader argued that "the only way to protect us is to prevent a war between the United States and China, and giving up *taidu* and working toward unification is the solution."[60] The prospect of more advanced-weapons sales to Taiwan by the United States and the possibility of increased U.S. military involvement now are viewed by newspapers and readers alike as alarming developments that would jeopardize the stability of China–Taiwan and U.S.–China relations. The *World Journal* urged Taiwan's government not to buy weapons from the United States—arguing that if Taiwan stops such purchases, China will likewise stop its development of advanced weapons. At the same time, it also exhorted Beijing to stay calm.[61] Most Chinese and Asian American newspapers, including the *World Journal*, *United Daily News*, and *AsianWeek*, remained optimistic during and after the 2000 elections that China–Taiwan and U.S.–China military tensions would not escalate no matter who was elected president.[62]

After George W. Bush entered the White House, Beijing discovered that the younger Bush is not a replica of his father, who, after serving as director of the U.S. Liaison Office in Beijing in the early 1970s, implemented modest policies toward the PRC and established friendly ties with Chinese officials. In talks with Chinese vice premier Qian Qichen, the new president antagonized China by saying that Washington would sell whatever arms it chose to Taipei. To Chinese Americans, weapons sales do little to protect Taiwan; they only damage U.S.–China relations. The *World Journal* has urged Beijing not to attack Taiwan under any circumstances, and advised Taiwan not to rely on the United States for security. The paper argued that, even if Washington provided Taiwan with advanced weapons, there is no guarantee that the United States would intervene on Taiwan's behalf if war ever broke out between China and Taiwan.[63]

The prolonged standoff over the collision of a U.S. spy plane and a Chinese fighter plane signals potential future trouble between the United States and China. Chinese American newspapers are aware that President George W. Bush is guided by Cold War warriors steeped in anti-Communist thinking. The Bush administration did back off in late April 2001 and announced that it would not sell Aegis-radar-equipped destroyers to Taiwan this time. However, the president's tough talk continued. On 25 April, Bush said unambiguously that the United States would do "whatever it took" to defend Taiwan if China attacked the island—even if that meant using U.S. military forces.[64] In spite of these messages, many Chinese Americans believe that

Bush will not sacrifice U.S. trade interests in the expanded China market and will moderate his rhetoric once his administration starts to experience the realities of international relations.[65] The future of U.S.–China relations under the George W. Bush administration is filled with uncertainty. However, this analysis of Chinese-community newspapers that reflect Chinese American views on U.S.–China relations suggests that a drastic change of China policy which increases tensions across the Taiwan Straits will surely alienate large numbers of Chinese Americans.

**Notes**

1. For sources regarding Chinese newspapers published in the United States, see *Chinese Newspapers Published in North America, 1845–1975*, compiled by Karl Lo and H.M. Lai (Washington, D.C.: Association of Research Libraries, 1977); Him Mark Lai, "The Chinese Press in the United States and Canada Since World War II: A Diversity of Voices," in *Chinese America: History and Perspectives* 14 (1990): 107–155. For other ethnic presses, see *Encyclopedic Directory of Ethnic Newspapers and Periodicals in the United States*, ed. by Lubomyr R. Wynar and Anna T. Wynar (Littleton, CO: Libraries Unlimited, 1976).

2. Lai, "Chinese Press," pp. 107–155.

3. J. Percy H. Johnson, ed., *Ayer Directory of Newspapers and Periodicals* (Philadelphia: N.W. Ayer & Son, 1940–1943).

4. For a more detailed discussion of Chinese-language and English-language community newspapers, see Xiaojian Zhao, *Remaking Chinese America: Immigration, Family, and Community* (Piscataway, NJ: Rutgers University Press, 2002), chapter 5.

5. Readers of Chinese-language newspapers often also subscribe to mainstream U.S. newspapers.

6. Benedict Anderson, *Imagined Communities: Reflections on the Origin and Spread of Nationalism*, rev. ed. (New York: Verso, 1991).

7. Zhao, *Remaking Chinese America*, chapter 5.

8. Joe Chung Fong, "Transnational Newspapers: The Making of the Post-1965 Globalized/Localized San Gabriel Valley Chinese Community," *Amerasia Journal* 22, No. 3 (1996): 68.

9. Xiao-huang Yin, "The Growing Influence of Chinese Americans on U.S.–China Relations," in *The Outlook for U.S.–China Relations Following the 1997–1998 Summits: Chinese and American Perspectives on Security, Trade, and Cultural Exchange*, ed. by Peter Koehn and Joseph Y.S. Cheng (Hong Kong: The Chinese University Press, 1999), p. 341.

10. Author's telephone interview with staff members of the newspaper's Los Angeles office, 3 April 2001.

11. Fong, "Transnational Newspapers," p. 73.

12. George Koo, "What Can We Say to Wen Ho Lee: His Daughter Alberta Speaks Out," *AsianWeek*, 30 September 1999, p. 6.

13. "Jianchi zhenpai banbao lichang, tigong youzhi zixuen fuwu" (Honest newspaper, reliable information), editorial, *World Journal*, 12 February 2001, p. A2.

14. See Zhao, *Remaking Chinese America*, chapter 7.

15. Gilbert Woo, "Informal Essays," *Chinese Pacific Weekly*, 3 September 1949, and 1 March 1957.

16. See the chapter by Tsung Chi in this volume.

17. Wu Jinfu, "Lin Yutang yugai mizhang" (Lin Yutang covers his mistake, but makes it more conspicuous"), *Chinese American Weekly*, 12 May 1955, pp. 6–7. There are a number of essays published in the *Chinese American Weekly* criticizing Lin's behavior. See Can Fu, "Lin Yutang zhi daxue" (Lin Yutang's university), 3 March 1955, p. 29; Gu Jun, "Lin Yutang zai nanda de fengbo" (The controversy involving Lin Yutang in Nanyang University), 14 April 1955, pp. 15–17; Lei Ming, with response from editor Wu Jinfu, "Lin Yutang qiao huaqiao zhugang" (Lin Yutang extorts money from overseas Chinese), 14 April 1955, p. 31; Zheng Feng, with response from editor Wu Jinfu, "Lin Yutang shi bei Beiping ganzou de ma?" (Was Lin Yutang driven out by Beijing?) 21 April 1955, pp. 31–32.

18. Jing Nan, "Pingpang waijiao" (Pingpong diplomacy), *Chinese Pacific Weekly*, 22 April 1971, in *Hu Jingnan wenji* (Selected works of Gilbert Woo) (Hong Kong: Xiangjiang chuban youxian gongsi, 1991), p. 677.

19. Maurice Chuck's *Shidai bao* (San Francisco journal), for example, started in 1972.

20. For a detailed discussion of the summits, see Harry Harding, "The Clinton–Jiang Summits: An American Perspective," in *The Outlook for U.S.–China Relations Following the 1997–1998 Summits*, ed. by Peter Koehn and Joseph Y.S. Cheng, pp. 29–48.

21. "Liangan rushi zaiwang, santong siwei ying tiaozheng" (Reconsidering communications and contact across the strait as China and Taiwan join the WTO), editorial, *World Journal*, 22 September 2000, p. A2. See also the editorial of 26 October 2000.

22. Harding, "The Clinton–Jiang Summits," p. 40.

23. "Jiang Zemin yanjiang, meirenshi zanshang" (American people praised Jiang Zemin's speech), *World Journal*, 9 September 2000, p. A3.

24. "Jiang Zemin gao gongguan" (Jiang Zemin's public relations diplomacy), *World Journal*, 21 September 2000, p. A9.

25. Ron Chepesiuk, "China and the WTO: The Impact on the Asian American Business Community," *AsianWeek* 8 September 2000, p. 2; and Ron Chepesiuk, "Asia in 2001: A Peak Ahead, Experts Have Reservations, Optimistic about Asian Economies," *AsianWeek*, 26 January 2001, p. 1.

26. Chepesiuk, "Asia in 2001," p. 1.

27. Ibid.

28. Bay Fang, "Taiwan Shows What Democracy Can Do: President-elect Soft-Pedals Independence," *U.S. News*, 3 April 2000, p. 31.

29. See editorials in *World Journal*, 11, 19, 20, 21 March 2000; editorial in *United Daily News*, 24 March 2000.

30. "Zhengfu xiuli renmin, qiye ruhe neng genliu Taiwan?" (How could businesses stay put in Taiwan when the government abuses its people?), editorial, *World Journal*, 27 October 2000, p. A2.

31. "Zhang Zhongmo: Jieji yongren ersha qiye shengji" (Zhang Zhongmo speaks out: the "be patient and endure" policy hurts Taiwan business prosperity); and "Dalu jingji meng chaoqian, Taiwan dangju kanbujian?" (Mainland economy leaps forward; is the Taiwan government blind?); "Jieji yongren bu songbang, liangan shuying yi

fenshao" (The "be patient and endure" policy is still in effect, but winner and loser is known), *World Journal*, 7 October 2000, p. A3.

32. Wen Xianshen, "Rang liangan wenti shimao hua" (Let the conflict between Mainland and Taiwan be resolved as it is in the WTO), *World Journal*, 26 September 2000, p. A6.

33. "Yi er san, jiu Taiwan" (One, two, three, save Taiwan), editorial, *World Journal*, 24 November 2000, p. A2.

34. Xiao Wei, "Cong minyi diaocha kan meiguoren dui liangan de guannian" (Polling American views on China and Taiwan), *World Journal*, 12 November 2000, pp. 24–25.

35. "Xinzongtong jiang liaojie tongqing Taiwan yao fu daijia" (The new president will learn that there is a cost for being sympathetic to Taiwan), news report, *World Journal*, 14 November 2000, p. A3.

36. "One Two Three, Save Taiwan," p. A2.

37. See *United Daily News*, 20 October 2000; "Liangan dongtai de weichi xianzhuang de xuhuan yu shiji" (Fantasy and reality for retaining the status quo between Mainland and Taiwan), editorial, *World Journal*, 11 October 2000, p. A2.

38. *World Journal*, 13 November 2000; "Zhonggong duitai zhengce mianlin xin zhuanzhe" (Communist China's Taiwan policy is facing a turning point), *World Journal*, 20 November 2000, p. A2.

39. Editorial, *United Daily News*, 21 February 2001.

40. "Cong Li Yuanzhe jianghua kan taidu lunshu the pohui" (Yuan Tze Lee's speech: Taiwan independence argument loses ground), editorial, *World Journal*, 7 September 2000, p. A2.

41. "One, Two, Three, Save Taiwan," p. A2.

42. "Shuangshijie, tantan haiwai de youguo xinqing" (Concern for the motherland on the double ten holiday), editorial, *World Journal*, 10 October 2000, p. A2.

43. "Zhengzhijia buyi wajing guantian" (Politicians should not view the world from the bottom of a well), editorial, *World Journal*, 30 October 2000, p. A2.

44. "Zhongwen yiyin de ji zhuanwan: zhuanye yiti you yancheng zhengzhi wenti" (A shift in Chinese romanization: another politicization of an academic topic), editorial, *United Daily News*, 9 October 2000, p. 2; Huang Biduan, "Yong sheme pinyin xitong haiyao chao ma?" (Why should we fight over pinyin systems?), *United Daily News*, 15 October 2000, p. 4, "Weibei zhuanye he chengxu: xinzhengfu ji pinyinan gao geming" (Against academic interest and procedures: is the new government using pinyin to start a revolution?) *United Daily News*, editorial, 30 November 2000, p. A2.

45. See essays under "Dajia tan: lianqing xiangzheng libiguan" (Readers' forum: pros and cons of celebrating two national holidays), *World Journal*, 8 October 2000, p. A13.

46. Yu Jianhong, "Liangan guanxi zhubu zhuanbian wei renmin neibu maodun" (Mainland-Taiwan relationship is transformed into differences among the people), *World Journal*, 15 February 2001, p. A7. See also discussions on 1 October 2000.

47. *World Journal*, 1 October 2000, "Liangan dangzhengzhe buyao rang Jin Dazhong zhuanmei yuqian" (Mainland and Taiwan leaders should not let Kim Dae Jung steal the show), editorial, 14 October 2000, p. A2.

48. "Asian American Group Seeks to Flex Political Muscle," *Los Angeles Times*, 27 August 2000, p. B1.

49. "Asian Group Backs Gore for President," *Los Angeles Times*, 28 August 2000, p. B1.

50. Sam Chu Lin, "80–20 Initiative Endorses Al Gore," *AsianWeek*, 8 September 2000, p. 1.

51. "Endorsement: President of the United States," *AsianWeek*, 3 November 2000, p. 1.

52. Chen Shiyao, "Huayi yiti zhichi Gaore he qinan" (It is difficult to get all Chinese Americans to support Gore), *World Journal*, 17 September 2000, p. 4.

53. "Kelindun kunhuo, Gaoer dui li an yinyou huashuo" (Clinton confused, but Gore should say something about Wen Ho Lee), editorial, *World Journal*, 18 September 2000, p. A2.

54. "Huaren ying nuli ba bianyuanpiao biancheng guanjianpiao" (Chinese Americans should use minority votes to make a difference), editorial, *World Journal*, 15 October 2000, p. A2; "Daxuan bianlun bufen shengfu, yayi xuanpiao burong qingkan" (Election debate produces no winner, but Asian American votes should not be ignored), editorial, 19 October 2000, p. A2.

55. Yin, "Growing Influence of Chinese Americans," p. 333.

56. Campaign committees have analyzed opinions in these papers to pinpoint concerns and voting patterns of Chinese Americans. During the 1992 election, for instance, the Democratic Party asked the author to provide such information.

57. "Huayi wuda guanxin wenti: Gaoer Bushi geshu jijian" (Gore and Bush on five issues concerning Chinese Americans), news report, *World Journal*, 4 November 2000, p. 4; "Bushi tan liangan, lichang hen mingque" (Bush's position on Mainland and Taiwan is very clear), news analysis, 8 November 2000, p. A3. See also, "Al Gore on Our Issues," and "George W. Bush on Our Issues," *AsianWeek*, 20 October 2000, p. 1.

58. See essays in "Nanjia luntan" (Southern California forum), *World Journal*, 10 September 2000.

59. Liu Tian, "Huaren canzheng de liangtiaotui" (Foundations for Chinese American political participation), *World Journal*, 21 January 2001, p. 4.

60. Huang Jingping, "Kuai qingxing ba, taishang de meiren!" (Wake up, Taiwanese Americans!), *World Journal*, 15 October 2000, p. A4.

61. "Meiguo yanpan liangan qingshi quhuan dayou xuanji" (U.S. research indicates improvement of Mainland and Taiwan), *World Journal*, 12 December 2000, p. A2.

62. "Zongtong daxuan yihou de meiguo yu shijie" (The U.S. and the world after the presidential election), editorial; and "Xinzongtong jiang liaojie tongqing Taiwan yao fu daijia," (The new president will know the cost of being sympathetic to Taiwan), *World Journal*, 14 November 2000, p. A3. See also editorials on 7 January and 8 February 2001.

63. "Bushi zhengfu dui taimei guanxi de dingwei he yingxiang" (The position and impact of the Bush administration's U.S.–Taiwan relations), editorial, *World Journal*, 20 February 2001, p. A2. Similar discussions are found in 17 and 25 February issues of the paper.

64. Steven Mufson, "Confusion over Bush Remarks on Taiwan," *San Francisco Chronicle*, 26 April 2001, p. 1.

65. "Xiao Bushi zhuyi: duihua zhengce fangwei ketiao fangxiang bubian" (Bush's idea is some adjustment of China policy, but in the same direction), editorial, *World Journal*, 9 January 2001, p. A2.

# Part III

# Expanding Networks and Prospects for Transnational Cooperation

# 9

# Chinese American Business Networks and Trans-Pacific Economic Relations Since the 1970s

*Wellington K.K. Chan*

The U.S. Immigration Act of 1965, which opened a floodgate for immigrants from non-European countries, has been rightly celebrated for its kaleidoscopic impact on the social and cultural fabric of American life during the last third of the twentieth century. Equally transforming are the changes that these immigrants have brought to many areas of the U.S. economy. From the first days of European settlement, each new wave of immigrants has provided a rich supply of energizing entrepreneurs who dare new visions and create jobs and wealth. However, since they generally were poor and not highly educated, most of those who ultimately succeeded required years, or even a full generation, of toil before they could build up businesses or be accepted into the professions.

The 1965 reforms, supplemented by the Immigration and Nationality Act of 1990, have made a difference by bringing immigrants of all races from all the continents of the world to the United States. They also created new sets of rules that included special quotas for individuals with special skills and educational credentials and, since the late 1990s, even special immigrant visas for those possessing the ability to invest $1 million (later reduced to $500,000) in enterprises that would provide a minimum of ten new jobs.[1] These developments, when combined with the emergence of economically strong countries in East and Southeast Asia, have attracted a new type of immigrant from these regions. Newcomers are arriving not only with entrepreneurial and technical skills, but with personal means and transnational economic networks that have contributed to the growth of trade, the exchange of investments, and the interplay of technology. These developments, reflecting an increasingly global economy, raise important issues about changing relationships among immigration, trade, and economic development.

## The Arrival of Chinese Entrepreneurs

The largest group of Asian-Pacific immigrants has been ethnic Chinese from Hong Kong, Taiwan, and, since the late 1970s, from Southeast Asia and the People's Republic of China as well. Many of these immigrants started new enterprises by rekindling the business networks they had forged in their homelands. Others came first as students who, upon graduation or the completion of professional training, took advantage of the new immigration laws to stay on. They became doctors, lawyers, CPAs, architects, financial consultants, and real estate brokers as well as scientists, college professors, and computer engineers. Since less than 15 percent of the several hundred thousand students from Taiwan and Mainland China have returned home, these young men and women have constituted a major new source of human capital for the United States.[2]

The inflow of Chinese immigrants more or less doubled each decade. Between 1960 and 1995, the Chinese population in the United States increased from under 240,000 to over 2 million. Critical masses of Chinese Americans formed in three metropolitan areas—Los Angeles, San Francisco, and New York. According to the 1990 U.S. Census, the Chinese American population for Southern California's six counties, from Ventura to San Diego, reached 324,274 (Los Angeles County alone stood at 245,033); for Northern California's five Bay-area counties, from San Francisco to San Jose, it amounted to 315,345; and for the greater New York metropolitan area, it numbered 261,722. As more and more of the new immigrants skipped or left the traditional Chinatown ghettos and spread out into suburban communities, there were large increases of Chinese- and Chinese American-owned businesses that catered to local and domestic needs in goods and services. Many of the entrepreneurs who settled in these communities also built on their trans-Pacific networks and focused in the international arena.

The intertwining of relationships between transnational corporations from the homelands and immigrant entrepreneurs allowed the latter to break through the limitations of a traditional ethnic-based-niche market and move directly into mainstream national and international markets. In this way, they rapidly expanded their economic scope and scale.[3] From the late 1970s on, as the number of Chinese immigrants doubled while the national economy also grew rapidly through a communication revolution and the globalization of trade and services, the new immigrants took advantage of the situation and greatly expanded their economic activities. In this effort, a new marketing trend started since the mid-1970s by major U.S. corporations played into their hands. The new approach concentrated on marketing to specific segments of the population—most often ethnic groups—in order that each targeted group of consumers would build up emotional attachment to certain products or services because of identifiable ties with them.[4] Thus, many immigrants, after starting a business that sold goods or services that carried clear ethnic identity, managed to broaden their niche to include the mainstream national market. At the same time, they vigorously tapped into the growing trans-Pacific economy by building on the personal and cultural networks they already possessed.

Although not all of these immigrants were wealthy or well educated,[5] a great many of them arrived with considerable funds and other assets. While stories about the average Chinese immigrant family bringing assets of $200,000 are overdrawn, many did so—or brought in more. From the mid-1980s through the mid-1990s, the Taiwan government's foreign-exchange reserves grew from about $50 billion to over $95 billion—second-largest in the world after Japan's.[6] Thus, it allowed each resident to take up to $5 million a year out of Taiwan. There is no accurate estimate of the total amount of capital that has been transferred to the United States by ethnic Chinese immigrants; speculations range widely, from 2–3 billion dollars to around several billion dollars each year from the late 1970s to the early 1990s. According to a report from Taiwan's Ministry of Economic Affairs, $1.5 billion of Taiwan's capital wound up in the Los Angeles area alone each year between 1985 and 1990. Hong Kong bankers suggest that, during essentially the same years, roughly 100,000 Hong Kong emigrants took at least $3 billion in direct investments from Hong Kong to Vancouver, Canada.[7] Without question, the net transfer of Chinese capital into the United States during these years must have been extremely large. One measure of the size and importance of the combined impact is reflected in the 20 to 30 community banks funded and operated by ethnic Chinese in each of the three metropolitan regions of concentrated Chinese immigrants by 1990.[8]

During the early 1990s, as the U.S. economy slowed down, the inflow of Chinese capital investments from Hong Kong and Taiwan receded somewhat, for the great majority of their capital outflow went to Mainland China and contributed significantly to its rapid economic growth since then. However, a new source of funds—the China Mainland—likely more than made up for this retreat. Although the official figure regarding Mainland Chinese investments in the United States is relatively small—around $3 billion as late as 1998 or 1999—the amount of funds that Chinese exporters unofficially have retained in this country from their earnings is sizable.[9] Most likely, it amounts to tens of billions of dollars. This situation resulted from the tremendous growth in bilateral trade between the United States and China during the 1990s—from $20 billion to almost $100 billion annually. By the end of the decade, the United States had accumulated an annual deficit in the $60–70 billion range from the U.S.–China trade imbalance —its largest deficit with any trading partner.[10]

Many of the first arrivals following the 1965 immigration reforms had relatives or family members already in the United States who, as citizens, could sponsor them. They generally came from the working or lower-middle class and lacked college education or managerial experience in modern business. This group of immigrants gravitated toward established Chinatown settlements. When they engaged in retail business, it tended to be of the traditional type—small groceries selling Chinese goods, tourist gift shops, restaurants, laundries, and the like. The majority among this group did not possess sufficient independent resources to start their own businesses; they simply found employment within the ethnic community or in locations nearby.[11]

However, there was a second group among these early post-1965 immigrants. Their backgrounds varied widely—from those rejoining families to those with refugee status to business prospectors. What this group had in common was experience in or exposure to modern business of some kind. Since Hong Kong and Taiwan—the two places where most of these immigrants came from—were just experiencing the "economic take off" phase of development, with a heavy emphasis on manufacturing goods and exporting them to the United States as their largest market, many among this group found it natural to be involved in some form of entrepreneurial activity that would maintain, strengthen, or in some way reconnect ties with their old homeland. They set up trading companies in major ports of entry, such as New York, San Francisco, or Los Angeles, to facilitate import–export exchanges between North America and the western Pacific. Then, as they tried to expand, they turned to their newly acquired networks to approach local banks for loans and increased credit facilities. In Los Angeles, ready support often came from several Chinese American banks already established in the community—especially those that had senior officers and investors from Hong Kong or Taiwan and, therefore, were far better able than larger mainstream banks, such as the Bank of America, to judge operation and creditworthiness.[12] This kind of mutually beneficial relationship accounts for the rapid growth of Chinese American banks during the 1980s.

The same entrepreneurs also encouraged, or were encouraged by, their former employers back in Hong Kong or Taiwan to open U.S. branch offices where they could be rehired as officers. By the late 1970s, many Hong Kong and Taiwanese businesses, especially those in textiles and the fashion industry, responded by opening up U.S. offices and warehouses as distribution depots located closer to consumers in order to better understand their latest fads and consumption habits. Besides rehiring former employees who had become immigrants, they also began to send in their own staff from the home offices, many of whom made use of work visas to change to immigrant status themselves. The growth of this trans-Pacific movement among Chinese firms from East Asia brought with it new transfers of capital and credit facilities.[13] By the late 1970s, some of these companies began to recruit local partners, including nonethnic Chinese, and set up affiliate, independently incorporated, U.S. firms to trade with them. One example is Styl-land, Inc., which opened for business in downtown Los Angeles in 1978 after the majority owner from a large Hong Kong garment manufacturer recruited a successful non-Chinese merchandiser from May Department Store to be a junior partner and CEO. Styl-land successfully designed and marketed a new line of casual wear for U.S. teenagers and young adults under the PCH (Pacific Coast Highway) trademark. The Hong Kong partners benefited from the increased orders for their manufacturing plants in East Asia, while Styl-land was assured of stable sourcing at competitive prices. By the late 1980s, Styl-land's annual sales in North America reached $200 million.[14]

## Changing Patterns of Immigration and Their Impact on U.S.–China Business Relations in the 1980s

Two additional factors simultaneously affected the dynamics of change in U.S.–China business relations during the 1980s. First, an enterprising middle class with savings and modern consumption habits arose in Taiwan and Hong Kong. Second, there was a dramatic increase in immigration by members of this class who departed mainly out of a concern over prospects for political instability at home rather than because of economic insecurity. For Taiwanese, the defining moment came when the United States switched its recognition of the regime in Taiwan as China to the government of the People's Republic of China in 1979, closed down the U.S. Embassy in Taipei, and opened a new one in Beijing. For Hong Kongers, concerns over prospects of political insecurity arose at about the same time as the British and the Chinese governments began to discuss the future of the Territory. In 1984, these discussions led the British government to agree to the return of Hong Kong to Chinese sovereignty by the year 1997. In 1986, the U.S. government increased the immigrant quota for natives of Hong Kong from 600 to several thousand per year. Hong Kongers born in the China Mainland already could immigrate under the 20,000 annual quota assigned to China. After 1979,

Taiwanese acquired their own 20,000 quota.[15] In addition, after the fall of Saigon in 1975, many ethnic Chinese from Vietnam, Cambodia, and Laos who had once been part of the enterprising middle class in these countries began arduous voyages as "boat people" and political refugees. Many would successfully land in the United States as immigrants. Taken together, these events greatly increased the number of immigrant slots available for ethnic Chinese and altered the predominant immigrant type.

Most ethnic Chinese immigrants who arrived during the 1980s brought along substantial savings that could be used for investment purposes. The great majority of new arrivals came with their families. They often purchased a residential home within the first few years of arrival. In Southern California, helped by local real estate brokerage firms using Chinese agents, they made use of their wealth and/or professional credentials to skip Los Angeles's Chinatown and to locate their residences and businesses in middle-class and upper-middle-class suburban neighborhoods. This led many to congregate in suburban neighborhoods in the San Gabriel Valley—a relatively compact area of about 15 miles north-south by 25 miles east-west—just to the east of the city of Los Angeles. Between 1980 and 1990, their number grew exponentially to about 170,000, or almost 70 percent of all ethnic Chinese living in Los Angeles County. In several townships—such as Alhambra, San Gabriel, Rosemead, and Arcadia—the proportion of Chinese Americans rose from 3–6 percent to 21–26 percent. Some even settled directly in exclusive upper-class neighborhoods like San Marino; indeed, San Marino's excellent schools became a magnet for those who could afford the town's expensive homes. The number of ethnic Chinese in this township rose from 4 percent (433) to 26 percent (3,355) during this period. As for Monterey Park, ethnic Chinese residents, almost all recent immigrants, reached 35 percent and generated such a political impact that the city voted in its first Chinese American city council member and mayor by 1990.[16]

As their numbers rose, property ownership by Chinese Americans in these towns increased even more markedly. For instance, individuals with Asian family names owned 40 percent of the residential and business properties in San Gabriel and at least two-thirds of those in Monterey Park by around 1990, and ethnic Chinese made up the overwhelming majority of all Asians in the area. Most striking, in the entire Los Angeles County, where ethnic Chinese made up below 3 percent of the total population, 19 percent of the home buyers surveyed for the year 1992 had a Chinese family name.[17] Similar ownership numbers appeared in the San Francisco Bay area: a 1990 report indicated that an ethnic Chinese purchased one out of every four homes sold there.[18]

Many of these new arrivals found real estate investments particularly attractive because they possessed few U.S. business networks and little knowledge of local rules and practices. From residential properties, they tended to move to investments in commercial property—in condominiums, hotels, office buildings, shopping malls, and warehouses. This strategy allowed some immigrants to remain passive investors who simply collected rents that ensured a steady income for the family; they left the leasing, managing, and marketing of the property to a management company. Others, however, used such investments to supply work and income for the entire family, while learning the business at the same time. During the 1980s, many Taiwanese immigrants bought individual motels with accompanying franchises from such chains as Comfort Inn and Quality Inn and ran them as family businesses. Others purchased individual liquor stores, 7–Elevens, or fruit markets, and ran them by themselves. Those with larger financial resources as well as those who could successfully leverage their earlier purchases because they had appreciated in value invested in bigger acquisitions: apartment buildings or condominiums, shopping centers, industrial parks, and downtown office buildings.[19]

As the strong U.S. real estate market continued, other affluent Chinese in Hong Kong, Taiwan, and elsewhere in Asia found, like many wealthy Japanese investors in Japan, that because the market value of their real estate properties at home had skyrocketed, the prices of comparable real estate in major U.S. cities appeared inexpensive by comparison. In the 1980s, Hong Kong and Taiwan pursued a similar path to rapid economic growth that, together with Singapore and South Korea, won them the sobriquet "Four Mini-Dragons."[20] Unlike Japanese investors who represented huge enterprise groups and bought up landmark downtown buildings (e.g., the Arco Towers in Los Angeles), and trophy golf courses (e.g., Pebble Beach Golf Course in Monterey Peninsula, California) at outlandish prices, Chinese investors, who had fewer resources to work with, proved more discriminate and circumspect in their purchases. By the end of the 1980s, when it was estimated that Japanese had bought up half of downtown Los Angeles and significant parts of New York, Chinese buyers reportedly only had acquired 10 percent of downtown San Francisco. Their acquisitions included the remodeling as well as purchasing of high-rise office buildings located in the city's financial district, shopping malls, expensive homes on and around Lombard Street, and several hotels—such as the Park Lane, the Meridien, and the Parc 55. Similar activities occurred in other parts of the United States. Increasingly, they involved large Chinese institutional buyers. In 1988, for instance, Hong Kong's Kowloon Wharf group took over the Omni hotel chain for $135 million. This was followed by another Hong Kong group, New World Properties, which bought all 825 Ramada Inns for

$540 million.[21] Los Angeles provided another major area for Chinese real estate activity.[22]

However, the bulk of Chinese American commercial and industrial development did not involve major players. By the late 1980s, small investors were particularly active in acquiring properties in the San Gabriel Valley. According to a survey conducted by one major brokerage firm, Lee & Associates, half of the purchasers of industrial buildings in the 5,000 to 25,000 square-foot size range carried ethnic Chinese names.[23]

The emphasis on property ownership for homes and for business also is reflective of core cultural values among ethnic Chinese; acquiring equity in real estate provides the immigrant with a sense of economic security and of taking root in a new society. This investment strategy further reflects the fact that more and more Chinese Americans have involved themselves in other forms of commercial and professional activity that require work space. As the number of Chinese immigrants in the three metropolitan areas reached a critical mass by the early or mid-1980s, mushrooming businesses provided an important ethnic-niche market for new arrivals who needed all kinds of services. In the San Gabriel Valley alone, the number of ethnic Chinese-owned businesses jumped from less than 1,000 in the early 1980s to over 10,000 by the early 1990s. Their services ranged from real estate brokering, medical and hospital care, and financial consulting, to construction contracting, insurance, tax accounting, and legal assistance.[24]

Many of these businesses demanded professional training that was not easily transferable. For example, those in health care, legal, and accounting work required credentialing that differed from their home country. Thus, they had to undertake new learning and to pass entry exams before they could practice in the United States. Other types of service tried to reproduce the comfort and familiarity of the old home. These included all types of eateries, groceries, Chinese-language newspapers and bookstores, movie houses, hairstyle salons, nightclubs, and flower shops. Like good entrepreneurs everywhere, many would adapt their business to the new local conditions. For instance, traditional restaurants in New York or San Francisco used to serve Americanized Cantonese food. New ones turned to hiring chefs directly from Hong Kong, Taiwan, or Shanghai to prepare more authentic dishes based upon these and other regional cuisines. Some, like Yujean Kang's in West Hollywood and in Pasadena, would follow the trendy Californian practice of fusion cooking, and serve what is described by the *Zagat Survey* as "an 'eclectic' amalgam of Californian and Modern Chinese cooking."[25] Similarly, in new suburban communities, supermarkets selling a full range of Asian foods first supplemented, then dominated, old-style grocery stores that were typical of those in Chinatowns.

## Immigrant Firms and Strategies

The overwhelming majority of these immigrant companies are small or medium in scale—each one employing a dozen or fewer workers, many of whom are likely to be family members or kin-related. For instance, a recent survey conducted for these firms in the San Francisco area indicates that over 90 percent are family owned.[26] Chinese business enterprises are also typically family-managed sole proprietorships, partnerships, or corporations of rather informal organization—headed by a family patriarch who has total authority to make decisions after consultations with a small group of senior staff and is constrained only by considerations of reciprocal relationships and obligations with family members and business associates. The small to medium scale, together with a loose, nonbureaucratic yet centralized two-tiered hub-and-spokes type of management structure, allows the enterprise to alter course or goals nimbly and, thus, to respond rapidly to changes in the marketplace. Even the publicly traded large, multinational corporations or corporate groups that are now quite plentiful in East and Southeast Asia—and found occasionally in the United States—follow the same basic informal organizational structure at the top.[27] What makes ethnic Chinese businesses in the United States different from those in East Asia is that they quickly learned that, even with a critical mass of ethnic Chinese to form the basis for a niche market, they needed to expand to include the regional, national, and, more often than not, trans-Pacific market.

This strategy can be illustrated by the garment industry, which has provided work for a large number of the new immigrants in all three major metropolitan areas. In the 1970s, when Chinese women formed a major portion of new immigrants for the first time, garment factories, at first mainly found in districts located outside of Chinatown and owned by non-Chinese, became a major source of work for them. By the late 1970s, as more Chinese immigrants learned the business, many took advantage of the subcontracting system used by major manufacturers such as Levi Strauss to start simple assembly-style garment factories of their own inside Chinatowns. Often, their friends or family members who had similar experience in Hong Kong or elsewhere helped them to start and, then, to expand their operations. During the 1980s, many followed the example of white owners who sold off their old garment factories in order to move production offshore where labor costs were cheaper. Several made use of old connections in Hong Kong and China to set up factories in China itself, while they turned their U.S. operations toward designing, marketing, and distribution.[28] Some of these operations grew into major transnational corporations. One example is Bugle Boy Industries, Inc., of Simi Valley, California. A first-generation immigrant, William Mow, founded Bugle Boy in 1977. Its trendsetting youth jeans had become widely popular by the early 1980s. By using modern production systems (Mow was an engineer by training), moving production offshore to East Asia, and setting up dozens of retail outlets in addition to wholesaling to upscale boutiques, department stores, and low-priced warehouse chains like Wal-Mart, Bugle Boy's annual sales topped $500 million by the early 1990s.[29]

## The Value of Trans-Pacific Networks

Beginning in the late 1980s, two interrelated developments involving ethnic Chinese immigrants and entrepreneurship again underlined the importance of the rich and complex web of networking among numerous cousins and friends on both sides of the Pacific for U.S.–China relations. Thus far, we have been concerned with the transfer of capital, the growth of business enterprises, and the spirit of entrepreneurial talent brought into the United States by Chinese immigrants and transnational corporations from East and Southeast Asia. However, there also has been an important reverse flow as large numbers of highly trained and experienced Chinese and Chinese American business managers, engineers, and scientists have returned to their former home or ancestral land since around 1990 to set up or to manage offices, high-technology production facilities, and science parks. Even those who are engineers and scientists and do not manage business enterprises are, like the owners and the managers, truly entrepreneurs in the sense that they too innovate, produce new products, and create wealth. The second development has been the striking success of a large number of Chinese immigrants, including many of the same entrepreneurs who have engaged in the reverse flow, in high-tech industries of California's Silicon Valley.

Taiwan's success story, rising from being a center of low-wage, low-value-added production in the 1970s to become an emergent new epicenter for design, high-tech manufacturing, and science by the late 1980s, is well known. Around 1990, as its government was putting in place what became the successful Hsin Chu Science Park just outside of Taipei, and preparing to launch a National Development Plan that included infrastructural and scientific projects valued at some $300 billion, it realized that Taiwan needed far more senior scientists and engineers as well as experienced managers than it had on hand. In order to fill this need, the government undertook serious recruitment efforts among ethnic Chinese in the United States and elsewhere. Its campaign turned out to be highly successful: from the United States, which provided around 90 percent of all returnees with postgraduate degrees, some 1,500 returned in 1989, 2,800 in 1990, and 4,200 in 1993. The Chinese Engineering and Science Association of Southern California reported in 1994 that 100 out of its 600 members had returned to Taiwan. Among the nonscientists, many had 15 to 20 or more years of management experience with U.S. companies.[30] The campaign's success can be attributed partly to Taiwan's improved working conditions, housing, and monetary compensation as well as to the emotional pull of relatives and friends. The island also had just ended decades of authoritarian military rule. More crucial for many, however, the decision to return was prompted by the unsettling feeling that they had reached the so-called "glass ceiling" within their U.S. corporation, and that, as middle or even senior managers, they had little or no prospect of further promotion to the boardroom or to the top tier of management. These perceptions are supported by statistics that clearly show that relative to their numbers at the staff level, Asian American representation in the middle and senior management ranks is far smaller in corporate America in comparison with other ethnic and racial groups.[31] Furthermore, their educational and professional accomplishments would win them much higher social status in Taiwan than in the United States. Finally, during the early 1990s, many Chinese Americans also were affected by the general U.S. economic slowdown—especially by the loss of aerospace and defense-related research jobs.

These thousands of highly accomplished returnees, mostly U.S. citizens, did not, however, pull up their roots in the United States when they moved to Taiwan. Although some brought their entire families with them, less than 5 percent intended to make Taiwan their permanent home. The great majority left their spouses and children in the United States, to continue in whatever professions or schooling they had chosen. For those with children still in secondary school or college, concern over education has meant that their offspring stayed behind.[32] Thus, together with thousands of other workers and job seekers who have returned to Hong Kong, China, or other fast-growing economies in East and Southeast Asia, they came to be known as *taikong ren* ("astronauts"—a pun with two possible literal meanings, "space persons" and "wives emptied-out persons"). They are constantly flying across the Pacific, between their place of work and the home where the rest of their family lives.

By their peripatetic mode of living, what the returnees have accomplished is not a simple reverse flow of technology, managerial experience, or entrepreneurial spirit. It also is more than a better-late-than-never attempt to redress the old truism that emigrant societies suffer "brain drain" because they give away their best and brightest to the societies that take them in. What has been achieved is the constant recharging of personal networks across different economies and institutional cultures, the cross-pollination of ideas and ways of doing things, and the gaining of up-to-date knowledge of local conditions—markets, science, politics, pop culture, latest fashions, and so forth.

AnnaLee Saxenian, who has carefully studied these "new immigrant entre-preneurs" in the Silicon Valley, argues that by making such trans-Pacific linkages, they have created a "brain circulation" that energizes both techno-logical advancement and marketing growth.[33] These linkages are particu-larly useful for a global entrepreneurship that requires instant information across vast distances, sensitivity to different cultural and national norms and practices, the renewal of old friendships, and the making of new ones. These transnationalists serve as facilitators as well as managers. Those working strictly on high technology are not just teachers dispensing state-of-the-art science; they also learn from their co-workers who come from different schools and institutional frameworks. In the end, the interplay of ideas helps to advance their final products.

There is no better illustration of the critical roles that the returnees and other Chinese immigrants have played than their contribution to high-tech industries in the Silicon Valley of California. Between 1980 and 1999, eth-nic Chinese, almost all first-generation immigrants, founded 17 percent of the 11,443 high-tech firms in the Silicon Valley—including some 40 pub-licly traded firms such as Jerry Yang's Yahoo! Inc.[34] A survey conducted in 1990 on the ethnicity and immigration status of all the scientists and engi-neers working in the Valley found that 32 percent were immigrants and that the ethnic Chinese among them alone made up one-third, or 11 percent of the entire professional workforce. Most of this group had originally come from Taiwan in the 1980s as students seeking graduate degrees in science or engineering.[35] When some of the more experienced among them joined the returnees in the early 1990s, they were attracted by the prospect of building partnerships with local firms, setting up new production lines and R & D facilities, and establishing new business relations in order to sell their U.S.-designed products. These Valley entrepreneurs typically mobilized venture capital through their connections in Taiwan, Hong Kong, and parts of South-east Asia. Although much of their investment has been handled informally and through individual partnerships, it is safe to conclude that the total to date is in the billion-dollar range.[36]

The pace of Chinese participation in the Silicon Valley quickened in the 1990s as new graduates who originally had arrived from China swelled the ranks of immigrant scientists and professionals. From 1980 to 1984, Chinese immigrants were responsible for 9 percent of the startups there; by 1995–1998, they accounted for over 20 percent. In 1998, Chinese or Chinese Ameri-cans managed 2,001 firms, employed 41,684 workers, and ran up $13.2 billion in sales. They accounted for 17 percent of all owners in the Valley, 10 per-cent of all its workers, and 13.5 percent of total sales.[37] These are impressive numbers for an ethnic minority that makes up less than 1 percent of the national population. They achieved this position only because of (1) the timely contributions of Taiwanese as partners or business associates—relationships that allowed them to become a world-class powerhouse in making mega-chips; and (2) the return to Shanghai in recent years of Chinese professionals of Mainland origin who forged comparable linkages with their Valley operations. Like the Taiwan government, the PRC government now is lending support to these efforts.

At the same time, Taiwanese entrepreneurs have extended their high-tech operations to China. By mid-2001, they and their employees already had reshaped an entire township, Kunshan, 35 miles west of Shanghai, in an ongoing effort to turn it into a smaller Hsin Chu Science Park. More than 900 high-tech firms from Taiwan have pledged $5.4 billion in new capital to set up plants and various related infrastructure there.[38] Given the new and renewed multipolar networks that are being formed and strengthened in the Silicon Valley, Hsin Chu, and comparable parks in the Shanghai area, Chinese entrepreneurs will exert even greater influence over trade and technology interplay between the United States and East Asia in the future.

## Conclusion

Chinese immigrants who have entered the United States during the last third of the twentieth century have demonstrated that newcomers, by employing a spirit of enterprise, can create jobs, markets, and wealth and can further economic linkages across nations that benefit not just their own communities, but the global economy as well. Their achievements belie the often-stated argument that immigrants take away jobs or affect the economy adversely.

These particular Chinese immigrants, however, have not been pioneers in this regard. Their forebears who migrated to Southeast Asia from the fourteenth century on already had charted a long tradition of establishing networks and managing successful businesses. Since they had to deal with different national and ethnic groups, cross boundaries, and negotiate with various European imperial powers at different times or simultaneously, they also had to adapt their operations and their web of relationships in order to succeed internationally.[39] The efficacy of such a transnational network also has been strengthened by the interaction among ethnic Chinese who migrate and then settle in the various national communities—for this allows Chinese entrepreneurs to have an edge over others who lack citizenship and often do not have intimate knowledge of each region's market conditions or practice.[40]

The accomplishments of Chinese Americans augur well for the future success of other immigrant groups who wish to achieve mutually beneficial relationships between transmigration and the host-country economy, break out of the confines of their own ethnic or enclave economies, and become successful partners and actors in world trade and the global economy. Such efforts will be helped immensely by mainstream America's new appreciation for cultural pluralism and ethnic diversity in place of the old emphasis on assimilation. Attaining such goals requires people of goodwill and leaders who are sensitive to different national interests and cultural idiosyncrasies and who avoid ideological blinders.

However, it would be too simple to stereotype ethnic Chinese immigrants as successful entrepreneurs and facilitators of the new global economy. The Wen Ho Lee case shows that Chinese immigrant scientists who maintain professional contact with counterparts in China can be subject to unfair suspicion and prosecution for treason based on unsubstantiated allegations of espionage. Issues of national security also have intruded ominously on international trade as the increasingly complex global economy opens up arcane areas that invite unwarranted sanction and even official abuse. Thus, a 1999 congressional report issued by U.S. Representative Christopher Cox and his investigative committee declared that "as many as 3,000 Chinese government-owned firms could be acting as fronts for the Chinese PLA (People's Liberation Army)."[41] In 1997, Representatives Duncan Hunter and Randy Cunningham and Senator James Inhofe blocked an offer, made by the Chinese state–owned COSCO (China Ocean Shipping Company)—one of the world's largest commercial liners, which already carried one-fifth of the transshipped cargo between China and the United States—to lease an old and unused naval base at Long Beach, California, out of fear that it would serve as a springboard for acquiring sensitive technology, smuggling arms, and conducting other operations injurious to U.S. national security.[42] The persistence of such unfounded suspicions seriously constrains the ability of Chinese Americans to maximize their entrepreneurial talents and connections through trans-Pacific operations, and ultimately undermines U.S.–China trade relations.[43]

On the other hand, one can point to many promising developments for the future of U.S.-China economic relations. As China and Taiwan are poised to join the World Trade Organization and participate even more fully with the United States in enhancing economic globalization, deeper and more complex relations will arise between the three political entities—making any alternative to cooperation and peaceful coexistence almost beyond contemplation for all parties. The China market remains a huge and largely untapped opportunity for U.S. firms, and the United States has much to offer in return, whether in terms of its natural and human resources or its economic and technological strengths. In trans-Pacific cooperative endeavors, networked Chinese American entrepreneurs will play a major role in facilitating business exchanges that benefit both sides.

## Notes

1. Bill Ong Hing, *Making and Remaking Asian America through Immigration Policy, 1850–1990* (Stanford: Stanford University Press, 1993); Ashley Dunn, "$1-Million Visas Seeking to Lure the Wealthy to U.S.," *Los Angeles Times*, 21 July 1991, pp. A1, 22–23.

2. Karl Schoenberger, "Breathing Life into the Southland," *Los Angeles Times*, 4 October 1993, pp. A1, 18, 19.

3. See Roger Waldinger, Howard Aldrich, and Robin Ward, *Ethnic Entrepreneurs* (Newbury Park: Sage, 1990). Much of the sociological literature on this subject, however, locates such entrepreneurs inside their enclaves, unable to break into mainstream markets. See, for instance, Alejandro Portes, ed., *The Economic Sociology of Immigration: Essays on Networks, Ethnicity and Entrepreneurship* (New York: Russell Sage, 1995). Until the mid-1970s, the Chinese American economy was largely a traditional enclave economy centered in the various Chinatowns.

4. Marilyn Halter, *Shopping for Identity: The Marketing of Ethnicity* (New York: Schocken Books, 2000), pp. 3–24.

5. Indeed, a 1990 survey showed that in the six core counties of Southern California, 15 percent of Chinese American families lived below the poverty level. See Paul Ong and Suzanne J. Hee, "Economic Diversity," in *The State of Asian Pacific America: Economic Diversity, Issues & Policies—A Public Policy Report*, ed. by Paul Ong (Los Angeles: Leadership Education for Asian Pacifics and Asian American Studies Center, UCLA, 1994), p. 34; Nancy Rivera Brooks, "Study of Asians in U.S. Finds Many Struggling," *Los Angeles Times*, 19 May 1994, p. A1. On issues of social polarization due to income disparities, see Xiao-huang Yin, *Chinese American Literature Since the 1850s* (Urbana and Chicago: University of Illinois Press, 2000), pp. 194–205.

6. The specific figures for Taiwan's foreign exchange reserves were $48.5 billion in 1986 and $95.6 billion in 1995. See World Bank, *World Development Report, 1988* (New York: Oxford University Press, 1988), p. 250, and World Bank, *World Development Report, 1997* (New York: Oxford University Press, 1997), p. 244.

7. Robert W. Gibson, "Networks of Chinese Rim Pacific," *Los Angeles Times*, 22 July 1990, pp. A1, 26, 27; Joel Kotkin and Yoriko Kishimoto, *The Third Century: America's Resurgence in the Asian Era* (New York: Crown, 1988), pp. 125–133. One public record that provides some sense of the total size of one segment of Chinese capital in the United States and its rapid rise during the late 1980s is the officially recorded holdings of U.S. stocks and other financial papers held by Hong Kong, Taiwan, and Singapore buyers. In 1984, these stood at $32.4 billion. By 1988, they more than doubled to $74.7 billion (see Gibson, "Networks of Chinese Rim Pacific"). While most of this amount represents investments by foreign Chinese individuals, corporations, and public institutions, many of these investors have migrated into or established businesses in the United States.

8. Joel Kotkin, *Tribes: How Race, Religion, and Identity Determine Success in the New Global Economy* (New York: Random House, 1993), pp. 165–200; Bernard Wong, *Ethnicity and Entrepreneurship: The New Chinese Immigrant in the San Francisco Bay Area* (Boston: Allyn and Bacon, 1998), pp. 39–40.

9. From Associated Press, "Stability Concerns Spark China's 'Capital Flight,' " *Los Angeles Times*, 16 December 1991, p. D7.

10. Evelyn Iritani, "Chinese in U.S. Shape Economy," *Los Angeles Times*, 17 October 1999, pp. A1, 22.

11. Wong, *Ethnicity and Entrepreneurship*, pp. 29–58.

12. Douglas Frantz, "New Banks Take Asian Customers into Account," *Los Angeles Times*, 9 November 1987, pp. IV 1, 2.

13. John Kao, "The Worldwide Web of Chinese Business," *Harvard Business Review* 71, No. 2 (March–April 1993): 24–36.

14. Interview with Steve Hogen, CEO of Styl-land, Inc., 10 November 1990, in Cerritos, California.

15. Luciano Mangiafico, *Contemporary American Immigrants* (New York: Praeger, 1988), pp. 118, 122–123.

16. Wellington K.K. Chan, "Chinese American Entrepreneurs Thrive in the [San Gabriel] Valley," *San Gabriel Business Journal* 2, No. 12 (1994): 15–16; Denise Hamilton, "A Patchwork of Ethnicity: The Changing Face of the San Gabriel Valley," *Los Angeles Times*, 25 December 1992, pp. J1, 4; Lee Romney, "Banker's Appointment to [San Gabriel] City Posts Signal Change for Asian Americans," *Los Angeles Times*, 4 November 1993, p. J1; Seth Mydans, "Asian Investors Create a Pocket of Prosperity: California Valley Avoids Region's Slide," *New York Times*, 17 October 1994, p. A8; Mark Arax, "Monterey Park: Nation's 1st Suburban Chinatown," *Los Angeles Times*, 6 April 1987; Timothy Fong, *Monterey Park: The First Suburban Chinatown* (Philadelphia: Temple University Press, 1994).

17. Schoenberger, "Breathing Life into Southland," p. A18.

18. Wong, *Ethnicity and Entrepreneurship*, p. 100.

19. Ibid., pp. 41–63, 100–101.

20. See Ezra F. Vogel, *The Four Little Dragons: The Spread of Industrialization in East Asia* (Cambridge: Harvard University Press, 1991).

21. Wong, *Ethnicity and Entrepreneurship*, pp. 89–92, 100–101; Gibson, "Networks of Chinese Rim Pacific."

22. Lilly V. Lee, a particularly successful real estate broker who worked out of her Beverly Hills office, began syndicating large land deals and major buildings to Chinese individuals in the late 1970s. Similarly, by 1977, an aggressive Chinese developer, Frederic Hsieh, served notice to the city leaders of Monterey Park that he was buying up as much property in the city as he could find, and predicted to a member of the city's Planning Commission that "Monterey Park was going to become the next Chinatown." See Myrna Oliver, "Businesswoman, Cultural Leader Lilly Lee Dies at 70," *Los Angeles Times*, 23 August 2000, pp. B1, 6; and Arax, "Monterey Park: Nation's 1st Suburban Chinatown."

23. Interview with Stephen Shatafian, vice president of Lee & Associates, 30 June 1993, in City of Industry, California.

24. Chan, "Chinese American Entrepreneurs Thrive in the [San Gabriel] Valley."

25. *Zagat Survey: 1998 Los Angeles/So. California Restaurants* (New York: Zagat Survey, LLC, 1998), p. 132.

26. Wong, *Ethnicity and Entrepreneurship*, p. 66.

27. Wellington K.K. Chan, "Tradition and Change in the Chinese Business Enterprise: The Family Firm Past and Present," *Chinese Studies in History* 31, Nos. 3–4 (1998): 127–144.

28. Wong, *Ethnicity and Entrepreneurship*, pp. 50–54.

29. Marla Dickerson and Abigail Goldman, "Bugle Boy Sinks Under Heavy Debt," *Los Angeles Times*, 2 February 2001, p. C1.

30. Mark Kendall, "Chinese Rediscover their Homeland: Some [San Gabriel] Valley Asians Return to Taiwan," *Pasadena Star News*, 1 February 1994, pp. A1, 4; Lee

Romney, "Homeland Beckons for Many Taiwanese," *Los Angeles Times*, 18 July 1993, pp. J1, 3; Andrea Chen, "Overseas Chinese Search for Fortune in East," *Free China Journal*, 23 October 1998, p. 7.

31. There is an extensive literature on the "glass ceiling." For purposes of the discussion here, see Paul Ong and Evelyn Blumenberg, "Scientists and Engineers"; and Ong and Hee, "Economic Diversity," *The State of Asian Pacific America: Economic Diversity*, pp. 177–183, 37–42. Also see AnnaLee Saxenian, *Silicon Valley's New Immigrant Entrepreneurs* (San Francisco: Public Policy Institute of California, 1999), pp. 18–20.

32. Romney, "Homeland Beckons for Many Taiwanese."

33. Saxenian, *Silicon Valley*, pp. vi, 9–26.

34. Ibid., p. 23.

35. Ibid., pp. 13–14.

36. Ibid., pp. 51, 61; Karl Schoenberger, "Networking Pays Off for Chinese," *Los Angeles Times*, 6 April 1994, p. A1.

37. Saxenian, *Silicon Valley*, pp. 23, 13–14.

38. Evelyn Iritani, "Chinese in U.S. Shape Economy," pp. A1, 22; "Kunshan: China's New Silicon," *The Economist*, 28 July–3 August 2001, p. 44.

39. Wellington K.K. Chan, "Chinese Business Networking and the Pacific Rim: The Family Firm's Roles Past and Present," *Journal of American–East Asian Relations* 1, No. 2 (1992): 171–190.

40. World Bank, *Entering the 21st Century: World Development Report 1999/2000* (New York: Oxford University Press, 2000), p. 40; Frankie Fook-Lun Leung, "Overseas Chinese Management: Myths and Realities," *East Asian Executive Reports*, 15 February 1995, pp. 6, 12–13.

41. Christopher Cox, Chairman of the U.S. Congressional Select Committee, *Report of the Select Committee on U.S. National Security and Military/Commercial Concerns with the P.R.C.* (Washington, D.C.: U.S. Government Printing Office, 1999), Vol. 3, p. 21.

42. Evelyn Iritani, "In Silicon Valley, China's Brightest Draw Suspicion," *Los Angeles Times*, 18 October 1999, pp. A1, 19.

43. Lars-Erik Nelson, "Washington: The Yellow Peril," *New York Review*, 15 July 1999, pp. 6–10.

# —— 10 ——

# A Neglected Minority in a Neglected Field

## The Emerging Role of Chinese American Philanthropy in U.S.–China Relations

*John J. Deeney*

Chinese American philanthropy has played an important role in ameliorating U.S.–China relations as well as in developing the respective civil societies. In this chapter, I address the relationship between civil society and philanthropy. I also describe, in considerable detail, the nature of Chinese philanthropy; assess the Chinese American community's giving patterns and their impact on U.S.–China relations; and conclude with some recommendations about how electronification of the traditional Chinese "bamboo network" can provide greater benefits all around through the world of e-philanthropy. Since Chinese American philanthropy is a relatively new field and not a great deal has been written on the subject, I have attempted to survey virtually all the published and unpublished literature.

### Philanthropy and Civil Society

Society conventionally is divided into the government, business, and not-for-profit sectors. Among Chinese Americans, the third sector is an important, but less studied, complement to the development of political, commercial, and cultural relations between the United States and China. While the nonprofit sector can never match the enormous sums of money that governments or the corporate world spend on developing societies, it can be a life-sustaining spirit and leavening conscience in the body politic. Perhaps the most compelling reason to support an increasing role for the not-for-profit sector around the world is the fact that many governments have been drastically cutting back their support for education and social welfare. Thus, the nonprofit sector—whether it be individual philanthropists and volunteers or well-organized foundations—is subject to increasing pressure to assume a greater role.

Philanthropy is understood here both in its conventional sense of charitable giving through the fundraising efforts of various individuals/groups and special foundations as well as in its broader sense of volunteering one's time and talents to benefit society. Although advocacy groups certainly have an important role to play in U.S.–China relations, this requires a special kind of skill and sensitivity. Given the political and commercial tensions that often exist between the United States and the People's Republic of China, constructive philanthropic activities can offer the most effective vehicle for bringing about mutually beneficial outcomes.

## Focal Points

In referring to U.S.–China relations and the role of Chinese American philanthropy in that relationship, Mainland China is the primary (although not exclusive) focus.[1] Since the main emphasis of this chapter is on how Chinese Americans relate to their respective ancestral lands (the China Mainland, Hong Kong, or Taiwan, etc.), the common ground of their traditional Chinese cultural heritage is most important when it comes to understanding their philanthropic activities. More specifically, this chapter takes most of its examples from the world of education.

Most Chinese Americans considered in this review either are American-born Chinese (ABCs) or Chinese immigrants who have become, or are in the process of becoming, U.S. citizens. While aspects of the cultural identity issue lie outside the scope of this chapter, they motivate many Chinese American philanthropists to be doubly generous—out of respect for both their Chinese ancestry as well as their adopted country.[2]

Another oft-neglected issue requires passing attention—the vast differences that exist among Chinese Americans in their knowledge of China. Understanding of traditional—or even contemporary—Chinese culture as well as having a command of spoken Mandarin, to say nothing of reading/writing ability, varies enormously. While this chapter supports the idea that Chinese Americans potentially are our best and most expansive bridge to improving relations with China, it is with the caveat that Chinese physical features do not necessarily guarantee immediate rapport and acceptance. In fact, in the presence of language/cultural deficiencies—to say nothing of political differences and sensitivities—overtures can be counter-productive. In looking for maximum philanthropic results, however, we are presuming that the "ideal" Chinese American has a relatively advanced degree of multi-linguistic/cultural skills at his/her command as well as interest in China.[3] Certainly, Chinese Americans have the economic wherewithal to make their presence felt since their median family income is approximately 20 percent higher than the national level and their average age is only 32.1.[4]

## Chinese American Giving: Historic Stereotypes and Current Prospects

The past century has not been kind to Chinese. A number of twentieth-century events generated huge population flows of refugees and exiles. For many Chinese immigrants, the nagging issue of mixed political loyalties and cultural allegiances to their respective homelands vis-à-vis their lives in the United States has been a constant source of unresolved anxiety and aggravation. Although a new stereotypical image has emerged on the scene of the well-educated, entrepreneurially sophisticated, technologically adept, more politically engaged Chinese American who lives on an income above the national median, many "uptown" Chinese Americans would add: "Oh yes, we have come a long way: from the bottom of the mine shaft to the 'glass ceiling.' "

In any event, Asian-Pacific Islanders (API) are the fastest growing population group in the United States (11.9 million), and Chinese are the largest ethnic group (over 2.8 million) within the API. The API population presently constitutes about 4 percent of the total U.S. population, but projections suggest that it will grow to 37.6 million and constitute 9 percent of the total by the year 2050. U.S. businesses owned by this group increased 56 percent between 1987 and 1992 (from 386,291 to 603,426)—with receipts generated by these businesses increasing 163 percent, from $36.5 billion to $96.0 billion. Among the API population, persons of Chinese origin owned the most U.S. firms in 1992 (153,096).[5] The fact that the vast majority of Chinese are located in two of the most influential states—California and New York—renders them a relatively easy ethnic group to target for nonprofit philanthropic endeavors (or marketing purposes).[6]

Notwithstanding a fair amount of continued stereotyping and negative publicity, Chinese Americans have made important contributions in virtually every area of U.S. society.[7] The prevailing attitude regarding Chinese Americans and philanthropy is based on mixed perceptions. On the one hand, there is a grudging acknowledgment of their hard-earned prosperity. This is offset by an uninformed bias that they are "selfish and clannish." Although little research has been undertaken on their giving patterns, "the prevalent presumption is that Chinese Americans lack a philanthropic spirit, that they are takers and not givers. For the most part, these misguided perceptions feed on historical stereotypes rather than contemporary facts."[8]

In assessing Chinese American philanthropy, it is important to recognize that contributions to many mainstream causes occur in a distinctively Chinese style. The practice of giving may not be referred to as philanthropy or volunteerism by Chinese Americans. Their tradition of sharing takes many informal forms—which often are simply referred to as "community work." Jessica Chao, a founding board member of Asian Americans and Pacific Islanders in Philanthropy, points out:

> Because most indigenous Asian-American philanthropy never passes through the normal radar of philanthropic activity in this country, many assume that interest and participation in civic and community welfare does not exist within these communities. Nothing could be further from the truth. Isolated from, or shut out of, the established community structure of the majority culture, Asian Americans create, support and participate in myriad parallel nonprofit structures. They give enormous amounts of time, skills and money to build these organizations. The obligation to help others is so ingrained in Asian-American cultures that many do not see gifts of money and time as philanthropy or describe their impulses to assist others as "generosity."[9]

In support of this assessment, Elaine Ko and Danny Howe found that Asian Americans in Seattle provided about 21 percent of their donations directly to Asian American nonprofit groups and the rest to religious causes and general nonprofit organizations. In addition, two-thirds did volunteer work for nonprofits and three-quarters served as board members of these organizations.[10]

Given these known giving patterns, the presentation set forth in this chapter will be comparative/contrastive. That is, similarities between the U.S. and Chinese understanding of philanthropy are explored while important differences simultaneously are investigated in order to identify specific Chinese American features and, therefore, to promote understanding and mutual learning.

## The Nature of Chinese American Philanthropy

Chinese American philanthropy is a continuing part of a centuries-old tradition of providing for the needy. The constant among the most important traditional values that continue to influence Chinese American giving is the overriding Confucian concept of *ren*—or benevolence, charity, love, and humaneness. The key Confucian ideal virtue of *ren* is reinforced by religious Buddhism (particularly by Guan Yin, the compassionate Goddess of Mercy) and the Taoist view about how all things, human and natural, are reciprocally related.

After stating that "the Asian American culture of giving [is] . . . an integral part of everyday life," Stella Shao explains that "philanthropy as such is not considered a separate and categorical concept. Asians give because of their understanding that benevolence, compassion, interdependence, and basic respect for humankind are necessary ingredients to living, first in their families, then in their own ethnic communities, and then in the greater society."[11] In the words of Robert Lee, "here we have the idea of corporate personality, not an isolated, insular self, but rather an ethos of interdependence."[12] This rather abstract notion of *ren* exhibits certain concrete characteristics that have served, in practice, to define four peculiarly Chinese ways of engaging in philanthropy: (1) *private* vs. public; (2) *personal* vs. professional; (3) *small* vs. large; and, (4) *networked* vs. independent.

### Private vs. Public

In most cases of genuine philanthropy, Chinese benefactors prefer to keep their generosity as a private matter, and shun publicity. Part of this tendency undoubtedly is due to their quiet deference and cautious reserve. Most Chinese are taught as children not to call attention to themselves and to remain apart from strangers, not to be too assertive or to take too much initiative. Most wealthy Chinese immigrants consider it unbecoming to flaunt their riches, for they do not want to call too much attention to themselves by excessive public display or media coverage.

In addition, public disclosure of one's assets invites trouble, not only from thieves and kidnappers, but from being hounded by others for numerous donations—to say nothing of zealous tax collectors. This does not mean that Chinese donors are indifferent to having their gifts recognized, as many buildings named after them amply testify. In fact, they rather expect recipients of their benefactions to keep in touch with them and to give indications regarding how their gifts are being utilized and appreciated. Furthermore, Joanne Scanlon, senior vice president of the Council of Foundations, reports that "Asian donors sometimes give to and volunteer as board members with mainstream nonprofit organizations in order to widen their social and business contacts. Involvement with renowned organizations also announces to the greater society that these donors are very successful."[13]

There is a preference, however, for appeals that are made by a friend, an acquaintance at work, or a family member—especially if these people occupy leadership positions and will invite one into their circle of wealthy and influential colleagues. This approach also is partly due to the common practice among Chinese Americans of donating to the chosen causes of friends who gave to one's own favorite causes—another example of the obligation of reciprocal giving.

Generally speaking, therefore, Chinese Americans take their philanthropy personally and often are emotionally engaged as well as willing to volunteer their own time for special causes. There is an informal group of Chinese American doctors and dentists in Pittsburgh, for instance, who have quietly teamed up to conduct periodic seminars and workshops in various hospitals and dental schools in China—introducing the latest techniques and demonstrating state-of-the-art equipment, much of which they carry with them. They do not do this as members of their respective associations, but in a private and personal way—to establish a new kind of rapport with the country of their ancestors.

### Personal vs. Professional

Closely related to the Chinese penchant for keeping things private is the notion of the personal. The Chinese pattern of giving usually is transacted in a personalistic or familial manner rather than through a separate organization with a professional staff. The maxim, "charity begins at home," although common to virtually all cultures, has a peculiarly Chinese force to it because of the traditional emphasis on the family unit in China. This emphasis easily extends itself to institutions that support the family spirit, such as schools and churches or temples. One outcome of the emphasis on family-centered living is that "it is customary during Chinese banquets following weddings, birthdays, child birth, anniversaries, funerals, or special celebrations, to mark the occasion with public announcements of donations to the family association, the Chinese hospital, or to one's favorite charitable organizations."[14]

Another time-honored consideration related both to the private and personal is at work among Chinese Americans. Ties of friendship and respect are all important; once they have been established, then personal trust counts more than anything else. Hence, many generous Chinese prefer that solicitations be made through family members or close friends rather than through impersonal direct mailings. They also generally eschew formal applications, detailed reports, and accounting details as tedious, unnecessarily complex, and time-consuming, and much prefer a more informal approach. Unless there is a major donation involved, once the gift is given, there is little, if any, follow-up expected or required.[15]

### Small vs. Large

The emphasis in the mainstream form of organized philanthropy is on extending numerous requests and following up. A large number of people serve on grant-making boards, or as staff who publicize mission statements and guidelines, screen and maintain records regarding sizable numbers of grant-seekers, and attend to the time-consuming accounting procedures and paper-work required to assure transparency and comply with tax laws. In contrast, most Chinese American foundations are deliberately kept small and possess few administrative resources or staff members to handle large numbers of inquiries or applications. According to Lee, "by mainstream standards, Chinese American foundations are quite small. The three largest have assets of $6.5, $6, and $5.87 million and ten others range from $1 to 4.5 million."[16] Of course, a trade-off is involved in staying small; such an approach does not attract large donors to support one's causes.

### Networked vs. Independent

What distinguishes U.S.-style independence from Chinese networking is summed up by the term *guanxi*—literally, relationships or connections. This concept is an extension of the friendship, trust, and obligation that comes from strong family unity. Indeed, Gary Hamilton maintains that Chinese society consists of "institutionalized webs of social relationships that identify people to whom participants in those networks are personally obligated."[17] There is no question about the importance of *guanxi* in successful fundraising.

### Chinese American Giving Patterns and U.S.–China Relations

The spontaneous outpouring of generosity on the part of Chinese Americans for disaster relief in the many tragic wars, floods, famines, earthquakes, and so forth, that have plagued their homelands and other countries is impressive. For instance, Lee cites specific examples where the Chinese American community of San Francisco contributed generously, not only to the victims of the deadly Yunnan earthquake (1988), but also to those devastated by the Mexico City earthquake (1985) and, closer to home, to quake relief in the 1989 San Francisco disaster—even though it left Chinatown virtually unscathed. He quotes a Salvation Army spokesman who remarked that "even though they may not have much themselves, . . . refugees donated because they know what it is like to be homeless and to lose everything."[18]

Education is another area that consistently receives an immense amount of support from Chinese Americans. Many Chinese donors want to acknowledge in some tangible way the institutions that contributed to their success. This should not come as a surprise, for China has been a literati culture for over two millennia and has always valued humanistic education. For centuries, the civil-service examination system (much of it based on the classics and literary texts) assured the government of a constant supply of elite officials to run all aspects of the vast bureaucracy. Moreover, inexperienced immigrants in the United States often invited distinguished scholarly types to serve as officials in early Chinatown associations because they assumed that the prestige attached to their civil-service examination degrees (more or less equivalent to Western master's or doctoral degrees), would be useful in economic, legal, and political disputes.

Chinese American giving patterns fall into four general categories: (1) individuals; (2) associations; (3) foundations; and (4) a variety of others (nonprofit charitable organizations, professional associations, social organizations, and a host of religious groups). The sections below select a few examples from each category, usually concentrating on education, to illustrate the impact of Chinese American philanthropy on U.S.–China relations.

### Individuals

One of the earliest examples of Chinese American philanthropy in the favored area of promoting education involves Yung Wing (Rong Hong, 1824–1912), a graduate of Yale College in 1854. He was probably the first Chinese and also the first Asian to become a naturalized citizen and the first to receive a U.S. college degree (incidentally winning two English composition competitions). He was a pioneer in sending 120 Chinese students to the United States from 1872 to 1875, primarily to master Western technology in order to help modernize China. The students, who ranged from 12 to 16 years of age, spent a full year preparing in China and expected to stay in the United States for fifteen years. However, when the U.S. government passed the exclusion act, these students returned to China and few arrived again until— with funds supplied by the Boxer Indemnity—after 1908. Although the U.S. government revoked Yung Wing's citizenship in the 1880s after the passage of legislation forbidding the naturalization of Chinese, he managed to return to the United States where he wrote his autobiography.[19]

An even more touching example involves Dean Lung, an immigrant to America employed as a domestic by General Horace W. Carpentier. Carpentier, a Columbia University graduate, was as irascible as he was generous. Once, when drunk, he beat his servant into unconsciousness. The general subsequently asked Dean Lung what he could do for him as an expression of gratitude for his years of patient and faithful service. According to author S.W. Kung, Lung replied "you pay me for my service. I desire for myself nothing more. But United States people know little about Chinese culture and philosophy. Could you do something about that?" Kung adds:

> General Carpenter [sic], deeply moved by the unique request, arranged with Columbia, and then gave an extremely large contribution to establish

the Chinese department and library. It is still recognized as one of the best Chinese foundations in the country. What was even more astounding was the gift of $12,000 from Dean Lung himself, representing his entire savings from his many years' labor.[20]

Columbia proceeded to establish a Chinese department and the Dean Lung Professorship of Chinese Studies.

In recent years, although any number of Chinese American philanthropists could be cited,[21] it would be hard to match Wang An, the founder of Wang Laboratories, whose personal wealth, estimated at $1.5 billion dollars in 1984, made him the fifth richest man in the United States. He started with $600 in savings to begin a company that grew into a $3 billion corporation and held forty patents in computer technology. Wang made generous gifts to his alma mater, Harvard University, through the John King Fairbank Center for East Asian Research, and, after his death in 1990, the family foundation gave a $4 million gift to the Boston Metropolitan Center that rescued it from bankruptcy. The concluding words of the chapter devoted to Wang An in James Joseph's *Remaking America* are a fitting tribute:

> On the jacket of Wang's autobiography, a *Wall Street Journal* quote describes him as "an industry phenomenon who combines the charity of a Rockefeller . . . with the public relations savvy of an Iacocca." Through all his success and fame, An Wang remained committed to the Confucian idea that humanity without benevolence invites its own destruction.[22]

Among contemporary Chinese American philanthropists who have contributed to education both in the United States and in China, the most well known is Charles B. Wang, founder and chairman of Computer Associates International, Inc.—the world's leading business software company with a net worth estimated at $25 billion. In 1996, he provided a $20 million donation to create an Asian American cultural center at the State University of New York–Stony Brook. In addition, in 1999, he gave $10 million for the famous "Smile Train" in his native China. The train will carry medical staff, equipment, and supplies to provide surgery for about 100,000 poor, disfigured children over a five-year period. In 1999, Wang also donated $5 million in funding and technology for the new headquarters of the National Center for Missing and Exploited Children (whose website receives over 2 million hits per day). Finally, he was one of the underwriters for the August 1999 PBS production of *The Chinese Americans*, which explores cultural history in a televised "family album"—with personal recollections by such celebrities as I.M. Pei (architect), David Ho (AIDS researcher and 1996 *Time* Man of the Year), Connie Chung (TV journalist), Martin Yan (chef), and David Henry Hwang (playwright).[23]

The total amount of contributions by individual Chinese Americans to the PRC are incalculable. Lee reports that the San Francisco Chinese Consulate's best estimate is that since normalization,

> Over 100,000 Chinese Americans have donated funds to support schools, day-care centers, orphanages, hospitals, clinics and libraries in the Toishan [Taishan] area alone. Over 200 new schools have been established with funds from Chinese Americans. The Consulate officer, who responded to queries, is from the Toishan area. He reports that the total amount of funds donated by Chinese Americans is approximately $3 million dollars. The largest gift by an individual, as reported in the local Chinese language press, was Stephen Lee's $400,000 to construct a school which is equipped with computer learning equipment in Toishan. Another large gift was from a group banded together to raise $150,000 to erect a television station in Toishan City.[24]

In addition, many Chinese American entrepreneurs who invest heavily in China are motivated by altruism to make individual contributions. Some are immigrants themselves, like Charles B. Wang, or descendents of immigrants who are eager to give something back to the sending land. They carry on the generous tradition of their much poorer ancestors who sent a steady stream of remittances to China to build schools and hospitals.

## Associations

In the early Chinatown days, immigrants formed various family clan or district associations to protect themselves in the rather hostile new environment as well as to gain a sense of security, financial and otherwise, regarding their basic needs. The important philanthropic role of Chinese American community associations often is overlooked. Lee points out, for instance, that "Chinese family associations have traditionally performed a welfare, benevolent and mutual assistance role, somewhat equivalent to foundations. Indeed, they may be regarded as surrogate foundations in the Chinese community."[25]

Chinese American associations have been deeply involved in giving to educational development in the homeland—especially when the reformers of the late Qing and early Republic were trying to modernize China. Associations developed "a rather sophisticated technique of money-collecting booklets." These booklets were "a kind of roster of donors with the stated purpose of collecting money for building schools" at the elementary and secondary levels.[26] Association efforts often had a sharp political edge. One of the best examples was the effort of Sun Yat-sen and his supporters to educate Chinese and non-Chinese about the need for a revolution in China—which eventually led to the overthrow of the Qing Dynasty in 1911. Dr. Sun himself made several trips to the United States, tapped into the well-organized family/clan associations, and supervised fund-raising groups already in existence in various Chinatowns. These same associations were active during World War II as well. I personally remember hanging on every word of Madame Chiang Kai-shek's radio broadcast to the American people before a joint session of Congress, passionately and eloquently appealing for funds to pursue the war against Japan. Him Mark Lai concludes that:

> Successive Chinese governments have successfully wooed . . . [association] support, as evidenced by the large amounts which the Chinese abroad have donated to various causes in the mother country. . . . The home government also encouraged remittances and investments in China, much of which went towards modernization of the native villages of overseas Chinese. Other amounts were invested in enterprises both in their native areas and in other parts of China.[27]

Of course, the many nineteenth-century associations organized in U.S. Chinatowns primarily looked after their own—for these early immigrants were barely able to survive. For instance, district and clan associations (*huiguan*), beginning in San Francisco and New York, would send bilingual representatives to meet the ships carrying immigrants, help them find a place to stay and a job, set up schools and hospitals, and provide some capital for business ventures—including a system of rotating credit. The most important of these groups became the famous Six Companies in San Francisco—which oversaw the Zhonghua Huiguan or Chinese Consolidated Benevolent Association (CCBA) and various other mutual-aid associations.[28] Since legislation prohibited Chinese from becoming U.S. citizens and from sending for their wives and children, they usually remitted whatever small amounts of money they could accumulate, through the *huiguan*, to their poorer families in China. These remittances have created ties that bind members of the Chinese American community to their homelands and have deepened relations between the United States and China.

During the past half-century, Chinese American associations have continued to flourish: there are over 100 in the San Francisco Bay area alone.[29] In New York City at the end of the century, for instance, the Fukien [Fujian] American Association (Meidong Fujian tongxianghui), with about 20,000 Fuzhou-native members, provided "services typical of community associations—modest scholarships for exceptional students, [etc.]. . . ."[30] Even though many Chinese Americans have become part of the middle-class establishment and have moved out of various Chinatowns across the nation, and mainstream social agencies as well as civic and political organizations have taken over many of the welfare and anti-discrimination tasks traditionally performed by the *huiguan*, a large number of these associations remain active in various fund-raising and philanthropic activities that often benefit new immigrants to the United States.

*Foundations*

Among the new generation of Chinese American professionals and entrepreneurs, we are beginning to see substantial efforts not only to give back to their respective homelands as well as to the Chinese community in the United States, but to donate to across-the-board U.S. philanthropies through numerous foundations. The bulk of the Chinese in America have moved from alienation to varying degrees of assimilation, from the lower income bracket to an increasing capacity to give. This development naturally makes many of them consider setting up private foundations for contributing to worthy causes and, to be sure, for enjoying tax breaks. Such independent family foundations usually are small endeavors focused on program areas that are stamped with the founders' personal intentions and often staffed by other family members.[31]

From my own limited experience, I know two Chinese professional women, one in California and the other in Massachusetts, who have worked with others to establish modest private foundations. Independently of one another, each of them is raising funds and engaged in curriculum upgrading for underprivileged primary- and secondary-school children in rural parts of the PRC. One is a university teacher and program director of the Soar Foundation—which has one of the most professionally run websites in this area.[32] It would not be surprising if a thousand or more such quiet and unobtrusive efforts exist among Chinese Americans on a nationwide scale.

After Lee's initial research efforts uncovered 124 Chinese American foundations in the United States by 1990, he noted that "most Chinese American foundations are located in the Western section of the nation: 38 in the San Francisco Bay Area, 22 in Los Angeles, 21 in Hawaii, 17 in New York and 26 scattered in states all across the nation. Total assets of the 124 Chinese American foundations amount to $64,588,155, while total grants awarded in 1988 were $4,891,403. . . ."[33]

The top ten Chinese American foundations are listed below. By and large, they are using their resources to start and maintain Chinese and Asian American studies programs. The first three place a special emphasis on relations with China. They favor scholarships and research grant awards and assist research centers as well as libraries and museums.

- Milton Shoong Foundation
- Tang Fund
- Li Foundation
- J.T. Tai & Co. Foundation
- S.K. Yee Foundation
- Hung Wo & Elizabeth Ching Foundation
- Tang Foundation
- Sit Investment Associates Foundation
- C.J. Wo Foundation
- Wang Family Charitable Foundation[34]

## Others

This section treats the wide variety of other Chinese American philanthropic activities that fall under different charitable groupings difficult to classify. There are, for instance, large numbers of small Christian, Buddhist, and Taoist groups who, if the general pattern among non-Chinese religious groups in the United States is any indication, account for over half of all philanthropic monies collected nationwide. Lee also refers to "myriad non-profit, charitable organizations which form part of the web of Chinese American community life."[35] These include agencies, clubs, and associations engaged in welfare, human services, cultural activities, and civil rights. Finally, he lists scores of professional associations and social organizations that provide scholarships, in-kind services, and monetary aid.[36]

As revealing background for this discussion, Roslyn Tonai's survey of 321 donors discovered that Asians are substantial givers (about 2.7 percent of their household income).[37] Mary M. Smith's research further documents contributions by Chinese (including Mainland, Taiwan, and Hong Kong) alumni from U.S. academic institutions to their alma maters and reiterates that Chinese philanthropy still is rooted in Confucian social philosophy. She reports that:

> A man who has a surplus is recognized as wealthy but it is imperative that he have a fondness for benevolence, that is to say, that he is philanthropic, concerned towards his fellow-man. The Chinese cannot just give lip-service to benevolence because it means for them the translation of benevolence into action. . . . It was clear through the conversations with the university alumni directors that the Chinese feel obliged to give, to receive and repay gifts that are both tangible and intangible in nature.[38]

Historically, when these small and diverse Chinese American philanthropic groups appeal to large, mainstream U.S. foundations for support, the response has been minimal.[39] In 1990, for instance, even support funding from the United Way for the San Francisco Bay area only met about 17.5 percent ($1,192,429) of the Chinese American community's needs. Just 14 groups (out of more than 75) received such support. These 14 groups had to come up with the other 82.5 percent ($5,621,451) on their own.[40]

On the other hand, the number of Asian American foundations is steadily increasing. Hence, as Susan Wegryn points out, because Asian Americans are viewed as an increasingly important, yet overlooked source of funds, organizations like the United Way are seeking more Asian American representatives on their boards and staff.[41]

Many China-related professional organizations are not, strictly speaking, Chinese American, but have Chinese Americans on their boards or among their trustees. A perusal of their websites reveals a wealth of educational programs involving Chinese Americans in efforts to improve relations with China through philanthropic and fund-raising activities.[42] It also is noteworthy that the Chinese American Kevin A. Fung of the Silicon Valley Mayfield Fund has become nationally prominent for initiating new approaches to philanthropy. Fung is a director of the Community Fund of Silicon Valley and the Silicon Valley II Social Ventures (SV2) group—created for young professionals to promote effective giving to nonprofit organizations by connecting venture philanthropy and venture stock. He and a colleague also established the Entrepreneur's Foundation—in which fifty-three early-stage companies they advise already have generated $4 million in value for the Foundation by giving it their founders' stock.[43] In other words, when a successful new company goes public, the increased value of the stock they donated to the Entrepreneur's Foundation benefits the Foundation's philanthropic causes. In addition, there are organizations such as the National Endowment for the Humanities (NEH) that support China-related projects "carried out by Chinese and Chinese American scholars and organizations. In term[s] of the subject matter, there are projects that specifically deal with China and those that are related to the Chinese American experience."[44]

## Recommendations for Chinese American Philanthropy in the Context of U.S.–China Relations

This review of Chinese styles of philanthropy suggests many attractive features that others could emulate. On the other hand, the U.S. style of philanthropy—*public, professional, large,* and *independent*—also has an impressive record.[45] Chinese American philanthropy will grow and further strengthen U.S.–China relations if Chinese Americans can maintain a balance in achieving the best of both worlds. Specifically, the impact of Chinese American philanthropy on U.S.–China relations can be enhanced if four steps are taken: (1) go public; (2) professionalize operations; (3) think globally; and (4) streamline networking. These ideas can be illustrated by the various ways in which Chinese American professional groups contribute to China and encourage reciprocal exchange from their counterparts.

## Go Public

Philanthropic dollars reach much farther if one is known and appreciated for certain good deeds. By going public, Chinese American philanthropists will become better known as such and be welcomed into the larger community of appreciative and practically helpful experienced peers. When Chinese American philanthropists are put in touch with their counterparts and share experiences, they are sure to become more confident and secure in giving that is not only charitable, but efficient and sustained.

For instance, Charles B. Wang got his "Smile Train" off to a good—and public—start by convincing former president George Bush personally to participate in this joint U.S.–China initiative by joining him and 1,200 physicians in Beijing for the First International Cleft Lip and Palate Symposium (March 2000).[46] Another means of going public with one's philanthropic activities is through publication. The Chinese American cancer researchers in the United States who collaborated with their counterparts in China in publishing a short report entitled "The China–America Connection" offer an example of this method. As Richard Stone reports, "the collaborators view this effort as more than just a research project. It's an opportunity to strengthen ties between Chinese-American scientists and their Pacific Rim counterparts."[47] These "go public" initiatives suggest approaches that other Chinese Americans involved in philanthropy could well imitate.

## Professionalize Operations

To professionalize does not mean that Chinese Americans have to abandon what has worked especially well for them by way of the traditional "private-personal-small-networked" approach to philanthropic practice. Just as the early and small *huiguan* evolved into larger, more professional umbrella organizations, so too can philanthropic potential be more fully realized by tapping into the professional expertise of successful fundraisers and foundation executives. Kevin Fung's ideas about "venture philanthropy" and his Entrepreneur's Foundation are examples of ideas a young professional can introduce from a business perspective.

Professionalization in the philanthropy world is relatively easy to achieve because there are scores of organizations like the Foundation Centers scattered around the United States, with excellent libraries and experienced staff, whose job it is to give advice on everything from setting up a foundation to running a board meeting and managing one's staff. Why not make use of the mechanisms and fund-raising devices they have perfected over decades of experience to improve one's own philanthropic efforts? More Chinese American philanthropists might consider pooling their resources and invest in hiring an experienced development professional (who also happens to be culturally in tune with Chinese American sensibilities) in order legally to establish a nonprofit organization and take it in the direction they want to go. This would be especially helpful in getting through the time-consuming and complicated start-up organizational period. In addition, many universities in the United States offer comprehensive and systematic programs in philanthropy and fundraising for training skilled staff members.[48] In short, Chinese Americans can capitalize on the rich resources available to complement traditional giving Chinese-style.

## Think Globally

The strength-in-unity appeal of the preceding section referred to the philanthropic efforts of Chinese Americans on the national level. Transnational efforts also are essential. China is sending some of its top scholars to the United States to explore philanthropic issues such as volunteerism on an international level.[49] Will the Chinese American community be there to cooperate with them as a professional group?

Globalization continues to be a buzzword for good reason, since many countries' economies are intricately dependent on one another. For some Chinese Americans, it has a special meaning because they have the challenging privilege of being mediators between the United States and China through philanthropic efforts that can benefit both sides.

## Streamline Networking

Internet communications provide an efficient and economical means of moving Chinese American philanthropy in a global direction. Streamlining one's networking capabilities by employing electronic media and adopting new technologies offers an approach with considerable potential if philanthropic efforts are to bear abundant fruit. Nevertheless, as Lee notes, among most Chinese

American groups to date, "there is no networking or sharing of experiences, no awareness of peer giving patterns, no information exchange or clearinghouse to learn from one another about mutual problems or potentialities among the foundations." Thus, "it would make sense to establish an 'Association of Chinese American Foundations,' as a loosely organized, self-sustaining vehicle to exchange ideas, coordinate programs, establish networking relationships and pool resources for more effective delivery of services."[50]

Chinese Americans are particularly well placed to make use of far-flung networks among overseas Chinese around the world. It is estimated that there will be a billion people on the Internet sometime in the year 2001. Much can be learned about philanthropy, in theory and practice, just by judiciously selecting from the valuable materials literally at one's fingertips through the Internet. Whether one is dealing with fellow Chinese Americans, other Chinese, or mainstream U.S. philanthropists, it is relatively easy to set up a website and tap into other existing sites. A great variety of appropriate software also is available.[51]

By taking the relatively simple steps suggested above, much can be done to improve relations between the United States and China in an unobtrusive but beneficial way. In particular, new technologies provide the means to reach a critical mass of time, talent, and wealth in order to surmount obstacles and transcend differences. As Wang Gungwu points out, "where China is concerned, it is clear that high-tech communications have enabled successful migrants to become role models for the young at home. The ability of these migrants to disseminate up-to-date information and new perspectives can even become a major intellectual source for China's modernization."[52] These goals are consistent with the expressed motives behind Charles B. Wang's $25 million donation for the establishment of an Asian American Center at the State University of New York–Stony Brook: "I want the Center to be a model of how information technology can be applied in the service of education. . . . These technologies will allow professors and students at Stony Brook and in Asia to conveniently interact and freely exchange ideas in real-time, regardless of their physical location."[53]

The challenge for Chinese American philanthropists is to see where they fit in this scheme and how they might mediate between Chinese and U.S. styles of philanthropy. Is it not the very essence of the spirit of philanthropy to share one's talents and resources in both directions for mutual benefit? Kevin Fung perhaps put it best in his White House Philanthropy Conference speech: "I think it's time to share, to stand for something that comes from the heart and is about giving back; [that is,] taking the principles of venture capital and bring that to the philanthropic world . . . not just with your dollars, but also with your time."[54]

The role of philanthropy in improving relations between the United States and China will center not only on monetary fundraising by Chinese Americans; it will be determined even more by efforts to recruit the vast number of talented members of the Chinese American community who are in a position to pursue this goal actively—whether their fields of expertise be political, commercial, managerial, research, or otherwise. The free flow of ideas through exchanges of personnel will ultimately result in the finest kind of philanthropic thought and action. Thus, the expansion of philanthropic exchanges initiated and sustained by Chinese Americans offers one of the firmest prospects for a harmonious, prosperous, and peaceful future for the two giants of the twenty-first century.

## Notes

1. I use the general term "China" to include important geographical areas where Chinese live in large numbers—such as Hong Kong, Macao, Taiwan, and other parts of Southeast Asia. Related to, but beyond the scope of, this chapter is the increasing attention given to research on East Asian and, particularly, Chinese philanthropy. Readers interested in how Chinese American philanthropists might cooperate with Chinese counterparts abroad would do well to consult Nick Young and Anthony Woo, *An Introduction to the Non-Profit Sector in China* (West Mailing, Kent: Charities Aid Foundation, 2000); and Asia Pacific Philanthropy Network (http://www.asianphilanthorpy.org).

2. Wang Gungwu, "Upgrading the Migrant: Neither *Huaqiao* nor *Huaren*," in *The Last Half Century of Chinese Overseas*, ed. by Elizabeth Sinn (Hong Kong: Hong Kong University Press, 1998), p. 28. Also see Wang Gungwu, *The Chinese Overseas: From Earthbound China to the Quest for Autonomy* (Cambridge: Harvard University Press, 2000); and Tu Wei-ming, ed., *The Living Tree: The Changing Meaning of Being Chinese Today* (Stanford: Stanford University Press, 1994).

3. Xiao-huang Yin, "The Growing Influence of Chinese Americans on U.S.–China Relations," in *The Outlook for U.S.–China Relations Following the 1997–1998 Summits: Chinese and American Perspectives on Security, Trade, and Cultural Exchange*, ed. by Peter H. Koehn and Joseph Y.S. Chang (Hong Kong: Chinese University Press, 1999), pp. 332–333.

4. *We the Americans: Asians* (Washington, D.C.: Superintendent of Documents, U.S. Government Printing Office, 1993), pp. 3, 7.

5. Statistics are taken from the annual "Census Bureau Facts for Features: Asian Pacific American Heritage Month" summary publication (typescript)—a product of the U.S. Department of Commerce, Bureau of the Census, Public Information Office (May 5, 2000); also at http://www.census.gov/population/estimates/nation/intfile3-1.txt and http://www.census.gov/Press-Release/www/2000/cb00–05.html. Statistics on "U.S. businesses" last appeared in the 1998 "Facts for Features" report, at http://www.census.gov/Press-Release/cb96-127.html. A considerably more attractive publication (with helpful graphs) is *We the Americans: Asians*. More comprehensive statistical information on Chinese Americans is available from the U.S. Census Bureau (http://www.census.gov).

6. David T.A. Chen, "Marketing to the Affluent Asian Americans" (paper presented at the Researchers Roundtable Seminar, Washington, D.C.: Council on Foundations, 1989).

7. See notes 21 and 23 below for references to distinguished Chinese Americans.

8. Robert Lee, *Guide to Chinese American Philanthropy and Charitable Giving Patterns* (San Rafael, CA: Pathway Press, 1990), p. 6. Lee's work is the most detailed and comprehensive study of Chinese American philanthropy.

9. Jessica Chao, "Asian American Philanthropy: Expanding Circles of Participation," in *Cultures of Caring: Philanthropy in Diverse American Communities*, ed. by Joanne Scanlon (Washington, D.C.: Council on Foundations, 1999), pp. 209–210. Also see http://www.cof.org/culturescaring.

10. Elaine Ko and Danny Howe, *The Asian American Charitable Giving Study: A Survey of Charitable Giving in King County's Asian American Community* (Seattle: United Way of King County, 1990). Another essay worth consulting is Stella Shao's "Asian American Giving: Issues and Challenges (A Practitioner's Perspective)," *New Directions for Philanthropic Fundraising* 8 (1995): 57–61. Shao dispels misconceptions about the supposed lack of giving by Asian Americans; they are, in fact, "substantial givers," and "give more per household income than the average population"— including to non-Asian causes.

11. Shao, "Asian American Giving," p. 56.

12. Lee, *Guide*, p. 143. For a much earlier treatment of Chinese philanthropy, see Yu-yue Tsu, *The Spirit of Chinese Philanthropy: A Study in Mutual Aid* (New York: Columbia University Press, 1912).

13. Joanne Scanlon, "Introduction," *Cultures of Caring: Philanthropy in Diverse American Communities*, p. 19.

14. Lee, *Guide*, p. 30.

15. Chao's research confirms that impersonal, direct mailings, or even telemarketing, are not effective. She adds that "even at lower levels, Asian Americans respond best to personal requests." Chao, "Asian American Philanthropy," p. 227.

16. Lee, *Guide*, p. 61.

17. Gary G. Hamilton, "The Theoretical Significance of Asian Business Networks," in *Asian Business Networks*, ed. by Gary G. Hamilton (Berlin: Walter de Gruyter, 1996), p. 288. For an amusing, but trenchant, summary of the pro and con arguments regarding the importance of "networking" in Chinese society, see Thomas Menkhoff's "Chinese Business Networks: A Hypothetical Dialogue," in the *Encyclopedia of the Chinese Overseas*, ed. by Lynn Pan (Cambridge: Harvard University Press, 1999), pp. 94–95.

18. Lee, *Guide*, p. 25.

19. For more about Yung Wing's distinguished career, see his autobiography, *My Life in China and America* (New York: Holt, 1909), and the index references in Shih-shan Henry Tsai, *China and the Overseas Chinese in the United States, 1868–1911* (Fayetteville: University of Arkansas Press, 1983). Also see Xiao-huang Yin, *Chinese American Literature Since the 1850s* (Urbana: University of Illinois Press, 2000), pp. 69–84. Yin takes up the question of Yung Wing's citizenship on pp. 81–82, note 45.

20. S.W. Kung, *Chinese in American Life: Some Aspects of Their History, Status, Problems, and Contributions* (Seattle: University of Washington Press, 1962), p. 234. In a note, the author states that the general contributed altogether $200,000 to Columbia. Shih-shan Henry Tsai's account claims that Carpentier's initial donation to Columbia in Dean Lung's name was $10,000, and says that the amount of money Dean

Lung donated to Columbia was $14,000, not $12,000. Shih-shan Henry Tsai, *The Chinese Experience in America* (Bloomington: Indiana University Press, 1986), p. 35.

21. The ten "philanthropy heroes" honored at the October 1999 White House Conference on Philanthropy included the Chinese American Rolland C. Lowe, M.D., chair of the Lawrence Choy Lowe Memorial Fund to which the Lowe family has contributed more than $600,000. Lowe also is the first Asian American President of the California Medical Association. The Conference cited his work in encouraging community involvement by physicians and in the establishment of a capital campaign for the Chinese Historical Society's museum. See http://www.whitehouse.gov/Initiatives/Millennium/Philan/html/bio.lowe.htm.

22. James A. Joseph, *Remaking America: How the Benevolent Traditions of Many Cultures Are Transforming Our National Life* (San Francisco: Jossey-Bass, 1995), p. 167. For Wang An's autobiography, see Eugene Linden and An Wang, *Lessons* (Reading, MA: Addison-Wesley, 1986).

23. On the website, http://www.goldsea.com/Profiles/100/100.html (2000), Charles B. Wang is named the number one Asian American businessman in "America's Top 100 Asian Entrepreneurs." For descriptions of his "Smile Train" and "Missing and Exploited Children" projects, see http://www.smiletrain.org and http://www.missingkids.com. For profiles of eminent Chinese Americans in all fields, see Hyung-chan Kim et al., eds., *Distinguished Asian Americans: A Biographical Dictionary* (Westport: Greenwood Press, 1999); and Franklin Ng and John D. Wilson, eds., *The Asian-American Encyclopedia* (New York: Marshall Cavendish, 1995). Finally, Lee's *Guide* provides a "Selective List of Prominent Chinese Americans," pp. 148–160.

24. Lee, *Guide*, pp. 122–123. An interesting account of economic ties between emigrants from Taishan and their home districts is found in June Y. Mei's "Researching Chinese-American History in Taishan," in *The Chinese-American Experience: Papers from the Second National Conference on Chinese American Studies (1980)*, ed. by Genny Lim (San Francisco: Chinese Historical Society of America and Chinese Culture Foundation of San Francisco, 1984), pp. 57–61. This joint project between a delegation (including Chinese Americans) from the University of California at Los Angeles and their PRC counterparts occurred in January 1979 and involved the first post-opening group of U.S. academics to visit China.

25. Lee, *Guide*, p. 32. Lee adds that family associations "went through a period of decline and now show some signs of strengthening with appeals to the younger generation."

26. Renqui Yu, "Chinese American Contributions to the Educational Development of Toisan 1910–1940," *Amerasia Journal* 10, No. 1 (1983): 55. Toisan [Taishan] refers to the city or county in Guangdong (Canton) Province from which the majority of Chinese emigrated in the early period.

27. Him Mark Lai, compiler, *A History Reclaimed: An Annotated Bibliography of Chinese Language Materials on the Chinese of America*, ed. by Russell Leong and Jean Pang Yip (Los Angeles: University of California, Asian American Studies Center, 1986), p. 9. Under the subtitles, "Contributions," "Remittances," and "Investments," Lai supplies over fifty annotated bibliographic entries (in English) referring to a variety of Chinese-language materials (pp. 12–17). From these numerous, though scattered, accounts of monies sent back to China through the *huiguan* (literally, association hall), and so forth, one can infer that they amounted to a substantial sum, and this is not counting the enormous amounts sent through private channels over the years.

28. For a thorough description of the complex subject of Chinese American associations, see Him Mark Lai's "Historical Development of the Chinese Consolidated Benevolent Association/Huiguan System," in *Chinese America: History and Perspectives* (San Francisco: Chinese Historical Society of America, 1999), pp. 13–51. For useful flow charts showing the structures and relations between various Chinese organizations in San Francisco's Bay area, based on the work of Lai, see Victor G. Nee and Brett de Bary Nee, *Longtime Californ': A Documentary Study of an American Chinatown* (New York: Pantheon Books, 1973), pp. 272–277. Also see Lee, *Guide*, p. 33. In an interesting article by L. Eve Armentrout Ma, "The Big Business Ventures of Chinese in North America, 1850–1930," the author describes both the negative and positive aspects of the *huiguan* and notes that almost all the major stockholders in twentieth-century business were originally from Taishan (p. 109). See *The Chinese American Experience*, ed. by Genny Lim, pp. 101–112.

29. Lee, *Guide*, pp. 32–33.

30. Marlowe Hood, "Little Fuzhou," in *The Encyclopedia of the Chinese Overseas*, ed. by Lynn Pan (Cambridge: Harvard University Press, 1999), p. 268.

31. Lee, *Guide*, p. 58.

32. The websites describing the activities of these two foundations can be accessed at: http://www.soaronline.org (California) and http://www.prelex.org (Massachusetts).

33. Lee, *Guide*, pp. 61, 66–89. Lee lists all 124 foundations, including their addresses, the head trustee, reporting date, gifts received, grants awarded, and assets.

34. For a paragraph-length profile of these "top ten," with some sample grants awarded, see "Spotlight: Ten Chinese-American Foundations," *Corporate Philanthropy Report* 6 (1991): 7. Incidentally, print and web searches—through *Yahoo!* browser, founded by Jeffrey Yang—suggest that none of these foundations possessed websites in 2000 nor e-mail contact addresses. The New York Foundation Center's website http://www.fdncenter.org can supply one-page printouts, giving basic information on each of these ten foundations (including mailing addresses, etc.).

35. Lee, *Guide*, p. 23.

36. Ibid., pp. 161–165. Also see Lai, *A History Reclaimed*, pp. 43–75, for his annotated list (with Chinese characters) of Chinese American organizations; the websites listed in notes 32 and 42.

37. Rosalyn Miyoko Tonai, "Asian American Charitable Giving: An Analysis of the Relationship Between Demographic, Attitudinal, and Situational Factors and Cash Contributions of Asian Americans to Nonprofit Organizations in San Francisco–Oakland Area" (Unpublished M.A. thesis, University of San Francisco, 1987). In 1988, the University of San Francisco's Institute for Nonprofit Organization Management, College of Professional Studies, published a twenty-page version of the thesis under the same title (Working Paper No. 4). Other useful studies that describe the customs of giving and sharing by Chinese, Japanese, Filipino, Mexican, and Guatemalan communities are: Bradford Smith, Sylvia Shue, and Joseph Villarreal, eds., *Asian and Hispanic Philanthropy* (San Francisco: Institute for Nonprofit Organization Management, 1992); and Julia Hsiao, "Asian Americans: Diversity in Giving," proceedings of the conference of the Council for the Advancement and Support of Education (CASE), *Fund Raising Strategies for Women, Minorities and Special Constituents* (Chicago: Council for the Advancement and Support of Education, May 1997). In the latter, the Chinese American community is singled out as an example of the role of immigrant status, wealth, and giving behaviors.

38. Mary Magnano Smith, "An Understanding of Gift Giving in Chinese Universities: A Hermeneutic of Philanthropy" (Ph.D. dissertation, University of San Francisco, 1992), p. 88.

39. Lee, *Guide*, p. 60.

40. Ibid., pp. 119–120. In total, U.S. foundation dollars given to Asian American organizations amounted to $34,660,040 between 1983 and 1990. As the largest numerical group within the Asian Pacific community, Chinese Americans captured the lion's share of $8,687,256 (25.1 percent). Susan B. Gall and Timothy L. Gall, eds., *Statistical Record of Asian Americans* (Detroit: Gale Research, 1993), p. 715. The source given for these statistics is: *Invisible and in Need: Philanthropic Giving to Asian Americans and Pacific Islanders* (San Francisco: Asian Americans and Pacific Islanders in Philanthropy [AAPIP], December 1992). Primary source: The Foundation Center (http://www.fdncenter.org) in New York, which classifies every grant over $5,000 reported to the Center. Another useful print source, including substantial sections on Chinese Americans, is Charles B. Montney, ed., *Asian Americans Information Directory, 1991–1995* (Detroit: Gale, 1994).

41. See Susan Wegryn, "Asian Americans Are Often-overlooked Source of Donations, According to Two New Reports," *NonProfit Times* 4 (November 1990): 3, 18. The two new reports referred to are Lee's *Guide* and Ko/Howe, *Asian American Charitable Giving Study*. Another useful report is sponsored by the Asian Americans/Pacific Islanders in Philanthropy and Leadership Education for Asian Pacifics: "Making the Invisible Visible: Strategies to Increase the Participation of Asian Pacific Americans in Philanthropy" (Unpublished report to the James Irvine Foundation, June 1996).

42. A sampling of websites related to Chinese American philanthropy and China, listed alphabetically, is as follows: The Asia Foundation: http://www.asiafoundation.org; AsiaNetwork: http://www.asianetwork.org.; The Henry Luce Foundation: http://www.hluce.org; The United Board for Christian Higher Education in Asia: http://www.unitedboard.org; The Yale-China Foundation: http://www.yale.edu/yalechin/home.html. One of the best websites on all things Chinese and Chinese American related to nonprofit organizations is http://www.chinasite.com. This frequently updated and comprehensive website is particularly useful in providing easy links to a broad spectrum of other related websites as well as links to the large number of Chinese American associations of professionals (science, medicine, economics, business, art, etc.). Another important website is that of the Organization of Chinese Americans (OCA), which can be reached at: http://www.ocanatl.org. At the end of the year 2000, America Online (AOL) launched a philanthropy website that already has over 630,000 sites and lists the 52 chapters of the OCA scattered throughout the United States along with 6 other organizations: http://www.helping.org.

43. Fung's speech on "New Giving for the New Millennium" at the 1999 White House Conference on Philanthropy, along with the entire conference transcript, can be downloaded at: http://www.whitehouse.gov/Initiatives/Millennium/Philan/html/conference/html.

44. Dai Sil Kim-Gibson, "NEH Funding," in Lim, *Chinese American Experience*, p. 327. The author cites examples of recent grants: $354,785 to the Chinese Culture Foundation of San Francisco to make documentary films on four cities in China; $60,000 to Washington University's Media Program to produce a documentary presenting Chinese writers talking about China's self-image, aspirations, and achievements.

As of November 2000, the "Sight First project," jointly sponsored by Lions Clubs International and the China Disabled Persons Federation, had trained some 4,000

Mainland doctors in surgical techniques and donated state-of-the-art equipment used to diagnose and treat eye diseases primarily in outlying areas of China. Elisabeth Rosenthal, "Blinded by Poverty: The Dark Side of Capitalism," *New York Times*, 21 November 2000, p. A4.

45. President Bill Clinton's radio address of 25 November 2000. The complete text for the President's radio talk is available at: http://www.whitehouse.gov/WH/html/Saturday_November_25_2000.html.

46. The Press Room of Wang's company, Computer Associates International, Inc., released a report on the Conference at: http://www.cai.com/press/2000/03/smile_train.htm.

To add to the publicity, Bill Gates and his wife, Melinda, who heard about the charity from Wang, also gave $1 million to the fund. See http://fdncenter.org/pnd/19980121/001901.html.

47. Richard Stone, "The China–America Connection," *Science* 262, No. 5132 (15 October 1993): 350. Another reference to such collaborative efforts can be found in Leo A. Orleans, *Chinese Students in America: Policies, Issues, and Numbers* (Washington, D.C.: National Academy Press, 1988), especially pp. 118–122. Jianyi Huang, in her book *Chinese Students and Scholars in American Higher Education* (Westport: Praeger, 1997), gives numerous examples in chapter 3 (pp. 49–57) of how students from China have benefited the U.S. education scene, especially in the fields of science and engineering, where they are welcomed as research and teaching assistants. They have received numerous awards and published books and articles in prestigious presses (both in English and in Chinese). In addition, they have established scholarships in China and, while in the United States, have inspired many Americans to become more interested in China and its relations with the United States.

48. There are numerous universities and research institutes in the United States offering courses that directly or indirectly are related to philanthropy and fundraising. The Center of Philanthropy at Indiana-Purdue University Indianapolis is considered by many as the nation's leading center on the theory and practice of philanthropy. About 50 students a year enroll in its graduate program. At least 50 other institutions offer courses in nonprofit management.

49. There is a new NGO Research Center at Tsinghua University (http://www.nporc.net). Several scholars at the Center are experts on volunteerism. They currently are editing a U.N. conference proceedings on the subject.

50. Lee, *Guide*, p. 62.

51. For a current review of Internet-related software products, see Martin B. Schneiderman, "Grants Management Software Moves to the Web," *Foundation News and Commentary*, July/August 2000, pp. 20, 22–23.

52. Wang Gungwu, "Introduction: Migration and New National Identities," in *The Last Half Century of Chinese Overseas*, ed. by Elizabeth Sinn (Hong Kong: Hong Kong University Press, 1998), p. 9.

53. The text of Wang's edited remarks, made on 9 December 1996, can be found at: http://www.aac.sunysb.edu/cbws12097.html.

54. See note 43.

# 11

# Improving Mainland Society and U.S.–China Relations

## A Case Study of Four Chinese American–led Transnational Associations

### Norton Wheeler

Chinese Americans are playing increasingly important roles as intermediaries in U.S.–China relations. Their activities in expanding trans-Pacific business ties and in shaping U.S. public opinion and official policies toward China have received considerable attention.[1] This chapter examines a particular expression of their intermediary role: associational activity directed toward the improvement of one or more aspects of China's economic, social, and political conditions. While there is a century-old tradition of U.S. reformers and Chinese Americans, acting individually and through traditional improvement associations, striving to improve Chinese society,[2] Chinese Americans recently have established new types of transnational associations for this specific purpose that deserve scholarly attention and public recognition.

Since the early 1970s, some political scientists have argued that national governments alone no longer can manage all the important interfaces among increasingly complex polities. In this situation, transnational (society-to-society) relations become an important complement to international (state-to-state) relations.[3] Along with the economic activities of transnational corporations, these theorists highlight cross-border circuits of ideas—especially those conveyed through various associational forms.[4] At the same time, a group of sociologists and anthropologists working primarily on migration studies have focused on the roles of transmigrants who use ethnic and familial ties to build and maintain social networks in two or more societies.[5] Both views of transnationalism are useful in understanding the contemporary impact of Chinese Americans on U.S.–China relations.

The subjects of this study are four transnational improvement associations—The 1990 Institute, the Committee of 100 (C-100), the Association of Chinese Professors of Social Science in the United States (ACPSS), and Human Rights in China (HRIC)—that have a prominent public presence (particularly, but not exclusively, in the United States), a predominantly (in one case exclusively) Chinese American membership, and have not been treated extensively or even partially in previous scholarly work. Collectively, they cover a broad spectrum in terms of issue orientation, immigrant cohort, and articulation between Chinese American identity and U.S.–China relations.

A critical review of the experiences, activities, and impact of these four associations can begin to answer several important questions. First, what motivates the members? Second, has the period of member immigration to the United States shaped perspectives on China and U.S.–China relations? Third, what is the relationship between the social position of the Chinese American members of these organizations and their China-improvement agendas? How do they leverage their position in U.S. society to pursue their agendas and/or vice versa? Fourth, what important commonalities and differences exist in issue orientations and positions? Finally, what impact are these transnational improvement associations having on China and on U.S.–China relations?

### Helping China Modernize: The 1990 Institute[6]

A group of Chinese Americans, many of whom were closely connected socially through the local chapter of a Chinese American fraternity, founded The 1990 Institute in San Francisco in April 1990. The Institute's founders were concerned that the tragedy at Tiananmen Square would set back China's social progress. Unlike many others, however, they sought a "nonpolitical" way to help the Chinese people. Specifically, they diagnosed the turmoil of 1989 as a symptom of an insufficiently modern society. Therefore, they developed an organizational plan to help China modernize. The Institute's mission statement explains its purpose: "To enhance understanding of the economic and social problems that are impeding China's modernization, and to contribute to the search for their solutions through independent, objective, and policy-oriented research for the benefit of the people in China, and peace and prosperity of the world."[7] By the end of 1991, the organization had established an ethnic mix of roughly two-thirds Chinese American and one-third non–Chinese American.

Rosalyn Koo, a future leader of the Institute, was visiting relatives in China in the spring of 1989, at the height of the pro-democracy demonstrations. A native of Hangzhou who came to the United States in the 1940s to study, Koo is currently director of an elderly self-help community organization in San Francisco. Unaware, because of the news blackout in China, of the full scope of the turmoil, she returned to San Francisco on the last plane out of Shanghai before the temporary suspension of flights. Back in the United States, Koo stayed glued to her television for days, soaking in news about the tragedy she had just left behind. "All of us [Chinese Americans] felt bad about the whole thing," Koo believes. In Chinatown, she continues, "there was a major organized movement, protesting the harsh treatment of the students."[8]

Another future 1990 Institute leader, website developer Wei-Tai Kwok, was born in the United States. His parents emigrated from Shanghai in the 1940s. Kwok spent two years in China in the late 1980s, returning to the United States in 1987. First, during a year at Fudan University, he studied Mandarin—which he had not learned while growing up in the United States. Then, he worked for a New York–based law firm that was organizing joint ventures in China. Both the reforms he observed firsthand and the democracy in the streets he later watched from across the Pacific raised Kwok's hopes for China's future. "But," he states, "it ended in great frustration by the summer of 1989."[9]

The central question for people like Koo and Kwok was, in the latter's words, "What can we do to help?" Eleven organizations quickly sprang up in San Francisco around a protest agenda. They bombarded local papers and the Chinese Consulate with press releases and petitions opposing the crackdown. Two individuals who sympathized with the protesters' outrage, nevertheless, took a different approach. Industrialist C.B. Sung and economist Hang-sheng Cheng independently formulated a strategy of research-based support for the continuation of China's economic reforms. Their shared premise was that economic problems were at the root of China's social and political unrest. Therefore, solving these problems held the key to a better life for the Chinese people. This vision became institutionalized with the formation of The 1990 Institute.[10]

By the time China opened its economy to foreign investment in the late 1970s, Sung had experienced a successful business career. After coming to the United States to study in the 1940s, he became the first Asian American vice president of a major U.S. corporation (Bendix) and, subsequently, a prosperous entrepreneur. Following China's opening to the West, Sung's company, Unison, became the foreign partner in the first U.S.–China joint venture, the Great Wall Hotel in Beijing. Unison later organized thirty-six joint ventures in the manufacturing sector. Sung sees U.S. investment in China as a way to benefit both countries. This perspective corresponds to his self-identification as a person with roots in two societies: "my motherland is

China, my fatherland is the U.S." In trying to help China, Sung wanted to avoid political controversy:

> We said the political is each country's own business. You shouldn't influence them. But the economic is worldwide, the social is worldwide. . . . We stay away from human rights, because human rights has one foot in the social aspect, but another foot in the political.[11]

In November 1989, Sung met Hang-sheng Cheng at a luncheon in San Francisco sponsored by the Business Council for International Understanding. Cheng had left Shanghai in the 1940s to earn a doctorate in economics in the United States. He taught that subject at Iowa State University for several decades before heading the Pacific Basin Program—a research project of the San Francisco Federal Reserve Bank—until his recent retirement. Tiananmen was a turning point in Cheng's life:

> [B]efore 1989, I always thought that I loved China, but I had not done anything [for it]. I enjoyed a good life in the United States, focused on my work and my family. I was quite contented with what I was doing. . . . But, June 4 . . . made me and many others sit up and realize how the people of China were still struggling.[12]

In the months after the Tiananmen incident, Cheng incubated a plan to team up ten economists from the United States with ten from China for the purpose of creating decision models for China's policymakers. The week after they met, Cheng wrote to Sung and proposed that the latter adopt the research project as his own. The urgency of Cheng's appeal stands out in his letter: "More than ever, it has become obvious that sustained concern about China's future must depend on those who are either themselves Chinese by origin or have made a long-term commitment to the interest of the Chinese people."[13]

Sung did adopt Cheng's proposal. He took it to the February meeting of F.F.—a Chinese American social fraternity in which he was and is active. F.F. was looking for a social-service project to mark its eightieth anniversary, and Sung persuaded his fraternity brothers to make Cheng's research plan, under the name The 1990 Institute, that project. Fraternity brother William Lee, who left Shanghai in 1946 to study in the United States and is now a retired architect, became a 1990 Institute board member and the project's number one booster within the fraternity. Lee's social connections, in both the United States and China, were important in getting The 1990 Institute off the ground.[14] Many early supporters, as well as future board member Wei-Tai Kwok, also came from the ranks of F.F. Realizing that the Institute had no one with administrative skills, Lee coaxed Rosalyn Koo (whose husband is an F.F. member) to attend a fraternity meeting and consider serving as the Institute's executive director. Koo got the group over the early hurdles of establishing bylaws, an Executive Committee, an office, and a fund-raising structure. She has remained active since.[15]

During the next year, the Institute expanded its organizational skills by recruiting Matilda Young and James Luce to its board. Young, a Shanghai native, had several decades of publishing experience in the United States. She has coordinated the publication of all Institute books. Luce's family has deep roots in China. His grandfather, Henry W., was a missionary there for several decades; his father, Sheldon, was born in Shandong Province and spoke Chinese before he learned English; his uncle, publisher Henry R., wrote extensively about China. Along with enthusiasm about China and U.S.– China relations, Luce brought his professional skills as an attorney to the Institute. In 1993, Cheng met University of California–Berkeley law professor Charles McClain at a World Affairs conference, and the board gained another energetic member. McClain has written a book about Chinese Americans' legal battles against discrimination during the nineteenth century, and is married to a third-generation Chinese American.[16]

The 1990 Institute divides its work into three phases. Phase I consisted of the publication of its first book, *China's Economic Reform*, in 1993. The book was the product of collaboration between teams of Chinese and American economists, according to Cheng's plan. Retired economist Walter Galenson, former director of research at the Social Science Research Council's Committee on the Economy of China, edited this work. The Institute provided modest stipends for the Chinese researchers involved in this project who had been studying in the United States in the spring of 1989 and had elected not to return after June 4. With the exception of a chapter on foreign trade by Cheng, the Institute recruited the other U.S. contributors, the majority of them Chinese Americans from academia, and most of these scholars donated their work. The Institute also collaborated with the Chinese Academy of Social Sciences (CASS) in order to publish a Chinese-language edition of the book for distribution in China.

In Phase II, The 1990 Institute commissioned U.S. scholars to write a series of research monographs, each focused on one dimension of China's reforms, that updated and expanded on the chapters in the first book. For example, it published *Foreign Business Law in China: Past Progress & Future Challenges* by Pitman Potter in 1995; *China's Ongoing Agricultural Reform* by Colin Carter, Funing Zhong, and Fang Cai in 1996; and *Fiscal Policy in China: Taxation and Intergovernmental Fiscal Problems* by Roy Bahl in 1998. Works on enterprise reform by Anthony Koo and Kung-Chia Yeh and on labor-market reform by Richard Freeman are forthcoming.

By the late 1990s, in Phase III, the Institute began to expand its scope of activity to include social as well as economic issues. In 1999, for example, it co-sponsored (with the Shanghai Academy of Social Sciences) an essay contest on "social ethics." One hundred college and university professors from cities throughout China submitted essays analyzing the role of social ethics as a counterbalance to the materialist individualism that has accompanied recent market reforms.[17] In April 2000, the Institute and the All-China Women's Federation co-sponsored a conference in San Francisco on "Women, Leadership, and Sustainability."

The reason for its new emphasis on social issues is threefold. First, Institute leaders believe that the accelerating pace at which China's own economists are developing economic-reform theories and policies diminishes (though it does not end) the need for and the feasibility of outside help. Second, as they observe the proliferation of social problems—like environmental degradation and urban unemployment—the Institute's leaders want to help formulate policy responses. Third, in order to broaden its base of active leaders, the Institute has turned to issues that can involve its directors and supporters, especially women who are not trained economists, but are concerned with social issues that affect people's everyday lives.[18]

Since its inception, The 1990 Institute has sponsored, co-sponsored, or participated in more than a dozen international conferences—roughly half of them in China. In March 1995, for example, Charles McClain organized a conference, with corporate sponsorship by Bank of America, called Foreign Business Law in China. Conference discussions were based on the research Pitman Potter conducted for the Institute. According to McClain, debates were livelier than he had anticipated. The following month, a similar conference was held in Beijing, co-sponsored with the Institute by China's Ministry of Foreign Trade and International Cooperation and Vision 2047 of Hong Kong. In July 1996, The 1990 Institute was invited to participate in the Symposium of [sic] China in the 21st Century and the New Generation of Overseas Scholars in Beijing, where Chinese president Jiang Zemin attended the opening ceremonies.[19]

Some of the economic-reform ideas set forth in The 1990 Institute's publications have found a receptive audience among China's policymakers. In 1998, Xu Xanda, then China's director of tax reform, was so eager to disseminate Institute ideas that he "organized a team of young tax officials to review the manuscript and, later on, to translate Roy Bahl's book [on tax reform] into Chinese and write a long introductory essay for the Chinese edition."[20] By 2000, after several promotions, Xu became deputy director of the State Tax Bureau of China. In April 2000, Xu received Institute chairman C.B. Sung when Sung visited China. During the thirty-minute session, Xu, in the presence of several aides, told Sung: "We are so impressed by this work that . . . I am going to give Bahl's book to Jiang Zemin and other top leaders."[21] This was not the first time The 1990 Institute found a receptive ear within China's policy establishment. In 1994, Chinese economist Wu Jinlian informed the Institute that Vice Premier Zhu Rongji had read *Institute Issue Paper* No. 10, "Should China Tolerate High Inflation?" by Thomas Mayer.[22] Wu reported that "Zhu . . . felt that this paper was very helpful and beneficial to this long term problem and should be read by more people in the academic and economics circles."[23]

Among the four organizations profiled here, influencing China's economic-reform policies is most central to the agenda of The 1990 Institute. As with think-tanks in general, however, its influence tends to be indirect and diffuse rather than direct and documentable.[24] While Institute members have built a growing web of connections with its target audience and can cite instances when key PRC officials have listened to its views and, in fact, actively sought them out, they can provide no hard evidence of specific policy changes introduced as a result of their influence. Thus, Hang-sheng Cheng offered this realistic assessment:

> People ask us, ask me: "How much effect have you had in China? Do you have any evidence that your research has affected policy?" I say: "I don't know. I cannot gauge the impact. . . ." I cannot say that a certain policy came from our thinking.[25]

## Advocates for Chinese Americans and U.S.–China Relations: The Committee of 100

Like The 1990 Institute, organizers founded the New York–based Committee of 100 (C-100) in 1990, at the height of concern that followed the Tiananmen killings of the prior year. There is some membership overlap between the two organizations and a substantial philosophical agreement about how to help China.[26] However, C-100 has its own distinctive membership, target audience, mission, and strategy. The most striking fact about the leadership of the Committee of 100 is their elite status. The chairman, Henry S. Tang, is general manager and vice president of Salomon Brothers, Inc., a major investment-banking company. Among C-100 governors are Yo-Yo Ma and I.M. Pei, world-famous musician and architect, respectively. Another governor, Shirley Young, is a General Motors vice president, and former director Leeann Chin is a well-known and successful restaurateur.

The Committee has a twofold mission. One part is domestic; the other, transnational. Government officials in the United States and China constitute its primary target audience. Its strategy largely consists of lobbying and publicity.

At first glance, the elite status of C-100 members obviates the need for the domestic half of the group's agenda, that is, "improving the environment for the full participation of Chinese Americans in all aspects of life in the United States."[27] However, as Henry Tang points out, entrenched barriers exist to full participation by Chinese Americans in U.S. society—even the elite among them. First, he explains how the current situation of Chinese Americans differs from that of African Americans and Hispanics. While the two latter groups face tremendous barriers to entry into institutions of higher education and the careers that follow, Chinese and other Asian Americans are welcomed to enter. After entry, however, they hit a glass ceiling. In Tang's words:

> To use an investment term, your yield or your dividend is a lot less than that for what other people invested in their lives. . . . After 25 years of life, that's when we begin to get short-changed, in a very big way, and almost to the point where you can't turn back and do anything about it. You're locked in.[28]

Tang punctuates his analysis with a story about a group of Chinese Americans he met in Chicago twenty years ago. All had earned doctorates in science, but, after ten or fifteen years, they realized that they had no opportunity for career advancement. He continues that "six of them decided at that time that it was more lucrative for them, not more intellectually stimulating, but more lucrative to hang up their Ph.D.s and open Chinese restaurants."[29]

A large part of the problem many Chinese Americans face is a popular perception that they are members of an alien group who lack the commitment to become loyal Americans. In an interview, Henry Tang discussed recent, highly publicized instances in which political authorities in the United States have acted upon—and reinforced—this perception through "ethnic profiling or, to use a common term, stereotyping."[30] The three most prominent examples have been the Senate's "Cox Report" (which implied that all Chinese Americans are potential spies), sensationalist reporting of any illegal political fundraising involving Chinese Americans (e.g., Johnny Huang, Johnny Chung, Al Gore at a Buddhist temple), and Wen Ho Lee's solitary confinement for mishandling Los Alamos computer files.[31]

Further analysis of the cloud of suspicion that hangs over Asian Americans, and Chinese Americans in particular, makes clear the connection between the domestic half of the Committee's mission and the international half—"enhancement of relations between the U.S. and the Greater China region." On the one hand, the "bicultural background" of its members positions the Committee "to serve as a bridge between the culture and systems of

Asia and America."[32] On the other hand, the stereotype of Asian Americans as disloyal, or potentially disloyal, deprives U.S. policymakers of their insights—abroad as well as at home.[33] Given that Asian Americans have never served in positions of assistant secretary or higher in the U.S. State Department, Tang asks rhetorically:

> Is it any wonder that, over the past 55 years, the U.S. has had conflicts with Japan, Korea, Vietnam, Cambodia and, to some extent, China? . . . Is it any wonder that it is in the mess it's in, when you might say it is by design that the country has chosen to exclude people who understand the situation much better?[34]

When National Security Advisor Sandy Berger, in a welcome departure from past practice, asked a group of Chinese American leaders to brief him on China prior to President Clinton's 1998 visit, Tang was "surprised at the elementariness of his questions."[35]

In spite of the history of neglect of their constituency's civic resources by the U.S. policy establishment, C-100 members continue to attempt to play a constructive advisory role aimed at improving U.S.–China relations. From their Chinese American perspective, they seek to be "cultural ambassadors" who can help each government better understand the motivations of the other. Committee members meet frequently with members of the legislative and executive branches of the U.S. government to share information and make policy recommendations. For instance, following a 1994 trip to China, a small C-100 delegation met with White House National Security Council staff, Commerce Department officials, and Cabinet members to discuss the findings of their trip and the Wirthlin Report—a survey, co-sponsored by the Committee, that compared the attitudes of Hong Kong residents to those of Americans regarding the impending reunification of Hong Kong with China. This survey found that the majority of Americans who knew about the impending change assumed that the people of Hong Kong were worried about their future, while the majority of Hong Kong residents expressed confidence about the changeover.[36] The Committee also has expressed support for "delinking the human rights issue from the U.S. trade policy (MFN) with China." In contacts with Chinese leaders, C-100 members promote a peaceful solution to the Taiwan problem, expanded cultural and economic relations with the United States, and bilateral collaboration on global defense and environmental issues.[37] They "encourage progress on human rights through quiet diplomacy and continue to encourage the release of prisoners of conscience."[38] The Committee is well connected at the top—both in China and in the United States. It hosted a luncheon and "fireside chat" for President Jiang Zemin during the latter's 1997 visit to the United States, and members have met periodically with other PRC leaders, as well as with the president and the premier of Taiwan.[39]

### Transnational Academic Research: The ACPSS

Founded in 1995, the main goal of the Association of Chinese Professors of Social Sciences in the United States (ACPSS) is to enhance career opportunities for Chinese American social science professors who are professionally marginalized. As former ACPSS president Li Xiaobing explained in an interview:

> It is hard for us to join the mainstream of [U.S.] academia. . . . If you want to present a paper at the Association of Asian Studies, usually you don't have a chance by yourself; probably, your paper will be declined. So, the only chance you have is if you put together a panel sponsored by an organization that is affiliated with the AAS. . . . As individuals it is hard, but an organization as a bridge helps them to connect.[40]

The structure and functions of the ACPSS suggest, in effect, the idea of an "academic enclave" as a support system for Chinese American scholars. While Li likely overstated the academic barriers that can be attributed to national background,[41] enclaves offer recent migrants protection in the short term and, over time, can facilitate integration (without requiring assimilation) into mainstream society.[42]

In March 1996, the ACPSS announced plans for the simultaneous publication in China and the United States of the organization's first book, *China's Road to Modernization*. The newsletter announcement asserted:

> There is no doubt that the Chinese version will reach a much larger audience and have more direct impact on China's modernization efforts. Therefore, the publication of the Chinese version in China will not only count favorably toward every author's professional development but also help realize your wish to contribute to the progress and development of modern China.[43]

Although ACPSS did not ultimately find a Chinese publisher for *China's Road to Modernization*, they subsequently published two scholarly works in Chinese for distribution in Taiwan, Hong Kong, and the China Mainland.[44] Members have presented papers at numerous ACPSS-sponsored and co-sponsored conferences in the United States, Taiwan, and the China Mainland. Many of the presenters, subsequently, have published in mainstream professional journals in the fields of economics, sociology, geography, urban planning, and so forth.[45] Further, the organization has sponsored an "American Studies" book series in China. Individual members have written books on various aspects of U.S. society such as media, economics, religion, popular culture, and Chinese Americans, and the prestigious Chinese Social Sciences Publishing House is publishing them. Eight titles, out of a projected twenty, had appeared in print as of July 2000.[46] In the summer of 2000, the Association published the inaugural issue of its journal, *American Review of China Studies*. Each contribution to the issue addresses some aspect of Chinese society, and many provide information not readily available in English. The contribution by Liu Yawei, for example, is entitled "Will Local Elections Lead to a New Political China? Status of China's Direct Elections at the Township and County Levels; A Field Report." While collaboration with Chinese counterparts has resulted in substantial Chinese participation at ACPSS-sponsored conferences—including opportunities for some to travel to the United States with ACPSS funding—the Association's publications almost exclusively are an outlet for Chinese American scholars. Of fifty-four contributors to the three major essay collections on Chinese reforms and U.S.–China relations, for example, all have Chinese surnames, but only seven co-authors are Chinese nationals.[47]

While advancing their own careers, ACPSS members simultaneously have furthered a second organizational aim—"supporting China's reform and opening to the world." To a considerable degree, this interplay between goals is a function of the Chinese American ethnicity of most members. In the first place, personal connections in China as well as bilingualism facilitate entry for ACPSS members into the Mainland discourse on Chinese modernity. Li Xiaobing emphasizes this point in discussing the "American Studies" book series:

> There are many books published in China about America, but most are written either by Chinese or by [non-Chinese] Americans. . . . People like us have the experience of living on both sides of the Pacific. We look at America through the eyes of Chinese Americans.[48]

In his introduction to the ACPSS book *Social Transition in China*, Li reiterates that their "cross-cultural background" puts the group's members in a "unique position to study Chinese society."[49]

In addition, access to archival and field data again, through a combination of *guanxi* and language facility, can give Chinese American scholars a research edge in their academic careers in the United States. From Li's perspective:

> Collaboration is very important for us because most ACPSS members base their research on China. That is their strength. We can't compete with [non-

Chinese] Americans. If I'm teaching history, I can't compete with an American professor of American history, but I can teach better in Chinese history. So, our resources are very important. . . . In my case, in history research, I can get some documentation, some unpublished papers that are not available to other American scholars.[50]

This statement captures the ACPSS perspective on U.S. barriers and the value of enclaves. In contrast, other Chinese American scholars have elected to teach China studies in order to be in a position to challenge the misleading Orientalist approach of some mainstream academics. Li's reference to competition with "American" scholars further suggests that Chinese *American* identity remains tenuous among ACPSS members. In fact, many Chinese American scholars have succeeded in teaching U.S. history and other subjects.

## Human Rights Without Borders: HRIC

By most accounts, a growing concern for human rights without respect to borders is both a hallmark of and a contributor to globalization.[51] Human Rights in China (HRIC) provides a notable organizational illustration of this concern. Its offices are in New York, but it describes itself as "an international non-governmental organization founded by Chinese scientists and scholars in March 1989."[52] While HRIC's full-time officers continue to be Chinese or Chinese Americans, sixteen of the thirty-four members of the current board of directors have non-Chinese surnames. Among the directors are well-known former Chinese dissidents such as journalist Liu Binyan and Tiananmen pro-democracy leader Wang Dan. Joining them are historians and other China scholars such as Orville Schell and Andrew Nathan.[53]

HRIC differs from the other organizations discussed here in several important respects: the background of its leading members; its open opposition to the Chinese government; and the global, or universal (as opposed to binational) space within which it seeks to relate to China. HRIC's top leaders suffered personal repression under the post-Mao government. Before he left China, HRIC president Liu Qing was a leader of the 1978–1979 Democracy Wall Movement and editor of the underground journal *April Fifth Forum*. The government sentenced him to a fifteen-year prison term for those activities. Labeled an "incorrigible counterrevolutionary," Liu was kept in solitary confinement until his release in 1991. According to HRIC, outside pressure won his family exit papers to the United States in 1992. Liu has been president of HRIC since soon after his arrival.

While Liu, born in 1945, came of age politically in 1978, Ge Yang is a generation older. Once a patriotic communist, she edited the liberal journal

*New Observer* that the government shut down during the Anti-Rightist Campaign of 1957. After spending twenty-two years in internal exile in the countryside, she reappeared publicly and resumed publication of *New Observer* during the relatively open climate of the 1980s. When the government cracked down on politically threatening individuals and movements in 1989, Ge and her journal were again targets. This time, however, she was in the United States at a conference on the May Fourth Movement of 1919. She heeded friends' advice to tear up her 20 May return ticket and has remained in the United States since. The PRC government has labeled her a "heroine of the turmoil" and a "black-hand of the democracy movement."[54]

Although its Chinese-origin members have lived in the United States nearly as long as ACPSS members, many in the HRIC consider themselves "Chinese forced to reside in the United States" rather than "Chinese American."[55] One staff member is an American-born Chinese (ABC), and several board members are naturalized U.S. citizens. Most others possess neither U.S. citizenship nor valid PRC passports. They are, in effect, "political exiles."[56] According to the HRIC leader I interviewed, most Chinese-origin members hope eventually to return to live in China—but only after the political climate changes so that "we would not be persecuted for speaking out."[57]

While other organizations profiled in this chapter rely to a greater or lesser extent on good relations with (or at least access to) Chinese government officials, HRIC criticizes governments and NGOs that, in their view, put bilateral trade and cultural exchange with China above internationally enforceable human rights standards.[58] The group aims to

> integrat[e] a human rights perspective into China's development program. . . . HRIC encourages victims of human rights abuse to seek redress under domestic law and assists them in seeking international intervention as a last resort. . . . [HRIC's] primary focus . . . is to encourage and empower the nascent grassroots human rights movement in China.[59]

Toward the latter end, the organization transmits Chinese-language broadcasts to China through Voice of America, BBC, Radio France Internationale, and Radio Australia; "mobilizes international pressure through the media, human rights organizations, UN bodies and governments"; maintains Internet contact with "more than 100,000 Chinese students and scholars worldwide"; and distributes the quarterly *China Rights Forum* (available in both Chinese and English) to 3,000 individuals and organizations worldwide—including many in China.[60]

One pointed example of external pressure is HRIC's recent circulation of a petition asking the Inter-Parliamentary Union (IPU) to exclude Chinese premier Li Peng from that group's United Nations–sponsored conference because of Li's role at Tiananmen. When the U.N. group did not exclude Li, the HRIC collaborated with the Center for Constitutional Rights to sue him for "crimes against humanity" during his visit to New York.[61]

HRIC occupies a social space that is partially, but not entirely, outside the modern system of nations. While it maintains its headquarters office in New York and possesses a substantial U.S. membership, the foundation of HRIC's vision of human rights is modeled not on the experience of the United States, or any other country, but on international human-rights standards. Its most active members do not possess close attachments to U.S. society—including Chinese American society.[62]

## Transmigrants, China's Modernization, and the Impact of Chinese American Transnational Improvement Associations on U.S.–China Relations

The foregoing profiles of four transnational associations reveal a multidimensional pluralism among Chinese Americans who actively concern themselves with China's development and with U.S.–China relations (see Table 11.1). There are points of commonality, and major differences. Motivation constitutes one area of commonality. Chinese American members of all four organizations affirm that emotional attachment to their nation of birth (or ancestry) inspires their efforts to improve life for China's people. They have reacted to momentous events in China—specifically, the internal and external opening of society since the Third Plenum of the Chinese Communist Party in 1978, the subsequent transition to a "socialist market economy," and a series of pro-democracy movements punctuated by the bloodshed at Tiananmen Square in 1989. Many HRIC members have the additional motivation of wanting to return permanently to China—if and when it adopts the changes they advocate.

Different periods of immigration, however, have molded divergent responses to those momentous events. Most Chinese American members of The 1990 Institute and the Committee of 100 came to the United States in the 1940s or, in the case of younger members, are ABCs. While their concern for China is intense, their search for solutions tends to be pragmatic— perhaps shaped by their long experience of U.S. political culture. Scholars in the ACPSS came to the United States in the 1980s. The post-Mao liberalization of Chinese society was a formative experience for them. Career pressures in the United States have channeled much of their desire to perpetuate China's reform movement into a search for publication venues. HRIC leaders arrived as political refugees—a specific category of immigrants that distin-

Table 11.1

**Comparative Organizational Characteristics: 1990–I, C-100, ACPSS, and HRIC**

| | Ethnicity of membership | Length of time in USA (for Chinese Americans) | Issue orientations | Posture toward PRC government |
|---|---|---|---|---|
| 1990 Institute (1990-I) | Chinese Americans and non-Chinese Americans | Most over 50 years, or since birth | Binational policy-oriented research in support of China's development and modernization. | Collaborative |
| Committee of 100 (C-100) | All Chinese Americans | Most over 50 years, or since birth | Dual focus—domestic (advocacy of full participation in U.S. society for Chinese Americans) and transnational (working as cultural ambassadors to improve U.S.–China relations). | Collaborative |
| ACPSS | Predominantly Chinese Americans | Most came between 1984 and 1989 | Promoting career and publishing opportunities for recent Chinese immigrant scholars, especially through research on China's modernization and U.S.–China relations. | Collaborative |
| HRIC | Chinese in the USA, non-Chinese Americans, and a few Chinese Americans | Most came between 1989 and 1992 | Advocacy in global forums on behalf of individual human rights as an inseparable element of social development in China. | Antagonistic |

guishes them from the two other cohorts. Their personal experience with political repression has shaped their activist style and their focus on individual political and social freedoms.

The social position of Chinese Americans within U.S. society also influences the articulation of ethnic identity and transnational agendas. Members of C-100 and (although not as part of their formal agenda) The 1990 Institute have the highest awareness of race relations in the United States and of the barriers that Chinese and other Asian Americans continue to face. ACPSS members, by contrast, attribute the career-advancement obstacles they face to limited (academic) resources, while most Chinese-origin members of HRIC simply do not focus on identity as Chinese Americans. On the other hand, the C-100 and 1990 Institute members have the most social and political resources available to them. The elite position of C-100 members helps them open doors to the halls of power in both the USA and the PRC. Similarly, Chinese Americans in The 1990 Institute have used their professional and business connections to assemble impressive participation in and support for their projects from non-Chinese Americans. Further, their success in U.S. society makes it easier for these two groups to activate family and personal ties in China in support of their binational projects. Lacking both the mainstream status and the career diversity of C-100 and The 1990 Institute, ACPSS and HRIC have had to find other ways to leverage their position in U.S. society. ACPSS scholars have used their academic credentials in the United States to gain access to primary research sources in China and have employed that access to bolster their careers in the United States. HRIC uses appeals to widely accepted global human-rights standards to supplement its members' personal networks in China.

In terms of organizational characteristics, most members of all four transnational associations are professionals, scholars, or business people. The leaders and active members of The 1990 Institute all live in the San Francisco Bay area. Thus, they are able to maintain a degree of group solidarity through frequent face-to-face interaction. The other three groups have a geographically dispersed membership and rely on a small staff and various forms of telecommunication. None receives government funding; all rely on some combination of individual, corporate, and foundation funding.

Issue orientation highlights not just pluralism, but a sharp divide among the four organizations. The 1990 Institute's policy research, ACPSS's academic research, and C-100's cultural ambassadorship all depend, to some extent, on acceptance of these associations by the Chinese government as legitimate partners in dialogue. HRIC, in contrast, has consistently criticized and antagonized the Chinese government in the course of its human rights campaigns. HRIC is also critical of organizations that take a "constructive engagement" approach to human rights in China, arguing that politeness undermines effectiveness. However, this difference over means to a particular end is a secondary theme. The deeper division is over the ends themselves. For The 1990 Institute, C-100, and ACPSS, human rights (as defined by HRIC) are a derivative goal, not a primary one. In their view, economic and social development in China are the primary objectives. Only on the foundation of a growing economy, institutionalization of the rule of law, and healthy relations with the United States, they believe, can China build a more democratic political culture. Responses to the June 4 events in Tiananmen Square highlight this division. Largely in reaction to those tragic events, members organized The 1990 Institute and the Committee of 100. While far from acting as apologists for the Chinese government's actions, the leaders of both organizations viewed the government crackdown as a symptom, rather than a cause, of institutional failure in China. Thus, they responded by pushing to reactivate reforms and to head off deterioration in relations between the United States and China.[63]

By combining elements of transnational associational activity and transmigrant ethnic networks, organizations like those examined here are able to increase their impact on binational relations. C-100 leaders possess knowledge and credibility that encourage leaders in both the United States and China to see them as helpful intermediaries. For similar reasons, Chinese think-tanks and policy advisors have sought pragmatic ideas and advice from 1990 Institute–sponsored researchers. While ACPSS's scholarly research, with its mainly academic target audience, is a step further removed from the policymaking process, its research is also contributing to binational dialogue. HRIC, through its extensive publicity activities, has become a prominent voice in global human-rights forums. However, its lack of influence with either the PRC or U.S. governments, coupled with many of its members' weak attachment to U.S. society, limits HRIC's impact on binational relations.

Based on his historical study of U.S.–China relations since President Richard Nixon's visit to Beijing in 1972, Harry Harding argues that both countries should eschew exaggerated visions of either a hostile relationship or an idealistic special relationship. Rather, they should work methodically, on multiple fronts, to build a normal relationship.[64] If a normal relationship continues to take root, it is likely that Chinese American–led transnational improvement associations will be important contributors.

### Notes

1. Lucie Cheng, "Chinese Americans in the Formation of the Pacific Regional Economy," in *Across the Pacific: Asian Americans and Globalization*, ed. by Evelyn Hu-Dehart (Philadelphia: Temple University Press, 1999), pp. 61–78; Evelyn Hu-

Dehart, "Introduction: Asian American Formations in the Age of Globalization," in *Across the Pacific: Asian Americans and Globalization*, pp. 1–28; Xiao-huang Yin and Zhiyong Lan, "Chinese Americans: A Rising Factor in U.S.–China Relations," *Journal of American–East Asian Relations* 6, No. 1 (1997): 35–57; Xiao-huang Yin, "The Growing Influence of Chinese Americans on U.S.–China Relations," in *The Outlook for U.S.–China Relations Following the 1997–1998 Summits: Chinese and American Perspectives on Security, Trade, and Cultural Exchange*, ed. by Peter H. Koehn and Joseph Y.S. Cheng (Hong Kong: The Chinese University Press, 1999), pp. 331–349.

2. For Chinese Americans, see, for instance, L. Eve Ma, *Revolutionaries, Monarchists, and Chinatowns: Chinese Politics in the Americas and the 1911 Revolution* (Honolulu: University of Hawaii Press, 1990); Yong Chen, *Chinese San Francisco, 1850–1943: A Trans-Pacific Community* (Stanford: Stanford University Press, 2000). For non-Chinese American reformers, see Shirley Garrett, *Social Reformers in Urban China: The Chinese Y.M.C.A., 1895–1926* (Cambridge: Harvard University Press, 1970); Randall E. Stross, *The Stubborn Earth: American Agriculturalists on Chinese Soil, 1898–1937* (Berkeley: University of California Press, 1986); Xiaohong Shen, "Yale's China and China's Yale: Americanizing Higher Education in China, 1900–1927," unpublished Ph.D. dissertation, Yale University, 1993.

3. See Daniel Mato, "On Global and Local Agents and the Social Making of Transnational Identities and Related Agendas in 'Latin' America," *Identities: Global Studies in Culture and Power* 4 (December 1997): 171.

4. For an early statement, see Robert Keohane and Joseph S. Nye, "Transnational Relations and World Politics: An Introduction," *International Organization* 25, No. 3 (1971): 329–349. For a later elaboration, see Thomas Risse-Kappen, "Bringing Transnational Relations Back In: Introduction," in *Bringing Transnational Relations Back In: Non-State Actors, Domestic Structures, and International Institutions*, ed. by Thomas Risse-Kappen (Cambridge: Cambridge University Press, 1995), pp. 3–33.

5. Nina Glick Schiller, Linda Basch, and Cristina Blanc-Szanton, eds., "Towards a Transnational Perspective on Migration: Race, Class, Ethnicity, and Nationalism Reconsidered," *Annals of the New York Academy of Sciences* 645 (1992): vii–259; Linda Basch, Nina G. Schiller, and Cristina S. Blanc, *Nations Unbound: Transnational Projects, Postcolonial Predicaments, and Deterritorialized Nation-States* (New York: Gordon and Breach, 1994); Nina G. Schiller, ed., "Transnational Processes/Situated Identities," special issue of *Identities: Global Studies in Culture and Power* 4, No. 2 (1997). For an innovative political-science approach to transnationalism that incorporates a role for transmigrants acting through personal and group ties to two societies, see Peter Koehn, "Greasing the Grassroots: The Role of Nongovernmental Linkages in the Looming U.S.–China Confrontation Over Global Petroleum Reserves," in *The Outlook for U.S.–China Relations Following the 1997–1998 Summits*, pp. 351–390.

6. The following discussion of The 1990 Institute is based on research conducted at the University of Kansas. A more thorough and nuanced study of the Institute's mission, members, and history will appear in my master's degree thesis, provisionally entitled "Identity and Modernity: The 1990 Institute in a Transnational Public Sphere" and due to be completed in 2001.

7. Introduced as "Our Mission," this statement has appeared on the back of each Institute newsletter since issue 5, No. 3 (December 1994). During the four-and-a-half prior years, similar formulations appeared in the organization's internal discussions and promotional literature.

8. Rosalyn Koo, interview with the author, 12 July 1999, San Francisco.

9. Wei-Tai Kwok, interview with the author, 11 July 1999, San Francisco.

10. The Institute's public relations got off to a shaky start when a San Francisco reporter implied that it, too, had a protest agenda. Frank Viviano, "Think Tank on China Reform Created in SF," *San Francisco Chronicle*, 4 April 1990, p. A1.

11. C.B. Sung, interview with the author, 10 July 1999, San Francisco.

12. Hang-sheng Cheng, interview with the author, 10 July 1999, San Francisco.

13. Letter from Hang-sheng Cheng to C.B. Sung, 5 December 1989.

14. When I attended The 1990 Institute's tenth anniversary dinner held 28 April 2000 in San Francisco, I had a firsthand opportunity to observe the strength of Lee's social network. At a table of ten, every other person was there because of some personal or family connection with Lee, with the exception of my wife and Institute Honorary Co-Chair T.Y. Lin.

15. Sung, interview, 10 July 1999, San Francisco; Koo, interview, 12 July 1999, San Francisco; William Ming Sing Lee, interview with the author, 11 July 1999, San Francisco; William Lee, "F.F. and The 1990 Institute" (Unpublished paper distributed to F.F., September 2000).

16. Matilda Young, interview with the author, 12 July 1999, San Francisco; James Luce, interview with the author, 11 July 1999, San Francisco; Charles McClain, interview with the author, 12 July 1999, Berkeley. The book is *In Search of Equality: The Chinese Struggle against Discrimination in Nineteenth-Century America* (Berkeley: University of California Press, 1994).

17. Cheng, interview, 10 July 1999, San Francisco; " 'Social Ethics in China': An Essay Contest Sponsored by The 1990 Institute and the Shanghai Academy of Social Sciences," *Issue Paper* No. 13 (San Francisco: The 1990 Institute, 1997).

18. Cheng, interview, 10 July 1999, San Francisco; C.B. Sung, telephone interview with the author, 10 September 2000, San Francisco.

19. McClain, interview, 12 July 1999, Berkeley; "Law Conferences in San Francisco and Beijing," *Newsletter: A Publication of The 1990 Institute* VI (July 1995): 1, 10; Wei-Tai Kwok, "Institute Participates in Major Beijing Conference of Overseas Scholars," *Newsletter: A Publication of The 1990 Institute* VII (October 1996): 7.

20. Cheng, interview, e-mail to the author, 25 February 2000.

21. Sung, interview, 9 September 2000, San Francisco.

22. Zhu, now premier, has been recognized since the mid-1990s as China's leading official organizer of economic reform. Wu, according to Sung, is "number one in Zhu's brain trust." Ibid.

23. Letter from Wu Jinlian to Hang-Sheng Chen, dated 7 October 1994, and published in *Newsletter: A Publication of The 1990 Institute* V (December 1994): 16. At the time, Wu was a visiting professor at Stanford University's Asia/Pacific Research Center and the Department of Economics.

24. With respect to successful think-tanks, James Smith concludes that "the expert rarely contributes the flash of insight that quickly and fundamentally transforms national policy or inspires an innovative law. Instead, experts work slowly, gradually building up intellectual capital. . . ." James A. Smith, *The Idea Brokers: Think Tanks and the Rise of the New Policy Elite* (New York: The Free Press, 1991), pp. 229–230.

25. Hang-sheng Cheng, interview with the author, 10 July 1999, San Francisco.

26. 1990 Institute Chairman C.B. Sung has chaired the Nomination Committee of the C-100 board since its inception. Global bridge builder T.Y. Lin is a director of the Committee of 100 and an honorary co-chair of the Institute, while Chang-Lin Tien is

a C-100 governor and 1990 Institute honorary co-chair. The Institute's Executive Committee minutes indicate that the two organizations have occasionally given endorsements and/or financial support to one another's projects and events.

27. "About Us," at Committee of 100 website, address http://www.committee of100.org., as of 27 August 2000.

28. Henry S. Tang, telephone interview with the author, 5 June 2000, New York.

29. Ibid.

30. Ibid.

31. Ibid. Anger over the Wen Ho Lee case may present the real threat to national security. The *New York Times* reports that academic organizations with Asian American constituencies are urging their members to boycott employment with all nuclear weapons laboratories. With Asian Americans accounting for one-fourth of the Ph.D.s awarded annually in science and technology at U.S. universities, the impact could be substantial. At Los Alamos, for instance, the number of Asian applicants has "dwindled to three in the first half of 2000 from an average of twenty-eight in 1998 and 1999." The article profiles several individual Asian American scientists, including Kalina Wong—whose family has been in the United States for five generations and who has worked at the Livermore Laboratory for more than two decades. Ms. Wong experienced "removal from sensitive projects and an unexplained erosion of authority." James Glanz, "Amid Race Profiling Claims, Asian-Americans Avoid Labs," *New York Times*, 16 July 2000, pp. A1, A14.

In his failed effort to refute charges that laboratory security officials have acted like " 'a highway patrolman suspecting someone merely by virtue of their physical characteristics'" (Tang, interview, 5 June 2000, New York City), former FBI chief of Chinese counterintelligence Paul D. Moore argued that "the Chinese government specifically courts ethnic Chinese in the United States when looking for potential spies. As a result, he admitted, counterintelligence agents focus on Chinese Americans. 'It's unfair,' he said, 'but what are you going to do?'" Glanz, "Race Profiling," p. A14.

32. "About Us." The phrase "bicultural background" is from the 19 June 1998 executive summary of a "U.S.–China Relations Background Paper" (available at the same website) presented to the U.S. Congress and President Clinton prior to the latter's trip to China. In "About Us," the equivalent expression is "Americans familiar with both Chinese and American cultures and systems."

33. Also see Yossi Shain, *Marketing the American Creed Abroad: Diasporas in the U.S. and Their Homelands* (Cambridge: Cambridge University Press, 1999).

34. Tang, interview, 5 June 2000, New York City.

35. Ibid.

36. "About Us."

37. Ibid.

38. "U.S.–China Relations Background Paper, Executive Summary," 19 June 1998, on "Published Works" page at Committee of 100 website, address http://www.committeeof100.org., as of 27 August 2000.

39. Tang, interview, 5 June 2000, New York City.

40. Li Xiaobing, telephone interview with the author, 6 July 2000.

41. In fact, the Association for Asian Studies accepts many paper proposals submitted each year by students and scholars with China backgrounds.

42. Min Zhou, testing a model developed by Alejandro Portes, found that an "urban ethnic enclave" generally improved Chinese Americans' economic opportunities in New York City by creating positive social values for ethnicity—as manifested in

job networks, "internal" and "external markets," and so forth. Min Zhou, *Chinatown: The Socioeconomic Potential of an Urban Enclave* (Philadelphia: Temple University Press, 1992). A similar dynamic seems to be at work in the scholarship strategy of the ACPSS.

43. Hongshan Li, "The Chinese Version of *China's Road to Modernization*," *ACPSS Newsletter* 1:2 (March 1996), pp. 2–3.

44. The titles are *Living with Differences: China–U.S. Relations Toward the 21st Century* (River Edge, NJ: Global Publishing, 1998); and *Taiwan in the 21st Century: The Mainland Chinese Scholars* (River Edge, NJ: Global Publishing, 1999).

45. ACPSS scholars whose research has entered mainstream academic channels in the United States include Guaqiang Tian, economist at Texas A&M; Yiping Wan, dean of the College of Education, Jersey City State University; Honggang Yang, dean of the Business College, Southern Florida State University. Li Xiaobing, e-mail to the author, 15 November 2000.

46. Yu Yanmin, "U.S. Book Series Off the Ground," *ACPSS News* 2 (November 1997): 1–2.

47. Jixuan Hu, Zhaohui Hong, and Eleni Stavrou, eds., *In Search of a Chinese Road Towards Modernization: Economic and Educational Issues in China's Reform Process* (Lewiston, NY: Edwin Mellen Press, 1996); Zhang Jie and Li Xiaobing, eds., *Social Transition in China* (Lanham, MD: University Press of America, 1998); Hongshan Li and Zhaohui Hong, eds., *Image, Perception, and the Making of U.S.–China Relations* (Lanham, MD: University Press of America, 1998).

48. Li Xiaobing, telephone interview with the author, 6 July 2000.

49. Li Xiaobing, "Introduction: Social-economic Transition and Cultural Reconstruction in China," in *Social Transition in China*, pp. 3–4.

50. Li Xiaobing, interview, 6 July 2000.

51. See, for example, Louis Menand III, "Human Rights as Global Imperative," in *Conceptualizing Global History*, ed. by Bruce Mazlish and Ralph Buultjens (Boulder: Westview Press, 1993), pp. 173–204.

52. "About HRIC," at the organization's website, http://www.hrichina.org, as of 19 July 2000.

53. "What Is HRIC's Organizational Structure?" at the organization's website, http://www.hrichina.org, as of 19 July 2000.

54. "About HRIC." Not all Chinese American leaders of HRIC have suffered to the extent of Liu and Ge. The organization's executive director, Xiao Qiang, born in 1961, studied in the doctoral program in astrophysics at the University of Notre Dame from 1986 through 1989. Shaken by the June 4th events, he returned to China on 6 June 1989 to bring contributions to the victims' families. Two months later, he returned to the United States, where he has remained a human-rights activist. Similarly, journalist Liu Binyan and scientist Fang Lizhi antagonized the PRC government by criticizing its actions in 1989, but they were able to come to the United States without prior harsh punishment.

55. HRIC leader, e-mail communication to the author, 6 September 2000. This leader asked to remain anonymous.

56. HRIC leader, telephone interview with the author, 13 September 2000.

57. Ibid. While non-Chinese American scholars like Andrew Nathan and Perry Link, as well as some Chinese exiles and Chinese Americans, have encountered difficulties in obtaining visas, China has permitted entry to a number of HRIC members, including my interviewee. Further, HRIC is able to operate with relative freedom in Hong Kong, where it maintains an office.

58. "From Principle to Pragmatism: Can 'Dialogue' Improve China's Human Rights Situation? A Human Rights in China Report, June 23, 1998." Linked to "HRIC Publication List," HRIC website http://www.hrichina.org, as of 19 July 2000.

59. "About HRIC."

60. Ibid.

61. For the petition, see "Press Release, 23 August 2000: June Fourth Victims Demand Exclusion of Li Peng," at HRIC's website: http://www.hrichina.org. For the civil law suit, see Edward Wong, "Chinese Leader Sued in New York Over Deaths Stemming from Tiananmen Crackdown," *New York Times*, 1 September 2000, p. A6.

62. My source at HRIC stated, "we are glad that several individual Chinese Americans have joined with us, but we have not gotten support from organizations of Chinese Americans. We have not really approached these organizations because our main emphasis is on the situation in China." HRIC leader, interview, 6 September 2000, New York.

63. For interpretations of the Tiananmen events that generally correspond to those of C-100 and The 1990 Institute, see Harry Harding, A *Fragile Relationship: The United States and China Since 1972* (Washington, D.C.: Brookings Institution, 1992), pp. 216–246; Richard Madsen, *China and the American Dream: A Moral Inquiry* (Berkeley: University of California Press, 1995), pp. 23–24.

64. Harding, A *Fragile Relationship*, pp. 22, 358–360. In a later formulation, following President Jiang's 1997 visit to the United States and President Clinton's visit to China, Harding says the two countries have "established a new framework for their relationship, regarding themselves neither as allies nor as adversaries, but as partners in addressing international issues." However, he warns that, if not properly nurtured, this "constructive strategic partnership" could dissolve into a zero-sum "competitive relationship." Harry Harding, "The Clinton–Jiang Summits: An American Perspective," in *The Outlook for U.S.–China Relations Following the 1997–1998 Summits*, pp. 41, 46.

# 12

# Chinese American Scientists and U.S.–China Scientific Relations

## From Richard Nixon to Wen Ho Lee

### Zuoyue Wang

When President Richard Nixon embarked on his historic journey to Beijing in February 1972, the trip not only opened a new era in U.S.–China relations, but also began an exciting process of mutual rediscovery among the two peoples. The end of the schism brought forth unprecedented exchanges in many walks of life—especially in academia.[1] Perhaps more than any other group, Chinese American scientists helped facilitate these post-Nixon interactions as contacts flourished and expanded in the 1970s and the 1980s. This intellectual "open door" proved to have profound social and political, as well as scientific, impacts as China emerged from the devastating Cultural Revolution (1966–1976).

Curiously, there has been little scholarly work on the role of Chinese American scientists in U.S.–China relations either in English or Chinese. Several excellent studies examine U.S.–China academic and educational exchanges, but they barely touch on the scientific components or the role of Chinese American scientists—thus obscuring the part they play in the developing relationship. Further, most studies focus on the effects of academic exchanges in the United States and leave the political, social, and cultural impact of such exchanges on Chinese society and on U.S.–China relations unexamined.[2] In the late 1990s and early 2000s, the case involving Wen Ho Lee, accused of passing nuclear secrets to China, did focus national media attention on U.S.–China scientific exchange and Chinese American scientists, but few in-depth historical studies have emerged among the numerous reports on the controversy.

In this chapter, I argue that Chinese American scientists and academics have played an important, but often neglected, role in re-opening the relationship and in the subsequent development of U.S.–China relations. In addition, the ensuing exchanges transformed Chinese American scientists from a secluded elite group within a marginalized "model minority" in U.S. society into agents of transnational technoscience possessing cultural and even political import in both societies—especially in China.

I aim to ground the experiences of Chinese American scientists in the context of the history of Chinese Americans and U.S.–China relations— exploring the influence of Chinese cultural nationalism, the Asian American civil-rights movement, and state-sponsored internationalism during and after the Cold War on the formation and identity of a distinct Chinese American scientific community. As members, if not representatives, of their respective generations, five Chinese American scientists figure prominently in this account of the community's evolution. In chronological order of arrival in the United States, these are Qian Xuesen (Hsue-shen Tsien), an aerodynamic scientist who came before World War II; Chen Ning Yang (C.N. Yang) and Tsung Dao Lee (T.D. Lee), physicists who arrived after World War II and rose to international academic prominence in the 1950s– 1980s; Chang-Lin Tien, a mechanical engineer who came via Taiwan and gained influence in the 1990s as chancellor of the University of California–Berkeley; and finally, Wen Ho Lee, a computer scientist who arrived in 1965 and has been at the center of national controversy over alleged Chinese espionage of U.S. nuclear secrets in the 1990s and early 2000s. Although the discussion in this chapter concentrates on physics, extensive exchanges took place in other scientific and technological areas—such as biology, mathematics, geology, and agriculture—and Chinese American scientists and engineers also played active roles in those fields.

My definition of a Chinese American scientist is intentionally broad due to the remarkable mobility these scientists enjoy or were forced to follow in the network of the Chinese Diaspora—which includes the United States, China, Hong Kong, and Taiwan. Qian, for instance, spent two decades of his scientifically most productive years in the United States, with plans for permanent settlement, until forced to return to China in the 1950s during the McCarthy period. He is included here as a Chinese American scientist because many of those who came after him view his academic success in the United States as trail-blazing. Another indication of the ease with which prominent Chinese American scientists crossed national boundaries in this diasporic network is the phenomenon of Chinese American scientists serving in top academic posts in Hong Kong, Taiwan, and, increasingly, in the China Mainland. Yuan Tze Lee, a Nobel laureate in chemistry and long-time professor at the University of California–Berkeley, for example, returned to Taiwan in 1994 to head its Academia Sinica.[3] In 2000, Paul

Ching-wu Chu, a Chinese American physicist at the University of Houston known for his breakthroughs in superconductivity, agreed to become president of the Hong Kong University of Science and Technology, replacing Chia-Wei Woo, another Chinese American physicist who formerly headed San Francisco State University.[4] Some of these Chinese American scientists later returned to the United States. Eugene Wong, a pioneer in database design and another long-time U.C. Berkeley faculty member who served as associate director of the White House Office of Science and Technology Policy from 1990 to 1993, for instance, moved to Hong Kong to become vice chancellor for research and development at Woo's university in 1994. Four years later, however, the National Science Foundation summoned Wong back to Washington to head the engineering directorate.[5]

It is as difficult to demarcate the boundary of Chinese American scientists by citizenship as it is by position. While Yuan Tze Lee gave up his U.S. citizenship when he returned to Taiwan in 1994, others, like Wong, kept theirs. Many other Chinese American scientists spent most of their careers in the United States, but remained Chinese citizens. In view of the ambiguity and fluidity that characterize key aspects in the identity of Chinese American scientists, I find it advisable to adopt an inclusive and functional definition. Thus, instead of relying on positions and citizenship, I use the term "Chinese American scientists" to denote all those scientists and engineers of Chinese ethnic origin who spent a significant portion of their careers in the United States. I also limit the subject of this study to those who have had an impact on the formation of the Chinese American scientific community and its role in U.S.–China relations. While much of the chapter is concerned with the Cold War years, the Wen Ho Lee case is included for what it reveals about the role of Chinese American scientists in post–Cold War U.S.–China relations.

Throughout this account, I use the experiences of individual scientists to gain a sense of the evolution of the role of Chinese American scientists in U.S.–China relations both before and after Nixon's trip in 1972. The chapter also looks at how the Cold War affected their status in U.S. society. This analysis provides important background to understanding the role of Chinese American scientists during the post-Nixon exchanges of the 1970s and 1980s and in the more recent era. The central question addressed is: how do Chinese American scientists affect U.S.–China relations by their actions as a unique subnational and transnational scientific community? In addition, the chapter examines the impact of the scientific exchanges on Chinese science and educational policy and on Chinese scientists—many of whom suffered persecution during the Cultural Revolution in China.

## Chinese Scientists in the United States

When C.N. Yang, then at the Princeton Institute of Advanced Study, and T.D. Lee, at Columbia University, won the Nobel Prize in Physics in late 1957, they not only brought pride to Chinese all over the world; they also gave some relief to Americans who worried that the West was losing the Cold War with the communist bloc in science and technology. Just days before, the Soviet Union had launched *Sputnik*, the first artificial satellite, touching off mass hysteria in the United States about a "missile gap" imperiling U.S. national security. *Sputnik*-inspired reforms led to the massive National Defense Education Act program to beef up U.S. science and education and to numerous measures aimed at expediting the immigration of foreign technical manpower.[6]

As science became a weapon in the Cold War, both for its military applications and for its symbolic importance as a measure of national prestige, Yang and Lee found themselves wooed on both sides of the iron curtain. The fact that they were not U.S. citizens (both traveled on Kuomintang Chinese passports) led U.S. government officials to keep "an anxious eye" on them when they flew to Sweden in December 1957 to receive their Nobel awards. The watchful officials breathed a collective sigh of relief when Yang announced in a speech at the Nobel banquet that "I am as proud of my Chinese heritage and background as I am devoted to modern science—a part of human civilization of Western origin." In the end, they were happy to see both prize winners return promptly to the States.[7]

The Nobel Prize celebration and media attention, however, only masked the deep social, cultural, and political tensions felt by Yang and Lee and many other Chinese scientists and engineers at the time. What first drew Chinese students to study science and technology in the United States, around the turn of the century, was their dream of building a strong, modern, and democratic China. The U.S. government encouraged such tendencies in an effort to influence the future direction of China. It stipulated in the early 1900s, for instance, that the United States would return part of the indemnity it received from China for the Boxer Rebellion of 1900 against foreigners only if the Chinese government used the funds to send students to the United States. The resulting Boxer fellowship program brought hundreds of elite Chinese students and scientists to the United States from the 1910s to the 1940s. Yang was one of these so-called Boxer scholars and, indeed, made the history of the Boxer program a central part of his address at the Nobel banquet in 1957. Recounting his ambivalent feelings about the Boxer program, Yang said, "I am in more than one sense a product of both the Chinese and Western cultures, in harmony and in conflict."[8]

Racial discrimination marked Chinese scientists' social experiences in the United States during the era of the Chinese Exclusion Act (1882–1943). Until the repeal of the last exclusion act in 1943, the U.S. government denied students from China rights to become permanent residents or citizens. Racism against Asian Americans persisted in the postwar period. Even as late as 1954, a developer refused to sell a house to Yang—then a member of the prestigious Institute of Advanced Studies at Princeton. The developer feared that "our being Chinese might affect his sales," Yang recalled.[9] Chang-Lin Tien recalled being "confused and scared" by drinking fountains labeled "white only" and "colored" when he arrived in Louisville, Kentucky, in 1956. At the University of Louisville, one of his professors called him "Chinaman"—supposedly due to difficulties pronouncing Chinese names. When Tien learned that it was a derogatory term, he confronted the professor and made him stop the practice: "If you can't remember my name, don't call on me anymore."[10]

International politics also complicated the lives and careers of Chinese American scientists. When the Chinese Communists won the civil war in 1949, many Chinese students decided to return to China. Having detested the corrupt Kuomintang government and experienced humiliating discrimination in the United States, these students placed great hope in a new China—whose government appeared to focus on national reconstruction and appreciate the role of science and scientists in the endeavor. The Korean War that broke out in the summer of 1950, however, soon closed the window of opportunity for Chinese students and scholars who wanted to return to their homeland. The U.S. government forbade Chinese nationals, especially those studying or specializing in science and engineering, from returning to China. The ensuing McCarthyist "Red Scare" targeted, among others, Chinese scientists suspected of left-wing activities and associations. These measures greatly alienated many Chinese scientists and engineers.

The best-known example of the disillusioned Chinese scientist is Qian Xuesen, an aerodynamic scientist at the California Institute of Technology. As a favorite student of Theodore von Karmen, Qian rose to the top of the profession in the 1940s, helped found the Jet Propulsion Laboratory, and contributed to U.S. weapons development during World War II. In the postwar period, Qian became a member of the influential Air Force Scientific Advisory Board—in spite of the fact that he retained his Chinese citizenship. He applied for U.S. citizenship in 1949.[11] Trust turned into suspicion during the McCarthy era, however, when he lost his security clearance. Humiliated, Qian decided to return to China, but the U.S. government charged him as a Communist Party member and spy for China and placed him under house arrest for five years—effectively prohibiting him from leaving the country.

At a dramatic hearing on Qian's case, an official asked him: "In the event of conflict between the United States and Communist China, would you fight for the United States?' " Qian, after a long pause, answered "my essential allegiance is to the people of China. If a war were to start between the United States and China, and if the United States war aim was for the good of the Chinese people, and I think it will be, then, of course, I will fight on the side of the United States."[12]

As a result of the Geneva Conference between the United States and China, the U.S. government eventually allowed Qian and hundreds of other Chinese scientists and engineers to return to China in the mid-1950s—in exchange for U.S. prisoners of war held in China.[13] However, Qian's experience, especially his treatment at the hands of the U.S. government, had a lasting impact on Chinese American scientists. Specifically, the persecution of Qian during the McCarthy era caused many Chinese American scientists to avoid political issues. To stay out of trouble, many in the Chinese American community, including scientists, adopted a strategy of striving for achievement in professional fields while shunning politics.[14] They fell silent and fearful, as Chang-Lin Tien put it, "as cicadas in cold weather" (*jinruo hanchan*). "When I came in the 1950s," Tien continued, "many (Chinese American) professors avoided meeting or talking to Chinese students. They dared not even speak Chinese."[15]

Among the thousands of Chinese American scientists who stayed, many, including C.N. Yang and T.D. Lee, became U.S. citizens in the 1950s and 1960s.[16] In the 1960s, the civil rights and anti–Vietnam War movements stirred Asian Americans to activism; they began to fight for their rights in mainstream society and culture.[17] The Asian American movement of the late 1960s and early 1970s, according to one commentator, "made Asian Americans more American and less Asian."[18] Chinese American scientists did not play a prominent role in the movement, but many began to change their earlier, conservative political stand and participated in the civil rights and, especially, the anti-war movements.[19] The emotional soul-searching that accompanied their decision to become U.S. citizens also led many of these scientists to discover the early, bitter history of Chinese Americans in the United States. They began to identify with the plights not only of early Chinese immigrants, but also of contemporary Chinese American communities cloistered in the different world of the Chinatowns in urban centers throughout the United States.[20] They often drew inspiration from examples of community solidarity by other ethnic groups, especially the African American civil rights struggle and Jewish American fight to remember the Holocaust.[21]

By all indications, prominent members of the nascent Chinese American scientific community grew active politically when the U.S.–China rapprochement took place in the early 1970s. A new generation of Chinese American scientists, such as Chang-Lin Tien, who left the China Mainland for Taiwan in 1949 and came to study in the United States in the 1950s, became politically active in the 1960s. They began to organize themselves during the *Baodiao* (Defending Diaoyutai Islands) Movement during the late 1960s and early 1970s. Diaoyutai, a group of islets near Taiwan and Okinawa that traditionally belonged to China, had been ceded, together with Taiwan itself, to Japan in the aftermath of the 1895 Sino-Japanese war. The U.S. military kept the islets as a training site instead of returning them to China as scheduled in 1945. In the late 1960s, Japan asserted ownership after the discovery of oil in the area. The U.S. government acquiesced to the Japanese claim when it turned over Diaoyutai (Senkaku in Japanese), along with Okinawa, to Japan. This action enraged Chinese Americans. In 1971, dozens of prominent scientists and scholars, including C.N. Yang and Chang-Lin Tien, signed an open letter to President Nixon and members of Congress asking them to "recognize Chinese sovereignty over these islands."[22]

The *Baodiao* Movement played a crucial role in the political activism of Chinese American scientists of Tien's generation. It stirred their Chinese nationalism and prompted them to organize themselves. During the movement, Tien and his fellow *Baodiao* activists became disillusioned with the weak response of the Kuomintang government in Taiwan. As a result, they looked favorably toward the Mainland government—which took a stronger stand against Japan's claim. Tien made his first visit back to China in 1973—shortly after Nixon's trip.

### Chinese American Scientists and U.S.–China Scientific Exchanges

The normalization of the U.S.–China relationship provided Chinese American scientists with a golden opportunity to satisfy their impulse to help their ancestral land and to assert their voice in U.S. society. The door for scientific and cultural exchange finally opened with Nixon's visit to China in 1972.[23] In the famous Shanghai Communiqué, science and technology figured prominently in the new bilateral relationship:

> The two sides agreed that it is desirable to broaden the understanding between the two peoples. To this end, they discussed specific areas in such fields as science, technology, culture, sports, and journalism, in which people-to-people contacts and exchanges would be mutually beneficial. Each side undertakes to facilitate the further development of such contacts and exchange.[24]

Both the United States and China saw scientific exchange as a neutral, nonideological route to mutual understanding after so many years of isolation. Of course, the U.S. government was aware of the military implications of technology transfer and its counterintelligence officials always kept their eyes on visiting Chinese scientists.[25] In the context of the heightened Cold War, however, the Nixon administration decided to take a calculated risk in the hope that a modernized China would provide balance against the Soviet Union and, thus, work in the U.S. national interest. In 1973, for example, Secretary of State Henry Kissinger secretly proposed to Premier Zhou Enlai that the United States would provide China with early-warning-intelligence information (satellite images) on Soviet missile launchings through a hotline. "We could also give you the technology for certain kinds of radars," Kissinger told Zhou, "but you would have to build them yourselves."[26]

Scientific exchanges carried great significance for Chinese leaders concerned with economic development—especially Premier Zhou and Deng Xiaoping. In many ways, Zhou became the gatekeeper in scientific exchange with the United States in the early 1970s. He personally negotiated the first formal academic exchange agreement with the U.S. Committee on Scholarly Communication with the People's Republic of China (CSCPRC) in 1973. The CSCPRC, a semi-official group formed in 1966 by the National Academy of Sciences, American Council of Learned Societies, and the Social Science Research Council, often worked through Chinese American scientists who were visiting China and meeting with Zhou Enlai or other Chinese science-policy makers to facilitate scientific exchanges.[27] In a 1973 meeting with Zhou, the CSCPRC presented a list of twelve items of exchange, and Zhou gave his blessing to nine of them—all in natural sciences. He excluded three social science projects (China studies, urban studies, and science and technology in China's development) as requiring further preparation.[28] Nevertheless, Zhou took great personal interest in scientific exchange with the United States and sought to ensure that the framework of exchange would survive personnel changes at the top of both governments—especially in view of Nixon's domestic political troubles.[29]

Interestingly, remarkably few Chinese American scientists exhibited much loyalty to Taiwan. Instead, they decided to travel to the China Mainland in spite of explicit expressions of displeasure by the Taiwan government. Some scientists even visited in the face of anonymous threats attributed to pro-Taiwan forces in the 1970s and 1980s.[30] Taiwan blacklisted Chang-Lin Tien, at the time professor of mechanical engineering at UC–Berkeley, for several years because of his trip to the Mainland in 1973.[31]

## *C.N. Yang and T.D. Lee*

Among Chinese American scientists, Yang and Lee were the earliest and most active in the U.S.–China scientific exchange. Yang was the first prominent Chinese American scientist to visit China in summer 1971, right after the Nixon administration lifted the ban on U.S. citizens' travel to China. In many ways Yang's trip set the precedent for other Chinese American scientists. Yang's father, Yang Wuzhi, was a U.S.-trained mathematician and professor in Shanghai. When he learned of his son's intention to come back for a visit, he was uncertain how the Chinese government would react. Therefore, he sent an inquiry to the State Council under Zhou Enlai. The State Council promptly approved the visit and asked the Chinese Academy of Sciences to host Yang in Beijing—hoping to attract other Chinese American scientists to return for visits as well.[32] Indeed, many Chinese American scientists, including T.D. Lee in 1972, followed Yang's footsteps.

As Yang and Lee visited China, each in his own way sought to revitalize Chinese science and society in the aftermath of the Cultural Revolution. When he visited Chinese universities in the early 1970s, Yang—by then a professor at the State University of New York–Stony Brook—was (like many other U.S. scientist visitors) impressed by the observed emphasis on practical applications. Even during his trip in summer 1971, however, he saw problems with the lack of attention to basic research. He raised the issue with Premier Zhou Enlai when Zhou hosted a banquet in his honor.[33] On his return visit in 1972, Yang made a stronger push for basic research.[34] Chinese scientists seized the opportunity afforded by Yang's and other visiting U.S. scientists' advocacy to advance not only the cause for basic research, but also the political fortunes of Chinese science in general.

Likewise, when T.D. Lee met with Zhou Enlai in Beijing on 14 October 1972, he encouraged Zhou to launch China's own basic research program in high-energy physics. He also urged Zhou to invite foreign scientists for visits and to send Chinese students and scientists abroad for study and research. Lee assured Zhou that CERN (European Center for Nuclear Research) and many other laboratories in the West would welcome Chinese scientists, and that such exchanges would not create a "two Chinas" problem because he did not believe that Taiwan was interested in high-energy research.[35] Later, Lee played a key role in the development of the Beijing Electron-Positron Collider. He has remained active in facilitating cooperation between Chinese and U.S. high-energy physicists.[36]

## Shared Motives, Different Visions

In many ways, Yang and Lee are representative of Chinese American scientists' home-country cultural nationalism. The most important contribution in his life, Yang said on 28 January 1995 in Hong Kong, was helping "Chinese change their perception that the Chinese were not as talented as others."[37]

In spite of their common goal of helping China, Yang and Lee held sharply different visions for the direction of Chinese science policy, which led them to give radically divergent advice to China's policymakers.[38] Generally speaking, Yang recognized the importance of basic research. He was instrumental in Zhou Enlai's drive to rehabilitate basic research in China. Yet, he came to believe that much more applied research should be undertaken. To Yang, applied research in areas such as computers or biochemistry served as a link in the chain that would transform scientific ideas into technologies and expedite national economic development. For this reason, he advised against China's undertaking an expensive high-energy physics program.[39] With memory of the first-half-of-the-twentieth-century sufferings in mind, Yang regarded poverty as the source of most of China's problems. "The most important thing for China," he said in 1986, is "to advance its economy." He did not want the PRC to engage in high-energy physics because it had nothing to do with economic development; it "might even have negative effects, because it is too expensive."[40]

Lee, on the other hand, consistently advocated that China invest in basic research. He thought that the PRC should develop its own high-energy physics program, including the building of accelerators, as a way to ensure that Chinese scientists keep abreast of advances at the frontiers of science and that China maintain a balanced infrastructure in science. Lee also created the popular China–U.S. Physics Examination and Applications (CUSPEA) program, which, from 1980 to 1988, annually brought about one hundred top Chinese physics students for graduate studies in the United States.[41] His other projects included a continuing special class for science prodigies at the University of Science and Technology of China in Hefei, establishment of the Chinese Center for Advanced Science and Technology in Beijing, initiation of a system of postdoctoral research in China, and, of course, the Beijing Electron-Positron Collider.[42]

## The Impact of Chinese American Scientists in China

In spite of divergence in their advice, the prominent role of the Chinese American scientists helped moderate concern in the PRC about the political and cultural values that accompanied scientific exchanges in particular and modernization and globalization in general. The fact that these Chinese American scientists acted out of nationalistic motives facilitated the transmission of such new values. The identification of Chinese American scientists with Chinese culture also helped alleviate any affront to national pride when they, rather than Westerners who were not ethnically Chinese, promoted ideas that challenged Chinese orthodoxy. Their international background and prominence further enabled them to speak out on sensitive issues with impunity; for similar actions, Chinese scientists would experience trouble. T.D. Lee, for example, told a group of Chinese graduate students in 1979 that he did not think that philosophy had any impact on physics.[43] In 1986, C.N. Yang similarly dismissed this privileged branch of scholarship in China: "Physics influenced philosophy, but philosophy never influenced physics."[44] Government officials denounced such views when advocated by people like Fang Lizhi, the Chinese astrophysicist-dissident who wrote a book entitled *Philosophy Is a Tool of Physics*, as efforts to undermine Marxism's guiding role in Chinese science and society.[45] Inconsistently, the government published both Lee's and Yang's speeches even after purging Fang from the Communist Party for expressing the same view.

Yang and Lee by no means were the only influential Chinese American scientists in China. Hundreds of other Chinese American scientists and professionals visited China in the 1970s. These included such prominent figures as the mathematician Shiing-shen Chern of Berkeley, architect I.M. Pei, and physicist C.S. Wu of Columbia, the first female (and Chinese American) president of the American Physical Society in 1975. Many of these Chinese American scientists were immigrants who had received an undergraduate education in China and had come to the United States in the 1930s and 1940s for graduate training—often with funding from the then Kuomintang government of China. In the 1970s, they participated in exchanges with China in the name of scientific internationalism, but their strongest motivation was cultural nationalism in the sense of identification with the developmental aspirations of their country of origin.[46] Their active participation in U.S.–China scientific exchanges constituted the single most important factor determining the success and character of the transnational scientific network. In turn, the U.S.–China reopening energized Chinese American scientists who, until then, had maintained an almost invisible presence among the U.S. scientific community and the public at large.

**Chinese American Scientists as a Transnational Community**

The U.S.–China reopening gave Chinese American scientists a sense of community for the first time and enabled them to gain a voice not only in science, but in public-policy making in the United States and China. Much networking went on among the widely dispersed Chinese American scientists and scholars in the early 1970s, when they sought to organize into groups to expedite their visits to China. They were impressed by the social and material progress in the People's Republic and, upon their return, became influential opinion makers in shaping the U.S. perception of the new China.[47] For the first time in the history of Chinese American scientists, they gained a voice in U.S. public-policy making. In 1971, for example, Yang met Edward David, President Nixon's science advisor, at a scientific meeting and told him about his recent visit to China. Later, David wrote a memorandum for Henry Kissinger concerning this conversation.[48]

Institutionally, Chinese American scientists, especially physicists, began to organize themselves at the national and, later, international levels. In 1977, Yang became the first president of the National Association of Chinese Americans (NACA). NACA, designed to lobby for normalization of the U.S.–China relationship, was composed mainly of scientists and other professionals.[49] Among other actions, the group paid for a full-page advertisement in the New York Times pushing for U.S.–China normalization. When Deng Xiaoping visited the United States in 1979, shortly after the two countries finally reestablished diplomatic relations, Yang organized a banquet for him on behalf of the NACA and other Chinese American organizations.[50]

Since the 1970s, common interests in the development of Chinese science, technology, and education and in improving U.S.–China relations have continued to unite Chinese American scientists. In Yang's words, it is "my responsibility to build a bridge of understanding and friendship between the two countries that are close to my heart. I also feel that I should help China in her drive toward developing science and technology."[51] In 1987, a Hong Kong journalist asked Yang what he thought should be done about continued Western restrictions on the export of high technologies to China. Yang replied:

> Ethnic Chinese scientists in the US in general care about the development of science and technology in China. They have requested that relevant agencies relax the restrictions on high-tech exports to China. However, the most important step toward solving this problem is (improving) China's own self-reliance. What we could do is help train China's scientific and technological talents.[52]

It should be understood that by working for enhanced Chinese science and education and improved U.S.–China relations in the 1970s and 1980s, Yang, Lee, and other Chinese American scientists were not in any way pursuing a secret agenda in conflict with that of the U.S. government. Indeed, many of the exchange programs resulted from official U.S.–China agreements when the Soviet Union's invasion of Afghanistan helped to sustain the Sino-U.S. strategic alliance in the early 1980s. Later, as the China Mainland under Deng Xiaoping launched economic reforms, the administration of President Ronald Reagan promoted scientific contacts as a way both to encourage Chinese reform and to expand the potential market for U.S. products and technology. In testimony before the Congressional Task Force on Science Policy in 1985, John P. McTague, deputy director of the White House Office of Science and Technology Policy, emphasized that "the most effective channel we have found for nations to cooperate has been through science and technology. The example . . . of the People's Republic of China may be the most spectacular success. . . ."[53] In response to questioning from congressmen, he explained that "by increasing technological capabilities in other countries, we then open up new markets for ourselves and, I think, help stabilize the world situation," and added, "it is clear that the People's Republic of China has decided to make a very major effort to utilize science and technology to modernize its nation, to increase its industrial base, to increase the standard of living for its people, to open its markets with the West."[54]

The influx of Chinese scientists and engineers who settled permanently in the United States after the reopening of U.S.–China relations also infused the Chinese American scientific community with much vitality. By the mid-1990s, according to one survey, there were over 1,000 academics above the rank of university lecturer in the United States who came from the China Mainland—about 800 in the sciences and engineering, 300 in social sciences and humanities, and 80 in other fields.[55] Their entrance into the research community also helped change the racial and gender structure of U.S. science, as the new Chinese American scientists and engineers increased the proportion of Asian Americans and a substantial percentage of them were women.[56]

While the Chinese government has been concerned over this obvious "brain drain," these science-trained expatriates are not a complete loss for China. Many of them became entrepreneurs who promoted U.S.–China trade and contributed to the Mainland economic boom of the 1990s.[57]

The loose connections among Chinese American scientists in the diaspora have developed into a powerful transnational network.[58] In 1980, a conference on particle physics theories in Guangzhou drew together, for the first time, many ethnic Chinese physicists from around the world.[59] In 1990, Chinese American physicists organized the Overseas Chinese Physics Association. OCPA includes physicists from the U.S., PRC, Taiwan, and Hong Kong. Its membership of more than 400 by July 2000 boasted several Chinese American Nobel laureates in physics—including C.N. Yang, T.D. Lee, Samuel Ting of MIT, and Daniel Tsui of Princeton, as well as the astrophysicist-dissident Fang Lizhi. The association organizes special "Physics without Borders" sessions at the annual meetings of the American Physical Society, maintains an e-mail network, sponsors workshops in the Asia-Pacific region, and acts as a clearinghouse of information on jobs for its members. It also gives the Outstanding Young Researcher and Achievement in Asia awards to recognize the talent of ethnic Chinese physicists and to promote scientific research in the Asia-Pacific region.[60] OCPA held the First International Ethnic Chinese Physics Conference in Shantou in 1995—just after the PRC conducted a series of menacing missile tests near Taiwan as a warning against the independence movement on the island. Many observers viewed conference attendance by scientists from the official Academia Sinica of Taiwan as an encouraging sign that scientists might play a crucial role in the eventual peaceful unification of China.[61]

*Tiananmen Setback*

The United States and many other nations imposed diplomatic and economic sanctions against China after the Tiananmen Incident on 4 June 1989. The U.S. scientific community interrupted bilateral scientific and technological exchanges in protest against the violence. The National Academy of Sciences and several other U.S. academic organizations suspended most of their joint projects with China in "outrage and sadness." While these measures received general approval, more radical forms of protest threatened far-reaching curtailment of scientific contact and, therefore, divided the scientific community in the West—including Chinese American scientists.

The dilemma facing many Chinese American scientists was how to demonstrate their disapproval of the PRC government's actions without isolating their colleagues in China. Proponents of radical measures—such as boycotting scientific exchanges with the Mainland—argued that only an unambiguous public stand could help the situation of scientist-dissidents. They urged colleagues to avoid meetings in the PRC and campaigned against holding future conferences there until the repression ceased. Business as usual, argued James C. Wang, a Chinese American professor of biochemistry and molecular biology at Harvard University, was unconscionable.[62]

On the other hand, there were scientists such as T.D. Lee, who insisted that a boycott would interrupt the free flow of scientists and scientific ideas, push China back into intellectual isolation, and hurt both Chinese science and scientists. While calling the Tiananmen Incident "a great tragedy," Lee—who was in Beijing as the host of a scientific seminar on June 4th—argued for maintaining U.S.–China scientific exchanges on grounds that "only through continuous contact with our colleagues in China can we help them in a genuine way."[63] Lee went back to Beijing in September 1989 and met with Deng Xiaoping in an effort to secure the government's lenient treatment of students and scientists who had been involved in the nonviolent protests. Many of his fellow Chinese American scientists criticized Lee's actions, however, when pictures of him holding hands with Deng made headlines all over the world. On the other hand, the U.S. government took his meeting with Deng seriously. On 17 October 1989, Lee met with President George Bush in the White House to convey Deng's message that he wanted to improve U.S.–China relations.[64] The fact that Lee played the messenger role at this critical juncture indicates that Chinese American scientists indeed had become a bridging and stabilizing force in bilateral relations.

Likewise, Yang pushed for resuming U.S.–China relations in the aftermath of Tiananmen. During a visit to Hong Kong in August 1989, he publicly opposed U.S. sanctions on China. Carefully avoiding comments on the Tiananmen Incident itself, Yang argued that continued attempts to punish China in this manner only threatened international stability.[65] His overriding concern for economic development led Yang to give priority to stability over political reforms (such as democratization and human rights). "Let the economy grow and later on reform," he told the New York Academy of Sciences' Committee on the Human Rights of Scientists in 1996. "Eventually we will reach a more open, more democratic society," Yang said, "but we don't want to go through the problems they had in the Soviet Union."[66]

In the debate over Tiananmen, other scientists believed that quiet diplomacy would be more effective than open sanctions. Sharp objections also arose over basing actions on the interests of scientists working in China rather than on those of dissidents or exiled scientists. In sum, the Chinese American scientific community, which led the way in establishing ties among scientists in the two countries, was highly polarized over scientific sanctions against the PRC.

By the end of the 1990s, as the political environment in the Mainland improved and interest in trade with China grew, scientific and technological exchanges resumed. However, the scars left by Tiananmen linger on in the new global political context of the post–Cold War era.

### The Wen Ho Lee Case

Post–Cold War international politics reshaped bilateral scientific relations in the 1990s. With the end of the Cold War in the early 1990s, some policymakers in Washington, D.C., increasingly viewed China as the primary threat to

U.S. interests and charged the PRC with weapons proliferation, human rights abuses, and illiberal trade practices. Such shifts in official attitudes paralleled the deterioration in U.S. public opinion toward China following the Tiananmen tragedy.[67] The loyalty of the entire Chinese American community came under question in the aftermath of the campaign-contribution scandal during the presidential election of 1996 when several Chinese Americans funneled illegal donations to the Democratic Party.[68] Domestic partisan politics and the sensation-seeking media helped make U.S.–China relations and the loyalty of Chinese Americans topics of national controversy in the post–Cold War era. In this new political climate, scientific exchange with China, and the role of Chinese American scientists therein, came under increased scrutiny in the United States.

In 1997, the Federal Bureau of Investigation arrested Peter Lee, a Taiwanese-born Chinese American physicist who once worked at the Los Alamos National Laboratory, on grounds that he had transmitted secret laser technology and techniques used in the detection of submarines to Chinese scientists. In a plea bargain, Lee admitted that he leaked classified information when he visited China, but insisted that it was unintentional—he had been carried away by his enthusiasm for scientific exchange. In light of his cooperation and the fact that the U.S. government soon thereafter declassified the information Lee had leaked, he received a lenient sentence—one year confinement in a halfway house. His case received scant media attention.[69]

In early 1999, the *New York Times* reported, based on leaked information from government sources, that China stole U.S. nuclear weapons secrets in the 1980s and that one scientist at the Department of Energy's Los Alamos weapons laboratory in New Mexico was under investigation as a Chinese spy.[70] The explosive report came on the heels of the unsuccessful impeachment trial of President Bill Clinton and completion of a classified investigation under Republican congressman Christopher Cox alleging Chinese thefts of U.S. nuclear and other military technologies. It generated great public and congressional pressure on the Clinton administration to take action. Three days after the *New York Times* reported the existence of a suspect at Los Alamos, Bill Richardson, secretary of the Department of Energy, fired Wen Ho Lee from the laboratory. Although Richardson had no evidence that Lee committed espionage, and fired him for "failure to properly notify Energy Department and laboratory officials about contacts with people from a sensitive country, specific instances of failing to properly safeguard classified material, and apparently attempting to deceive lab officials about security matters," the *New York Times* and other media sources immediately identified Lee as the primary suspect in the Chinese espionage case.[71] Thus began the national political controversy over the Wen Ho Lee "spy case," which, along with U.S. bombing of the Chinese embassy in Belgrade and the subsequent attacks by Chinese students on the U.S. embassy in Beijing, led to a rapid decline in U.S.–China relations during the spring of 1999.

Wen Ho Lee, born in Taiwan in 1939, came to the United States for graduate studies at Texas A&M University in 1965 and received his doctorate degree in mechanical engineering in 1969. He became a U.S. citizen in 1974, and worked for a variety of industrial and government research firms before moving to the Los Alamos laboratory in 1978—where he worked on applied mathematics and fluid dynamics involving computer simulations of nuclear explosions from 1978 to 1999.[72] In 1996, the FBI began investigating Lee as the prime suspect in the leaking of the design of W-88, the most advanced U.S. nuclear warhead, to the PRC. After his firing in March 1999, the FBI searched his office and home and found evidence that he had improperly downloaded classified computer codes onto unclassified computers and tapes.[73] On 10 December 1999, prosecutors indicted Lee on 59 counts of illegally removing classified nuclear data at Los Alamos.[74] Lee, pressured to confess his crime under the threat of execution, spent the next nine months awaiting trial in solitary confinement under harsh conditions.

As the Lee case evolved, Chinese Americans became alarmed over the racial and political overtones of the investigation, which was code-named "Kindred Spirit" at one time to reflect the perceived Chinese practice of using Chinese Americans as spies. Many in the Asian American community believed that government officials had singled out Wen Ho Lee because of his Chinese ethnic background and used him as a scapegoat for national security problems, real or imagined, amid a background of domestic partisan politics and increasing U.S.–China tensions. On 1 April 1999, the Overseas Chinese Physics Association, of which Wen Ho Lee was a member, wrote a letter requesting that President Bill Clinton take action to prevent "the deterioration of the working environment of Chinese-American scientists" and damage to U.S.–China scientific exchanges due to the fallout from the Lee case:

> We urge you as the President to speak out to set the Los Alamos incident in its proper perspective and let the public know that the overwhelming majority of the Chinese-Americans scientists are law-abiding, that they have contributed significantly to the advancement of science in the United States, and that scientific exchanges between the United States and China related to basic research also serve American interests.[75]

Likewise, the 80–20 Initiative, an Asian American political action committee with Chang-Lin Tien among its founders, questioned whether the government followed due process of law when it fired and prosecuted Wen Ho Lee.[76]

In July 1999, responding to increased criticism that Wen Ho Lee was a victim of racial profiling, President Clinton issued a statement decrying discrimination against Asian American scientists. Using the occasion of his appointment of Chang-Lin Tien as a member of the National Science Board, Clinton praised Tien and other Asian Pacific American scientists for their contributions to U.S. science and society:

> Asian Pacific American scientists and engineers have long made major contributions to our country, to our national security, and to our unmatched scientific enterprise. . . . That is why it is intolerable that the patriotism of Asian Pacific American scientists be questioned in the wake of recent allegations of espionage at one of our national laboratories. Security matters are of the highest priority in my administration, but history has shown the damage to the lives of our citizens and to our society that results from the destructive grip of prejudice, suspicion and discrimination. Racism and stereotyping have no place in our One America in the 21st century.[77]

Such reassurance, though welcome by Chinese Americans, did not turn the tide of widespread suspicion. In May 1999, Congress released an unclassified version of the Cox report, which stated that "threats to national security can come from PRC scientists, students, business people, or bureaucrats, in addition to professional civilian and military intelligence operations." Several congresspersons questioned whether such incendiary language might be used unfairly to question the loyalty of all Asian Americans.[78] By mid-2000, as Lee languished in pre-trial detention, handcuffed and shackled, Asian American scientists began to leave or avoid jobs at nuclear weapons laboratories.[79] "The labs are having great difficulty recruiting Asian [American] scientists and engineers, and many who are there are considering other jobs," reported Bob H. Suzuki, president of the California State Polytechnic University at Pomona and, with Tien, another Asian American member of the National Science Board.[80] In August 2000, the National Academy of Sciences, the National Academy of Engineering, and the Institute of Medicine openly expressed their dissatisfaction with Wen Ho Lee's treatment while in detention and with the government's handling of the entire case in an open letter to Attorney General Janet Reno.[81] These academies together represent the most prominent bodies of U.S. science, technology, and medicine—with dozens of Chinese Americans among their membership.

After a series of dramatic turns and twists, the case against Lee unraveled as government investigators admitted making false statements and as the prosecutors failed to turn up any evidence of espionage. Wen Ho Lee's lawyers and the prosecutors reached a plea-bargain agreement in September 2000. Under the agreement, Lee pleaded guilty to one count of mishandling national security data and received a sentence for time already served, while the prosecutors dropped the other 58 counts against him.[82]

Chinese American scientists greeted Lee's release with relief. Nevertheless, they still harbored deep concern about what is perceived to be deepseated racism exposed by the case. The Committee of 100, a nonpartisan organization of some of the most prominent Chinese American professionals formed in 1990 by Chang-Lin Tien, the architect I.M. Pei, the musician Yo-Yo Ma, and others, expressed two paramount concerns:

> The Committee of 100 remains deeply concerned about two remaining issues. First, there is "racial profiling," particularly as practiced by federal personnel at the national laboratories and in the defense industries. Americans of Chinese descent are unjustly singled out solely because of their ancestry. Second, the Committee fears that the anti-Chinese hysteria . . . which led to Dr. Lee's indictment and prosecution may reappear wherever tensions or disagreements arise between China and the United States.[83]

While the debate over the Wen Ho Lee case continues against a background of U.S.–China tensions, domestic partisan politics, and the media's thirst for sensational reporting, it is clear that the case has had a chilling effect on the morale of Chinese American scientists and on the atmosphere for cross-national scientific communication between the United States and China that they worked hard to create.[84] It likely will result in more stringent restrictions in weapon-related exchanges—especially in view of the new George W. Bush administration's more cautious policy toward the PRC. There is no evidence, however, that fallout from the Wen Ho Lee case has caused a Tiananmen-like disruption of U.S.–China scientific exchanges. Collaborative projects outside of sensitive areas continue to flourish. In January 2001, for example, the National Academy of Sciences/National Research Council sponsored a major joint study with the Chinese Academy of Engineering on the future of personal transport in China that considers environmental, energy, and health effects.[85]

## Conclusion

In spite of recent setbacks, Chinese American scientists have had and continue to have a profound impact on U.S.–China scientific and political relations. Geopolitical considerations initially motivated the United States and China to encourage their efforts to promote scientific exchanges between the two countries. However, neither the scale of the subsequent exchanges nor the enthusiasm of the participants can be explained solely in terms of the interest of the state. The activism of Chinese American scientists, motivated by Chinese cultural nationalism and traditional beliefs in science as an international activity, gave the exchange programs drive and momentum. Individually and collectively, Chinese American scientists played a crucial nongovernmental role in bringing tens of thousands of Chinese students and scientists to the United States who, whether they stayed or returned to China in the end, helped further promote mutual scientific understanding. Some of these scientific-exchange personnel became involved in setting up companies engaged in trans-Pacific business and trade and, in no small measure, are responsible for the growing commerce between the two countries and for advancing China's economic development.

The dominance of states in international science does not mean that traditional, informal ties among scientists, such as the connections between Chinese American scientists and their colleagues in China, will disappear from the scene. In the case of U.S.–China scientific relations, the state and private actors entered into a new era of intricate interactions. While the U.S. and PRC governments often utilized Chinese American scientific networks to accomplish their geopolitical goals, Chinese American scientists took advantage of official cooperation to promote their own agenda—including the advancement of science in their country of birth and improved relations between the two countries. Trips to China by Chinese American scientists often took on a spirit of Chinese cultural nationalism as they tried to moderate the country's radical, Cultural Revolution–inspired science and educational policy and to encourage Chinese interaction with the outside world. At the same time, Chinese American scientists' active role in PRC science and educational policy and in U.S.–China relations helped them create a sense of their own distinct scientific community.[86]

Ironically, the Chinese nationalism that motivates many Chinese American scientists to promote U.S.–China scientific exchanges also undermines the authority of the Chinese nation-state. Consciously or unconsciously, the extensive scientific and cultural interactions they encourage introduce liberal-democratic ideas and values that challenge the orthodoxy of Marxist ideology. PRC officials cannot control every step of the exchange process, nor can they keep an iron grip on whom to send abroad (in terms of ideological correctness), where to send them, and what they will be exposed to. Thus, scientific exchanges have promoted meritocracy and facilitated the creation of a de-ideologized civil-society sphere.

A comparison of U.S.–China scientific exchanges with those between the United States and the Soviet Union, which analysts have judged less successful, helps illuminate the important role of Chinese American scientists.[87] Historical ties between senior members of the Chinese and U.S. scientific communities and the active role of Chinese American scientists gave U.S.–China exchanges an emotional appeal that was missing in the U.S.-Soviet case. Similarly, the China–Soviet Union exchanges of the 1950s failed, at least in part, due to the absence of a transnational community like that created by Chinese American scientists. While some Soviet advisors offended national pride by acting in an arrogant and patronizing manner with senior Chinese scientists, the participation of culturally sensitive Chinese American scientists in U.S.–China exchanges mitigated or avoided such situations.

The intermixing role of Chinese American scientists is likely to be of even greater importance in future U.S.–China scientific and political relations. As an ethno-international scientific community, Chinese American scientists helped blur national boundaries in science—even at the height of the Cold War. They will play an even more prominent post–Cold War role as the United States becomes increasingly involved in the Asia-Pacific region, as Asian Americans increase in number and political influence in the United States, as China, Taiwan, and Hong Kong enjoy more intimate interactions, and as globalized commerce and technology further remove geographic and cultural barriers.

Modern science, born at about the same time as the modern nation-state, helped break the grip of sovereignty through the threat of nuclear war.[88] Cross-national scientific exchanges offer a safer, more positive route to the goal of "peace through science." In the post–Cold War era, U.S.–China scientific cooperation will be crucial in meeting major global challenges involving the environment, energy, and the proliferation of nuclear weapons.[89] In these vital collaborative endeavors, Chinese American scientists, as agents for transnational exchange, have played and will continue to play a crucial role. Nevertheless, the Wen Ho Lee case reminds us that the influence of the nation-state over scientific communication will not end in the foreseeable future.

## Notes

This chapter draws in part on my article "U.S.–China Scientific Exchange: A Case Study of State-sponsored Scientific Internationalism During the Cold War and Beyond," in *Historical Studies in the Physical and Biological Sciences* 30:1 (1999): 249–277. I thank the University of California Press for permission to reprint portions of the article.

1. A. Doak Barnett, *China and the Major Powers in East Asia* (Washington, D.C.: Brookings Institution, 1977), p. 178. See also Harry Harding, *A Fragile Relationship: The United States and China Since 1972* (Washington, D.C.: Brookings Institution, 1992); Leo A. Orleans, *Science in China and U.S.–China Scientific*

*Exchanges: Assessment and Prospects* (Washington, D.C.: U.S. Government Printing Office, 1976), p. 11.

2. David M. Lampton, *A Relationship Restored: Trends in U.S.–China Educational Exchanges, 1978–1984* (Washington, D.C.: National Academy Press, 1986); and Leo A. Orleans, *Chinese Students in America: Policies, Issues, and Numbers* (Washington, D.C.: National Academy Press, 1988). Also, see Kathlin Smith, "The Role of Scientists in Normalizing U.S.–China Relations, 1965–1979," in *Scientific Cooperation, State Conflict: The Roles of Scientists in Mitigating International Discord*, ed. by Allison L.C. de Cerreno and Alexander Keyan (New York: New York Academy of Sciences, 1998), pp. 114–136; and Richard P. Suttmeier, "Scientific Cooperation and Conflict Management in U.S.–China Relations from 1978 to the Present," in *Scientific Cooperation, State Conflict: The Roles of Scientists in Mitigating International Discord*, pp. 137–164; Denis F. Simon, "The Role of Science and Technology in Chinese Foreign Relations," in *China and the World: Chinese Foreign Policy in the Post-Mao Era*, ed. by Samuel S. Kim (Boulder, CO: Westview Press, 1984), pp. 293–318.

3. Julia Sommer, "Yuan T. Lee Receives Clark Kerr Award," *Berkeleyan*, 3 March 1999, accessed from its website: http://www.berkeley.edu/news/berkeleyan/1999/0303/lee.html on 5 February 2001.

4. On Chu, see Gary Cheung, "Presidential Challenge for Houston Scientist," *South China Morning Post*, 16 December 2000, p. 5. On Woo, see Howard LaFranchi, "A University President Determined to Integrate Education, Everyday Life," *Christian Science Monitor*, 4 May 1984, p. 19; and Elaine Woo, "Hong Kong University Gets Cal State S.F. Head," *Los Angeles Times*, 7 November 1987, p. 32.

5. Elisabeth Tacey, "Ex-Bush Adviser Appointed to Top University Position," *South China Morning Post*, 3 June 1994, p. 6; "Eugene Wong Named to NSF Post," *Berkeleyan*, 6 May 1998, accessed from its website: http://www.berkeley.edu/news/berkeleyan/1998/0506/wong.html on 15 February 2000.

6. Barbara B. Clowse, *Brainpower for the Cold War: The Sputnik Crisis and National Defense Education Act of 1958* (Westport: Greenwood Press, 1981); Benjamin Zulueta, "Forging the Model Minority: Chinese Immigrant Intellectuals, American Science, and the Cold War, 1949–1965" (Unpublished Ph.D. dissertation, University of California, Santa Barbara, 2002).

7. Anon., "These Chinese Choose," *Newsweek* 50 (23 December 1957): 36; C.N. Yang, "Prof C.N. Yang's Address at the Nobel Banquet, 1957," in C.N. Yang, *Ningqiao wuzhuo: Yang Zhenning fangtan lu* (Interviews with C.N. Yang), ed. by Pan Guoju and Han Chuanyuan (Singapore: World Scientific, 1988), n.p.

8. Yang, "Address at the Nobel Banquet," n.p.

9. Chen Ning Yang, *Selected Papers with Commentary* (San Francisco: W.H. Freeman, 1983), p. 57.

10. Elizabeth Venant, "A Position of Prominence," *Los Angeles Times*, 27 August 1990, p. E3.

11. Iris Chang, *Thread of the Silkworm* (New York: Basic Books, 1995), p. 143.

12. Ibid., p. 170.

13. Ibid., p. 189; Jin Chongji, editor in chief, *Zhou Enlai zhuan, 1949–1976* (Biography of Zhou Enlai, 1949–1976), vol. 1 (Beijing: Zhongyang wenxian, 1998), p. 235.

14. Interview with Chang-Lin Tien by Zuoyue Wang, 19 March 1999, Berkeley. Chang, *Thread of the Silkworm*, pp. 196–198.

15. Interview with Chang-Lin Tien by Zuoyue Wang, 19 March 1999, Berkeley.

16. Yang, *Selected Papers*, pp. 56–57. Also see Li Peishan, "Science and Technology: U.S. Impact on China," *Beijing Review* 34 (18 November 1991): 35–37.

17. William Wei, *The Asian American Movement* (Philadelphia: Temple University Press, 1993).

18. Shih-shan Henry Tsai, "Review of *The Asian American Movement* by William Wei," *Pacific Historical Review* 64 (February 1995): 154–155.

19. Interview with Chang-Lin Tien by Zuoyue Wang, 19 March 1999, Berkeley; Chi-Kung Jen, *Recollections of a Chinese Physicist* (Los Alamos: Signition, 1991).

20. Yang, *Selected Papers*, pp. 56–57. Yang, "My Reflections on Some Social Problems," a speech delivered to the Hong Kong Student Association in New York on October 3, 1970, in Yang, *Dushu jiaoxue sishinian* (Forty years of studying and teaching) (Hong Kong: Sanlian, 1985), pp. 55–61.

21. Yang, "My Reflections on Some Social Problems." Ruan Beikang and Ouyang Yingzi, "Zhongmei de huagong yanjiu he yingyong: fang Wei Qianguang jiaoshou," (Research and applications of chemical engineering in China and the United States: an interview with Professor James Wei on 21 August 1978) in Ruan Beikang and Ouyang Yingzi, eds., *Xueren zhuanfang lu* (Interviews with scholars) (Hong Kong: Tiandi Tushu, 1980), p. 124. The experience of Chinese American scientists in many ways paralleled that of Chinese American writers. See Xiao-huang Yin, *Chinese American Literature Since the 1850s* (Urbana: University of Illinois Press, 2000), pp. 185–194.

22. "An Open Letter to President Nixon and Members of the Congress," full-page ad in *New York Times*, 23 May 1971, p. E7. When Yang visited China in 1971, the Chinese government regarded Yang's signature on the letter as a sign of his concern for his native country even after he had acquired U.S. citizenship. See the diary entry of Zhu Kezhen, vice president of the Chinese Academy of Sciences, on 12 July 1971, in Zhu Kezhen, *Zhu Kezhen riji* (Zhu Kezhen diary), v. 5 (Beijing: Science Press, 1990), p. 464. The dispute over Diaoyutai Islands has not been resolved to date.

23. Henry Kissinger, *White House Years* (Boston: Little, Brown, 1982), pp. 693, 705; Harding, *Fragile Relationship*, pp. 35–36, 394–395.

24. Cited in Kissinger, *White House Years*, p. 1492.

25. For instance, the Central Intelligence Agency hired Sylvia Lee, wife of Wen Ho Lee and an employee at the Los Alamos weapons laboratory, to report on the activities of Chinese scientists visiting the laboratory in the 1980s. See Mathew Purdy, "The Making of a Suspect: The Case of Wen Ho Lee," *New York Times*, 4 February 2001, p. A1; and Mathew Purdy with James Sterngold, "The Prosecution Unravels: The Case of Wen Ho Lee," *New York Times*, 5 February 2001, p. A1.

26. Memorandum of Beijing conversation between Kissinger, Zhou, and others, 13 November 1973, in William Burr, ed., *The Kissinger Transcripts: The Top-Secret Talks with Beijing and Moscow* (New York: New Press, 1998), p. 204. The Chinese government did not follow up on the offer.

27. When the Chinese American mathematician Shiing-shen Chern visited China in 1972, he brought a letter from the CSCPRC seeking exchanges with the Chinese Academy of Sciences. See Zhu Kezhen diary entry for 14 September 1972, in Zhu, *Zhu Kezhen Diary*, v. 5, p. 553.

28. See Glenn T. Seaborg, "China Journal: Report of a Visit to the People's Republic of China, 22 May–10 June 1973" (Unpublished manuscript courtesy of Professor Seaborg, 1973), pp. 29–39.

29. See Zuoyue Wang, "U.S.–China Scientific Exchange: A Case Study of State-

sponsored Scientific Internationalism during the Cold War and Beyond," *Historical Studies in the Physical and Biological Sciences* 30, No. 1 (1999): 255–256.

30. See Jen, *Recollections*.

31. Interview with Chang-Lin Tien by Zuoyue Wang, 19 March 1999, Berkeley; Venant, "Position of Prominence," p. E3.

32. Zhu Kezhen diary entry on 12 July 1971, in Zhu, *Zhu Kezhen Diary*, v. 5, p. 464.

33. Wu Heng, *Keji zhanxian wushinian* (Fifty years on the scientific and technological front) (Beijing: Keji wenxian, 1992), p. 351; Yang, *Selected Papers*, pp. 76–77.

34. Yang, "Commentary (on 'What Visits Mean to China's Scientists')," in Yang, *Selected Papers*, pp. 77–78.

35. Wu Heng, *Keji zhanxian wushinian*, pp. 368–369. In addition, Lee described U.S. institutional and cultural approaches to the promotion of science and technology—including the peer-review process and the relative autonomy of the scientific community. See Wang, "Scientific Exchange," p. 263. Zhou also relied on Lee to certify discoveries made by Chinese physicists. At a meeting, Zhang Wenyu asked Zhou whether Chinese scientists should publish the discovery of a new particle and Zhou said that he would need to discuss it with Lee first. See Zhu Kezhen diary entry for 5 October 1972 in Zhu, *Zhu Kezhen Diary*, v. 5, pp. 558–559.

36. On Lee and BEPC, see Liu Huaizu (chief editor), *Beijing zhengfu duizhuangji* (Beijing electron positron collider) (Beijing: Keji chubanshe, 1994). On Lee's continued involvement in U.S.–China high-energy-physics policy, see Lee to Jiang Zemin, 13 October1994, reprinted in Lee, *Li Zhengdao wenlu* (Essays of T. D. Lee) (Hangzhou: Zhejiang wenyi, 1999), pp. 60–67. The book also contains Lee's recollections of his interactions with Mao Zedong and Deng Xiaoping.

37. C.N. Yang, *Dushu jiaoxue zhai shinian* (Ten more years of learning and teaching) (Taipei: Shibao Press, 1995), back cover.

38. The difference reflected in some ways the well-known personal animosity between the two early collaborators. See, for example, T.D. Lee, "Broken Parity," in T.D. Lee, *T.D. Lee Selected Papers*, ed. by G. Feinberg (Boston: Birkhauser, 1986), vol. 3, pp. 487–509.

39. Zhu, *Zhu Kezhen Diary*, vol. 5, p. 544, entry for 4 August 1972.

40. C.N. Yang, "Tantan wulixue yanjiu he jiaoxue: zai beijing zhongguo kexue jishu daxue yanjiushengyuan de wuci tanhua" (On research and teaching in physics: five talks at the graduate school of the University of Science and Technology of China in Beijing, 27 May–12 June 1986), in C.N. Yang, *Yang Zhenning yanjiang ji* (Speeches of C.N. Yang) (Tianjin: Nankai University Press, 1989), p. 149.

41. William Sweet, "Future of Chinese Students in US at Issue; CUSPEA Program Nears Its End," *Physics Today* 41 (June 1988): 67–71; Robert Novick, ed., *Thirty Years Since Parity Nonconservation: A Symposium for T.D. Lee* (Boston: Birkhäuser, 1988), p. 169.

42. See articles by or about T.D. Lee in *Zuji* (Footprints: C.N. Yang's, T. D. Lee's, Samuel Ting's, and Yuan Tze Lee's routes to success) (Beijing: Beijing Language College Press, 1989), pp. 95–166; and Lee, *Essays of T.D. Lee*.

43. T.D. Lee, "Wulixue ji qita" (Physics and beyond: a talk with graduate students at the graduate school of the University of Science and Technology of China, Beijing, 12 May 1979), in *Footprints*, p. 101.

44. Yang, "On Research and Teaching in Physics," p. 151.

45. See Fang Lizhi, *Bringing Down the Great Wall: Writings on Science, Culture,*

*and Democracy in China*, ed. and principal translator James H. Williams (New York: Knopf, 1991). On the great ideological and political debate over philosophy and physics in the 1970s and 1980s, see H. Lyman Miller, *Science and Dissent in Post-Mao China: The Politics of Knowledge* (Seattle: University of Washington Press, 1996).

46. Chinese leaders, especially Zhou Enlai, adroitly tapped into the home country nationalism of Chinese Americans. During a meeting with C.S. Wu (Wu Jianxiong) and her physicist husband, Luke Yuan (Yuan Jialiu), for instance, Zhou showed his deeply moved guests a map indicating how much Chinese territory formerly under Russian control he was able to get back from the Soviet Union through negotiations in the 1950s. See Jiang Caijian, *Wu Jianxiong: Wuli kexue de diyi furen* (C.S. Wu: the first lady of physical science) (Shanghai: Fudan University Press, 1997), p. 279.

47. See *Qishi niandai* (The seventies) journal editors, *Liumei huayi xuezhe chongfa zhongguo guangan ji* (Reflections on revisiting China by Chinese American scholars) (Hong Kong: The Seventies Press, 1974).

48. Edward David, Jr., to Henry Kissinger, September 22, 1971, on "Visit of U.S. Physicist, C.N. Yang, to the People's Republic of China," in National Archives, Nixon Presidential Materials, White House Central Files, Subject Files, FG 6–9, box 1, folder "(EX) FG 6–9 Office of Science and Technology 1/1/71–." David suggested that Kissinger call Yang for a briefing but it never took place. Yang e-mail to author, 6 November 1997.

49. Nie Huatong, "Wo suo zhidao de Yang Zhenning" (The C.N. Yang that I know), reprinted in *Ningzhuo wuqiao: Yang Zhenning fangtan lu* (Interviews with C.N. Yang), ed. by Pan Guoju and Han Chuanyuan, pp. 101–119.

50. Xu Shenglan and Meng Dongming, *Yang Zhenning zhuan* (A biography of C.N. Yang) (Shanghai: Fudan University Press, 1997), pp. 123–129.

51. Yang, "Commentary," p. 77.

52. C.N. Yang, "Fahui qiaoliang zuoyong" (Playing the role of a bridge), in Ning Pingzhi, Tang Xianmin, and Zhang Qinghua, eds., *Yang Zhenning yanjiangji* (A collection of C.N. Yang's Speeches) (Tianjin: Nankai University Press, 1989), pp. 196–197.

53. Testimony of John P. McTague, 20 June 1985, in *International Cooperation in Science, Science Policy Study—Hearings* Volume 7, Hearings before the Task Force on Science Policy of the Committee on Science and Technology, House of Representatives, 99thCongress, 1st session (Washington, D.C.: U.S. Government Printing Office, 1985), pp. 235–236.

54. Ibid., p. 249.

55. Wang Xi, "Dalu lumei xueren ziyuan yu ershiyi shiji zhongguo de fazhan" (Mainland scholarly personnel in the United States and China's development in the twenty-first century), *Shijie ribao* (World journal), 9 November 1997, p. A5.

56. According to a survey conducted by the American Institute of Physics in 1996, women made up 12 percent of the 144 Asian or Pacific Islander U.S. Ph.D. physicists, while only 6 percent of the 1,942 other U.S. Ph.D. physicists were women. E-mail from Raymond Chu of AIP to author, 5 March 1998.

57. See the chapters by Sufei Li and Norton Wheeler in this volume.

58. Shih-shan Henry Tsai uses the term "subnationalism" to depict the activism of Chinese immigrants who are occupied with and try to influence developments in their old country. Shih-shan Henry Tsai, *The Chinese Experience in America* (Bloomington: Indiana University Press, 1986).

59. See, for example, Yang, *Forty Years of Studying and Teaching*, p. 89.

60. On the association, see its website at http://www.ocpaweb.org. On Yang's role in the founding of the association, see Tung-Mow Yan, "Professor C.N. Yang's Impact on Physics," in C.S. Liu and S.T. Yau, eds., *Chen Ning Yang, A Great Physicist of the Twentieth Century* (Boston: International Press, 1995), pp. 451–456.

61. Ted Plafker, "Physics Meeting Unites the Two Chinas—Briefly," *Science* 269 (18 August 1995): 916.

62. James C. Wang, "U.S. Scientists and China," letter to the editor, *Science* 246 (22 December 1989): 1547.

63. T.D. Lee, "U.S.–China Relations," letter to the editor, *Science* 246 (17 November 1989): 873.

64. "Why Is This Man Smiling?" *Science* 246 (13 October 1989): 214; Nicholas D. Kristof, "Deng Reappears, Saying China Will Seek Change," *New York Times*, 17 September 1989, p. A5; Don Oberdorfer, "Chinese Plan Effort to Heal Relations, Bush Is Told," *Washington Post*, 18 October 1989, p. A27.

65. "Yang Zhenning huyu mei jieshu dui hua 'zhicai'" (C.N. Yang calls on the United States to end sanctions against China), *People's Daily*, overseas edition, 11 August 1989, p. 5.

66. Burkhard Bilger, "Holding Pattern: Chinese Science Has Arrived, but the Fate of Dissident Scientists Is Still up in the Air," *Sciences* 36, No. 4 (July–August 1996): 10–11.

67. On the vicissitudes of U.S.–China relations, see James Mann, *About Face: A History of America's Curious Relationship with China, from Nixon to Clinton* (New York: Knopf, 1999); and Steven W. Mosher, *China Misperceived: American Illusions and Chinese Reality* (New York: Basic Books, 1990).

68. See L. Ling-chi Wang, "Race, Class, Citizenship, and Extraterritoriality: Asian Americans and the 1996 Campaign Finance Scandal," *Amerasia Journal* 24, No. 1 (Spring 1998): 1–21.

69. See Eric Lichtblau, "Physicist Admits Passing Laser Secrets to Chinese Scientists," *Los Angeles Times*, 9 December 1997, p. B1. A group of Chinese scientists who hosted Lee have denied that Lee passed any military secrets. See the open letter by Wang Ganchang et al., *People's Daily*, overseas edition, 11 February 1998, p. 4. See also Rone Tempest, "Chinese Scientists Defend Southland Spy," *Los Angeles Times*, 11 February 1998, p. A4; James Brook, "An Earlier China Spy Case Points Up Post–Cold War Ambiguities," *New York Times*, 13 March 1999, p. A4; Jeff Gerth and James Risen, "Reports Show Scientist Gave U.S. Radar Secrets to China," *New York Times*, 10 May 1999, p. A1.

70. James Risen and Jeff Gerth, "China Stole Nuclear Secrets for Bombs," *New York Times*, 6 March 1999, p. A1.

71. James Risen, "U.S. Fires Nuclear Scientist Suspected of Spying for China," *New York Times*, 9 March 1999, p. A1.

72. Information from http://wenholee.org/whois.htm, accessed on 1 January 2001.

73. James Risen and Jeff Gerth, "U.S. Says Suspect Put Data on Bombs in Unsecure Files," *New York Times*, 28 April 1999, p. A1.

74. David Johnson and James Risen, "Nuclear Weapons Engineer Indicted in Removal of Data," *New York Times*, 11 December 1999, p. A1.

75. Cheuk-Yin Wong, Chairman of Overseas Chinese Physics Association, to President William J. Clinton, 1 April 1999, available on OCPA's website: http://www.ocpaweb.org/newsitems/1999/ocpa2clinton.txt. OCPA sent a similar letter to Jerome Friendman, President of the American Physical Society. See Ye Guochao,

"Quanqiu huaren wuli xuehui jueyi" (Resolution of the Overseas Chinese Physics Association), *World Journal*, 22 March 1999, p. A1.

76. Xu Minzhi, "80/20 cujinhui wei Li Wenhe baobuping" (80–20 Initiative protests the treatment of Wen Ho Lee), *World Journal*, 18 March 1999, p. A4.

77. "Science Board Member Chang-Lin Tien and Contributions of Chinese American Scientists," statement by the White House press secretary, 29 July 1999, accessed at http://www.whitehouse.gov/WH/New/APA/tien.html in December 2000 (a printout is in the author's possession).

78. The United States House of Representatives Select Committee, *U.S. National Security and Military/Commercial Concerns with the People's Republic of China* (The "Cox Report"), U.S. House of Representatives, 106th Congress, 1st session (Washington, D.C.: U.S. Government Printing Office, 1999). The full text is available on the U.S. House of Representatives website: http://www.house.gov/coxreport/. The quote is from chapter 1 of the report. On congressional discussions of the report, see *The Cox Committee: Report of the Select Committee on U.S. Security and Military/Commercial Concerns with the People's Republic of China*, Hearing before the Subcommittee on Asia and the Pacific of the Committee on International Relations, House of Representatives, 106th Congress, 1st session, on May 26, 1999 (Washington, D.C.: U.S. Government Printing Office, 1999), esp. pp. 32–38, 43–47. See also Michael M. May, Alastair I. Johnston, W.K.H. Panofsky, Marco Di Capua, Lewis Franklin, *The Cox Committee Report: An Assessment* (Stanford: Stanford University Center for International Conflict and Cooperation, 1999), available from http://cisac.stanford.edu.

79. James Glanz, "Amid Race Profiling Claims, Asian Americans Avoid Labs," *New York Times*, 16 July 2000, p. A1.

80. Usha Lee McFarling, "Case's Legacy Is Distrust in Scientific Community," *Los Angeles Times*, 14 September 2000, p. A16.

81. Bruce Alberts, William A. Wulf, and Kenneth I. Shine to Janet Reno, 31 August 2000, available on http://www4.nationalacademies.org.

82. James Sterngold, "U.S. to Reduce Case against Wen Ho Lee to a Single Charge," *New York Times*, 11 September 2000, p. A1.

83. "Statement of Committee of 100 on Wen Ho Lee's Release," 13 September 2000, available at http://www.committee100.org/news/whl_pr.htm. A printout is in the author's possession.

84. See Xiao-huang Yin, "The Lee Case Shakes Asian Americans' Faith in Justice System," *Los Angeles Times*, 24 September 2000, pp. M1, M7. In December 2000, the FBI turned its investigation to Wen Ho Lee's connections with Taiwan. See Walter Pincus, "Investigators Now Focusing on Lee's Ties to Taiwan," *Washington Post*, 24 December 2000, p. A3. On the media's role in the Wen Ho Lee case, see the *New York Times'* critical self-evaluation in "The *Times* and Wen Ho Lee," written by its editors, *New York Times*, 26 September 2000, p. A2. On congressional calls for curtailing international scientific exchange, see James Brooke, "Senator Tells Nuclear Bomb Labs to End Foreign Scientists' Visits," *New York Times*, 13 April 1999, p. A14.

85. Information on "The Future of Personal Transport Vehicles in China" can be found on the National Academy of Sciences' website: www.nas.edu. Among the U.S. participants in the project is Feng An—an environmental scientist at the Center for Transportation Research, Argonne National Laboratory. He represents a new generation of Chinese American scientists who came to the United States from the China Mainland in the 1980s.

86. After all, for many overseas Chinese, "the state, either Nationalist or Commu-

nist, controls the symbolic resources necessary for their cultural identity." Tu Wei-ming, "Cultural China: The Periphery as the Center," *Daedalus* 120 (Spring 1991): 16.

87. On U.S.-Soviet academic and scientific exchanges, see Linda L. Lubrano, "National and International Politics in U.S.-U.S.S.R. Scientific Cooperation," *Social Studies of Science* 11 (1981): 451–480; Robert F. Byrnes, *Soviet-American Academic Exchanges, 1958–1975* (Bloomington: Indiana University Press, 1976).

88. See, for example, Richard Rhodes, *The Making of the Atomic Bomb* (New York: Simon and Schuster, 1986).

89. See, for example, U.S. National Academy of Sciences Panel on Global Climate Change Sciences in China, *China and Global Change: Opportunities for Collaboration* (Washington, D.C.: National Academy Press, 1992). In the mid-1990s, the NAS launched a joint project with the Chinese Academy of Sciences on "Cooperation in the Energy Futures of the United States and China." See National Academy of Sciences, Chinese Academy of Sciences, and Chinese Academy of Engineering, *Cooperation in the Energy Futures of the United States and China* (Washington, D.C.: National Academy Press, 2000), which can be accessed at http://www.nap.edu/catalog/9736.html. See also Peter Koehn, "Chinese+Americans and U.S.–China Relations: Domestic Politics and Transnational Sustainable-Development Projects," paper delivered at the 51st Annual Meeting of the Association for Asian Studies, Boston, March 1999, and Koehn's chapter in this volume.

# 13

# The Role of Cross-nationally Competent Chinese+Americans in Environmental-interdependence Challenges

## Potential and Prospects

*Peter H. Koehn*

### Cross-national Competence and U.S.–China Relations

This chapter is launched with the premise that fundamental aspects of U.S.–China relations today are shaped largely by the actions or inactions of cross-nationally competent civil-society actors. The first section outlines critical dimensions of cross-national competence and inquires into the extent of its presence within the Chinese American community. The next section presents a framework for identifying civil-society access points in transnational relations that can be applied to contemporary networks and interfaces between the China Mainland and the United States. The end goal of analysis, which is developed in the final sections, is to offer an informed estimate of the likely participation of cross-nationally competent Chinese Americans in addressing twin interdependence challenges of escalating urgency—environmental protection and natural-resource depletion—across the range of available influence arenas.

In the wake of late-twentieth-century globalization, the welfare of local communities in China and the United States increasingly involves linked rather than separate destinies. A concomitant development is that nongovernmental actors, operating along and across porous nation-state boundaries through civil-society networks and micropolitical processes, have become key players in transterritorial relations.[1] Coincidently, the worldwide skill revolution has dramatically enhanced the ability of individuals, acting on their own or through organized groups, to address interdependence challenges.

## The Skill Revolution and Cross-national Competence

Spurred by advances in information technology and means of human mobility, people throughout the world are experiencing a skill revolution that is transforming international relations in myriad ways.[2] The explosion of interpersonal interactions across nation-state boundaries ensures that the expansion of cross-national competence will constitute an increasingly important dimension of the skill revolution.

Cross-national competence requires mastery of analytic and behavioral skills. *Analytic competence* requires knowledge of the beliefs, values, and practices of host and heritage cultures—including political sensitivity,[3] the ability to link host-country developments to one's own circumstances and vice versa, and the ability to discern effective transaction strategies among a complex range of alternative cultural paths. *Behavioral competence* involves communicative facility (proficiency in and use of the other's spoken/written language, ability in and use of culturally appropriate nonverbal cues, effective listening, facilitating mutual self-disclosure[4]) and functional adroitness (the ability to relate to counterparts and to apply/adapt knowledge about and sensitivity to host and heritage values, customs, rules, and practices effectively—i.e., cross-national efficacy). Table 13.1 presents illustrations of both dimensions of cross-national competence.

Individuals, organizations, and communities in China and the United States possess these skills in varying degrees and in different mixes. Based upon systematic research, each transnational actor could be located analytically on a continuum that ranges from cross-nationally proficient to incompetent, with adequately competent and pre-competent as in-between points. What is particularly important when considering future China–U.S. relations is evidence that dramatically expanded numbers of people on both sides of the Pacific are moving in the transnationally competent direction. Among the most important factors accounting for this development are permanent and circular migration from East and Southeast Asia to the United States along with the rise of global electronic networks and frequent intercontinental travel by transmigrants "who live their lives across national borders, participating in the daily life and political processes"[5] of both China and the United States.

### Cross-nationally Competent Chinese+Americans

In spite of the absence of nationwide survey data that specifically address cross-national competence, it is possible to gain valuable insights regarding

Table 13.1

**Illustrations of Cross-national Competence**

*Analytical competence*

Possession of reasonably complete understanding of the central beliefs, values, and practices of counterpart culture(s) and society(ies)—including political and ethnic sensitivity

Ability to discern effective cross-national transaction strategies and to learn from past successes and failures

*Behavioral competence*

*Communicative facility*

Fluency in and use of counterpart's spoken/written language

Proficiency in and relaxed use of culturally appropriate nonverbal cues and codes

Ability to listen to and discern different cultural messages

Ability to facilitate mutual self-disclosure

*Functional adroitness*

Ability to relate to counterpart(s) and to develop and maintain positive interpersonal relationships

Ability to overcome problems and accomplish goals when dealing with cross-national challenges

---

relevant skills currently possessed by Chinese Americans. The most useful source for this purpose is the May 1997 survey of Chinese in Southern California conducted by the *Los Angeles Times*.[6] This source is supplemented here by reference to data collected in a small-scale summer 2000 exploratory study carried out among North Carolina Chinese Americans.

*Analytical Skills*

Currently, well over 2 million people of Chinese descent live in the United States. About 70 percent of these residents are foreign-born.[7] Their awareness of developments in China is sustained at a high level via frequent contact with family members living in the homeland and physical return to the place of birth.[8] The activities of adaptive associations[9] and the instantaneous transplantation of the "Chinese world" in the United States[10] enhance the analytic skills of American-born Chinese (ABCs) and reinforce those of the immigrant population.

Analytic competence in U.S. society and culture is not problematic for most ABCs.[11] Moreover, among the Chinese immigrants surveyed by the *Los Angeles Times*, roughly 80 percent had lived at least six years in this country by 1997. Only 10 percent of all respondents reported that cultural differences are "holding back" Chinese in Southern California. Among the North Carolina respondents in the summer 2000 survey, 81 percent had lived in the United States for nine years or longer and over 90 percent reported "excellent, "good," or "fair" knowledge of beliefs, values, and practices in the United States.[12] When considered together, these findings suggest that most Chinese Americans possess considerable cross-national (U.S.–China) analytic competence.

*Behavioral Skills*

The *Los Angeles Times* survey data are especially revealing in terms of the crucially important dimension of behavioral competence. Employing (1) *use of Chinese at home and English outside the home and at work*, (2) *social interaction with Chinese and non-Chinese in the United States*,[13] and (3) *the maintenance of close ties with relatives and friends in the homeland* as indicators of communicative and participatory facility, and extrapolating from the 1997 findings, we can surmise that over 60 percent of the total Chinese American population (i.e., more than 1.4 million U.S. residents) possess considerable cross-national behavioral competency. The summer 2000 North Carolina survey data reported in Table 13.2 reinforce the 1997 Southern California findings. Among this group, the vast majority of surveyed Chinese Americans use Mandarin and English and are reasonably fluent in both, interact socially and professionally with mainstream Americans and socially with Mainland Chinese nationals, maintain annual contact with at least one individual in the PRC, and are able to function effectively on both sides of the Pacific.[14]

*Scope and Implications*

In sum, the large and diverse Chinese American population includes hundreds of thousands of persons who possess a high degree of cross-national competence. Moreover, immigrant and native-born Chinese American professionals increasingly are inclined to perceive their bicultural heritage as an asset rather than a liability in today's world and to become involved in influential transnational and national capacities involving the China Mainland.[15] To highlight the advantages—both at home and abroad—conferred by bicultural backgrounds[16] and cross-national competence, and to erase, rather than minimize, "any negative connotation associated with bilaterality,"[17] the "plus"

Table 13.2

**Behavioral Skills Reported by Chinese Americans in North Carolina**

| Cross-national Behavioral Skill | Number | % Total |
|---|---|---|
| Speak Mandarin most frequently at home | 31 | 81.6 |
| Use Chinese frequently/occasionally away from home | 25 | 65.8 |
| "Excellent/good" spoken ability in most familiar Chinese dialect | 31 | 81.6 |
| Use English frequently away from home | 29 | 76.3 |
| "Excellent/good" spoken ability in English | 28 | 73.7 |
| Mainstream Americans among 5 closest friends | 18 | 51.4 |
| Mainland Chinese nationals among 5 closest friends | 24 | 68.6 |
| Mainstream Americans among 5 work most closely with | 26 | 83.9 |
| Mainland Chinese nationals among 5 work most closely with | 10 | 32.3 |
| Contact 1 or more Chinese in Mainland at least 1x per year | 24 | 63.2 |
| "Good/fair" ability to function in China Mainland | 23 | 65.7 |
| "Excellent/good" ability to function in USA | 22 | 61.1 |

*Source:* Data collected by the author in conjunction with Yuhang Shi's summer 2000 survey. Total number of respondents = 38.

sign will be used when referring to this sizable and expanding group throughout the rest of this chapter.

## Civil-society Access Points

There are clear limits to what nation-states, acting on their own or through multilateral institutions, are able to accomplish in addressing interdependence issues. An extensive and diverse array of civil-society actors—including individuals, large-scale and small-scale (international and domestic) nongovernmental organizations (NGOs), and transnational social movements—have demonstrated that they can fill key gaps at international, national, and local levels of political action along interstate frontiers where domestic and foreign issues converge and "people sort and play out the many contradictions presently at work on the global scene."[18]

Civil-society interactions are particularly dense along domestic-foreign frontiers when actors address *interdependence challenges* that "by their very nature do not fall exclusively within the jurisdiction of states and have rendered the Frontier increasingly porous."[19] In terms of environmental-interdependence issues, nongovernmental change agents possess important capabilities that are not available to states—at all levels of political action.[20] Moreover, "ordinary people working through largely voluntary organizations . . . have acted decisively for human well-being, while the established power structures were either blind to the perils or actively promoting them."[21]

Figure 13.1 **Civil-society Actors along the U.S.–China Frontier**

|  | | Basis for Affiliation | |
|---|---|---|---|
|  | | *Achieved/principled* ◄──────────────── | *Ascribed/self-interested* ──────────► |
| ▲ **SIZE** ┃ ▼ | *Larger* | Multinational corporations | |
|  |  | Social movements (national and transnational) | Social networks |
|  |  | Advocacy/activist networks | |
|  |  | Religious networks | |
|  |  | Internet networks | |
|  |  | Epistemic communities | |
|  |  | Professional organizations and contacts | |
|  |  | Improvement associations | |
|  |  | Philanthropic foundations | |
|  |  | Benevolent associations | Ancestral-place networks |
|  |  | Domestic business | |
|  |  | Alumni clubs | |
|  |  | | Kinship/family networks |
|  | *Smaller* | Personal friendship networks | |
|  |  | Bicultural individuals | |

## Civil-society Actors and Networks

In broad terms, the civil-society actors that operate on the world stage include international organizations, NGOs (both transnational and national), social movements (transterritorial as well as domestic), and individuals.[22] Nongovernmental actors range from large, bureaucratic, and impersonal institutions to "intimate circles and small networks."[23] In this chapter, we are primarily interested in roles that can be performed by cross-nationally competent Chinese+Americans—acting one-on-one, through small and intimate networks, and as key participants in NGOs and transnational social movements—in domestic and transterritorial civil-society capacities across interconnected influence arenas. Figure 13.1 offers a conceptualization of the discrete civil-society actors expected to be involved in addressing environmental-interdependence issues along the U.S.–China frontier.[24]

At the start of the new millennium, a dense array of nongovernmental networks and ties bind the peoples of China and the United States. The principal actors creating and pursuing the vision required to address the linked destinies of the United States and the PRC are not official emissaries from Beijing and Washington, D.C., but the "multitude of diverse Chinese and Americans interacting within the fertile spaces on the edges of both societies. . . ."[25] Although they are predominantly members of a settled U.S. community,[26] Chinese+Americans actively participate in a rich variety of civil-society forums along the U.S.–China frontier. Their participation ranges from individual contacts with family members and professional/business colleagues to involvement in influential organizations such as the U.S.–China Association, the China Business Council, the Washington Center for China Studies,[27] and various human-rights groups and philanthropic foundations.[28]

## Influence Arenas

Civil-society actors perform crucial roles in addressing interdependence issues by becoming involved in four double-edged (domestic and transnational) influence systems:

- international-agreement shaping;
- policymaking and international-agreement implementation at national and subnational levels;
- local/community project initiation and implementation;
- value sharing and change.

A single actor (e.g., NGO) can be active in more than one influence arena and on one or both sides of the Pacific. Whether a specific civil-society actor opts to become involved in a U.S.–China interdependence challenge depends, in part, on the nature of the issue at stake. Once a nongovernmental actor decides to engage an issue, the focus and geographic locus/locuses of activity are determined by the individual/organization's ability to exert leverage within the activated influence systems. Thus, individuals are most likely to affect the value-change influence system (e.g., by serving as role models) and least likely to influence agreements that require inter-nation negotiation. Nevertheless, while the latter outcome is rare, it is not unheard of—as evidenced by the personal "Track II diplomacy" single-handedly accomplished by the cross-nationally savvy Korean+American academic, K.A. Namkung, in brokering a 1993 agreement dealing with nuclear arms between the Democratic Republic of Korea and the United States.[29]

Furthermore, civil-society actors can devote attention to intergovernmental arenas (international forums and organizations) as well as to national and subnational contexts in both countries in the process of attempting to influence environmental and natural-resource challenges. The increasingly linked nature of international, domestic, and foreign considerations as well as demands for reciprocity and mutual accommodation mean that two or more influence systems frequently need to be approached simultaneously. In the process, contacts will be developed and coalitions forged with state, multistate, substate, and other nongovernmental actors. One outcome is to provide actors in domestic struggles with new transnational resources.[30]

## Cross-nationally Competent Chinese+Americans and Environmental-interdependence Challenges

The cross-national competence of Chinese+Americans can be employed with important effect to a number of crucial and complex interdependence challenges. In these domains—which include peace and security, trade and investment, human rights, population transmigration, environmental protection, health care, and resource consumption—state-to-state relations either are unable by themselves to ensure harmonious interactions or are likely to exacerbate tensions. In particular, the continued preoccupation of political leaders in the United States and China with twentieth-century sensitivities of military-strategic superiority and economic advantage threatens to foreclose actions that would address pressing environmental and natural-resource threats. In this milieu, civil-society actors can perform decisive cross-boundary roles that are not being filled by state players in the contemporary global arena.

The list of interdependent environmental and sustainable-development issues that are likely to present serious challenges to U.S.–China relations in the twenty-first century is lengthy. In addition to ozone depletion,[31] global warming,[32] and petroleum exploitation/importation,[33] the challenges include air and water pollution,[34] forest management and biodiversity,[35] food availability,[36] and the consumption of material goods.[37] This chapter focuses on issues related to sustainable development and nonrenewable-resource consumption to illustrate the increasingly linked destinies of the peoples of the China Mainland and the United States as well as prospects for collaboration.

The challenge of sustainable development involves providing for " 'development that meets the needs of the present without compromising the ability of future generations to meet their own needs.' "[38] Total world population multiplied by per capita consumption provides a critical measure of stress on the global environment and on each country's natural-resource base.[39] At present, most population growth occurs in the South (led by China and India) while about three-fourths of "the world's total goods and services are consumed in the highly industrialized countries" (led by the United States).[40] Earth's nonrenewable resources are not inexhaustible.[41] Known global oil reserves, for instance, are inadequate to satisfy the levels of petroleum consumption projected for China and the United States alone for 2015.[42]

The twentieth century drew to a close on the interrelated global notes of population proliferation and natural-resource depletion. Taken together, the United States and China are responsible for an immense share of the current and projected environmental-interdependence challenge. Nonrenewable global resources are particularly threatened by prevailing excessive consumption patterns in the United States and by population size coupled with consumption trends in China.[43] As Judith Banister points out, "when an enormous population rapidly multiplies its per capita income, the impacts can be massive and ecologically destabilizing." At the same time, "greater income and wealth give the PRC a variety of options for ameliorating the ecological impacts of the added people."[44]

In terms of future challenges facing the people of the United States, maintaining a high standard of living is likely to be a priority. For the bulk of the China Mainland population, the critical future challenges are finding/maintaining remunerated work[45] and achieving improved living conditions. Under prevailing predilections, the consumption dynamics inherent in both undertakings rely on a common core—a fossil-fueled economy. In the United States, per capita energy consumption and automotive-fuel burning has returned to its peak level.[46] While China also is developing a growing thirst for petroleum—particularly to fuel the rapid growth in automobiles—the level of U.S. oil consumption is roughly five times greater than estimates for the Mainland even though China's population is five times larger than that of the United States.[47] If per capita car ownership and usage in the PRC should reach U.S. levels, China would require 80 million barrels of petroleum daily—16 million barrels more than recent worldwide production.[48] Moreover, the generation of rural employment in the Mainland has been dependent on expansion of jobs in energy-inefficient, resource-wasteful, and "massively polluting" township and village enterprises.[49] In sum, China and the United States are among the largest contributors to global nonrenewable-resource-depletion trends,[50] and their participation is essential if international cooperation is to succeed in effectively addressing sustainable-development challenges.

Historically, however, the governments of the two countries have been inclined to pursue opposing policies and approaches and to play leadership roles that emphasize confrontation and competition rather than partnership in addressing resource-consumption issues. For instance, China took the lead in organizing and coordinating the positions of Southern states both in preparation for and during the United Nations Conference on Environment and Development (UNCED) in Rio de Janeiro.[51] From the perspective of many Southern activists and state-policy makers, international proposals for environmental or resource protection frequently threaten sovereignty over Third World resources and appear to be designed to extend or deepen the structural inequalities embedded in the prevailing international economic order. China's traditional environmental diplomacy embraces this perspective. One of the major principles officially articulated in 1990 for the PRC's formal international negotiating position holds that "the sovereignty of natural resource rights must be respected. No country can interfere with the decisions of another with regard to the use of its natural resources."[52] From 1995 to 1997, moreover, the Chinese media frequently suggested that "sustainable development was part of a master plan by the advanced industrialized countries (and especially the United States) to contain China by forcing it to slow the pace of economic growth in order to protect the environment."[53] For its part, the U.S. government, under the administration of former President George Bush, "blocked secretariat proposals for change in industrialized countries' consumption patterns . . ." at the time of UNCED in Rio and "was prepared to veto any initiatives that could be viewed as redistributing economic power at the global level. . . ."[54] The energy policy adopted at the onset of the new George W. Bush administration notes that the United States, "which now consumes more than 25 percent of the oil produced worldwide, will find itself increasingly in competition for oil with rapidly industrializing countries like China." Its approach emphasizes development of and improved U.S. access to unexploited petroleum fields around the world as well as avoiding any commitment to domestic measures that would address global warming.[55]

If the next millennium affords a window of opportunity for transition to an ecologically sustainable world, the actions and reactions of the most populous nation and the most gluttonous one will exert an immense influence on the human condition. Cooperation between the United States and China is crucial because of the disproportionate impact (and dependence) of the two societies on the global environment and on natural-resource use, because of the irreparable harm that would result from their conflict over nonrenewable resources[56] and/or failure to reach agreement on environmental-protection measures and approaches, and because of the powerful message that their partnership in sustainable development would send to the rest of the world.

To date, however, both governmental and nongovernmental actors have failed to overcome divisive gulfs between China and the United States over how to deal with environmental-interdependence challenges. Political leaders have tended to resist symbolic or policy compromises—particularly in terms of addressing conditions affecting climate change—that would enable major breakthroughs, and many nongovernmental actors active in addressing sustainable-development issues lack the requisite intercultural sensitivity and competence that would inspire widespread and fundamental behavioral and value change. Failure to overcome the fundamental China–U.S. polarization on urgent environmental and resource-depletion issues risks perpetuating the consumption race and smothering potentially powerful incentives to curtail or eliminate abusive and unsustainable practices. Thus, new forms of cooperation are essential if the interdependence challenge of sustainable development is to be addressed effectively in the twenty-first century.

One objective of this chapter is to demonstrate that cross-nationally competent actors are strategically positioned to fill the required U.S.–China bridging niche—particularly, although not exclusively, via civil-society networks. This prospect has been overlooked or underestimated by scholars of international relations.[57] With close ties to both societies, nonstate actors occupy a privileged vantage point from which to identify and carry out effective strategies of communicating about and exerting influence over interdependence issues in places of origin and residence. Successful transnational actors pursue strategies that are adapted to the domestic political structure and political culture of the target state(s).[58]

Although they are not the only cross-nationally competent actors at work along the China–U.S. frontier, we are particularly interested here in the potential of Chinese+Americans—both those born in the United States and elsewhere—to bridge the existing chasm with respect to policy, practice, and values related to pressing environmental-interdependence challenges. The following sections explore the challenge of nonrenewable-resource consumption with reference to the potential impact of Chinese+Americans on *international-agreement making* by the governments of the PRC and the United States; *national environmental and natural-resource policymaking and international-agreement implementation* in China and the United States; *sustainable-development projects* in the PRC and the United States; and *resource-use-values change* in both countries. Each section also provides illustrations of promising roles and strategies based on assessments of prevailing political institutions and culture as well as on evaluations of national and transnational experiences and the potential impact of civil-society actors. In light of the emerging and uncharted nature of critical linking relationships along domestic-foreign frontiers, the discussion presented here is intended to be suggestive rather than definitive.

### International-agreement Shaping

An international convention on the sustainable use of the world's natural resources—which likely would include the imposition of "some limits on total worldwide consumption"[59] linked with effective population control—remains to be initiated.[60] Although the PRC is not likely to take a leadership role with respect to international agreements that are perceived to constrain its development potential,[61] the government has not denied the existence or potential significance of particular global environmental problems and has shown willingness to agree to cooperative undertakings in response to financial incentives.[62] The principle of *common but differentiated responsibility* for the global environment, which separates "the question of where abatement should be undertaken from who should pay for it,"[63] provides one promising basis for international agreements.

### Potential Civil-society Roles for Chinese+Americans

With roots in both China and the United States, Chinese+Americans are uniquely positioned to broker the kinds of mutually acceptable compromises that are required to overcome formidable gulfs in official perspectives—for instance, an international agreement "that would establish targets for limiting both population and consumption."[64] They will need to act simultaneously on both sides of the Pacific and through international forums. Success in these influence arenas is likely to require attention to securing acceptance of the principle of common-but-differentiated responsibility for natural-resource conservation and to ensuring that U.S.–China relations basically are characterized by constructive and pragmatic partnership.[65] It also depends on effectuating change in the perspective of key state actors—especially the president and Congress of the United States and the Chinese Communist Party (CCP) leadership.[66]

In selecting roles as well as change strategies, Chinese+Americans will need to draw upon their insights regarding the two political systems and the prevailing political cultures. In the international-agreement-shaping arena, the potentially most effective nonstate roles are likely to stem from involvement in national and cross-national epistemic communities. Epistemic communities are networks of knowledge-based experts who possess expertise, competence, and an "authoritative claim to policy-relevant knowledge" within a particular domain or issue area.[67] Since 1972, "many Chinese American scientists and engineers have contributed their knowledge and skills to universities, research institutes, government agencies, and special projects in the People's Republic of China."[68] Chinese+American scientists—including, for instance, the 800 members of the Chinese-American Engineers and Scientists Association of Southern California[69]—are well situated to participate in addressing resource-interdependence issues. One promising avenue open to Chinese+American scientists interested in filling cross-national brokering roles is via linkages with the environmentally proactive expert community in China. The latter, many of whom developed their expertise through participation in international training forums, tend to support the internationally cooperative, domestically uphill efforts of China's "techno-diplomats" to advance meaningful environmental protection as a foreign and domestic priority.[70]

Transnational and national NGOs, acting directly as well as through alliances and long-term coalitions, also perform important agreement-initiating and -ratifying roles in international forums and in target countries.[71] To the extent that China is actively seeking to raise its status in the international system, "moral leverage" can be relevant.[72] Within the United States, participation in social movements and advocacy networks, and professional-association[73] involvement can be effective with respect to interdependent resource-use challenges. Chinese+Americans are likely to be most influential in civil-society roles if their actions are based on the understanding that a necessary, if often insufficient, condition for U.S. government accession to international agreements has been pressure from a coalition of industry and environmental actors.[74]

## Strategic Options, Strengths, and Opportunities for Chinese+Americans

The choice of strategies to utilize in bringing about change in the position of the United States and China depends on the cross-nationally competent actor's assessments and insights regarding roles and resources, the nature of the specific issue at stake, and the political system/culture. Effective strategies generally available to members of epistemic communities include (1) information-sharing and educating; (2) providing evidence and advice about the cause-and-effect relationships involved in complex interdependence problems[75] and about the likely outcomes of various courses of action; (3) defining policy alternatives[76] and proposing specific policy prescriptions and standards;[77] (4) framing issues in ways that influence negotiations;[78] (5) building transterritorial coalitions through persuasion in support of selected policies;[79] and (6) contributing to the "creation and maintenance of social institutions  that guide international behavior."[80] Members of transnational and national NGOs influence international agreements by (1) defining, redefining, and strategically framing issues; (2) advancing proposals, preparing background papers/reports, and providing drafts of convention text; (3) organizing consumer boycotts and topical/ educational campaigns; and (4) lobbying and/or demonstrating during international negotiations.[81] Activists in transnational advocacy networks (1) mobilize and deploy timely, well-documented, and dramatic information in order to create new issues and exert maximum impact; (2) persuade, pressure, and leverage organizations and governments; (3) attempt to transform the terms of policy debates; and (4) serve as sources of information and testimony.[82]

The particular strategic strengths of the cross-nationally competent actor in this arena include analytical understanding of foreign-policy-making processes,[83] reliably identifying the party or parties responsible for the given state of affairs, proposing solutions that are credible and acceptable in both cultures, discerning the kinds of testimony and/or actions that will impress targeted policymakers, relating testimonials (typically about identifiable victims being physically harmed) in a convincing manner in both societies, and mobilizing resources that can be used as financial incentives.[84] These special capabilities can be applied through institutions or through personal diplomacy to broker agreements acceptable to both governments. Some Chinese+American scholars have already served as "go-betweens for Washington and Beijing."[85] In short, considerable potential exists for cross-nationally competent and strategically astute Chinese+Americans, acting individually, through epistemic networks, or through NGOs, to fulfill major international-agreement-shaping roles with respect to resource-interdependence issues. Prospects that Chinese+Americans will perform these roles in the China Mainland are enhanced by the opportunity to draw upon the Confucian legacy of approaching international relations in an informal and interpersonal (rather than an interstate) manner that emphasizes pragmatic personalized diplomacy.[86]

### Domestic-policy Shaping

Beyond international agreements, attention needs to be devoted to the enactment and enforcement of domestic policies that promote resource conservation. Examples of promising U.S. and PRC policies include:

- institution of energy taxes that encourage efficient consumption practices;
- elimination of hidden subsidies for the operation of cars and trucks;[87]
- installation of cogeneration equipment that uses waste heat to generate extra electricity from coal;
- enforcement of stricter standards for energy-efficient improvements;
- acceptance of measures that preclude discrimination against renewable-energy sources by eliminating fossil-fuel subsidies and imposing carbon taxes;
- promotion of emerging technologies such as fuel cells and solar/wind power;[88]
- application of community-energy-management policies and practices.[89]

The formulation and approval of China's *Agenda 21* action plan to implement a policy of sustainable development (based on the UNCED consensus *Agenda 21* document) constitutes an important domestic-policy development in this arena.[90] However, China's enforcement system is weak and its implementation capacity remains problematic.[91] The prevailing traditional perspective of the government supports the twin principles that "environmental protection should not be achieved at the expense of the economy" and that the PRC should only begin to implement serious environmental-protection measures—in exchange for foreign assistance—when it has attained an appropriate level of economic development.[92] In the United States, meanwhile, policymakers continue to resist adopting domestic measures that would apply substantial constraints to fossil-fuel-energy usage and to the consumption of other nonrenewable resources.[93]

*Potential Civil-society Roles for Chinese+Americans*

Based on their understanding of living conditions and available natural resources in both China and the United States, a large number of
Chinese+Americans are positioned to propose and/or broker reciprocal, long-
term arrangements that simultaneously would result in the adoption and
implementation of effective domestic environmental-protection and resource-
conservation policies on both sides of the Pacific. In particular, the dual frame
of reference maintained by transmigrants facilitates constant comparisons of
the situation in one location with that experienced in the other.[94]

Success in the Mainland and U.S. domestic-policy-shaping arenas ultimately depends upon changing the perspectives held by state actors at the
national, regional/state, and local levels. In selecting civil-society roles as
well as intervention strategies, cross-nationally competent Chinese+Americans
will need to draw upon their insights regarding the two distinctive political
systems and political cultures. In *state-dominated systems* such as the PRC,
prospects for bringing about policy change are advanced by the activation of
influential semi-governmental actors (such as think-tanks and research laboratories) and by gaining initial access to and generating winning coalitions
with state authorities. Once the penetration obstacles are overcome, the policy
impact can be profound.[95] Indeed, "those with close government links often
play a more direct role in policy formulation than their counterparts [do] in
many other countries. . . ."[96] In the absence of permitted institutional channels for public involvement in policymaking and for broad consultation in
regulatory processes,[97] however, state and nonstate environmental-protection
advocates find the support and pressure that respected transnational civil-
society actors can provide particularly useful for countering entrenched bureaucratic resistance.

It is important to note in this connection, first, that associations in China's
contemporary "semi-civil society" simultaneously overlap with the state and
possess partial autonomy.[98] Overlapping includes " 'double posting' [*jianzhi*],
whereby all or a portion of the leading positions in a social organization are
filled by people who also hold formal positions in the department in charge
or in an affiliated department."[99] Association members themselves " 'blur'
the demarcation between the state and associations, or 'sacrifice' their autonomy" as a deliberate strategy "in order to survive and develop, or to change
the structure or policy of the state from within."[100] Tony Saich further shows
that while the PRC's 1998 *Regulations on the Registration and Management
of Social Organizations* "attempt to incorporate social organizations more
closely with existing party-state structures," the state lacks the human and
financial capacity to enforce the regulations effectively, and social organiza-

tions have devised strategies (such as registration as a "secondary organization" or not registering at all and functioning as an informal group) that evade government control. Hence, "social practice reveals a pattern of negotiation that minimizes state penetration and allows such organizations to reconfigure the relationship with the state in more beneficial terms that can allow for policy input or pursuit of members' interests and organizational goals."[101] Furthermore, in light of official moves to downsize government by establishing social organizations that provide employment for laid-off department bureaucrats and, then, to phase out state financial obligations over a three-year period, Saich expects that these new social organizations "will develop an identity independent of the state and will become increasingly dependent on society and the business sector for funding."[102]

In the second place, China's fragmented political system and overwhelming pace of economic growth and reform limits the capacity of central government units, including ministries, to ensure the implementation of international agreements and domestic policies, laws, and regulations at subnational levels.[103] In fact, township, county, city, and provincial government bodies often possess powerful incentives for noncompliance—including dependence, for financial resources and pollution levies, on enterprises that are among the least compliant.[104] Kenneth Lieberthal cites instances where territorial governments pass on tax breaks that are roughly equivalent to the amount of pollution fines. He concludes that "the entrepreneurs (local territorial officials) typically control the regulators (local environmental officials)."[105] Moreover, "environmental law is an area in which problems of distorted decision-making stemming from Party influence, corruption, selective implementation of rules, the difficulties of confronting local political leaders, and the low status of those involved in administering the system and so on appear to be particularly serious."[106] However, in the wake of the widespread failure to stem serious domestic environmental deterioration, the *central* government has demonstrated growing willingness to place equal emphasis on environmental protection and economic development.[107] This situation highlights the importance of strengthening transnational linkages at subnational levels and of focusing attention (and adequate incentives) on improvements in *local* policy/practice and on compliance efforts.[108] For instance, some local governments are "developing their own Agenda 21 bureaus to ensure that sustainable development principles are incorporated in urban planning."[109] Chinese+Americans are most likely to succeed in influencing Mainland policies and implementation outcomes when their sustainable-development recommendations address contemporary domestic problems and satisfy the nationalistic inclinations of PRC environmental specialists and political leaders who increasingly recognize that escalating damage to the country's ecological carrying capacity threatens China's national interests.[110]

Prior success in the international-agreement-shaping arena also has an important effect on domestic policy because "the more the respective issue-area is regulated by international norms of cooperation, the more permeable should state boundaries become for transnational activities."[111] In this regard, international and multinational actors have had an important softening impact on China's domestic environmental-policy-making environment. The new domestic institutions and processes required for participating in global environmental regimes have advanced the status and interests of actors within the PRC who "advocate more stringent environmental protection laws and improved enforcement efforts" as well as reform of the pricing system for natural resources.[112]

Based on these three related Mainland developments, strategic coalition-building in China is likely to involve a mix of scientific and policy personnel affiliated with the Chinese Academies of Sciences and Social Sciences, the NPC's State Commission on Environmental and Natural Resources Protection and the State Council Committee for Environmental Protection,[113] universities and affiliated research labs and postdoctoral stations, energy and environmental-protection bureaus and enterprises, and research institutes attached to the State Council, the State Science and Technology Commission, the State Planning Commission, the State Environmental Protection Administration, and provincial/local governments.[114] By working with and through government-organized NGOs (GONGOs) such as the China Council for International Cooperation on Environment and Development (CCICED), the China Environmental Protection Foundation, and the China Society of Environmental Science;[115] the Beijing Energy Efficiency Center created in 1994 with U.S. financial support;[116] the China National Cleaner Production Center and the Environmental Management Committee of China Registration Board of Auditors under the Chinese Research Academy of Environmental Sciences;[117] the 200-plus energy-conservation technology-service centers scattered across the country;[118] ad hoc grass-roots groups along with provincial/local scientific committees;[119] local environmental-supervision groups (*huanbao jiandu xiaozu*) and street environmental committees (*jiedao huanweihui*);[120] local environmental-dispute-resolution bodies (including people's mediation committees and lawyers' negotiations);[121] and emerging environmental NGOs,[122] Chinese+Americans also are likely to be able to contribute to the adoption and implementation of resource-conservation policies. For instance, CCICED, established in 1992 to identify problems/causes and assess policies and programs, currently has 54 councilors—20 PRC government officials, 7 Mainland scholars or specialists, and 27 foreign members representing industry, international environmental NGOs, foundations, governments, research institutes, and international organizations.[123] It set up a Working Group on Trade and Sustainable Development in 1994. At the close of its December 1998 meeting in Beijing, CCICED submitted a series of important policy recommendations dealing with resource issues to the government.[124]

In the domestic-policy-shaping sphere, therefore, the potentially most effective civil-society roles are likely to come from involvement in national and cross-national epistemic communities,[125] NGOs,[126] professional organizations,[127] corporations with international operations,[128] multilateral donor and credit organizations,[129] foundations, social movements, advocacy/activist networks (United States), and from participation in social networks (China). Among these, Chinese+Americans are particularly well represented in national and transnational epistemic networks.[130] Roughly 70,000 Chinese scholars holding advanced degrees—including a high proportion of those earning doctorates in science and engineering fields—have settled in the United States.[131] Many of these "highly skilled and biculturally savvy" scholars retain strong professional and family ties in the Mainland and frequently travel to China.[132] Given the breadth of disciplinary expertise of relevance in addressing environmental-interdependence issues, a large proportion of Chinese+American scholars possess knowledge and skills of considerable value in terms of domestic policy and law making,[133] training,[134] and the implementation and enforcement of international agreements along the U.S.–China frontier. At present, moreover, a "unified and aggressive" environmental-epistemic community exists within the PRC[135] for Chinese+American scientists to link up and collaborate with.

*Strategic Options, Strengths, and Opportunities for*
*Chinese+Americans*

National and transnational NGOs can influence domestic policies by (1) organizing consumer boycotts and educational efforts; (2) lobbying; (3) monitoring compliance with international conventions; and/or (4) calling for accountability to promised policies and principles.[136] Margaret Keck and Kathryn Sikkink suggest that in political systems "where participatory channels are blocked or limited," citizens are likely to turn to transnational networks and NGOs in order to advance their claims. In such situations, NGOs and transnational social-movement organizations typically endeavor to "transform state understandings of their national interests" and to convince targeted governments that the advocated action is not costly or is less costly than not acting.[137]

Friends of Nature offers an exceptional illustration of how effective an indigenous environmental NGO can be in the PRC "when it is run by an energetic, charismatic individual who has a powerful vision" and is well connected with influential political leaders. Skillfully led by Liang Congjie, Friends of Nature used student vigils, local-area lobbyists, expert scientific arguments, letters and petitions to officials, and media publicity to protect the habitat of the golden snub-nosed monkey in Yunnan by extracting a commitment from local authorities to support sustainable development by enforcing the ban on illegal logging practices.[138]

The particular strategic strengths of the cross-nationally competent Chinese+American actor in the domestic-policy formation and implementation arena include expanding public understanding of environmental issues and correcting misinformation; helping to broker reciprocal agreements; activating social networks and regional/kinship economic networks[139] in China; using their understanding of "behind-the-scenes negotiations" in the PRC to forge winning coalition strategies;[140] mobilizing resources that can be used as financial incentives for implementation efforts; and serving as an information conveyor belt for monitoring activities. One prospect that merits consideration is to pursue such strategic actions in cooperation with the Mainland's nascent indigenous "citizens' movement" for change in environment and development policies.[141] In the United States, Chinese+Americans influence public opinion through publications in prestigious journals such as *Foreign Affairs*, by appearances on prime-time TV programs, and by their contributions to mainstream magazines and newspapers.[142] The influential Committee of 100, composed of citizens of Chinese descent who hold leadership positions in a wide range of professions, could play an important policy-shaping role on both sides of the Pacific with respect to interdependent resource-conservation challenges.[143]

### Sustainable-development Projects

The sustainable-development project arena allows for a multitude of change opportunities. In general terms, such projects encompass *research* into innovative and sustainable approaches; *applications* of energy-saving and renewable-energy technology; *exchanges* of proven conservation-sensitive methods and approaches that possess adaptive potential in the other country; and *interventions* that promote economically viable and environmentally sound undertakings. Most of these efforts would be small-scale and community-based.[144] In terms of promoting the adoption of energy-saving options, for instance, both sides need to cooperate in identifying and adapting approaches, incentives, and technological breakthroughs that will maximize the introduction of solar power, wind power, geothermal power, small-scale hydroelectricity, combined-cycle natural-gas turbines, biogas, fuel cells, tidal and wave power, and organic farming for petroleum-based approaches. Wind turbines alone offer the prospect of providing a major share of the total required energy supply in both countries.[145]

U.S. institutions have been the largest external contributors to the sustainable-development projects generated to date by China's *Agenda 21* plan.[146] Additional Mainland-based projects commenced in 1998 as part of the U.S.– China Energy and Environment Cooperation Initiative agreed to by Presidents Bill Clinton and Jiang Zemin during the 1997 Summit.[147]

*Potential Civil-society Roles for Chinese+Americans*

As a result of understanding living conditions in both China and the United States and possessing access to local knowledge about successful sustainable-resource-management approaches, a sizable number of Chinese+Americans are uniquely positioned to recommend, arrange, and participate in transterritorial and exclusively domestic projects (to be initiated in the United States as well as in China) that apply valuable lessons from one country in the other. For instance, there is much of environmental, health, and resource-conservation value that U.S. drivers who value individual mobility could learn from China's designated citywide bike lanes;[148] free or inexpensive, convenient, and guarded bike-parking areas; extensive system of sidewalk bicycle-repair stations; cyclist-commuter subsidies; and bicycle load carrying, delivery, and advertising.[149] Since "the most energy-intensive activities people engage in are those involving travel"[150] and motor vehicles (primarily automobiles) consume roughly two-thirds of the petroleum used in the United States "simply in their use,"[151] the provision of cyclist- and pedestrian-friendly routes and the curtailment of short car trips—particularly during peak traffic hours—can bring about a substantial reduction in nonrenewable-energy consumption.[152] While China's urban and rural populations already are experienced with the "vehicle of the future" (the bicycle), U.S. bikes are more likely to collect dust in the garage than be used for commuting or shopping.[153] On the other side of the Pacific, Chinese+Americans can initiate projects that demonstrate, based on U.S. experience, that environmental protection and sustainable development are employment-generating rather than employment-reducing undertakings.[154] They also can share experience with adaptable ways of reducing the negative impacts of motorization—such as telecommuting.[155]

In the project arena, the potentially most effective nonstate roles open to Chinese+Americans are likely to come from involvement in national and cross-national epistemic communities (scientific research),[156] professional organizations (technical applications),[157] environmental and development NGOs,[158] multinational corporations, environmental joint ventures,[159] domestic businesses and consulting firms, philanthropic foundations,[160] kinship and/ or ancestral-place networks,[161] friendship ties,[162] and religious networks. Chinese+American specialists could propose innovations, assist with renewable-energy-technology transfers,[163] provide training in new technologies and approaches, and share diagnosis and monitoring experience on projects designed to assist (1) China's effort to improve township, local- and state-enterprise, and household-energy efficiencies,[164] and (2) moves to adopt renewable-energy alternatives.[165] Another promising project initiative would involve the establishment by Chinese+American specialists of independent, but affiliated, Mainland-based applied-research centers on sustainable resource management patterned along the lines of the Beijing University–attached Center for Chinese Economic Research or Battelle Lab's energy-efficiency centers.[166] Home-district investments in sustainable-development undertakings by U.S.-based native-place associations are likely to be supported enthusiastically in China.[167] A particularly proactive approach in this arena would involve the creation of a Chinese+American Transnational Resources Corps, patterned on the U.S. Peace Corps, that would apply the insights of committed and skilled participants to innovative small-scale demonstration projects and awareness-building efforts in both countries.

*Strategic Options, Strengths, and Opportunities for Chinese+Americans*

The current absence of deeply rooted conceptual screens with regard to China among the U.S. public[168] opens opportunities to frame U.S.–China relations in terms of cooperative projects (such as renewable-energy schemes, recycling and repair/reuse ventures, waste-heat utilization and district heating[169]) that address environmental and natural-resource interdependence challenges. The particular strategic strengths of the cross-nationally competent Chinese+American actor in the U.S. and PRC project arenas are likely to include contributing insights based on local knowledge and practice regarding viable approaches, encouraging participation through persuasion based on trust and cross-cultural knowledge and understanding, leveraging resources for initial investments, mobilizing and cooperating with kinship, native-place, friendship, and religious networks at the local level in China, identifying qualified and reliable Mainland partners who are committed to sustainable development, and initiating demonstration schemes.

One particularly ambitious initiative in this arena would involve

Chinese+Americans in the establishment of and transnational funding for a China–USA foundation specifically devoted to promoting (1) reciprocal fossil-fuel energy conservation and (2) collaborative projects designed to facilitate transitions to safe, affordable, and renewable alternative-energy sources in both countries. Among other projects, the new foundation could help to underwrite China's interest in "expanding scientific research and exchanges in the study of energy conservation" and in sustainable development.[170] This initiative also could include a specific program component that facilitates the return of Chinese+American experts to the Mainland on short-term research, training, and consultancy projects[171]—similar to the less focused assignments for U.S.-based Chinese scholars supported since 1993 by the Washington Center for China Studies.[172]

## Value Change and Mutual Learning

The double-edged arena of resource-use values change is at once the most important and the most difficult for nonstate actors (or state actors for that matter) to affect. First, people must recognize a compelling need to transform production processes and to adopt sustainable-consumption values and life-styles. Such shifts are facilitated by convincing proof that failure to change will produce proximate danger,[173] by unwillingness to depend on the arrival of technological fixes, by "a feeling of responsibility for one's children and subsequent descendants" or future generations,[174] and/or by appreciation for the immediate and long-term personal benefits associated with a frugal and simple life-style.[175] Then, publics must be convinced that any personal sacrifices required by sustainable-consumption behavior will not be negated by the behavior of others—either domestically or globally.

Chinese+Americans can play crucial roles in all of these resource-curtailment respects—especially with regard to the intrinsic satisfactions involved (in terms of quality of life, sense of well-being, close interpersonal relationships, etc.) as well as the reciprocal personal sacrifices required in both societies. The magnitude of this adjustment challenge should not be underestimated, however. Decreased per capita consumption is an ambitious goal. At present, most residents of the United States, who consumed 24 percent of the world's used energy while constituting only 5 percent of its population in 1990, are not acting to curtail their consumption behavior.[176] In China, the global "priests and prophets of the culture of competition and consumption" have been working arduously to instill the value of "self-expression through consumption of material goods."[177] Many Mainland Chinese, at 22 percent of the world's population but using only 8.5 percent of its energy in 1990, aspire to use their newly acquired wealth to increase their access to consumables—including electrical appliances, motorized transport, heating and air conditioning, and status items such as camcorders and cellular phones.[178] In addition, the ostentatious consumption standards established by wealthy and middle-class trendsetters "have created new demands for environmentally damaging products."[179]

It is likely that some of the movement of people between the Mainland and the United States has "transformed lower consumers into higher consumers . . . [who] then transfer these values and aspirations back to their places of origin during their periodic returns to home areas."[180] At the same time, Chinese+Americans are presented with an unprecedented opportunity to transform transcontinental migration networks into two-way avenues for transmitting and reinforcing energy-conservation and sustainable-consumption sensitivities and values. Many more people in the United States—especially young people—embraced attitudes favorable to environmental protection and resource conservation by the end of the twentieth century. Between 1976 and 1990, for instance, the percentage of U.S. Americans who agreed with the statement "we must sacrifice economic growth in order to preserve and protect the environment" in *Cambridge Reports'* surveys increased from 38 percent to 64 percent.[181] In the mid-1990s, Willet Kempton, James Boster, and Jennifer Hartley found overwhelming support for protecting the environment even when they explicitly connected this position to a reduced "standard of living today" or to returning to "a less materialistic way of life." The vast majority of their respondents also were convinced that "Americans are going to have to drastically reduce their level of consumption over the next few years."[182] Earlier research conducted by Raymond De Young indicated that a substantial proportion of the small-town residents surveyed in the U.S. Midwest associated "forms of intrinsic satisfaction with a reduced consumption lifestyle."[183] Many Mainland Chinese are acutely aware of the seriousness of China's environmental problems[184] and still derive considerable personal satisfaction from the frugal use of resources in everyday living.[185] Carlos Lo and Sai Wing Leung report that strong "green values" are widely held at the personal level among residents of Guangzhou—one of China's most industrialized cities. In their 1996 survey, "94.2 percent of respondents agreed or strongly agreed that they ought 'to save water and electricity'; 72.9 percent felt that they ought 'to buy environmentally friendly products'; 68.4 percent advocated 'separating household waste for recycling'; 61.6 percent thought it was right 'to bring one's own shopping bag'; and 55.5 percent felt that 'to spend more on environmentally friendly products is worthwhile.'"[186] Chinese+Americans are positioned to build on this foundation by constructing appealing local visions of resourceful living that respond to Tu Wei-ming's call for ways of life that are "not only commensurate with human flourishing but also sustainable in ecological and environmental terms."[187] Openness to the mutually satisfying possibilities inherent in conservation-value exchanges will extend further among both populations as analytical and conceptual skills expand[188] and as publics increasingly recognize the unsustainability of high-energy-consumption life-styles and automotive-centered economies.[189]

Although difficult value and behavioral adjustments are required among both populations, the first step toward embracing and implementing a low-energy-intensive and sustainable-consumption life-style rests with the United States. Unilateral curtailment by the world's most inveterate consumer would dissolve political obstacles that have deterred China from implementing adjustments that are in the long-term interest of its own population. For instance, participating in an early and massive transition to renewable-energy sources would enable China to avoid expensive investments in obsolete fossil-fuel-driven systems.[190]

After demonstrating initiative in adopting low-energy-consumptive lifestyles (including drastically reduced use of gasoline-operated motor vehicles) and in shifting to renewable sources of energy, state and nonstate actors in the United States will be in a stronger position to "help China follow its example."[191] It is encouraging in this connection that China's *Agenda 21* white paper foresees rejection of the industrialized-country development model and acceptance of "appropriate consumption and a low energy-consuming production system."[192] China also will need to undertake additional efforts that address population control and reduction.[193]

## Potential Civil-society Roles for Chinese+Americans

In selecting civil-society roles as well as effective change strategies, Chinese+Americans will benefit from drawing upon their insights regarding the two political systems and the prevailing political cultures. In the linked values arena, the potentially most effective nongovernmental roles include involvement in national and cross-national epistemic communities (scientific research, educational efforts), professional organizations, national and transnational NGOs and social movements, advocacy/activist networks, philanthropic foundations, native-place networks, benevolent associations,[194] friendship networks, social networks, religious networks, kinship networks, and Internet networks. Individuals also can act directly through personal contacts.

Advocacy/activist networks, for instance, strive to inculcate widespread ecological sensibility so that decisions and actions affecting life-styles, consumer behavior, fashion, workplace habits, building construction, domestic politics, and so forth, are made "in deference to environmental awareness."[195] Transnational social movements likewise devote considerable emphasis and energy to the "'deep politics' of shaping individuals' thinking and actions. . . ."[196] Perseverant individuals can serve as influential role models.[197] In general, nonstate actors occupy critical positions from which to advance a notion of security that shifts the traditional preoccupation with "politico-military threats" to an emphasis on the threat of worldwide environmental degradation.[198]

In terms of value and behavioral changes affecting resource use, Chinese+Americans might find it useful to pursue participation in Consumers International (CI).[199] Partnering with women's NGOs in China and the United States on educational programs designed to raise awareness regarding the societal and intergenerational virtues and personal benefits associated with recycling, public and nonmotorized transportation, sustainable-consumption practices, "making purchasing decisions based upon [product] source reduction characteristics of durability, repairability and reusability,"[200] and participation in helping to preserve natural resources,[201] offers another promising role for Chinese+Americans. As Liao Xiaoyi, the director of a Chinese women's NGO engaged in precisely these kinds of efforts, explained to President Bill Clinton in Guilin, "women are consumer decision makers" and their choice of the three R's of an environmentally friendly life style—"reduce, recycle, and reuse"—would provide an invaluable force for change.[202] Another Mainland prospect involves linkages with the self-identified "citizen's movement" for change in environment and development policies. One part of this group's 26 August 1998 open letter/petition asserts that "the so-called high growth economics that waste resources and pollute the environment come at too high a price. They have brought severe consequences to our nation and must be stopped right away."[203]

The questions directed to President Clinton in Guilin in July 1998 reveal that considerable grass-roots interest exists in China today in securing external assistance for environmental-education efforts—ranging from television programs warning the Chinese people not to copy U.S. mistakes and describing how to organize an effective environmental movement,[204] to the publication of children's guides to sustainable consumption.[205] At the 1998 Summit, moreover, China and the United States agreed to undertake a program of multiweek secondary-school student and teacher exchanges.[206] This initiative, scheduled to commence on a pilot basis in fall 2001, aims to "develop linkages between schools and communities in the U.S. and China for the purpose of mutual education and the development of student participation in community affairs." According to guidelines issued on 8 June 2000 by the Bureau of Educational and Cultural Affairs, "each one-to-one school partnership will choose a theme relevant to their communities; students will work together [via Internet connectivity and exchanges of 3–4 weeks in duration] to complete a joint project related to this theme."[207] The broad mandate of this new cooperative venture presents an opportunity for participating Chinese and Chinese+American secondary-school students and teachers to become involved in transnational awareness-building concerning the urgency of resource conservation and sustainable consumption and the link between energy efficiency and environmental benefits.[208]

In short, there are a growing number of potential state and nonstate partners in China who are challenging the view that resources are inexhaustible and are committed to emphasizing the importance of maintaining natural resources for future generations in place of pursuing maximum economic growth and conspicuous consumption.[209] The environmental-education-oriented NGOs and GONGOs that have emerged as potential in-country partners include Friends of Nature, the China Forum of Environmental Journalists, Women and the Environment, the Guangzhou Environmental Science Foundation, the Yunnan Man and Nature Foundation, and the Global Village Environmental Culture Institute of Beijing.[210]

In the United States, cross-nationally competent Chinese+Americans could connect with a host of respected NGOs for the promotion of mutual learning. As one example of how this might work, the local chapter of the League of Women Voters could join with the Silicon Valley Chinese Engineers' Society or the New York–based Chinese Association of Science and Technology to offer a series of town meetings on the topic of nonrenewable energy consumption trends and conservation prospects in both countries.[211] Moreover, through participation in U.S. universities, think-tanks, churches, professional associations, human-rights organizations, labor alliances,[212] and service clubs, Chinese+Americans can engage in a "people-to-people dialogue"[213] over U.S.–China perspectives on and approaches to sustainable development. These efforts will be most effective when they occur at the local level—where members of the Chinese+American community are well known, trusted, and respected. This opportunity dovetails with the propensity for permanent settlement among recent immigrants and the growing tendency of Chinese Americans to become involved politically in "ethnically mixed neighborhoods and communities."[214] Within Chinese+American immigrant communities, existing community-organized workshops on issues such as worker and immigrant rights and domestic violence can be augmented by grass-roots environmental-education efforts.[215]

## Strategic Options, Strengths, and Opportunities for Chinese+Americans

In the United States, a basic prerequisite for mutual learning is to break down unidimensional and overly simplistic perceptions of the PRC.[216] Furthermore, it is necessary to be vigilant in countering negative stereotypes regarding the role of Chinese+Americans in U.S. science and society.[217] Beyond creating open-minded predispositions about contemporary China and the important contributions of Chinese+Americans, progress in achieving sustainable consumption and averting conflict over scarce resources depends on the capacity of actors along the China–United States frontier to promote understanding on both sides that common interests are at stake, that the factors contributing to resource depletion and environmental degradation are nearby as well as distant, and that far-reaching civil-society exchanges and cooperation are vital in order to deal with "powerful global trends that transcend the control of any single nation-state."[218]

The particular strategic strengths of the Chinese+American actor in the (USA and PRC) value arena are likely to include possession of a dual frame of reference, essential and in-depth cross-cultural knowledge and understanding,[219] the generation of valuable insights for mutual learning and transformation that are derived from transnational encounters, and persuasion based on trust;[220] the ability to access and to engage social, kinship, native-place, community, friendship, economic, and religious networks at the local level in China; skill in simultaneously invoking insider and outsider identities[221] and in linking existing environmental values to specific and effective responses;[222] and setting examples, by serving as a role model, that inspire resource-sensitive behavior in both societies. Aside from a few transcultural values with global resonance, such as protection of infants and children from bodily harm, environmental and resource issues need to be framed in ways that fit with culturally specific "belief systems, life experiences, and stories, myths, and folk tales."[223] Cross-nationally competent Chinese+Americans are particularly capable of assisting transnational NGOs and scientific/professional networks in addressing this strategic challenge.[224] In recognition of the "risk-aversion" tendencies that prevail in Chinese culture, for instance, they would be likely to approach value change in the Mainland by emphasizing the magnitude of potential losses rather than the probability of positive outcomes. In contrast, the benefits for the individual associated with personal frugality and participation in a linked community–global conservation movement would be stressed among relatively "risk-prone" U.S. decision makers.[225] Moreover, the Mainland-public-interest motives of many

Chinese+American scientists and their identification with Chinese culture mean that their efforts to transmit resource-curtailment values are likely to encounter a receptive audience.

## Likely Involvement by Chinese+American Advocates of Sustainable Consumption

The transnational foundation required to cope with potentially contentious U.S.–China interdependence challenges exists today in the form of extensive and vibrant networks of civil-society actors that are active along shared political, economic, cultural, and scientific boundaries. As Chinese+Americans adopt a shared vision of the double-sided problem of sustainable consumption "and see themselves, collectively, as part of the solution, they become [active] stakeholders"[226] along the U.S.–China frontier. By contributing their special insights and skills in the arenas of international-agreement shaping, domestic-policy making, development-project implementation, and value exchange, cross-nationally competent Chinese+Americans can play exceptionally influential, even decisive, roles in addressing environmental-interdependence challenges.[227]

Whether or not they actually participate in resource-conservation efforts in the United States and the PRC will depend on at least three factors: personal commitment, willingness to address key issues, and perceived ability to influence relevant decision making. In the absence of communitywide research regarding the presence or absence of these factors, the summer 2000 North Carolina findings provide a suggestive framework for analysis—particularly since 80 percent of these respondents are scientists, educators, professionals, or business managers/owners.

The findings reported in Table 13.3 indicate that about two-thirds of the North Carolina respondents identify themselves as sustainable-consumption advocates.[228] While only 27 percent of all those surveyed (25 percent of the advocates) demonstrated willingness to initiate discussion about curtailing consumption in the PRC, half of the advocates of sustainable consumption (38 percent overall) are inclined to take that step in the United States. In addition, substantial majorities reported some ability to influence local-level decision making in both countries—particularly the United States.[229] On the whole, the exploratory findings presented in Table 13.3 suggest the possibility that a substantial segment of the Chinese American community is positioned—in terms of value orientation, willingness to act, and self-perceived ability to organize and execute influential courses of action—to promote resource conservation and sustainable consumption through participation in civil-society roles in the PRC and (especially) the U.S. influence arenas.

Table 13.3

## Sustainable-consumption Commitments, Discussion, and Perceived Influence Among North Carolina Chinese Americans

| Item and responses | Number | % Total |
|---|---|---|
| "In general, I am an advocate of sustainable consumption." | | |
| Agree | 22 | 64.7 |
| Disagree | 12 | 35.3 |
| | | |
| "When/if in China, I am likely to initiate discussion about reducing/limiting consumption." | | |
| Agree | 9 | 27.3 |
| Disagree | 24 | 72.7 |
| | | |
| "In the United States, I am likely to initiate discussion about reducing/limiting consumption." | | |
| Agree | 12 | 37.5 |
| Disagree | 20 | 62.5 |
| | | |
| Self-assessed ability to influence local-level decisions in the China Mainland | | |
| Good/Fair | 11 | 31.4 |
| Poor | 10 | 28.6 |
| None | 14 | 40.0 |
| | | |
| Self-assessed ability to influence local-level decisions in the United States | | |
| Excellent/Good/Fair | 16 | 44.4 |
| Poor | 13 | 36.1 |
| None | 7 | 19.4 |

*Source:* Data collected by the author in conjunction with Yuhang Shi's summer 2000 survey.

Table 13.4 provides independent support regarding the ability of Chinese+Americans who are advocates of sustainable consumption to make a difference in both societies. Using a scale that measures language ability and usage, social and work interactions, along with self-assessed knowledge, ability to function, and influence in the PRC/United States, the Table 13.4 data show that the most cross-nationally competent Chinese+American respondents are far more likely than the least competent respondents are to identify as a sustainable-consumption advocate (72 percent and 33 percent, respectively).[230] Thus, to the extent that cross-national competency makes a difference in contemporary transnational relations, one would expect to see Chinese+American advocates of sustainable consumption playing more influential civil-society roles relative to nonadvocates. Furthermore, 88 percent of the North Carolina respondents who have voted in a U.S. election

Table 13.4

**Advocates/Nonadvocates of Sustainable Consumption by Cross-national Competency: North Carolina Chinese Americans**

| | Position on sustainable consumption | | | |
| | Advocate | | Nonadvocate | |
| Score on cross-national competency scale | No. | % Total | No. | % Total |
|---|---|---|---|---|
| Not competent (1 to 5 points out of 16) | 2 | 33.3 | 4 | 66.7 |
| Competent (6 to 13 points out of 16) | 20 | 71.5 | 8 | 28.6 |

*Source:* Data collected by the author in conjunction with Yuhang Shi's summer 2000 survey.

*Note:* Scale construction awarded one point for each of the following: excellent/good English-language ability; excellent/good ability in Chinese dialect most familiar with; use English away from home frequently/occasionally; most frequently speak Mandarin, Cantonese, or another Chinese dialect at home; one or more mainstream Americans among five closest friends; one or more Mainland Chinese among five closest friends; one or more mainstream Americans among five work most closely with; one or more Mainland Chinese among five work most closely with; contact with three or more Mainland Chinese in China per year; contact with Mainland Chinese in China at least once per month; excellent/good knowledge of beliefs, values, practices in China Mainland; excellent/good knowledge of beliefs, values, practices in USA; good ability to function in China Mainland; excellent/good ability to function in USA; good ability to influence local-level decisions in China Mainland; excellent/good ability to influence local-level decisions in USA.

identify as sustainable-consumption advocates.[231] Support for sustainable consumption is most widespread among those who report their current political-party affiliation to be Democrat (83 percent), followed by independents and Republicans (67 percent and 53 percent, respectively). Respondents who believe that the U.S. government should do more to improve relations with the PRC are more likely to advocate sustainable consumption than are those who do not share this belief (72 percent versus 56 percent). Fully 82 percent of those who are members of secular Chinese American organizations are advocates, while only 57 percent of those who do not belong to such organizations identify in this manner. With the important exception of business managers/owners (100 percent nonadvocates), majorities identify as sustainable-consumption advocates among all occupational groups represented in the North Carolina study—particularly professionals (83 percent) and information-technology specialists (75 percent)—and respondents possessing total annual family incomes of US$70,000 and higher are more likely to be advocates than are those with less family income (73 percent versus 55 percent).[232]

## Conclusion

The analysis presented in this chapter has shown that Chinese+Americans are strategically positioned to engage in effective civil-society actions that address interdependent environmental and natural-resource challenges that will be of escalating concern to China and the United States in the trans-Pacific century. When civil-society actors accept personal responsibility for addressing interdependence issues, they are able to effectuate change through "a myriad [of] small contributions."[233] The extent of their impact on direction setting and ultimate outcomes will depend upon the degree to which far-sighted community members are motivated to participate in each arena, able to mobilize the requisite skills, information, and resources, and succeed in employing appropriate strategies for effectuating change.

Most of the nongovernmental roles identified in this chapter would not be highly visible and primarily would be filled out of concern for human welfare in both countries rather than in pursuit of narrow ethnic-community interests. Sustainable-consumption advocacy along the China–U.S. frontier addresses an interdependence challenge that simultaneously is a crucial mainstream issue affecting other communities[234] and of nationalistic concern. However, involvement in these roles would not be risk-free. As Paul Watanabe warns, "in a dominant society that is suspicious of activists' true allegiances, aggressive actions, particularly against prevailing trends, tend to validate in many people's minds fears of divided loyalties."[235] One immediate outcome of the U.S. government's prosecution of Wen Ho Lee has been signs of reluctance on the part of some Chinese+American scientists to travel to the Mainland or even to attend China-related events out of concern that any association with the PRC might target them for FBI or INS investigations and actions.[236] Prospects for cooperation will worsen if the George W. Bush administration relates to the PRC in ways that are consistent with its highly publicized "strategic competitor" characterization.

Chinese+Americans engaged in promoting resource conservation at transnational, national, and subnational levels are likely to encounter suspicions and state-imposed political obstacles both in the PRC and in the United States. While the challenges are formidable, growing numbers of Chinese+Americans are positioned to influence U.S.–China environmental interdependence in the twenty-first century as a result of transterritorial civil-society network building, enhanced activism, and cross-national competency.

## Notes

1. See James N. Rosenau, *Along the Domestic-Foreign Frontier: Exploring Governance in a Turbulent World* (Cambridge: Cambridge University Press, 1997), pp. 5–6; Thomas Risse-Kappen, "Structures of Governance and Transnational Relations: What Have We Learned?" in *Bringing Transnational Relations Back In: Non-State Actors, Domestic Structures and International Institutions*, ed. by Thomas Risse-Kappen (Cambridge: Cambridge University Press, 1995), p. 280; Daniel Mato, "On

Global and Local Agents and the Social Making of Transnational Identities and Related Agendas in 'Latin' America," *Identities* 4, No. 2 (1997): 171.

2. The ideas developed in this section build on the pioneering work of James N. Rosenau. See James N. Rosenau, "Enlarged Citizen Skills and Enclosed Coastal Seas," in *Saving the Seas: Values, Scientists, and International Governance*, ed. by L. Anathea Brooks and Stacy D. VanDeveer (College Park: University of Maryland Press, 1997), pp. 349–350; James N. Rosenau and W. Michael Fagen, "A New Dynamism in World Politics: Increasingly Skillful Individuals?" *International Studies Quarterly* 41, No. 4 (December 1997): 660. Also see the complete framework for understanding transnational competence set forth in Peter H. Koehn and James N. Rosenau, "Transnational Competence in an Emergent Epoch," *International Studies Perspectives* 3, No. 2 (2002): 105–127.

3. Norman Dinges, "Intercultural Competence," in *Handbook of Intercultural Training*, Vol. II, ed. by Dan Landis and Richard W. Brislin (New York: Pergamon, 1983), p. 178.

4. On the latter, see Guo-ming Chen and William J. Starosta, "Intercultural Communication Competence: A Synthesis," *Communication Yearbook* 19, No. 3 (1996): 368.

5. Nina G. Schiller, "The Situation of Transnational Studies," *Identities* 4, No. 2 (1997): 158.

6. Internet findings, Study No. 396 of 29 June 1997.

7. See Xiao-huang Yin, "The Growing Influence of Chinese Americans on U.S.–China Relations," in *The Outlook for U.S.–China Relations Following the 1997–1998 Summits: Chinese and American Perspectives on Security, Trade, and Cultural Exchange*, ed. by Peter H. Koehn and Joseph Y.S. Cheng (Hong Kong: Chinese University Press, 1999), pp. 341–342.

8. *Los Angeles Times*, Study No. 396.

9. Edgar Wickberg, "Overseas Chinese Adaptive Organizations, Past and Present," in *Reluctant Exiles? Migration from Hong Kong and the New Overseas Chinese* ed. by Ronald Skeldon (Hong Kong: Hong Kong University Press, 1994), p. 73.

10. See Yin, "Growing Influence of Chinese Americans," pp. 341–342.

11. See Yu-wen Ying, "Life Satisfaction Among San Francisco Chinese-Americans," *Social Indicators Research* 26, No. 1 (1992): 18.

12. The complete breakdown is 14 percent "excellent," 32 percent "good," 46 percent "fair," and 8 percent "poor" (N=37). Data collected by the author.

13. U.S. Census Bureau estimates for 1999 indicate that 83 percent of the 2.4 million Chinese Americans speak their native language at home. Cited in Stuart Elliott, "Ads Speak to Asian-Americans," *New York Times*, 6 March 2000, p. C1. For a study of factors promoting and discouraging ethnic-language learning among ABCs aged 5–13 enrolled in four "Chinese-language schools" in Salt Lake City, Utah, see Simon H. Cheng and Wen H. Kuo, "Family Socialization of Ethnic Identity Among Chinese American Pre-adolescents," *Journal of Comparative Family Studies* 31, No. 4 (2000): 476–478.

Yu-wen Ying concludes that the most demanding and revealing measure of cross-cultural competence is "the formation of significant and intimate interethnic relationships. . . ." In this late-1980s study of 143 Chinese-American adults living in San Francisco (two-thirds of whom were foreign-born), 30 percent listed both Chinese and non-Chinese among their three closest friends. Yu-wen Ying, "Cultural Orientation and Psychological Well-Being in Chinese Americans," *American Journal of Community Psychology* 23, No. 6 (December 1995): 906, 901.

14. In fact, 53 percent of the N.C. respondents contact three or more people in the China Mainland at least once per year.

While based on a small, nonrepresentative sample, these exploratory findings suggest, in contrast to the expectation set forth in 1996 by Yu-Wen Ying, that Chinese Americans living in parts of the United States that lack "access to a large Chinese American community" are more rather than less likely to live a "full bicultural life. . . ." See Yu-Wen Ying, "Immigration Satisfaction of Chinese Americans: An Empirical Examination," *Journal of Community Psychology* 24 (January 1996): 11, 14.

15. See, for instance, Lucie Cheng, "Chinese Americans in the Formation of the Pacific Regional Economy," in *Across the Pacific: Asian Americans and Globalization,* ed. by Evelyn Hu-DeHart (New York: Asia Society, 1999), p. 75; Ying, "Life Satisfaction," 18; Yin, "Growing Influence of Chinese Americans," pp. 332–336.

16. See Myrtle P. Bell and David A. Harrison, "Using Intra-national Diversity for International Assignments: A Model of Bicultural Competence and Expatriate Adjustment," *Human Resource Management Review* 6, No. 1 (September 1996): 50–59.

17. See Sau-ling C. Wong, "Denationalization Reconsidered: Asian American Cultural Criticism at a Theoretical Crossroads," *Amerasia Journal* 21, Nos. 1 & 2 (1995): 7.

18. Rosenau, *Along the Domestic-foreign Frontier,* pp. 5–6.

19. Ibid., p. 72.

20. See Gareth Porter and Janet W. Brown, *Global Environmental Politics,* 2d ed. (Boulder: Westview Press, 1996), p. 51; Paul Wapner, *Environmental Activism and World Civic Politics* (Albany: State University of New York Press, 1996), p. 2; Margaret E. Keck and Kathryn Sikkink, *Activists Beyond Borders: Advocacy Networks in International Politics* (Ithaca, NY: Cornell University Press, 1998), pp. 10, 213–214; Paul Wapner, "Politics beyond the State: Environmental Activism and World Civic Politics," *World Politics* 47 (April 1995): 336–337; Sally Morphet, "NGOs and the Environment," in *"The Conscience of the World': The Influence of Non-Governmental Organisations in the UN System,* ed. by Peter Willetts (Washington, D.C.: Brookings Institution, 1996), pp. 131–133; Thomas Princen and Matthias Finger, "Introduction," in *Environmental NGOs in World Politics: Linking the Local and the Global,* ed. by Thomas Princen and Matthias Finger (London: Routledge, 1994), pp. 1–9, 11.

21. Paul Ekins, *A New World Order: Grassroots Movements for Global Change* (London: Routledge, 1992), pp. 164–165. Also see Wapner, *Environmental Activism,* p. 149; Thomas Princen and Matthias Finger, "Preface," in *Environmental NGOs in World Politics: Linking the Local and the Global,* pp. x–xi; Princen and Finger, "Introduction," pp. 10–11; Thomas Princen, "NGOs: Creating a Niche in Environmental Diplomacy," in *Environmental NGOs in World Politics: Linking the Local and the Global,* pp. 30–31.

22. See Richard W. Mansbach, Yale H. Ferguson, and Donald E. Lampert, *The Web of World Politics: Nonstate Actors in the Global System* (Englewood Cliffs, NJ: Prentice-Hall, 1976), pp. 26, 39–41.

23. Ulf Hannerz, *Transnational Connections: Culture, People, Places* (London: Routledge, 1996), p. 89.

24. Multinational corporations and domestic business firms are relevant in this connection when they promote "principled ideas as well as knowledge" rather than seek "instrumental, mainly economic, gains. . . ." Thomas Risse-Kappen, "Bringing Transnational Relations Back In: Introduction," in *Bringing Transnational Relations Back In,* p. 8.

Gary Hamilton maintains that members view Chinese society as consisting of "institutionalized webs of social relationships that identify people to whom participants in those networks are personally obligated." Gary G. Hamilton, "The Theoretical Significance of Asian Business Networks," in *Asian Business Networks*, ed. by Gary G. Hamilton (Berlin: Walter de Gruyter, 1996), pp. 287–289. Also see Alan Smart and Josephine Smart, "Transnational Social Networks and Negotiated Identities in Interactions Between Hong Kong and China," in *Transnationalism from Below*, ed. by Michael P. Smith and Luis E. Guarnizo (New Brunswick: Transaction, 1998), pp. 104, 107–108.

On the networking role of evangelical Protestant churches in North America, see Wickberg, "Overseas Chinese Adaptive Organizations," p. 82. On Internet networks, see Yu Yunmin, "The Development of Communication Information Infrastructure: A Revolution in Networking," in *Social Transition in China*, ed. by Zhang Jie and Li Xiaobing (Lanham, MD: University Press of America, 1998), pp. 171–173, 183. The official number of registered Internet users in China, estimated at 1.2 million in 1998, reached 9 million early in 2000 and, according to one source, leaped to 16.9 million by mid-2000. Maggie Farley, "China Tries 'Cyberdissident,' " *Missoulian*, 3 December 1998, p. C2; Elisabeth Rosenthal, "China Lists Controls to Restrict the Use of E-mail and Web," *New York Times*, 27 January 2000, p. A12; Li Cheng, "China in Year 2000: A Year of Strategic Rethinking," *Asian Survey* 41, 1 (January/February 2001): 87. Between 20 and 30 persons often share one account in China's universities and research centers, and cybercafes attract a growing clientele. Thus, the actual number of Internet users is much higher than the official figure. See Yu Yunmin, "Revolution in Networking," pp. 173–174. Although the government issued new regulations prohibiting the posting and distribution of "state secrets" on 26 January 2000, control over Internet messages will be difficult to enforce. Rosenthal, "China Lists Controls," pp. A1, A12; Elisabeth Rosenthal, "Web Sites Bloom in China, and Are Weeded," *New York Times*, 23 December 1999, p. A10. Also see Yu, "Revolution in Networking," pp. 177–182. On improvement associations and philanthropic foundations, see the chapters by Norton Wheeler and John J. Deeney in this volume. On alumni clubs, see Wickberg, "Overseas Chinese Adaptive Organizations," p. 74.

Hamilton concludes that "networks spawned by regional collegiality and by kinship" constitute the basic units linking Chinese economic activity. Family ties include extended and immediate families with members living in both countries—including those holding U.S. passports by birth or naturalization. Gary G. Hamilton, "The Organizational Foundations of Western and Chinese Commerce: A Historical and Comparative Analysis," in *Asian Business Networks*, ed. by Gary G. Hamilton (Berlin: Walter de Gruyter, 1996), pp. 53–54. The children of influential figures in the PRC also fit here. See Elisabeth Rosenthal and Erik Eckholm, "On Unofficial Level, At Least, Chinese Value Ties to the U.S.," *New York Times*, 27 May 1999, p. A6.

25. Richard Madsen, *China and the American Dream: A Moral Inquiry* (Berkeley: University of California Press, 1995), p. 228.

26. See Philip Q. Yang, "Sojourners or Settlers: Post-1965 Chinese Immigrants," *Journal of Asian American Studies* 2, No. 1 (February 1999): 72, 85–86.

27. John J. Jia and Kyna Rubin, "A Potential Bridge over Troubled U.S.–China Waters," *Chronicle of Higher Education*, 7 March 1997, p. A56.

28. See the chapters by Deeney and Wheeler in this volume.

29. Leon V. Sigal, "Look Who's Talking: Nuclear Diplomacy with North Korea," *Items* [SSRC] 51, 2/3 (June/September 1997): 35–36. Also see Peter Koehn, "Cross-

National Competence and U.S.–Asia Interdependence: The Explosion of Trans-Pacific Civil-Society Networks," in *Tigers' Roar: Asia's Recovery and Its Impact on the Global Economy*, ed. by Julian M. Weiss (Armonk, NY: M.E. Sharpe, 2001), p. 230.

30. See Keck and Sikkink, *Activists Beyond Borders*, pp. 1–4; Samuel S. Kim, "Chinese Foreign Policy in Theory and Practice," in *China and the World: Chinese Foreign Policy Faces the New Millennium*, ed. by Samuel S. Kim (Boulder: Westview Press, 1998), p. 23.

31. See Elizabeth C. Economy, "China's Environmental Diplomacy," in *China and the World: Chinese Foreign Policy Faces the New Millennium*, ed. by Samuel S. Kim (Boulder: Westview Press, 1998), p. 270; Porter and Brown, *Global Environmental Politics*, pp. 4, 8.

32. See Economy, "China's Environmental Diplomacy," p. 270; Mark Seis, "Protection of the Atmosphere," in *Introducing Global Issues*, ed. by Michael T. Snarr and D. Neil Snarr (Boulder: Lynne Rienner, 1998), p. 211; Todd M. Johnson, "Foreign Involvement in China's Energy Sector," in *China Joins the World: Progress and Prospects*, ed. by Elizabeth Economy and Michel Oksenberg (New York: Council on Foreign Relations, 1999), p. 267; Kim, "Chinese Foreign Policy," p. 7; Porter and Brown, *Global Environmental Politics*, p. 150.

33. Peter H. Koehn, "Greasing the Grassroots: The Role of Nongovernmental Linkages in the Looming U.S.–China Confrontation over Global Petroleum Reserves," in *The Outlook for U.S.–China Relations Following the 1997–1998 Summits: Chinese and American Perspectives on Security, Trade, and Cultural Exchange*, pp. 351–390; Erica S. Downs, "China's Thirst for Oil: Energy Security and Interdependence" (paper presented at the 51st Annual Meeting of the Association for Asian Studies, Boston, March 1999, pp. 4, 6, 9; Lin Gan, "Energy Development and Environmental Constraints in China," *Energy Policy* 26, No. 2 (1998): 120, 122–123.

34. Vaclav Smil, "China's Energy and Resource Uses: Continuity and Change," *China Quarterly* 156 (December 1998): 940–941; John Leicester, "Green Crusaders: Activists Emerge from China's Polluted Environment," *Missoulian*, 25 November 1998, p. E2; Nicholas D. Kristof, "A Vast Disaster Is in the Air," *International Herald Tribune*, 29–30 November 1997, p. 13; Kim, "Chinese Foreign Policy," p. 7. Recently, for instance, U.S. Geological Survey ecologists have discovered that global air movements result in the accumulation of "persistent organic pollutants" traceable, in part, to China's industrial enterprises that threaten high-elevation ecosystems in Colorado, Montana, Washington, and the Canadian northwest. Michael Jamison, "Dirty Secrets in the Snow," *Missoulian*, 25 March 2001, p. E1.

35. Porter and Brown, *Global Environmental Politics*, p. 126; James Harkness, "Recent Trends in Forestry and Conservation of Biodiversity in China," *China Quarterly* 156 (December 1998): 911–936.

36. Lester R. Brown, *Who Will Feed China? Wake-up Call for a Small Planet* (New York: W.W. Norton, 1995).

37. Porter and Brown, *Global Environmental Politics*, pp. 3–4, 26, 113; Elizabeth Economy, "The Environment and Development in the Asia-Pacific Region," in *Fires across the Water: Transnational Problems in Asia*, ed. by James Shinn (New York: Council on Foreign Relations, 1998), pp. 45, 64–65; Wapner, *Environmental Activism*, pp. 104–105.

38. *1987 World Commission on Environment and Development Report* cited in Stephen Collett, "Environmental Protection and the Earth Summit: Paving the Path to

Sustainable Development," in *Introducing Global Issues*, p. 242.

39. Porter and Brown, *Global Environmental Politics*, pp. 3–4. On the global threat of human-induced degradation of the earth's land resources (soils, forests, biodiversity, fresh water), see Collett, "Earth Summit." For China, see People's Republic of China, State Council, *China's Agenda 21: White Paper on China's Population, Environment, and Development in the 21st Century* (Beijing: State Council, 1994), p. 54.

40. Porter and Brown, *Global Environmental Politics*, pp. 3–4, 26, 113; also see Wapner, *Environmental Activism*, pp. 104–105. China's population is expected to climb from 1.3 billion to 1.6 billion by 2030—"the equivalent of adding four Japans." Brown, *Who Will Feed China?* p. 29. The U.S. population, which is growing three times faster than the average for other industrialized countries due to in-migration and its far higher fertility rate, could total 333 million by 2025. *International Herald Tribune*, 11 November 1997, p. 8; Barbara Crossette, "Against a Trend, U.S. Population Will Bloom, U.N. Says," *New York Times*, 28 February 2001, p. A6.

41. On "nonrenewable" resources, see Karrin Scapple, "Cooperation and Conflict over Natural Resources," in *Introducing Global Issues*, pp. 225–226.

42. See Koehn, "Global Petroleum Reserves," pp. 359–363.

43. On the latter, see Brown, *Who Will Feed China?* p. 36; PRC, State Council, *China's Agenda 21*, p. 51; Joseph C.H. Chai, "Consumption and Living Standards in China," in *The Chinese Economy Under Deng Xiaoping*, ed. by Robert F. Ash and Y.Y. Kueh (Oxford: Clarendon, 1996), p. 272. Also see Porter and Brown, *Global Environmental Politics*, pp. 112–113.

44. Judith Banister, "Population, Public Health, and the Environment in China," *China Quarterly* 156 (December 1998): 986, 1010, 1014. Also see Clem Tisdell, "Protecting the Environment in Transitional Situations," Working Paper No. 29 (Brisbane: Department of Economics, University of Queensland, November 1998), pp. 8–9, 20.

45. Banister, "Population and Environment," pp. 1012–1014.

46. Allen R. Myerson, "U.S. Splurging on Energy After Falling Off Its Diet," *New York Times*, 22 October 1998, p. A1; Keith Bradsher, "Fuel Economy for New Cars Is at Lowest Level Since '80," *New York Times*, 18 May 2001, p. A15. Moreover, U.S. automobile production accounts for about 13 percent of the country's steel consumption, "16 percent of the aluminum, 69 percent of the lead, 36 percent of the iron, 36 percent of the platinum, and 58 percent of the rubber (both natural and synthetic)." Matthew Paterson, "Car Culture and Global Environmental Politics," *Review of International Studies* 26 (2000): 260.

47. See Koehn, "Global Petroleum Reserves," pp. 360–361, 374–375; Nicholas Lenssen, *Empowering Development: The New Energy Equation*, Worldwatch Paper 111 (Washington, D.C.: Worldwatch Institute, November 1992), pp. 22–23; Brown, *Who Will Feed China?* p. 58; Downs, "China's Thirst for Oil," pp. 5–6; Stephen Stares and Liu Zhi, "Motorization in Urban China: Issues and Actions," *China City Planning Review* 12, No. 1 (1996): 13–16; Qing Shen, "Urban Transportation in Shanghai: Problems and Planning Implications," *International Journal of Urban and Regional Research* 21, No. 4 (1997): 593–594.

48. *South China Morning Post*, 12 January 1998, p. 15. According to Vaclav Smil, "even if the average fuel consumption of Chinese cars could be just half the current U.S. mean, China would need about 300 Mt of petrol a year, roughly twice as much as its current annual crude oil consumption." Smil, "China's Energy," 950n.

49. Banister, "Population and Environment," pp. 1012–1013.

50. See Economy, "China's Environmental Diplomacy," p. 265; Seis, "Protection of the Atmosphere," pp. 211, 216.

51. Economy, "China's Environmental Diplomacy," pp. 272–273.

52. Cited in ibid., pp. 271–272.

53. Ibid., p. 281.

54. Porter and Brown, *Global Environmental Politics*, pp. 118, 122, 128.

55. Joseph Kahn, "Excessive Regulation Is Blamed for Energy Woes," *New York Times*, 18 May 2001, p. A15.

56. See, for instance, Koehn, "Global Petroleum Reserves," p. 366.

57. In 1974, however, Ali Mazrui recognized one direction of this two-way shaping process when he noted that "the 'brain drain' from the developing into the developed world could one day become a source of Southern influence within the North. . . ." Ali A. Mazrui, "The New Interdependence: From Hierarchy to Symmetry," in *The U.S. and World Development: Agenda for Action 1975*, ed. by James W. Howe (New York: Praeger, 1975), p. 126.

58. Risse-Kappen, "Structures of Governance," p. 310.

59. Porter and Brown, *Global Environmental Politics*, p. 26.

60. The 1992 Rio Conference did produce *Agenda 21*. *Agenda 21* addresses production, population, and overconsumption, and is intended to provide a road map that points the way toward sustainable development. At the urging of the General Assembly, moreover, the U.N. Economic and Social Council (ECOSOC) set up a high-level Commission on Sustainable Development to follow up on UNCED initiatives. See Morphet, "NGOs and the Environment," pp. 136–138, 140–141.

61. Lester Ross, "China and Environmental Protection," in *China Joins the World: Progress and Prospects*, ed. by Elizabeth Economy and Michel Oksenberg (New York: Council on Foreign Relations, 1999), pp. 299–300.

62. See Economy, "China's Environmental Diplomacy," p. 273; Ross, "China and Environmental Protection," pp. 300, 317–318. However, "it has disputed the amount and terms of its contributions." Ross, "China and Environmental Protection," p. 318.

63. See Scott Barrett, "Montreal Versus Kyoto: International Cooperation and the Global Environment," in *Global Public Goods: International Cooperation in the 21st Century*, ed. by Inge Kaul, Isabelle Grunberg, and Marc A. Stern (Oxford: Oxford University Press, 1999), pp. 210–211; also see Porter and Brown, *Global Environmental Politics*, pp. 122–127.

64. Porter and Brown, *Global Environmental Politics*, p. 122.

65. See Economy, "China's Environmental Diplomacy," p. 281; Peter H. Koehn and Joseph Y.S. Cheng, "The Outlook for U.S.–China Relations in the 21st Century: Regional Security, Trade and Information, and Cultural Exchange," in *The Outlook for U.S.–China Relations Following the 1997–1998 Summits*, pp. 3, 5, 9.

66. Robert Ross suggests that the current "absence of foreign policy imperatives creates expanded opportunities" for interest groups to influence policymakers—particularly in the United States—on issues involving U.S.–China relations. Robert S. Ross, "The Strategic and Bilateral Context of Policy Making in China and the United States: Why Domestic Factors Matter," in *After the Cold War: Domestic Factors and U.S.–China Relations*, ed. by Robert S. Ross (Armonk, NY: M.E. Sharpe, 1998), p. 34.

67. Peter M. Haas, "Introduction: Epistemic Communities and International Policy Coordination," *International Organization* 46, No. 1 (Winter 1992): 2–4, 16–20.

68. L. Ling-chi Wang, "Roots and the Changing Identity of the Chinese in the

United States," in *The Living Tree: The Changing Meaning of Being Chinese Today*, ed. by Tu Wei-ming (Stanford: Stanford University Press, 1994), p. 201. Also see the chapter by Zuoyue Wang in this volume.

69. James Sterngold, "For Asian-Americans, a New Political Resolve," *New York Times*, 22 September 1999, p. A21.

70. Economy, "China's Environmental Diplomacy," pp. 265–271, 274–277, 281–282; Lester Ross, "China: Environmental Protection, Domestic Policy Trends, Patterns of Participation in Regimes and Compliance with International Norms," *China Quarterly* 156 (December 1998): 835. Also see Yong Deng, "The Chinese Conception of National Interests in International Relations," *China Quarterly* 154 (June 1998): 329. The 1998 Summit agreement to "initiate a dialogue on climate change" among senior-level U.S. and Chinese experts further enhanced prospects along these lines. See United States, White House, Office of the Press Secretary, "Fact Sheet: Achievements of U.S.–China Summit" (Beijing: 27 June 1998).

71. See Porter and Brown, *Global Environmental Politics*, pp. 53–54; Morphet, "NGOs and the Environment," p. 141; Tadashi Yamamoto, Pranee Thiparat, and Abul Ahsan, *America's Role in Asia: Asian Views* (New York: Asia Foundation, 2001), p. 35.

72. See Liu Yongtao, "Norms, Identity, and Prospects of Sino-American Security Cooperation," in *The Outlook for U.S.–China Relations Following the 1997–1998 Summits*, pp. 131–132; Keck and Sikkink, *Activists Beyond Borders*, p. 29.

73. Such as the National Association of Chinese Americans, which is "composed mostly of scientists and other professionals and designed to lobby for the normalization of the U.S.–China relationship." Zuoyue Wang, "U.S.–China Scientific Exchange: A Case Study of State-sponsored Scientific Internationalism During the Cold War and Beyond," *Historical Studies in the Physical and Biological Sciences* 30, No. 1 (1999): 271.

74. See Elizabeth R. DeSombre, *Domestic Sources of International Environmental Policy: Industry, Environmentalists, and U.S. Power* (Cambridge: MIT Press, 2000), pp. 10, 245.

75. Kim, "Chinese Foreign Policy," p. 24.

76. Haas, "Introduction," pp. 6, 15–16.

77. Kim, "Chinese Foreign Policy," p. 24; Emmanuel Adler and Peter M. Haas, "Conclusion: Epistemic Communities, World Order, and the Creation of a Reflective Research Program," *International Organization* 46, No. 1 (Winter 1992): 375, 378.

78. Haas, "Introduction," p. 5.

79. Ibid., p. 16; Risse-Kappen, "Structures of Governance," p. 312.

80. Haas, "Introduction," p. 4.

81. Porter and Brown, *Global Environmental Politics*, p. 54; Wapner, *Environmental Activism*, p. 3; Keck and Sikkink, *Activists Beyond Borders*, pp. 6–7; Morphet, "NGOs and the Environment," p. 134; John D. McCarthy, "The Globalization of Social Movement Theory," in *Transnational Social Movements and Global Politics: Solidarity Beyond the State*, ed. by Jackie Smith, Charles Chatfield, and Ron Pagnucco (Syracuse, NY: Syracuse University Press, 1997), pp. 244–247; Chadwick F. Alger, "Transnational Social Movements, World Politics, and Global Governance," in *Transnational Social Movements and Global Politics: Solidarity Beyond the State*, pp. 264–265.

82. Keck and Sikkink, *Activists Beyond Borders*, pp. 2–3, 16, 19, 23, 25.

83. David Bachman suggests that foreign-policy formulation in the PRC increas-

ingly will involve "extensive bargaining, negotiations, and deal-making" among multiple and competing players and that "compromise and consensus building will be the key political processes. . . ." David Bachman, "Structure and Process in the Making of Chinese Foreign Policy," in *China and the World: Chinese Foreign Policy Faces the New Millennium*, ed. by Samuel S. Kim (Boulder: Westview Press, 1998), p. 50. Also see Michel Oksenberg and Elizabeth Economy, "Introduction: China Joins the World," in *China Joins the World: Progress and Prospects*, p. 24.

84. Adapted from Keck and Sikkink, *Activists Beyond Borders*, pp. 19, 132.

85. Yin, "Growing Influence of Chinese Americans," p. 335. See the thorough historical discussion of the cross-border roles filled by Chinese+American scientists—particularly Cheng-ning Yang, Nobel laureate in physics, and T.D. Lee—found in Wang, "U.S.–China Scientific Exchange," pp. 257, 260–265, 268–269.

86. See Hongying Wong, "Chinese Culture and Multilateralism," in *The New Realism: Perspectives on Multilateralism and World Order*, ed. by Robert W. Cox (Tokyo: United Nations University Press, 1997), pp. 156–157.

87. See Paterson, "Car Culture," pp. 266–267; Marcia D. Lowe, *The Bicycle: Vehicle for a Small Planet*, Worldwatch Paper 90 (Washington, D.C.: Worldwatch Institute, 1989), pp. 7, 41–44; Stares and Zhi, "Motorization in Urban China," pp. 16–17, 26; Shen, "Urban Transportation in Shanghai," p. 603.

88. See, for instance, Porter and Brown, *Global Environmental Politics*, pp. 122, 149–150; Willett Kempton, James S. Boster, and Jennifer A. Hartley, *Environmental Values in American Culture* (Cambridge: MIT Press, 1995), pp. 160–161; Zhongxiang Zhang, "Decoupling China's Carbon Emissions Increase from Economic Growth: An Economic Analysis and Policy Implications," *World Development* 28, No. 4 (2000): 748.

89. See Bryn Sadownik and Mark Jaccard, "Sustainable Energy and Urban Form in China: The Relevance of Community Energy Management," *Energy Policy* 29, No. 1 (2001): 55–65. The de-densification programs being pursued in most major Chinese cities, coupled with the disappearance of state-provided and enterprise-based housing, promote increased levels of motorization and petroleum consumption. Stares and Zhi, "Motorization in Urban China," p. 16; Shen, "Urban Transportation in Shanghai," pp. 597–598. China's municipal governments would play a particularly vital role in shaping and implementing community-energy-management policies that promote accessibility. See Shen, "Urban Transportation in Shanghai," pp. 599–603.

90. See PRC, State Council, *China's Agenda 21*, p. 55; Carlos Wing Hung Lo and Sai Wing Leung, "Environmental Agency and Public Opinion in Guangzhou: The Limits of a Popular Approach to Environmental Governance," *China Quarterly* 163 (September 2000): 678. Moreover, the 4th Session of the Eighth National People's Congress endorsed the principle of sustainable development in 1996. Szu-chien Hsu, "International Linkage and China's Environmental Policies" (Paper presented at the 51st Annual Meeting of the Association of Asian Studies, Boston, March 1999), p. 8; Chang-chin Chen, "Beijing's Environmental Protection Strategy," *Issues & Studies* 33, No. 7 (July 1997): 84; Michael Palmer, "Environmental Regulation in the People's Republic of China: The Face of Domestic Law," *China Quarterly* 156 (December 1998): 791–792.

91. Bruce Tremayne and Penny de Wall, "Business Opportunities for Foreign Firms Related to China's Environment," *China Quarterly* 156 (December 1998): 1020–1025; Ross, "China and Environmental Protection," p. 313; Economy, "China's Environmental Diplomacy," pp. 278–280. Changes are occurring in some places, however. In

Guangzhou, "a tougher stand in law enforcement . . . led to the close-down of more than 150 polluting factories between August 1996 and March 1997" and to increases in "the amount of pollutant discharge fees collected, the number of development projects subject to EIA review, and the number of enterprises investigated for violating environmental rules and regulations." Lo and Leung, "Environmental Governance," p. 700.

92. Economy, "China's Environmental Diplomacy," pp. 271, 269; Lo and Leung, "Environmental Governance," p. 677.

93. See Kahn, "Excessive Regulation Is Blamed," p. A15.

94. Luis Guarnizo, "The Emergence of a Transnational Social Formation and the Mirage of Return Migration Among Dominican Transmigrants," *Identities* 4, No. 2 (1997): 310.

95. Risse-Kappen, "Introduction," pp. 25–26.

96. Tony Saich, "Negotiating the State: The Development of Social Organizations in China," *China Quarterly* 161 (March 2000): 139.

97. Lo and Leung, "Environmental Governance," pp. 679, 700–704; Tisdell, "Transitional Situations," pp. 5–6.

98. See Baogang He, *The Democratic Implications of Civil Society in China* (London: Macmillan, 1997), pp. 8–13, 150–153, 169; Gordon White, "Prospects for Civil Society: A Case Study of Xiaoshan City," in *China's Quiet Revolution: New Interactions Between State and Society*, ed. by David S. Goodman and Beverley Hooper (New York: St. Martin's Press, 1994), pp. 202–215.

99. White, "Civil Society," p. 207. Also see Lo and Leung, "Environmental Governance," p. 701.

100. He, *Civil Society*, p. 8; White, "Civil Society," p. 214.

101. Saich, "Social Organizations," pp. 129, 125, 130–140.

102. Ibid., p. 134. Also see Gordon White, Jude Howell, and Shang Xiaoyuan, *In Search of Civil Society: Market Reform and Social Change in Contemporary China* (Oxford: Clarendon, 1996), pp. 98–127.

103. Kenneth Lieberthal, "China's Governing System and Its Impact on Environmental Policy Implementation," China Environment Series 1, Environmental Change and Security Project, Woodrow Wilson International Center for Scholars, 1997, http//ecsp.si.edu/ecsplib.nsf; Hsu, "China's Environmental Policies," pp. 2, 25; Michel Oksenberg and Elizabeth Economy, "China: Implementation Under Economic Growth and Market Reform," in *Engaging Countries: Strengthening Compliance with International Environmental Accords*, ed. by Edith B. Weiss and Harold K. Jacobson (Cambridge: MIT Press, 1998), pp. 355, 358, 390, 392; Palmer, "Environmental Regulation," pp. 796–800, 805–806; Wang Xi and Robert F. Blomquist, "The Developing Environmental Law and Policy of the People's Republic of China: An Introduction and Appraisal," *Georgetown International Environmental Law Review* 5 (Fall 1992): p. 25–75; Ross, "China," p. 826.

104. Michael Palmer ("Environmental Regulation," p. 806) reports that local environmental-protection authorities fail to impose financially stringent penalties because "they are as much concerned with securing an income from the fines as they are with protecting the environment. . . ." Also see Hsu, "China's Environmental Policies," p. 26; Oksenberg and Economy, "China," pp. 358–359; Lo and Leung, "Environmental Governance," p. 691; David N. Campbell, "The Maoist Legacy and Environmental Implementation in China," *Asian Survey* 37, No. 9 (September 1997): 860–862, 873.

105. Lieberthal, "China's Governing System."
106. Palmer, "Environmental Regulation," p. 806.
107. Hsu, "China's Environmental Policies," pp. 8, 22, 29; Oksenberg and Economy, "China," p. 354; Palmer, "Environmental Regulation," p. 807; Ross, "China," pp. 813–814, 829–830, 834; Lo and Leung, "Environmental Governance," pp. 677, 700.
108. See Hsu, "China's Environmental Policies," pp. 2, 23–24; White et al., *Civil Society*, p. 127.
109. Economy, "China's Environmental Diplomacy," pp. 276–277.
110. See Hsu, "China's Environmental Policies," pp. 22–24; Chen, "Environmental Protection Strategy," pp. 80–81, 85–90; Ross, "China," p. 834.
111. Risse-Kappen, "Introduction," p. 7.
112. Economy, "China's Environmental Diplomacy," pp. 265–269, 274–278.
113. See Palmer, "Environmental Regulation," p. 793.
114. Zijin Wu, "The Origins of Environmental Management in China," in *Learning from China? Development and Environment in Third World Countries*, ed. by Bernard Glaeser (London: Allen & Unwin, 1987), pp. 116–117; Richard L. Edmonds, *Patterns of China's Lost Harmony: A Survey of the Country's Environmental Degradation and Protection* (London: Routledge, 1994), pp. 234–245; Palmer, "Environmental Regulation," pp. 794–795; Carlos Wing-hung Lo, Jack Man-keung Lo, and Kai-chee Cheung, "Institutional Reform in Environmental Governance System of the People's Republic of China: Service Organizations as an Alternative for Administrative Enhancement," *Policy Studies Review* 18, No. 1 (Spring 2001): 37–58; Jia and Rubin, "Potential Bridge," p. A56; Economy, "China's Environmental Diplomacy," p. 266.
115. Hsu, "China's Environmental Policy," p. 11; Lo and Leung, "Environmental Governance," p. 679n; Elizabeth Knup, "Environmental NGOs in China: An Overview," China Environment Series 1, Environmental Change and Security Project, Woodrow Wilson International Center for Scholars, 1997, http//ecsp.si.edu/ecsplib.nsf; PRC, State Council, *China's Agenda 21*, p. 238, 4; Ross, "China and Environmental Protection," p. 299.
116. John Byrne, Bo Shen, and Xiuguo Li, "The Challenge of Sustainability: Balancing China's Energy, Economic and Environmental Goals," *Energy Policy* 24, No. 5 (1996): 460.
117. Ross, "China and Environmental Protection," pp. 313–314; Ross, "China," p. 828.
118. Zhang, "Decoupling," p. 744.
119. Robert P. Taylor, *Decentralized Renewable Energy Development in China: The State of the Art* (Washington, D.C.: World Bank, 1982), pp. 27–28; *China Rights Forum* (Spring 1998): 16–17, 19–21. Semi-official science and technology associations in Xiaoshan are organized according to disciplines, skills, and research topics. White, "Civil Society," pp. 204–205.
120. Lo and Leung, "Environmental Governance," pp. 693–694.
121. Palmer, "Environmental Regulation," p. 805.
122. Including the Green Students' Forum. See Bo Wen, "Greening the Chinese Media," China Environment Series 2, Environmental Change and Security Project, Woodrow Wilson International Center for Scholars, 1998, http//ecsp.si.edu/ecsplib.nsf; Economy, "China's Environmental Diplomacy," pp. 265, 277; Leicester, "Green Crusaders," p. E2; White et al., *Civil Society*, pp. 112–113..
123. Hsu, "China's Environmental Policies," p. 11; Earl Drake, "China Council

for International Cooperation on Environment and Development," China Environment Series 1, Environmental Change and Security Project, Woodrow Wilson International Center for Scholars, 1997, http//ecsp.si.edu/ecsplib.nsf; and http://www.harbour.sfu.ca/dlam/members.html.

124. See Hsu, "China's Environmental Policies," pp. 11–12; Drake, "China Council."

125. See Ross, "China and Environmental Protection," p. 316.

126. See Porter and Brown, *Global Environmental Politics*, p. 52.

127. Such as the China Association of Science and Technology (CAST). See White et al., *Civil Society*, pp. 107–108. Also see Daniel Kane, "The Social and Intellectual Elite," in *China's Quiet Revolution: New Interactions Between State and Society*, ed. by David S. Goodman and Beverley Hooper (New York: St. Martin's Press, 1994), pp. 138–139.

128. Ross, "China and Environmental Protection," p. 306.

129. Ibid., pp. 306–313.

130. See Wang, "Scientific Exchange," pp. 265, 270–272.

131. Beth McMurtrie, "No Welcome Mat for the Chinese? U.S. Visas Seem Harder to Get," *Chronicle of Higher Education*, 24 September 1999, p. A59; Sufei Li's chapter in this volume. By the mid-1990s, over 1,000 academics born in Mainland China occupied positions above the rank of lecturer at U.S. universities. Cited in Wang, "Scientific Exchange," p. 271.

132. Jia and Rubin, "Potential Bridge," p. A56.

133. For one perspective on needed reforms in China's environmental law, see Palmer, "Environmental Regulation," p. 792.

134. Michel Oksenberg and Elizabeth Economy maintain that training at national, provincial, and local levels by technically proficient experts stationed in the PRC is essential in order for China to succeed in implementing international agreements. Oksenberg and Economy, "China," pp. 391–392.

135. Economy, "China's Environmental Diplomacy," p. 275.

136. Porter and Brown, *Global Environmental Politics*, pp. 54, 165; Keck and Sikkink, *Activists beyond Borders*, pp. 3, 16, 24; Wapner, *Environmental Activism*, pp. 126, 146; Princen, "NGOs," p. 35; Ross, "China and Environmental Protection," p. 318.

137. Keck and Sikkink, *Activists Beyond Borders*, pp. 201–203; Wapner, *Environmental Activism*, p. 142.

138. Saich, "Social Organizations," pp. 136–138; Knup, "Environmental NGOs." In 1999, Friends of Nature lobbied successfully to have the headwaters area of the Yangtze River designated as a state nature preserve. Jiang Wandi, "Friends of Nature: China's New Environmental Watchdog," *Beijing Review* 99, No. 32 (5–11 August 1999): 18–19.

139. See Hamilton, "Asian Business Networks," pp. 286–290.

140. Lieberthal, "China's Governing System."

141. See Jiang Qisheng and Zhu Rui, "Protect the Yangtze, Our Mother River: An Open Letter to the Chinese People," *China Rights Forum* (Fall 1998): 32–34.

142. Yin, "Growing Influence of Chinese Americans," p. 334.

143. Xiao-huang Yin and Zhiyong Lan, "Chinese Americans: A Rising Factor in U.S.-Chinese Relations," *Journal of American–East Asian Relations* 6, No. 1 (Spring 1997): 35–36. At the Committee's annual conferences in Washington, D.C., members meet with U.S. congressmen and congresswomen and with high-ranking officials in the executive branch. Paul Y. Watanabe, "Asian American Activism and U.S. Foreign

Policy," in *Across the Pacific: Asian Americans and Globalization*, ed. by Evelyn Hu-DeHart (New York: Asia Society, 1999), p. 118.

144. See, for instance, Porter and Brown, *Global Environmental Politics*, pp. 51–53; Princen, "NGOs," p. 34. Ronnie Lipschutz argues that resource conservation and sustainable development can be accomplished most effectively "through efforts at the local level" and "changes in micro-level practices." Ronnie D. Lipschutz, "Networks of Knowledge and Practice: Global Civil Society and Protection of the Global Environment," in *Saving the Seas: Values, Scientists, and International Governance*, ed. by L. Anathea Brooks and Stacy D. VanDeveer (College Park: University of Maryland Press, 1997), pp. 433–440, 445, 455.

145. See Byrne et al., "Challenge of Sustainability," p. 459; Jeffrey S. Logan and Jiqiang Zhang, "Powering Non-Nuclear Growth in China with Natural Gas and Renewable Energy Technologies," China Environment Series 2, Environmental Change and Security Project, Woodrow Wilson International Center for Scholars, 1998, http//ecsp.si.edu/ecsplib.nsf; Johnson, "Foreign Involvement," p. 289; Matthew L. Wald, "U.S. Aims to Have 5% of Electricity from Wind by 2020," *New York Times*, 20 June 1999, p. A25. Small-scale fuel-cell development holds out the promise of providing an energy bridge from fossil fuels to abundant and clean-burning hydrogen. See William McCall, "Flush with Success: Methane Gas from Decomposing Waste Used to Create Electricity," *Missoulian*, 21 January 2001, p. D1. China's special needs, which can be assisted by U.S.-based expertise, include expanding rural energy supplies through small-scale hydro-electrification schemes and extensive afforestation of fuelwood trees. Michael B. McElroy and Chris P. Nielsen, "Energy, Agriculture, and the Environment: Prospects for Sino-American Cooperation," in *Living with China: U.S.-China Relations in the Twenty-first Century*, ed. by Ezra F. Vogel (New York: W.W. Norton, 1997), p. 244; Smil, "China's Energy," 950; Tremayne and de Waal, "Business Opportunities," 1035.

146. Economy, "China's Environmental Diplomacy," pp. 276–277.

147. U.S., White House, "Fact Sheet."

148. In Beijing, according to observational studies conducted by Walter Hook in 1996, "bicycle traffic moves at 6–8 kilometers per hour, and the bicycle lanes move 900 more people per lane per hour than the . . . mixed motor lanes." In China's flat cities, Hook foresees that roller blades "could be the wave of the future." Walter Hook, "China Mustn't Copy Western Transport," *China Daily*, 15 October 1996, p. 4.

149. See Koehn, "Global Petroleum Reserves," p. 375; Alan T. Durning, *How Much Is Enough? The Consumer Society and the Future of the Earth* (New York: W.W. Norton, 1992), p. 79; Jun-meng Yang, "Bicycle Traffic in China," *Transportation Quarterly* 39, No. 1 (January 1985): 93–104; Lowe, *The Bicycle*, pp. 20–21, 31–33; Elisabeth Rosenthal, "Who Needs TV? They Pedal Hard to Peddle Ads," *New York Times*, 3 February 2000, p. A4. Bicycle ridership is declining in the United States (down from 56 million in 1995 to 43.5 million in 1998) and, while 22 percent of U.S. children are obese (according to the Centers for Disease Control), less than 1 percent of those aged 7 to 15 ride bicycles to school. Peter T. Kilborn, "No Work for a Bicycle Thief: Children Pedal Around Less," *New York Times*, 7 June 1999, p. A1. Also see Greg Patent, "Fattening the East: China Succumbing to Western High-Fat Diets," *Missoulian*, 13 November 2001, p. C1.

150. Lee Schipper, Sarita Bartlett, Dianne Hawk, and Edward Vine, "Linking Life-Styles and Energy Use: A Matter of Time?" *Annual Review of Energy* 14 (1989): 317.

151. Petroleum also is a major component in asphalt and, hence, in highway con-

struction and repair. Paterson, "Car Culture," p. 260; also see Lowe, *The Bicycle*, pp. 16, 20; Kempton, Boster, and Hartley, *Environmental Values*, p. 142.

152. See Schipper et al., "Energy Use," pp. 316–317. According to William Dietz, director of the Division of Nutrition and Physical Activity at the Centers for Disease Control and Prevention, "a quarter of all trips taken by Americans are under a mile, but 75 percent of those trips are done by car." Cited in Jane E. Brody, "Planning Healthier Suburbs, Where Cars Sit Idle and People Get Moving," *New York Times*, 17 October 2000, p. E1.

153. Lowe, *The Bicycle*, pp. 7, 10–18.

154. Also see Chen, "Environmental Protection Strategy," p. 90. Lieberthal ("China's Governing System") maintains that the type of environmental-protection projects that are most likely to succeed in China will be job-creating initiatives supported by foreign technology and funding.

155. See Shen, "Urban Transportation in Shanghai," p. 603.

156. In 1998, the Chinese Academy of Social Sciences (CASS) and the Social Science Research Council (SSRC) signed an agreement of cooperation that is designed, in part, to respond to CASS's interest in problem-oriented studies. Mary B. McDonnell, "Building Bridges with the Chinese Academy of Social Sciences (CASS)," *Items* 53, No. 1 (1999): 13. Chinese-American scientists are experienced in establishing exchange programs with PRC scholars. See Yin and Lan, "Chinese Americans," 53.

157. For instance, a growing number of organizations for Chinese+American scientists and engineers, such as the 1,500-member Society of Chinese Bioscientists in America and the 1,000-member Chinese-American Chemical Society, are strengthening linkages to China that involve training Mainland scientists in the United States and placing Chinese+American experts in positions in Asia as part of an overall effort to "develop more researchers who can contribute scientifically on both sides of the Pacific." Richard Stone, "The Chinese-American Connection," *Science* 262, No. 5132 (15 October 1993): 350.

158. Such as the solution-focused World Wildlife Fund–China, which opened a Beijing office in 1996, and the South-North Institute for Sustainable Development, which helps peasant farmers construct small-scale biogas-generating systems in cooperation with The Nature Conservancy. See Bo, "Greening the Chinese Media"; Chen Qing, "Building Local Partnerships: The South-North Institute for Sustainable Development," in *Green NGO and Environmental Journalist Forum* (Washington, D.C.: Woodrow Wilson Center, 2001), p. 14; Jennifer L. Turner, "Promoting a Great Green Leap Forward? The Growing Role of U.S. Green NGOs in China" (Paper presented at the 43rd Annual Convention of the International Studies Association, New Orleans, March 2002).

159. See Tremayne and de Waal, "Business Opportunities," p. 1040.

160. For instance, the Rockefeller Brothers Fund has supported a small-scale organic-farming project in Nanjing. "Financing Environmental Protection in China: The Role of Foundations and NGOs," China Environment Series 2, Environmental Change and Security Project, Woodrow Wilson International Center for Scholars, 1998, http//ecsp.si.edu/ecsplib.nsf.

161. See Graham E. Johnson and Woon Yuen-Fong, "The Response to Rural Reform in an Overseas Chinese Area," *Modern Asian Studies* 31, No. 1 (1997): 45–49, 55.

162. For instance, committed Chinese+Americans could initiate small-scale sustainable-development projects in the Mainland through existing sister-city ties. See Michael H. Shuman and Hal Harvey, *Security Without War: A Post–Cold War Foreign Policy* (Boulder: Westview Press, 1993), p. 223.

163. See Johnson, "China's Energy Sector," p. 277.

164. See Koehn, "Global Petroleum Reserves," pp. 367, 385n–386n; Smil, "China's Energy," pp. 947–948. China's township enterprises are notorious for "high rates of consumption of raw materials and energy . . . and serious environmental pollution." Ma Xia, "Changes in the Pattern of Migration in Urban China," in *Migration and Urbanization in China*, ed. by Lincoln H. Day and Ma Xia (Armonk, NY: M.E. Sharpe, 1994), p. 214. Todd Johnson ("China's Energy Sector," p. 289) maintains that "the biggest potential for energy efficiency [in China] is in the widespread dissemination and adoption of fairly low-tech, higher-efficiency equipment, including small electric motors and pumps, steam traps, and insulation."

165. See Koehn, "Global Petroleum Reserves," pp. 368, 386n.

166. See Jia and Rubin, "Potential Bridge," p. A56; Elizabeth Economy, "The Environment and Development in the Asia-Pacific Region," in *Fires across the Water*, p. 67. The Beijing Environment and Development Institute, established in 1995 by Ma Zhong, "focuses on applied research on environmental issues. . . ." Projects undertaken by the Center for Biodiversity and Indigenous Knowledge, affiliated with the Kunming Institute of Botany, include research on conservation and development and working with rural communities on the sustainable management of natural resources. See Knup, "Environmental NGOs."

167. See Wickberg, "Overseas Chinese Adaptive Organizations," p. 79.

168. Steven M. Teles, "Public Opinion and Interest Groups in the Making of U.S.–China Policy," in *After the Cold War: Domestic Factors and U.S.–China Relations*, ed. by Robert S. Ross (Armonk, NY: M.E. Sharpe, 1998), pp. 42, 52, 57.

169. See Gan, "Energy Development," pp. 126–127.

170. PRC, State Council, *China's Agenda 21*, p. 130; Zhongxiang Zhang, *The Economics of Energy Policy in China* (Cheltenham: Edward Elgar, 1998), p. 135; Chen, "Environmental Protection Strategy," p. 87; Gan, "Energy Development," p. 125.

171. Also see Harry Harding, *A Fragile Relationship: The United States and China Since 1972* (Washington, D.C.: Brookings Institution, 1992), p. 353.

172. Jia and Rubin, "Potential Bridge," p. A56.

173. See Rosenau, "Enlarged Citizen Skills," pp. 340–341, 352; Durning, *How Much Is Enough?* p. 25.

174. Kempton, Boster, and Hartley, *Environmental Values*, pp. 12–13, 95–96, 101.

175. See Raymond De Young, "Some Psychological Aspects of Living Lightly: Desired Lifestyle Patterns and Conservation Behavior," *Journal of Environmental Systems* 20, No. 3 (1990/1991): 215–216, 226; Kempton, Boster, and Hartley, *Environmental Values*, pp. 101, 136; Durning, *How Much Is Enough?* pp. 137–139, 149.

176. See Koehn, "Global Petroleum Reserves," pp. 368, 386n; Kempton, Boster, and Hartley, *Environmental Values*, p. 220; Durning, *How Much Is Enough?* pp. 28–29.

177. Madsen, *China and the American Dream*, pp. 166, 171–172. On the Mainland impact of overseas Chinese from the commercialized and consumption-oriented societies of Taiwan and Hong Kong, see Smart and Smart, "Transnational Social Networks," p. 114; Mayfair M. Yang, "Mass Media and Transnational Subjectivity in Shanghai: Notes on (Re)Cosmopolitanism in a Chinese Metropolis," in *Ungrounded Empires: The Cultural Politics of Modern Chinese Transnationalism*, ed. by Aihwa Ong and Donald M. Nonini (New York: Routledge, 1997), p. 304. Derived, in part, from the life-style of early-twentieth-century Shanghai, Hong Kong's culture of consumption, with its emphasis on the overt display of material wealth, has also permeated Chinese communities in North American cities. See Katharyne Mitchell,

"Transnational Subjects: Constituting the Cultural Citizen in the Era of Pacific Rim Capital," in *Ungrounded Empires*, pp. 231–232, 236–237.

178. Benjamin R. Barber, *Jihad vs. McWorld* (London: Random House, 1995), pp. 294–295; Edmonds, *China's Lost Harmony*, p. 256; Brown, *Who Will Feed China?* p. 31; Banister, "Population and Environment," p. 1014; Conghua Li, *China: The Consumer Revolution* (Singapore: John Wiley & Sons, 1998), pp. 54–55, 62–63, 131, 156–157, 186; Deborah S. Davis, "Introduction: A Revolution in Consumption," in *The Consumer Revolution in Urban China*, ed. by Deborah S. Davis (Berkeley: University of California Press, 2000), pp. 2, 4; Hanlong Lu, "To Be Relatively Comfortable in an Egalitarian Society," in *The Consumer Revolution in Urban China*, p. 134; Chai, "Consumption and Living Standards in China," pp. 256–257, 274, 276; Shen, "Urban Transportation in Shanghai," p. 595. The Mainland is expected to have 155 million cell-phone users by 2002. In the words of the general manager of Jegaxunlian store in Guangzhou, "Everyone in China wants to own a mobile phone. For men, it's like having a cigarette lighter. For women, it's like wearing an accessory." Mark Landler, "Selling Status, and Cell Phones," *New York Times*, 24 November 2000, p. C1.

179. Oksenberg and Economy, "China: Implementation," p. 354. Also see David S. Goodman, "The New Middle Class," in *The Paradox of China's Post-Mao Reforms*, ed. by Merle Goldman and Roderick MacFarquhar (Cambridge: Harvard University Press, 1999), pp. 259–260; Durning, *How Much Is Enough?* p. 52.

180. Ronald Skeldon, "Of Migration, Great Cities, and Markets: Global Systems of Development," in *Global History and Migrations*, ed. by Wang Gungwu (Boulder: Westview Press, 1997), p. 211.

181. Another 21 percent reported that they "don't know." Cited in Willett Kempton, "Will Public Environmental Concern Lead to Action on Global Warming?" *Annual Review of Energy and the Environment* 18 (1993): 222; also see pp. 223–224.

182. Kempton, Boster, and Hartley, *Environmental Values*, pp. 99, 134.

183. De Young, "Living Lightly," p. 226. Also see Durning, *How Much Is Enough?* pp. 38–39, 41–43. Durning adds (pp. 145–146) that "even in the United States, now arguably the most wasteful society in human history, thrift and frugality are the buried touchstones of the national character."

184. See Lo and Leung, "Environmental Governance," pp. 683–685, 691–693, 699.

185. The items De Young ("Living Lightly," p. 222) used to operationalize "frugality" included "keeping things running past normal life," "finding ways to avoid waste," "repairing rather than throwing away," "saving things I might need someday," and "finding ways to use things over and over."

186. Lo and Leung, "Environmental Governance," p. 689. Also see Richard Madsen, "Epilogue: The Second Liberation," in *The Consumer Revolution in Urban China*, pp. 316–318; Lu, "Comfortable," p. 141.

187. Tu Wei-ming, "Cultural China: The Periphery as the Center," *Daedalus* 120, No. 2 (Spring 1991): 10, 14.

188. Rosenau, "Enlarged Citizen Skills," pp. 350–351. Although some enhancement of conceptual tools is occurring and cultural models that would lead to more effective consumer choices exist, Kempton, Boster, and Hartley conclude, on the basis of an extensive anthropological study, that people in the United States "have serious misunderstandings about global environmental issues, which skew public support for policies for irrelevant reasons." Kempton, Boster, and Hartley, *Environmental Values*, pp. 219, 225.

189. Paterson, "Car Culture," pp. 258–260; Durning, *How Much Is Enough?* pp.

82–84; Thomas Homer-Dixon, *The Ingenuity Gap* (New York: Alfred A. Knopf, 2000), pp. 398–399.

190. Also see Ryan and Flavin, "Facing China's Limits," pp. 129, 115; Vaclav Smil, *China's Environmental Crisis: An Inquiry into the Limits of National Development* (Armonk, NY: M.E. Sharpe, 1993), p. 202; Hsu, "China's Environmental Policy," pp. 29–30.

191. Edmonds, *China's Lost Harmony*, p. 257; Lenssen, *Empowering Development*, p. 37; Ekins, *New World Order*, pp. 163–164; Durning, *How Much Is Enough?* p. 137.

192. PRC, State Council, *China's Agenda 21*, p. 55.

193. Smil, *China's Environmental Crisis*, pp. 135–137.

194. See Wickberg, "Overseas Chinese Adaptive Organizations," p. 78.

195. Wapner, "Politics Beyond the State," pp. 322–326; Wapner, *Environmental Activism*, p. 15.

196. Jackie Smith, Ron Pagnucco, and Charles Chatfield, "Social Movements and World Politics: A Theoretical Framework," in *Transnational Social Movements and Global Politics: Solidarity Beyond the State*, pp. 70–74.

197. Albert Bandura, "Exercise of Personal and Collective Efficacy in Changing Societies," in *Self-efficacy in Changing Societies*, ed. by Albert Bandura (Cambridge: Cambridge University Press, 1995), pp. 2–3.

198. See Hugh C. Dyer, "Environmental Security as a Universal Value: Implications for International Theory," in *The Environment and International Relations*, ed. by John Vogler and Mark F. Imber (London: Routledge, 1996), p. 31.

199. CI is developing links with consumer groups affiliated with the semi-official central Chinese Consumers Association. Dongfang Han, "A Road to Nowhere: International Exchanges and Trade Union Rights for Chinese Workers," *China Rights Forum* (Winter 1997–98): 29.

200. De Young, "Living Lightly," p. 221.

201. Ibid., pp. 221–222.

202. United States, White House, Office of the Press Secretary, "Remarks by the President on the Environment to the People of Guilin Area" (Guilin: 2 July 1998). Another specific venue for the consideration of such values would be the symposiums on "opportunities and challenges for women and children stemming from economic globalization" sponsored by the Shanghai Women's Federation in cooperation with overseas women's organizations and/or scholars. Zheng Ye, "Friendly Sisterhood," *Women of China* (August 2000): 29.

203. Jiang Qisheng and Zhu Rui, "Protect the Yangtze, Our Mother River: An Open Letter to the Chinese People," *China Rights Forum* (Fall 1998): 33.

204. On the role of the media in promoting environmental awareness in China in recent years, see Bo, "Greening the Chinese Media." Former citizens of China who have settled overseas are likely to be favored in televised programming when the ban on media joint ventures is lifted. Willy Wo-Lap Lam, "'Unmuzzle Media Watchdog' Appeal," *South China Morning Post*, 3 June 1998, p. 9. Also see Knup, "Environmental NGOs." The U.S.–China trade agreement reached in November 1999 opened the door to overseas Chinese investments in Mainland Internet businesses. Erik Eckholm and David E. Sanger, "Watershed Pact," *New York Times*, 16 November 1999, pp. A1, A11.

205. According to Bruce Tremayne and Penny de Waal ("Business Opportunities," p. 1026), "there is growing recognition [in China] of the need to raise public awareness and improve environmental education in the schools."

206. U.S., White House, "Fact Sheet."

207. U.S. Department of State, Bureau of Educational and Cultural Affairs, "U.S.–China Youth Exchange Initiative: Pilot Project Request for Proposals," Public Notice 3332 (8 June 2000).

208. On the latter, see Kempton, Boster, and Hartley, *Environmental Values*, p. 160. On the incorporation of environmental protection into the kindergarten, primary, and secondary curriculums and the establishment of "green groups" in Guangzhou schools, see Lo and Leung, "Environmental Governance," p. 693.

209. See Economy, "China's Environmental Diplomacy," pp. 274–276, 280, 282; Leicester, "Green Crusaders," p. E2; Jiang and Zhu, "Protect the Yangtze," p. 33.

210. Economy, "China's Environmental Diplomacy," p. 277; Leicester, "Green Crusaders," p. E2; Palmer, "Environmental Regulation," p. 796; Lo and Leung, "Environmental Governance," p. 693; Knup, "Environmental NGOs." Saich ("Social Organizations," p. 137) reports that Mainland social organizations "working in the field of education and environment have been permitted or have negotiated relatively free space."

211. Adapted from Jia and Rubin, "Potential Bridge," p. A56.

212. See Mae M. Ngai, "Who Is an American Worker? Asian Immigrants, Race, and the National Boundaries of Class," in *Audacious Democracy: Labor, Intellectuals, and the Social Reconstruction of America*, ed. by Steven Fraser and Joshua B. Freeman (Boston: Houghton Mifflin, 1997), pp. 178–179.

213. Jia and Rubin, "Potential Bridge," p. A56.

214. Wei Li, "Building Ethnoburbia: The Emergence and Manifestation of the Chinese *Ethnoburb* in Los Angeles' San Gabriel Valley," *Journal of Asian American Studies* 2, No.1 (February 1999): 21; also see Sterngold, "A New Political Resolve," p. A21.

215. To mention one possibility, environmental education could be included as a UNITE project among the Sunset Park Chinese community in Brooklyn, New York. See Ngai, "Who Is an American Worker?" pp. 180–181.

216. Robert S. Ross, "Forward," in *After the Cold War*, p. xi; Steven I. Levine, "Sino-American Relations: Practicing Damage Control," in *China and the World: Chinese Foreign Policy Faces the New Millennium*, ed. by Samuel S. Kim (Boulder: Westview Press, 1998), p. 93.

217. Asia Society, *Bridges with Asia: Asian Americans in the United States*; *Summary Report* (New York: Asia Society, 1997), pp. 6–7, 55; Evelyn Hu-DeHart, "Introduction: Asian American Formations in the Age of Globalization," in *Across the Pacific: Asian Americans and Globalization*, ed. by Evelyn Hu-DeHart (Philadelphia: Temple University Press, 1999), p. 14; Xiao-huang Yin, "The Lee Case Shakes Asian Americans' Faith in Justice System," *Los Angeles Times*, 24 September 2000, p. M1. On the steps taken by the 450-member Overseas Chinese Physics Association in the wake of media, government, and public reaction to allegations that Wen Ho Lee leaked nuclear-weapons secrets to China, see Colin Macilwain, "U.S. Societies Fear Clampdown on Visits by Foreign Scientists," *Nature* 398, No. 672 (April 1999): 448; and "Playing Dirty with the China Card," *Nature* 398, No. 672 (April 1999): 445. Also see Sandra Blakeslee, "Circling Los Alamos Inquiry: Specter of Science as a Sieve," *New York Times*, 12 March 1999, p. A1; Hoyt Zia, "Well, Is He a Spy—or Not?" *New York Times*, 26 May 1999, p. A31; William J. Broad, "Bias Is Called Key to Naming Suspect in China Spy Case," *New York Times*, 18 August 1999, p. A1; "Effort Begun for Asian-American Scientists," *New York Times*, 20 January 2000, p. A11; James Sterngold, "Defense Argues Ethnicity Made Scientist a Suspect," *New York Times*, 16 August 2000; James Sterngold, "Accused Scientist to Go Free on Bail in Los Alamos Case," *New York Times*, 25 August 2000, p. A1.

In general, Chinese+American scientists with Mainland experience can help "shape the American perception of the new China by giving public lectures and writing articles in the mass media." Wang, "U.S.–China Scientific Exchange," p. 270.

218. Madsen, *China and the American Dream*, p. 216.

219. See Kempton, "Public Environmental Concern," p. 225.

220. On the latter, see Keck and Sikkink, *Activists Beyond Borders*, p. 214; Adler and Haas, "Conclusion," p. 386; Guarnizo, "Transnational Social Formation."

221. See Smart and Smart, "Transnational Social Networks," p. 115.

222. Kempton, "Public Environmental Concern," p. 239; Kempton, Boster, and Hartley, *Environmental Values*, p. 220.

223. Keck and Sikkink, *Activists Beyond Borders*, pp. 204–205.

224. Also see Jia and Rubin, "Potential Bridge," p. A56.

225. See Wen-Qiang Bian and L. Robin Keller, "Chinese and Americans Agree on What Is Fair, but Disagree on What Is Best in Societal Decisions Affecting Health and Safety Risks," *Risk Analysis* 19, No. 3 (1999): 442.

226. Cynthia Hardy, "Underorganized Interorganizational Domains: The Case of Refugee Systems," *Journal of Applied Behavioral Science* 30, No. 3 (September 1994): 279.

227. Also see Peter Koehn, "Chinese Americans and U.S.–China Relations in the 21st Century: Applications of Cross-national Competence to Interdependent Resource-consumption Challenges," *Journal of American–East Asian Relations* 9 (Spring 2000): 16-17.

228. However, these self-identifications are qualified by the observations that (1) 86 percent of this group (in comparison with only half of the nonadvocates) disagreed with the statement that "people in the United States should rely more on bicycles for transportation like people in the China Mainland do," and (2) only 38 percent of the advocates (versus 60 percent of the others) disagreed that "people in the China Mainland should acquire labor-saving devices that allow a standard of living similar to that available to most persons in the United States."

229. The self-identified advocates of sustainable consumption in this study proved more likely than did the nonadvocates to assess their ability to influence local-level decisions in the United States as "excellent," "good," or "fair" (48 percent and 33 percent, respectively). The two groups showed little difference in terms of perceived capacity for local-level influence in China.

230. Moreover, 89 percent of the non-native-born respondents who have lived in the United States for more than 20 years are advocates. Only 58 percent of those with 20 years or less of U.S. residence identify in this manner.

231. Another interesting finding is that 71 percent of both the naturalized U.S. citizens and those who are neither citizens nor permanent residents are advocates, while only 33 percent of the U.S. permanent residents identify in this manner.

232. In the North Carolina study, moreover, majorities of those over 40 and between 18 and 30 support sustainable consumption; 63 percent of those in the 31–40 age bracket disagree. Women also are more likely than men are to be sustainable-consumption advocates (77 percent versus 57 percent).

233. Smil, *China's Environmental Crisis*, p. 203.

234. See Sanford J. Ungar, "America's New Immigrants: Can 'Fresh Blood' Lead to a Fresh Foreign Policy?" in *Bridges with Asia: Asian Americans in the United States*; *Summary Report* (New York: Asia Society, 1997), p. 37.

235. Watanabe, "Asian American Activism," pp. 119–120.

236. See Wei Qing, "'Huafu dangan' de gangxian" (Afterthoughts on the documentary film *Chinatown Achieves*), *Qiaobao* (China express), 21 October 2000, p. A3.

# ——— Conclusion ———

# Transnationalism, Diversity, and the Future of U.S.–China Relations

## Peter H. Koehn and Xiao-huang Yin

Like the multiple reference points reflected in Christine Choy's stereotype-shattering art,[1] the authors featured in this book present the role of Chinese Americans in U.S.–China relations in its manifold complexity. For readers who are interested in understanding the impact of globalization and/or the effects of transnational networks on the receiving society and its recently arrived members, there is much to learn from the diverse practices and experiences of Chinese Americans in the expanding arena of U.S.–China relations.

### The State and Transnational Involvement

In all fields of human endeavor, cross-nationally competent Chinese Americans (and non-Chinese Americans) are eluding nation-state controls. The scope and persistence of their dynamic transnational networks indicate that many Chinese Americans, especially those of the first generation, deserve to be reconceptualized as "transmigrants."[2] As they literally and virtually traverse boundaries between the place of their current residence and the place from which they or their ancestors came, one finds indications in all of the contributions to this volume of cross-national involvement and competence among a substantial portion of the rapidly expanding Chinese American population. Through a multitude of transterritorial commitments, the growing number of first-generation immigrants as well as many ABCs are building ever-denser bridges across the Pacific.[3] That Chinese Americans as a whole are also becoming more openly involved in U.S.–China relations is reflected in Tsung Chi's discussion of the pro-Taiwan lobby, in the attention commanded by the dissident community, and in the changing attitudes of American-born Chinese toward China-related affairs. As Nancy Yao's chapter indicates, many ABCs have been transformed from "bystanders" to "participants" in the relationship. Among other developments, therefore, the extensive and expanding network of economic and other nonstate ties among Chinese and Chinese Americans reduces the capacity of government policymakers on both sides of the Pacific to engage in more than rhetorical hostilities.

Nevertheless, the state "is not going away."[4] It remains influential in shaping the nature of Chinese American involvement in U.S.–China relations. Thus, Chinese Americans today are more deeply involved in transnational activities partly because of the evolving post–Cold War role of the U.S. government in world affairs and the "deepening U.S. involvement in Asia."[5] As Xiaojian Zhao's historical analysis of the views of Chinese-language newspapers confirms, the views of Chinese Americans typically are congruent with mainstream-society trends when it comes to open participation in the bilateral relationship.[6] This response reflects motivations for involvement in China-related affairs that extend beyond a sense of ethnic consciousness and concern for the ancestral land. The desire to enhance their marginal status and expand their influence in the receiving society also attracts Chinese Americans to contribute in visible ways to the U.S.–China relationship. However, few community members have gained entry to the higher ranks of the U.S. foreign-policy establishment even though many respected Chinese Americans have demonstrated personal commitment to mainstream values of free-market economics, democracy, pluralism, and human rights.[7] Moreover, the advent of a Republican administration symbolically committed to redefining relationships with the PRC in terms of competition rather than partnership threatens to curtail the already limited public and state-related involvement of Chinese Americans.

## Diversity and Transnational Possibility

In novel and interesting ways, the contributors to *The Expanding Roles of Chinese Americans in U.S.–China Relations* confirm that the Chinese American population has become increasingly diverse, and that transnational possibilities affect members of the community differentially. In Lucie Cheng's words, "among Chinese Americans we have the exploited and the exploiters; people who live in poverty and people who spend cash to buy mansions; racists and victims of racism; people who are proud when white Americans compliment them on their fluency in English, which has taken them twenty years to achieve, and those who are angered by the same compliment, because English is their native language."[8] Specific categories among this population are "unequal in their capacity . . . to take advantage of others . . . [by] availing themselves of family and *guanxi* network resources to accumulate various kinds of capital" that can be "converted into personal power. . . ." [9] Caught in an oppressive world of poverty, sweatshops, gangs, and drugs, "downtown" Chinese Americans experience U.S. life and the impact of transnational activity quite differently from their "uptown" counterparts.[10] In addition to calculating benefits, therefore, there is a need to address the costs of differential transnational advantage incurred by migrant workers, displaced rural women, and the "home-bound."[11]

As a consequence of their divided interests and differential status, Chinese Americans today maintain diverse and conflicted attitudes toward China-related issues. For some, their views reflect professional interests and/or personal stakes in the development of U.S.–China relations. While those who are active in the dissident movement often support a confrontational policy toward China in the hope of quickly bringing down the Beijing regime, others—especially those who work in China-related professions—prefer a more constructive U.S.–China relationship. Thus, in contrast to some other established and recently empowered diasporas, Chinese Americans have not been successful in "uniting and mobilizing their community . . . by pursuing causes directly relating to their homeland."[12]

In addition, it is noteworthy that the growing importance of transboundary activity has reinforced cleavages based on place of upbringing and Chinese-language facility. As an Asian American scholar convincingly argues, "native-born Chinese Americans who refused to learn Chinese and who rejected Chinese culture in an earlier configuration of race and economy in the United States—when biculturalism and bilingualism were stigma rather than virtues—are finding themselves left out of the new opportunities."[13] It comes as no surprise, therefore, to discover that local and transnational responses to globalization coexist and alternate among Chinese and Asian American populations.[14]

Chinese Americans are not immune from the "underside of globalization."[15] Both externally and internally, some Chinese *guanxi* relationships and family networks employ "tactics of domination, violence, exploitation, and duplicity." Such networks exclude numerous others "with whom one has no acknowledged relationship—such as a female clerical employee, a non-Chinese manual laborer, [urban and township residents afflicted by environmental pollution and destruction,] or a poorer customer to whom one sells adulterated goods. These people can be legitimately taken advantage of, exploited, disciplined, abused, or cheated." Within the Chinese American community, "the supposed equality or benign status difference euphemizes relations of domination where de facto differences in power and capital are misrecognized or not acknowledged in public by both sides."[16]

In the current century, therefore, the key issue will concern the uses to which Chinese Americans put their cross-national linkages. Oppressive forces underlie certain network developments and some of the transterritorial problems that fall through the cracks of foreign-policy establishments.[17] One cannot dismiss the involvement of some Chinese immigrants in human-trafficking networks that stretch to the United States through the China Mainland, Taiwan, Hong Kong, Thailand, Latin America, and Canada. In the face of massive debts owed to smugglers, illegal entrants "become virtual slaves, often being forced by the smuggling ring into criminal activities. Failure to pay results in brutal sanctions" applied against the immigrant and/or her/his homeland family members.[18]

By and large, however, the contributors to this volume emphasize the positive side of Chinese American involvement in U.S.–China relations. With the important exception of direct participation in foreign-policy making, the authors foresee that Chinese Americans will become more deeply involved as nongovernmental actors—both in constructive Mainland activities and in a host of different mutually rewarding transboundary interactions.

## Potential Future Impact

In the post–Cold War, terror-focused environment of the twenty-first century, the nature of the U.S.–China relationship will assume even greater global importance. Although outbreaks of nationalistic sentiment are likely to continue to capture headlines, "the more pervasive dynamics are those that span, transgress, or otherwise undermine long-standing boundaries."[19] While not ignoring the oppressive forces unleashed along the underside of global capitalism, the contributors to this volume demonstrate convincingly that many Chinese Americans can play central, even decisive, roles in helping Chinese and Americans "create a common home in the intricately interdependent world of the twenty-first century."[20] In some cases (e.g., scientific exchanges, environmental-interdependence challenges, advancing human rights), their transsovereign[21] struggles are dependent upon success in building "coalitions based on a politics of [current] location, those with an eye toward the homeland, *and* those *outside* both of these configurations."[22]

Some circularity is at work in the relationship between socioeconomic status and participation in China–U.S. linkages. Given the common conviction, noted by several contributors to this volume as well as by Adam McKeown,[23] that the status and treatment of Chinese in the United States is directly connected to "the status of China within the international system," the efforts of Chinese Americans to improve relations between China and the United States can be based on personal/community interest as well as on concern for binational and/or global harmony and security. While the risk of suspect loyalties has not disappeared, demographic trends and the institutionalization of multicultural appreciation[24] allow Chinese Americans (as well as other Americans) increasing flexibility to promote and nurture close and constructive ties with the PRC and to engage in trans-Pacific civil-society collaboration across virtually all dimensions of human activity not directly related to military advantage or the threat of terrorism.

### Transsovereign Movements and Asian American Studies

Scholars working in Asian American studies increasingly emphasize the historical and contemporary centrality of transsovereign movements and concerns.[25] Networks in Asia figure prominently in current research and discourse along with other transboundary continuities and domestic solidarities.[26]

As many of the essays in this book highlight, once ties with the country of origin assume a central place in Asian American studies, then the knowledge and insights contributed by Asian studies scholars are essential for complete and accurate inquiries regarding social phenomena. This approach affirms rather than denies the difference between the Asian and Asian American. It recognizes, however, that in a society that has experienced substantial and sustained in-migration from Asia, knowledge about and understanding of the source context provides a vital reference point for Asian American studies and enables scholars, interested domestic students, and place-bound U.S. residents to remain current with critical developments in sending countries.[27]

At the same time, the involvement of Chinese Americans in the extensive and exploding array of transterritorial civil-society undertakings uncovered by the authors who contributed to this volume suggests that Asian Americans increasingly frame social, economic, and political developments of interest in "the study of Asia and its subjects."[28] The overwhelming weight of the evidence and insights shared by contributors to *The Expanding Roles of Chinese Americans* affirms that the cross-national networks and informal roles of Chinese Americans in U.S.–China relations will continue to expand and assume growing influence in the Pacific century.

### Notes

1. See Asia Society, *Bridges with Asia: Asian Americans in the United States*, Summary Report of a 1996 Conference in New York (New York: Asia Society, 1997), p. 45.

2. Charles Hirschman, Philip Kasinitz, and Josh DeWind, "Theories and Concepts of International Migration," in *The Handbook of International Migration: The American Experience*, ed. by Charles Hirschman, Philip Kasinitz, and Josh DeWind (New York: Russell Sage Foundation, 1999), p. 18.

3. The prospect that such ties will drive bilateral relations and limit foreign-policy options is overlooked in Manfred Jonas's argument that acculturation is a necessary precondition for exerting an impact on U.S. foreign policy. See Manfred Jonas, "Immigration and U.S. Foreign Policy: The Interwar Period," in *Immigration and U.S. Foreign Policy*, ed. by Robert W. Tucker, Charles B. Keely, and Linda Wrigley (Boulder: Westview Press, 1990), pp. 58, 67–68.

4. Maryann K. Cusimano, Mark Hensman, and Leslie Rodrigues, "Private-sector Transsovereign Actors—MNCs and NGOs," in *Beyond Sovereignty: Issues for a Global Agenda*, ed. by Maryann K. Cusimano (Boston: Bedford/St. Martin's, 2000), p. 280.

5. Myron Weiner, "Asian Immigrants and U.S. Foreign Policy," in *Immigration and U.S. Foreign Policy*, ed. by Robert W. Tucker, Charles B. Keely, and Linda Wrigley (Boulder: Westview Press, 1990), p. 193.

6. Also see Jonas, "Immigration and U.S. Foreign Policy," p. 68.

7. Yossi Shain, *Marketing the American Creed Abroad: Diasporas in the U.S. and Their Homelands* (Cambridge: Cambridge University Press, 1999), pp. x, 8, 49–50.

8. Lucie Cheng, "Chinese Americans in the Formation of the Pacific Regional Economy," in *Across the Pacific: Asian Americans and Globalization*, ed. by Evelyn Hu-DeHart (Philadelphia: Temple University Press, 1999), p. 70.

9. Donald M. Nonini and Aihwa Ong, "Chinese Transnationalism as an Alternative Modernity," in *Ungrounded Empires: The Cultural Politics of Modern Chinese Transnationalism*, ed. by Aihwa Ong and Donald M. Nonini (New York: Routledge, 1997), pp. 24, 22.

10. See Xiao-huang Yin, "The Two Sides of America's 'Model Minority,' " *Los Angeles Times*, 7 May 2000, pp. M1, M7. Also see Susumu Awanohara, "Tyros, Triads, Tycoons: Chinatown Ghettos Versus Arriviste Suburbs," *Far Eastern Economic Review*, 153, No. 29 (18 July 1991): 51; Evelyn Hu-DeHart, "Introduction: Asian American Formations in the Age of Globalization," in *Across the Pacific: Asian Americans and Globalization*, p. 18.

11. Aihwa Ong and Donald M. Nonini, "Toward a Cultural Politics of Diaspora and Transnationalism," in *Ungrounded Empires: The Cultural Politics of Modern Chinese Transnationalism*, p. 327.

12. Shain, *Marketing the American Creed*, p. xi.

13. Cheng, "Chinese Americans," p. 66.

14. See Sau-ling Cynthia Wong, "Denationalization Reconsidered: Asian American Cultural Criticism at a Theoretical Crossroads," *Amerasia Journal* 21, Nos. 1 & 2 (1995): 17.

15. Hu-DeHart, "Introduction," p. 18; also see David Palumbo-Liu, *Asian/American: Historical Crossings of a Racial Frontier* (Stanford: Stanford University Press, 1999), p. 362.

16. Nonini and Ong, "Chinese Transnationalism," p. 22; Aihwa Ong, "Chinese Modernities: Narratives of Nation and of Capitalism," in *Ungrounded Empires: The Cultural Politics of Modern Chinese Transnationalism*, p. 192.

17. See Maryann K. Cusimano, "Beyond Sovereignty: The Rise of Transsovereign Problems," in *Beyond Sovereignty: Issues for a Global Agenda*, p. 7.

18. Awanohara, "Triads," 51. Roy Godson and Phil Williams note that Chinese

transsovereign criminal organizations operate "an extensive range of enterprises incorporating traditional criminal activities such as extortion and prostitution and more novel ventures such as the smuggling of illegal aliens or nuclear materials." Roy Godson and Phil Williams, "Strengthening Cooperation against Transsovereign Crime: A New Security Imperative," in *Beyond Sovereignty: Issues for a Global Agenda*, p. 114. According to a National Security Council report released in December 2000, "China's Big Circle Gang deals in drugs, alien smuggling, vehicle theft, financial crimes, and computer hacking as part of a horizontal network that links cells in nearly every Chinatown worldwide." Joseph Kahn and Judith Miller, "Getting Tough on Gangsters, High Tech and Global," *New York Times*, 15 December 2000, p. A7. Also see Ko-Lin Chin, *Smuggled Chinese: Clandestine Immigration to the United States* (Philadelphia: Temple University Press, 1998).

19. James N. Rosenau, *Along the Domestic-Foreign Frontier: Exploring Governance in a Turbulent World* (Cambridge: Cambridge University Press, 1997), p. 447.

20. Richard Madsen, *China and the American Dream: A Moral Inquiry* (Berkeley: University of California Press, 1995), p. 228.

21. Maryann Cusimano presents a compelling argument for privileging the term *transsovereign* over *transnational* "in order to keep clear the distinction between sovereign states and national groups." Cusimano, "Beyond Sovereignty," p. 3.

22. Palumbo-Liu, *Asian/American*, p. 390 [emphasis in original].

23. Adam McKeown, "Conceptualizing Chinese Diasporas, 1842 to 1949," *Journal of Asian Studies* 58, No. 2 (May 1999): 326.

24. Shain, *Marketing the American Creed*, pp. xi, 9.

25. Somini Sengupta, "Asian American Programs Are Flourishing at Colleges," *New York Times*, 9 June 1999, p. B11.

26. Wong, "Denationalization Reconsidered," pp. 7–8.

27. Also see Peter Koehn, "Convergence of Global and Multicultural Education: The Socio-political Context," *International Education Forum* 12, No. 1 (Spring 1992): 14–15.

28. Hu-DeHart, "Introduction," p. 11.

# About the Editors and Contributors

## The Editors

**Peter H. Koehn** (Ph.D., Political Science, University of Colorado, 1973) is Professor of Political Science at the University of Montana–Missoula. He was recently named a Fulbright New Century Scholar. During the 1997–1998 academic year, he served as Director of Research and Development at the Hong Kong–America Center and Visiting Professor in the Department of Government and Public Administration, Chinese University of Hong Kong. He taught as an exchange professor at Shanghai International Studies University during 1996–1997. From 1987 to 1996, he served as the University of Montana's founding Director of International Programs. Dr. Koehn's scholarship includes *The Outlook for U.S.–China Relations Following the 1997–1998 Summits: Chinese and American Perspectives on Security, Trade, and Cultural Exchange*, co-edited with Joseph Y.S. Cheng (1999), and *Refugees from Revolution: U.S. Policy and Third-World Migration* (1990).

**Xiao-huang Yin** is Professor and Chair of the American Studies program at Occidental College. He received a Ph.D. from Harvard University and has taught at Harvard as a visiting professor of history and ethnic studies. Specializing in interdisciplinary studies of the Asian American experience and U.S.–China relations, Dr. Yin is the author of *Chinese American Literature since the 1850s* (2000), an advisory editor of and a contributor to *New Americans: Immigrants Since the 1960s* (2003), a contributor to *Babel in American: Essays on Language, Immigration, and Ethnicity* (2002); *Not English Only: Redefining "American" in American Studies* (2002); *Multilingual America: Transnationalism, Ethnicity, and the Languages of American Literature* (1998); *Asian American Encyclopedia* (1996); and many other books. In addition, Dr. Yin is a frequent contributor on Chinese/Asian Americans and U.S.–China relations to the *Los Angeles Times*.

## The Contributors

**Wellington K.K. Chan** (Ph.D., Harvard), Professor of History and Chair, Department of History, Occidental College, has published extensively on

Chinese social and economic history both in the United States and overseas. His *Merchants, Mandarins and Modern Enterprise in Late Imperial China* (1977) was translated into Chinese and published by the Chinese Academy of Social Sciences, Beijing, China, in 1997. His recent publications include "Tradition and Change in the Chinese Business Enterprise: The Family Firm Past and Present," *Chinese Studies in History* 31, Nos. 3–4 (1998), and "Introduction to Historical Patterns of Chinese Business," *Journal of Asian Business* 14, No. 1 (1998).

**Tsung Chi** (Ph.D., Political Science, Michigan State University, 1993), is Associate Professor and Chair of the Department of Politics at Occidental College. He specializes in comparative politics, Chinese politics, and research methodology. His publications include: "Allocating Scarce Resources: A Comparative Analysis of the Distributive Principles in China's Cadre System and Taiwan's Civil Service System," *Journal of Contemporary China* 8, No. 20 (March 1999), and (in Chinese with Carl Huang) *The Negotiation Process Between the Chinese Nationalist Party and the Communist Party Between 1945 and 1949* (1995).

**John J. Deeney** is Center Associate, University Center for International Studies, University of Pittsburgh. He has taught Anglo-American as well as comparative literature and translation at universities in the United States, Taiwan, Hong Kong, and the PRC for over thirty years. Dr. Deeney has served as Director of the Hong Kong-America Center, organizer of a wide range of U.S.–China cultural and educational activities, and as promoter, fund raiser, and administrator of numerous academic exchanges involving PRC scholars and graduate students. He is the founder of the Philanthropy/Fundraising Resource and Advisory Unit in Hong Kong.

**Him Mark Lai** has taught Asian American studies at the University of California, Berkeley and at San Francisco State University since 1969. He is the author of *From Overseas Chinese to Chinese American* (1992), co-translator/ editor of *Island: Poetry and History of Chinese Immigrants on Angel Island, 1910–1940* (1980), and compiler of two bibliographies on Chinese American newspapers and Chinese-language publications in the United States. He is also a contributor on Chinese and Asian Americans to *Harvard Encyclopedia of American Ethnic Groups, Asian American Encyclopedia, The Encyclopedia of Chinese Overseas*, and many other books.

**Sufei Li** is Associate Director of Educational Credential Evaluation, the Knowledge Company in Washington, D.C. She is a graduate of Nanjing

University, the University of London, and the University of Maryland at College Park, and member of the National Association of International Educators–NAFSA, and the American Association of Collegiate Registrars and Admissions Officers (AACRAO). Ms. Li specializes in comparative higher education. At the Knowledge Company, she oversees corporate operations and reviews and approves educational credentials from Asia, all Commonwealth countries, the Middle East, and Spanish-speaking countries.

**Haiming Liu** (Ph.D., Comparative Culture, University of California–Irvine, 1995) is Associate Professor, Department of Ethnic and Women's Studies, the California State Polytechnic University, Pomona. He specializes in Asian American history, social history, and diaspora studies. His publications include articles on the Chinese family and Chinese herbalists in America in *Amerasia Journal* and the *Journal of Asian American Studies*.

**Qian Suoqiao** is Assistant Professor in the Department of Chinese, Translation, and Linguistics at City University of Hong Kong. He received his Ph.D. degree in Comparative Literature from the University of California–Berkeley in 1996 and was Mellon Postdoctoral Fellow in the Humanities at Barnard College from 1997 to 1999. Dr. Qian has published a number of articles in both English and Chinese, and currently is working on a book manuscript on Lin Yutang and U.S.–China cross-cultural issues.

**James Jinguo Shen** is Assistant Professor and Coordinator of the Communication Program at the Richard Stockton College of New Jersey. He received his Ph.D. degree in mass communication from Ohio University in 1995. His presentations and publications in the United States, China, Taiwan, and Hong Kong cover a variety of topics in international communication, Asian affairs, information technologies, and critical cultural studies. He is a member of the National Communication Association (NCA), and a national officer and editor of the newsletter for the Association for Chinese Communication Studies—an official affiliate of the NCA.

**Yuhang Shi** teaches political science and public administration at Florida State University. His scholarly interests include the impact of new technology on political behavior and public administration and the influence of interracial and interethnic relations on public policy at the state level and on political behavior at the individual level. His recent publications include "Citizen Participation and Direct Democracy through Computer Networking" in *Handbook of Public Information Systems*, ed. by David Garson (1999), and "A Test of Reverse Causality in the Democratic Peace Relationship" in *Journal of Peace Research* 36, No. 3 (November 1999).

**Zuoyue Wang** (Ph.D., University of California–Santa Barbara, 1994) is Assistant Professor of History, California State Polytechnic University, Pomona. His scholarly interests include Chinese American scientists and science and politics in the United States and China in the twentieth century. Dr. Wang's scholarship includes "Science, Technology, and Foreign Policy," in Alexander DeConde et al., eds., *Encyclopedia of American Foreign Policy: Studies of the Principal Movements and Ideas* (forthcoming), and "Between the Devil and the Deep Sea: C.K. Tseng, Mariculture, and the Politics of Science in Modern China," co-authored with Peter Neushul, *Isis* 91 (March 2000): 59–88; and "U.S.–China Scientific Exchange" *Historical Studies in the Physical and Biological Sciences* 30, No. 1 (1999): 249–277.

**Norton Wheeler** has been a business executive for twenty years. His professional activities include substantial involvement with China. His contribution draws, in part, on research currently being undertaken in a doctoral program at the University of Kansas.

**Nancy Yao** was born and raised in New York City. She received her A.B. in Diplomacy and World Affairs with a concentration in East Asia from Occidental College and her M.B.A. from the School of Management, Yale University. Prior to attending Yale, she was Research Associate for China at the Council on Foreign Relations in New York. She also served as associate producer for CNN International's coverage of the handover of Hong Kong to the PRC in 1997. Ms. Yao currently is an associate in the investment banking division of Goldman Sachs (Asia) in Hong Kong.

**Xiaojian Zhao** (Ph.D., University of California–Berkeley, 1993) is Associate Professor in the Asian American Studies Department, University of California–Santa Barbara. She is the author of *Remaking Chinese America: Immigration, Family, and Community, 1940 to 1965* (2002), and is exceptionally knowledgeable about Chinese-language newspapers published in the United States.

# Index

Compilation of the index is funded by the Louis and Hermione
Brown Humanities Support Fund at Occidental College

Diaoyutai Islands (Fishermen's Islands), 127, 213
Diasporic hummingbirds, xxi, 53
Diasporic patriotism. *See aiguo*
Doctoral degrees earned by foreigners (table), 28
"Does My Future Lie in China or America," 9
Double posting (*jianzhi*), 249
Downtown Chinese, xxxv *n30*, 286
DPP. *See* Democratic Progressive Party

*The Eavesdropper*, 38–40, 41–42
80–20 Initiative, xxv, 80 *n5*, 89–90
circularize candidates, 136
election activity, 135–136
issues, 136
and Wen Ho Lee Case, 223
Electron-Positron Collider, 215, 216
Embassy of the PRC, Belgrade,
and ABCs, 90, 91
bombing of, 223
Embassy of the PRC, Washington,
returning students and professionals, 22
Energy-conservation technology-service centers, 251
English language use, 126
English-language newspapers, 126
2nd generation opinions, 126
Entrepreneur's Foundation, 175, 177
Environmental-interdependence issues/ challenges, xxx, 244
Environmental protection
education efforts, 259–260
local dispute-resolution bodies, 251
local supervision groups (*huanbao jiandu xiaozu*), 251
Ethnic discrimination, 62, 224
Ethnic identity, 126
Ethnic press
classified, 128
coverage, 127
entertainment sections, 127–128
opinions, 126–127

Exclusion Era
discrimination against Chinese scholars/ scientists, 211
family residency, migration, reunification, xxxvi *n45*, 3, 34 *n26*
and immigrants, 4
Executive order 12711, 12, 27–28

Falun Gong, xiv
*Facai* (making money, realizing the American Dream), 38, 49–50
Family migration, residency. *See* Exclusion era
Family reunification
and immigrant students/professionals, 11
program
misunderstood, 10
preference, 5, 11
and Tiananmen Square Incident, 12–13
Fang Lizhi, 217, 220
FAPA. *See* Formosan Association for Public Affairs
FAPR. *See* Formosan Association for Public Relations
Federal Bureau of Investigation (FBI), 222, 223
F.F. (Chinese American social fraternity), 188–189
Financial support for students and scholars, 25–26
First International Ethnic Chinese Physics Conference, 220
FOB (fresh off the boat), 50
Fochler, Julia Z. *See* Zhou Li
*Foreign Affairs*, 115, 252
Formosan Association for Public Affairs (FAPA), xxv, 121
and American Israel Public Affairs Committee (AIPAC), 113
and FAPR, 117
goals, 114
Grassroots Campaign Workshop, 117
legislative influence, 114
legislative priorities, 115
lobbying efforts, 115, 116